CW00391976

I THINK I AM

Other Books by Laurence A. Rickels
Published by the University of Minnesota Press

Acting Out in Groups

The Case of California

The Devil Notebooks

Nazi Psychoanalysis
　　I. Only Psychoanalysis Won the War
　　II. Crypto-Fetishism
　　III. Psy Fi

Ulrike Ottinger: The Autobiography of Art Cinema

The Vampire Lectures

I THINK I AM
Philip K. Dick

LAURENCE A. RICKELS

University of Minnesota Press

Minneapolis

London

The research for this book was supported by the Alexander von Humboldt Foundation in 2004 and Berlin's Center for Literary Research (Zentrum für Literaturforschung) in 2005.

Copyright 2010 by the Regents of the University of Minnesota

All rights reserved. No part of this publication may be reproduced, stored in a retrieval system, or transmitted, in any form or by any means, electronic, mechanical, photocopying, recording, or otherwise, without the prior written permission of the publisher.

Published by the University of Minnesota Press
111 Third Avenue South, Suite 290
Minneapolis, MN 55401-2520
http://www.upress.umn.edu

Library of Congress Cataloging-in-Publication Data

Rickels, Laurence A.
  I think I am : Philip K. Dick / Laurence A. Rickels.
  p.   cm.
  Includes bibliographical references.
  ISBN 978-0-8166-6665-2 (acid-free paper) — ISBN 978-0-8166-6666-9 (pbk. : acid-free paper)
  1. Dick, Philip K.—Criticism and interpretation. 2. Science fiction, American—Philosophy. 3. Philosophy in literature. I. Title.
  PS3554.I3Z854   2010
  813'.54—dc22   2009016366

Printed in the United States of America on acid-free paper

The University of Minnesota is an equal-opportunity educator and employer.

16 15 14 13 12 11 10   10 9 8 7 6 5 4 3 2 1

Contents

Introjection 1

Part I

Endopsychic Allegories 19
*Radio Free Albemuth, Valis, The Divine
Invasion, The Transmigration of Timothy Archer,
Confessions of a Crap Artist*

Schreber Guardian 46
Time out of Joint

Belief System Surveillance 58
A Scanner Darkly

Part II

Deeper Problems 79

Veil of Tears 85
*The Cosmic Puppets, Eye in the Sky, The Man
Who Japed, The Man in the High Castle*

Go West 99

Dick Manfred 106

Timing 112
Martian Time-Slip

Glimmung 120
*Galactic Pot-Healer, Nick and the Glimmung,
A Maze of Death*

Part III

Spiritualism Analogy   133

Imitating the Dead   152
Dr. Bloodmoney, Voices from the Street,
Mary and the Giant

Indexical Layer   159
Deus Irae

Ilse   168

Hammers and Things   183
Vulcan's Hammer

Crucifictions   190
The World Jones Made, Counter-Clock World

Over There   200
Solar Lottery, Our Friends from Frolix 8

Martyrology   210

Can't Live, Can't Live   221
The Game-Players of Titan, Clans of the Alphane
Moon, Now Wait for Last Year

Lola   237

Umwelt, Mitwelt, and *Eigenwelt*   245
The Simulacra

Outer Race   261
The Crack in Space, The Ganymede Takeover

The German Introject   269
The Penultimate Truth, Lies, Inc.

Part IV

Materialism, Idealism, and Cybernetics   279

Startling Stories   285

A Couple of Years   292
Do Androids Dream of Electric Sheep?
The Zap Gun

Android Empathy   308

Homunculus and Robot   322
We Can Build You

ALL OF YOU ARE DEAD. I AM ALIVE.   334
The Three Stigmata of Palmer Eldritch, Ubik

Go with the Flow   348
   Flow My Tears, the Policeman Said

Part V

Room for Thought   361

Caduceus   367
   Dr. Futurity

Jump   371

Still   374

A Wake   381

Spätwerk   392

Let the Dead Be   399

Play Bally   403

Das Hund   409

Notes   419
Bibliography   431

Introjection

Philip K. Dick died in the spring quarter of my first (academic) year in California. For many years during my tenure at the University of California, students would claim to recognize Dick's influence in my classes. They were each time surprised that I had never read any of his works. I should proceed directly to this, that, or the other title. I was not surprised that all these proclamations of soul mating (or murder) led me not to read Dick. Soon extramural readers of my work noted its uncanny compatibility with Dick's work. In time for the new millennium I finally broke down and read *The Divine Invasion,* responding less to any pressure, accumulated or otherwise, behind the prompt than to the pointer that the book included representations of the Devil. In the course of overcoming one large chunk of resistance—I had carefully left the infernal prince out of my casting call for occult figures to play in my mourning show—I was very much aided by the recommendation (by one of the students attending my German science fiction class) of Arthur C. Clarke's *Childhood's End.*

The Divine Invasion did not help me with my interpretation of the Devil. But its placement within a trilogy brought me to both its book-ends. As a trio it convinced me to continue. Through the trilogy alone (in which psychosis as science fiction and fantasy as untenable redemption value are ultimately undermined or conjoined through Spiritualist communication with the other side) I was already able to fold out of Daniel Paul Schreber, Walter Benjamin, and Freud my "endopsychic allegory."[1] In the subsequent novels of my long-deferred reading assignment I realized that in addition to all the reasons that crossed my mind with regard to the proclaimed compatibility between us—and all those reasons were indeed represented in Dick's novels—what really took me by surprise was the foregrounding of a frame of reference made in Germany for his staging area of future worlds that, essentially and recognizably, never left the field of representation called California.

Certainly Germanicity as the open book of evil politics, in which Dick also often inserts his place marker, is not at all a surprising prop in forecast fiction. As I argued in *Psy Fi* (volume 3 of *Nazi Psychoanalysis*), Nazi Germany was, in addition to everything else, to some gratuitous point of excess, one big science fiction.[2] Plus, investments to this day in maintaining the good war as ongoing frame of reference necessarily require that Nazi Germany keep on winning: loss only entered the field, then, because the winning was/is otherwise limitless. What is unique to Dick's Californian future, however, is that the German introjects are psychically installed with ambivalence—right up against the ego ideal or its missing place. In the future that Dick foretells, high culture, music, literature, science, philosophy, you name it, are overwhelmingly German, for better or worse. The American or Terran language (in other words, Globalese) includes on its vocabulary list, like *kindergarten* or *blitzkrieg,* such words as *Selbstmord, Geheimnis, Gift,* and *Augenblick.* That American would go global simply because anyone can stumble through it and still be understood and, same thing, because it is no one's mother tongue is part of Dick's accurate forecasting. That the global prospecting of all things Californian (as the teen field of representation) inside the American global language would require a certain ascendancy of Germanicity (as dead language culture) is the part of the forecast that boggles my mind. As I already argued in my first book *Aberrations of Mourning,* via the Melanesian Cargo Cult, which refers to Djaman in this function, and as the future word of Philip K. Dick confirms, German is, inside Californian or Globalese, the language of the dead.

The art world fool who claimed that, because I include typos among the materials and effects of my critical reading, I have a problem with projection[3] was dead-head wrong but, beside his point, just the same in my court. I've always had a problem with identification, no doubt aggravated by traumatic circumstances in childhood. The corollary to this problem is that, for me, projection is no problem—my unproblem. Like Dick, I enjoy accuracy and "safety" with my projections.

While Nicolas Abraham and Maria Torok restored the recognition value of "introjection," gave it back change in currency, they were also setting it up as fall guy for turning up a contrast whereby "incorporation" could be dramatically defined. The hierarchical difference in dosage between incorporation and introjection doesn't balance its act over and against projection, which Sandor Ferenczi guaranteed would remain introjection's parallel universal. Just as projection, which traverses haunting, mourning, melancholia, psychosis, and politics, distinguishes itself not in or from itself but only site-specifically, so introjection is differentiated only by its schedule or timing. Projection, as the theorization in psychoanalysis that Freud himself reported missing, proves the placeholder of all the doctrines of haunting that fold out from its lost and found office. To this end introjection must be recognized as the alternate mechanism without which projections cannot be made or followed.

Many "people" have been lodged inside me to varying degrees of inclusion or occlusion. But isn't this the situation of adolescence, the new frontier that artists and thinkers, for example, attempt to invest with staying power? By this I don't refer to the psychopathology of perpetual adolescence but rather to the artist's or thinker's revalorization of the flash in the attention span of brilliant insight—the traumatizing condition of adolescent "energy"—as building block of an oeuvre that's here to stay. Become who (or what) you are, Nietzsche counsels. But beginning in adolescence we discover that the breach of boundaries such an opening requires also makes one available for foreign body switches. Thus one cannot become who one is without at the same time becoming, over and again, who (or what) one isn't. How often have I been left crying out, at the climax of some accomplished moment, "This is not my life!"

The onset and career of identification requires that you not recognize your own provenance as host to guests or ghosts. But in time you do finally see the brand name attached to what you assumed was properly your own in flashback or as insight always accompanied by a groan or yelp. I refer to these moments of catching up with identification, like all those other moments of recall of extreme embarrassment, as "scream memories." But these are the identifications that can be assigned. This after-the-fact predicament of never quite undoing your assignment leads you into assuming, once again wrongfully, that identification is always a contact sport. That "first contact" is what identification, beside itself, can be shown to commemorate holds true in cases of mourning or unmourning. But what about the world of no difference out there that organizes itself in circumvention of mourning?

Theodor Adorno already pointed out that in the mass media Sensurround to recognize and identify a product is already to identify with it, consume it (openly and secretly) as your own. Desublimated access to all the names in history or on the shelves in a store characterizes the psychotic break as tearing of the subliminal veiling of direct contact with the techno-mass-mediatic pressures that are on us. Thus it is not so much that cognitive or linguistic association is loosened as that fundamental defense filtering has been knocked out of the running of reception, which opens wide as coextensive with the mass media Sensurround (but unveiled, like the phallus—or like Hitler—in Lacan's *Hamlet* essay). The question this big picture of identification raises is that of redefining the contact that identification replaces and emplaces. The contact that mourning implies or excludes is grounded (and ground up) at the busy intersection between singularity and iterability. The prospect of first contact, though untenable, cannot be abandoned. It is the very prospect to which the medium of writing owes its impulse, its admission.

I sign in with "my Freud," which includes his influence in both Frankfurt School thought and deconstruction. But for the revalorization of (Dick's) schizophrenia, I recruited Benjamin in particular and like never before. Schreber's *Memoirs of My Nervous Illness (Denkwürdigkeiten eines Nervenkranken)* and Freud's study of this document of psychotic break and consolidation stand behind Benjamin's identification speculations from *Origin of the German Mourning Play (Ursprung des deutschen Trauerspiels)* through his media essays and into the construction site of the *Arcades Project (Das Passagen-Werk)* (where all the advance previews or projections were to be reclaimed). But what I have thereby determined is that, from start to finish, Benjamin's allegorical reading administers the supplement to my Freudian approach.[4]

I had a Devil of a time getting from there to here: Freud's commitment to secularism and (or as) transference does not make him mutually excluded from consideration of religion in the ruins of former functions or in psychosis. It is not only that I was able to join Freud at the remove of Devil's advocacy in contemplation of the process of Christianity. But even more to the point was my acceptance that religion could not be excluded from Freud's explicit withdrawal of "worldviews" into the underworld of psychoanalysis. Like his focus on the shifting borderline with regard to the legibility of psychosis, Freud's bottoms-up view of religion had all along reserved a place for the Benjaminian supplement, which I take as vital to my Freudian reading. Benjamin's revalorization of allegory (and all that follows from it in his diverse work) leads back to and through Freud's frame for world reading, namely endopsychic perception, as elaborated in his study of Schreber's *Memoirs*.

The limits Freud admitted with regard to the legibility of psychosis, in which, bottom line, he saw reality testing and transference circumvented as condemned sites under reconstruction, are the links to follow. In projective summation, then, mourning (or unmourning) is the restriction placed on passage across the borderline inside psychosis. For this book passage, reality testing will be left subsumable in loss—loss conceived, however, as the test of the reality it itself is (like no other).

The test situation, which Dick famously foregrounded, but in more settings than the one future world projected as *Blade Runner,* has been raised to consciousness as ongoing present tension within a relay of contexts by Avital Ronell in *The Test Drive.*[5] When I take the association with test, I'm already thinking of Jung's attempts to crack the code of schizophrenic speech. But in the first place I think of Benjamin's testing rapport with and through the film medium or Freud's fundamental notion of reality testing. In both cases the test subject seems to be identified on an upbeat. On second thought, however, I recall Schreber's "basic" notion of tested souls (a notion, in other words, of unpurified, unredeemed ghosts), which, among many other moments in Schreber's delusional system and alongside Freud's analysis of the anxieties involved in being tested,[6] seem to give funereal foundation to the connection between Benjamin and Freud. Dick assigns Freud to the world the psychotic loses in the break, though the test of the viability of each new delusional order or insight will be the renewed compatibility with the Freudian reality test, which, as Dick and I hope ultimately to have shown, maps out where the dead are within the loss it recognizes, scans, and plumbs as real.

To inhabit the compatibility between us, consciously for a change, I have organized a multilayered reading of y(our) oeuvre. I relied on intertexts that were for Dick trying but true. Freud, Carl Jung, and Ludwig Binswanger mainly inhabit this range of reading. Since Dick claimed to be fascinated by any theoretical or clinical work on schizophrenia, I have consulted studies by other clinicians, which Dick would or could or should have encountered. What Dick took up philosophically and theologically he did so mostly indirectly, but regularly, via encyclopedia articles. I do not mean to undervalue encyclopedic discourse: the new world could not have been colonized without it. That's the spirit that, from California to Mars, continues to stamp the survivability of the frontier: do it yourself, but with instruction manual in hand. Just the same, I have represented his strong philosophical tendencies not methodically but by proxy, via Gotthard Günther, the German philosopher of cybernetics, Hegel, and then some. Though he remains unnamed in Dick, his articles on the philosophy of science written for the American science fiction magazine *Startling Stories* in the 1950s during the time of his exile from Nazi Germany (his wife was Jewish) comprise the foreign body it takes to know one. It's true, Günther's reflections fold out of a corner of the science fiction community from which Dick felt excluded (though he did publish one early story in *Startling Stories*). I am not, however, terribly dependent on whether or not Dick knew about these remarkable essays. Through Günther's articles I allegorize that commitment of science fiction to philosophy that Dick took too seriously by half—on the better behalf of his investment in the condition and concept of schizophrenia.

According to Fredric Jameson, the objective of Dick's "absolute formalism"—the approximation of the writer's concrete social and psychic content—is end to the mere means of the work's so-called meanings, which belong instead among the work's raw materials. Dick's motifs solve problems of representation inherent in their content (365). "Thus the elective affinities between Dick's writing and the most traditional theological figures and figurations need not be interpreted in any conventionally religious way, unless religion is itself nothing more than just such an intense aesthetic and formal obsession with representation as such" (370). What counts for the religious themes goes double for the secular ones like psychosis. "It would be possible to show, I think (and here the works of Philip K. Dick would serve as the principal exhibits), that the thematic obsession, in SF, with manipulation as social phenomenon and nightmare all in one may be understood as a projection of the form of SF into its content" (263). But if, following Jameson's argument, we therefore enter into the manipulation to the full extent of submission to the authority of the author, who alone is the source of unity or disunity in the work, then we can also see that in science fiction we remain inside a singular (and secular) mind. Only if it is of one mind can the unhousing or unhinging of reality—the crisis of uncanniness—prove legible as world. A mind is a terrifying thing to waste upon the reader, who is of the two minds, but each wrapped up in the other. I thus give priority to the legible borderline passing through psychosis along which Dick unfolds his thought experiments on the way to giving them form. What Dick's science fiction has in common with the theories of psychoanalysis and with certain survival tracts housing the memoirs of psychosis is self-analysis.

As I commenced reading P. K. Dick in 2004, I found his science fiction fundamentally bound up with a certain staging or foregrounding of Freud's encounters with psychosis. Dick's frame of reference is locally based in California but seeks the wide open via readings of Goethe and Schiller. Dick immediately became the Californian correspondent of my new three-way reading of Benjamin's *Origin of the German Mourning Play,* Schreber's *Memoirs of My Nervous Illness,* and Freud's interpretation of Schreber's *Memoirs.* But I also recognized Dick as the living proof of my earlier work, notably *The Case of California.* There are more ways of traversing an inheritance or transmission of knowledge than is allowed by the interpersonal models or methods applied in our classrooms. Even the transmission of the superego skips the generational link and is mediated instead by the transferential borderzone Freud assigned to telepathy: up close it is always the parental superego of our parents we encounter as "first" contact with our inheritance (*Standard Edition* 22:67).

All that's left of the section Schreber earmarked for tell-all discussion of "soul murder," after his family managed to delete everything in which its system was recognizable, was the literary reference to Faust's pact with the Devil among the techniques whereby existence is prolonged at the expense of another's. Before he died, Dick was planning his ultimate Faust novel. While Dick cited or summoned Goethe's *Faust* regularly in his published works—to the extent that *A Scanner Darkly* and *Galactic Pot-Healer,* at least, could be considered as Faust novels—only in this projected narrative would the issue of lifetime's extension have been addressed. To cut to the chase after a second lifetime (which is what Goethe's Faust obtains as the span wide enough for mounting an affirmation of life) Dick introduces the biochip, which allows thought to live on with another's body, in time at that body or brain's expense. But that "life" can in turn be slipped as biochip into another host. Like the superego, then, each biochip would skip (a) generation while forwarding its survival beyond lifetime but still in spans of finitude that stagger the relation between self and other. Joe Chip is the name of the protagonist of *Ubik,* the novel in which Dick gives the longest heir extensions to lifetime at the breaking point when self and other lose and rescue each other through the interminable infrastructure "half-life" of finitude, which Dick called "half-life."

I discovered in Philip K. Dick a precursor. My one and only practical critique over the years has been to inquire of every system of thought and belief what it does with and for the dead. Dick posed my question regarding the location of the dead relentlessly and from the ready, set, and the get-go. Now, for the duration of the memoirs of our encrypted states, it is our question to raise, not to bury.

In his essay on the *Doppelgänger,* Otto Rank cites Pausanias's intervention in the Narcissus myth: young man Narcissus sees in the reflecting surface his dead sister (who is his double or twin).[7] That narcissism is circuited through the other's loss and that the undead loved one fits the crypt-compatible shape of twin fold out of this niche of an exception within the self-relational reception of the tight spot in which Narcissus finds himself and which will not wash out. Sadger's understanding of your homosexuality as identification with the missing mother via assumption of her love for you (as little one or the Big One) also contributes to the prying loose of a melancholic space internal to narcissism, the libidinal foundation, after all, for every object relation.[8]

Philip K. Dick was born as twin of his sister Jane, who died a few weeks after their premature birth. Dick's loss of his twin sister doesn't qualify as your usual case of melancholia, not because he was only a baby at the time of (no) impact but because his mother didn't play the role of secret sharer in the transmission of loss. It would seem instead that she faced motherhood already on psychotic turf. Dick's reminiscences of his mother, which he shared in an interview with Gregg Rickman (whose diagnosis of Dick's early sexual abuse must be viewed as 1980s-typical circumvention of this uncanny turf report of crisis), lays out a delegation of murder threat as the thread of psychotic "mourning":

I didn't go to her funeral. I was sent a ring that she had worn all her life that her father had given her and I give it away to the first girl I met. I asked for it and deliberately give it away. I deliberately asked for it to give it away.... She bordered on psychosis all the time. She bordered on paranoia all the time. I even remember as a little child hearing her tell me that she knew that I... had hidden her medication so she would die.... When she first started telling me about my dead sister, she said "It's just as well she's dead," and I said "Why?" and she said "Well, she would have been lame." I said, "Well, what do you mean?" and she said "Well, we burned her with a hot water bottle so she would have been crippled for life, so it's a good thing that she's dead."... When I tell that, all of a sudden it gets to the point. They burned her seriously enough so they know she should be in a hospital and they don' t take her there and she would have been crippled from that burn and they, she's dying of starvation, she died of malnutrition. See. And I hate her for that. Because I grew up an only child without that sister and all those years she'd make sure I knew about that dead child. My twin. (She) showed me a lock of her hair, told me what color her hair was. And said "It's a good thing she's dead." And the rest of that message is, "And why aren't you dead?" (Rickman, *To The High Castle,* 3–4)

But how does this fit a life history? Dead Jane is what the industry refers to as a continuity error, a plot point that all P. K. Dick's subplots, and all P. K. Dick's themes cannot put back together again with the larger narrative.

At age six Dick developed a symptomatic inability to swallow. The attending physician thought it was necessary to separate the "hysterical" child from his mother (his parents had separated the year before). But when he nearly starved to death at boarding school, he was brought back home. The comparison that is always available in the grid of these reminiscences is that animals, too, will simply refuse to eat—unto death. "As he told me, it's 'true of many animals, you know, when they're in mourning. Anorexia is common, is common to grief but now that I mention it, that is what she died of, she died of malnutrition' " (47). This is how Philip Dick's father Edgar Dick recalls what he takes to be the origin of P. K.'s love of cats. Mother and son had gone west. A cat Edgar had nursed back to health impeded his ability to follow. When he tried to give the animal away, it just wouldn't eat. Dorothy urged him to put the cat to sleep. "Leaving the cat at his home for the vet to drop by and kill, he 'felt something in his back' and 'dropped the phone' as if 'I had a stroke' while at work that day. Calling home he was told that the animal had 'just been put to sleep.' The old man concluded that this was 'the beginning of Philip's love for cats,' although it is hard to see how" (27–28). What is hard to know, at any given point in the narrative of P. K.'s childhood, is who's crazy now. As cat lover, P. K. Dick allows his twinned other to love dogs (and thus be other). As we will see, this division of work of mourning is clearly demarcated between Provoni and Morgo in *Our Friends from Frolix 8*. P. K.'s earliest work, a poem, dated November 11, 1940, and titled "He's Dead," marks the onset of his writing, as cat lover, with a dirge for the other's missing other, totemically mediated as a dog's life. "Our dog is dead / He's here no more. / No longer is he / At the door, / To send us to our / Work each day" (in Rickman, *To The High Castle*, 392). The poem, which continues along the way stations of leave-taking and reminiscence, receives a more complete orchestration in *Flow My Tears, the Policeman Said*, in which the animal component of *Do Androids Dream of Electric Sheep?* so often overlooked in the reception folding out of the assembling line of projected androids, is redeposited as the other's mourning. But first there was his very first story "Roog," in which Dick opened the dog's I view of garbage disposal as murderous threat from outer space against which our best friend seeks to defend us. What we don't see but the barking dog does is that we are unwittingly paying protection to aliens who, once they tire of this regular offering in a can, will proceed anaclitically to take us in as takeout. As Dick recalls in "How to Build a Universe That Doesn't Fall Apart Two Days Later":

> The story was about a real dog, and I used to watch him and try to get inside his head and imagine how he saw the world. Certainly, I decided, that dog sees the world quite differently than I do, or *any* humans do. And then I began to think, Maybe each human being lives in a unique world, a private world, a world different from those inhabited and experienced by all other humans. And that led me to wonder, If reality differs from person to person, can we speak of reality singular, or shouldn't we really be talking about plural realities? And if there are plural realities, are some more true (more real) than others? What about the world of a schizophrenic? Maybe it's as real as our world. (260–61)

Alternate present reality began as a dog's world.

Dick's footing with psychosis allowed him to immerse himself in the legacy of melancholia or narcissism, the deep end of mankind's traditions/transmissions in all talk of life (and death). Like the fourth dimension of Spiritualism, the psychotic/mythic perspective allows a view of loss, not this time as the other's safe deposit, or rather, yes, this time as that death charge, but doubly so or from both sides now. The question of the reception of loss is at the same time the question of reality testing (in psychosis). For Dick, loss isn't simply transitive, linear, or for life but the other reality of relationality at the core of our greatest narcissistic resistance to influence or contact. Here loss isn't bigger than the two of us. Instead self and other are encompassed by one loss through which both, each lost to the other, fall and, as continuity error, continue to fall.

P. K. Dick was frequently convinced that the other so-called reality was a mass delusion: you think you are. Only God exists. However, the corollary argument is advanced in *Valis* that the death of a pet is argument enough against believability in and desirability of God's existence.

In his last words in an interview published posthumously and way belatedly (in 2000!) as *What If Our World Is Their Heaven? The Final Conversations of Philip K. Dick,* the soon-to-die author looked forward to his next novel, the Faust novel he would never write (or had always already been writing), and reflected on his state of recovery from his (in every sense) last novel, *The Transmigration of Timothy Archer,* the non-science-fiction volume concluding his Valis trilogy. In this trilogy Dick staggered as seemingly separable phases the elements he metabolized all together now in works like *Ubik* and *The Three Stigmata of Palmer Eldritch*. *The Trans-migration of Timothy Archer* concludes with the outside chance that dead Archer lives on in Billy, the schizophrenic son of his assistant and lover, whose death, like the earlier death of his son, was mourned by Archer while still alive by staying in touch through Spiritualism. What was miss-ing from this conclusion was affirmation of the science fiction that Dick built up out of all the psy fi doubles of the genre. This is what the unwritten novel would have delivered.

But there is looking back. The projection of a new novel folds out between the lines of his completed or introjected works. He decides that he now will write his version of the Faust story: "it is almost the paradigm of the writer" (67).

In Dick's last conversations we can follow out a mapping of incor-poration. The multiple senses of encryptment rise up from Germany as ambivalent introject (Beethoven *and* World War II), while Dick's Faustian striving is introduced and enacted as soul murder. But *The Transmigra-tion of Timothy Archer,* the bookend of this reopening that the projected book would never close, introduced soul murder as the double duty of crypt carrying that communication with the realm of the dead levies. As wife of Timothy Archer's son, Angel is the only figure without model in the true story of Bishop Pike's sojourn in Spiritualism before up and dying in or for the secularization of mysticism (which as itinerary covers much of Dick's science fiction). Dick's own involvement with the Bishop is a blank she could be seen to fill. And yet he can't fill her shoes. Angel Archer is Dick's one exogamous choice in the recycling between life and fiction. Angel became for Dick evidence of foreign embodiment whereby he could write down or describe what he couldn't understand or otherwise come up with. "I mean, half my time is spent reading what Angel is thinking, this is all her thoughts, you know, her thoughts throughout—and she is liter-ally real to me. And now OK, where did she come from? She didn't come from my mind. She did not come from my mind, because it's impossible, unless I somehow contain another human being" (58). The relationship to haunted Angel, whose part in his novel exceeds the whole for which Dick stands surety, suggests the possibilities of a relationship of dictation between figures who never knew one another, who never came into any kind of interpersonal contact.

I suddenly realized that the character in the book, Angel Archer, was literally as real to me as my own girlfriend. And I thought, . . . "This is absolutely impossible," because there is no such person as Angel Archer. . . . Where did she come from? (58)

Or again:

I almost died writing that Angel Archer book.... After I finished the Angel Archer novel, I was convinced I could write anything.... If I could write from the standpoint of a character smarter than me, more rational than me, more educated than me, funnier than me, I said OK, I can do anything. (66)

The work of survival was to be the Faust novel based on thoughts he couldn't follow. To get around this impasse—or pass the baton to Angel—Dick enters it as encryptment.

First Dick comes up with the reversal of the notion of the oxymoron, the notion or diagnosis that a concept is self-contradictory. Dick focuses on the self-reflexivity: "You don't have to know anything but the statement to know that it is wrong, because it contradicts itself" (77). He concludes that if there are assertions that contradict themselves, then "there also must be self-*authenticating* statements" (79). Dick switches from Aristotle to World War II encoding and decoding. In addition to the code books, British agents behind the lines needed some way of authenticating the encoded transmissions as coming from them—and not for example from German soldiers who had overrun the British agent. In one instance the Germans figured out the extra twist of self-authentication:

They picked up these codebooks, the Germans did, and they transmitted the most looned-out material to England for years. And the English never caught on. So what the Germans wound up doing is whatever things they were short on—trucks,... whatever they needed, parts of some kind, ball bearings and that kind of stuff—they would transmit a request for these parts. They'd say we really—... the underground, the French, the maquis...—need ball bearings in this particular size, whereupon the RAF would fly over and parachute down ball bearings to them. *(laughs)* Germans were restocking their shortages from England that way, by overrunning the cipher book. (81)

This laugh from the crypt of Dick's identifications tracks the ultimate German fantasy and limitation each time, at Germany's invitation, the world came to war: transmutation of running out of reserves as running on empty. The takeoff of rocket flight was the ultimate fetish triumph over the castrational depletion of supplies. It is a condition Germany at World War II would share with Heidegger's inquiries into technology and with a recognizable lexicon for the analysis of the schizophrenic process.[9]

While trying to analyze what would be a self-authenticating factor in a cipher transmission, Dick "shorted out" (82). The long before the short of it was that whereas, before, for Dick to write something down was to be done with it, now he found himself reading over what he had written and finding it all too difficult. "I could invent them, but I couldn't understand them after I'd invented them" (82). He was now inventing in advance of his ability to understand his inventions—ultimately of the other. Via his book on Spiritualism as an encapsulated form of psychosis, Dick made contact with an other inside him—he invented her—who is just the same uncontrollably on her own and in nowise subsumed by him, if only because her ability to understand remains in advance of his own. They share the excess of his invention but from divergent vantage points. Now he can invent thoughts or figures that are beyond him, but which internalized others can receive, compute, and transmit. Thus he doesn't greet Angel as the ultimate embodiment of his once and future undead. Angel is rather the proof that he is his own living on in excess of himself in time, in excess of lifetime. She is the placeholder for a relay of others, human and alien, as melancholic chip on the unknown other's shoulder.

He gets around the impasse of "them" by entering the thought experiment—the work-to-be—as encryptment. The new novel would subscribe to and through the viewpoint of a nonhuman entity, which, by our standards, would be mute and deaf. "It would begin in another star system on a planet with a civilization . . . where there is no atmosphere such as we have, and as a result speech has never developed; . . . and as a result . . . they have no art that is predicated on sound" (88). More precisely, they have "no collective atmosphere": "What they had was pockets. Each is in a self-contained atmosphere" (94). The aliens use different color frequencies for language. Just as human mysticism imagines light as prefiguring the next world, since visual language is the limit concept of our world of words, ciphers, and music, so the aliens would have mystical visions of the other world, but precisely not as "vision" but as supernatural experience of music, of sound. Thus each civilization across interstellar distances would be the other's next world. But the disconnection between them, as loss, can be conveyed in both directions only as encryptment.

So now, these people who have never used sound, . . . even when they can transduce it electronically into something, they still are unable to grasp what's going on. Except when they experience a religious breakthrough. And for them, it's a mystical experience, which is completely incomprehensible. (100)

Well, now they encounter a planet where there is sound, and not only is there sound, there is music. Well, to them, this would be a sacred planet. This would be . . . like finding God. The only problem is, they can't experience it. Except one way. There is only one way it can be done.... They would have to enter a symbiotic relationship with a human being. There's no way an electronic technological interface would work, because music is conceptual. And the electric interface would only give them the bare bones.... If they can patch into a human brain, in a symbiotic relationship, then they can use the human brain to conceptualize the music. (103–4)

The biochip is the greatest breakthrough in information storage... The biochip is alive; when it is implanted in the brain it will grow into the nervous system of the brain. It will grow into the neural tissue. (106)

And the lovely thing is... when the host dies you pull the biochip out, and it's now got the host's memories. Which you could then insert in another host. (108)

At this point in the novel-to-be viewpoints will be switched: the alien decides to biochip himself and enter a human host brain as symbiote.

We switch viewpoints to the human being who is a composer. Now, that host for a symbiote from this alien planet would be a person who is involved with music all the time.... We'll have him be a very routine composer, but financially successful... He writes the music for cheapo science fiction movies. You know, these clones of *Star Wars*. And he makes a lot of money. But he has no original ideas. None whatsoever. And they have this really rotten science fiction film about this detective who's tracking down these androids. And this guy is writing this schmaltzy score to go with this movie.... Now, it's easy to track him down because he's well known. They stick the biochip of the alien life form into his brain. OK, now, the bioform is alive and it is essentially the mind of the alien—he's on that biochip.... The biochip lives there passively for a while, and that is the psyche of the alien, ... but this guy does nothing but listen to the dullest music available on the planet.... Well, it has a remedy. There's a remedy for the biochip and that's to take control of the guy's... actions.... What finally happens is that the biochip develops a system where it begins to feed the guy mathematical ideas which the guy then converts into music... which then passes back to the biochip, which the biochip then remembers. So it is now taking an active role in the creating of musical compositions.... This thing, this biochip has got the guy writing night and day on these really difficult compositions.... It is evolving through... hierarchical layers, evolutionary layers of music where greater complexity, greater originality, greater artistic merit, whatever axis you want to describe—it's evolving like Beethoven's music did from period to period to period. It becomes evident very soon that this is going to kill the host brain. (112–20)

But before death there are symptoms, scanners, and physicians: the biochip is discovered. Once the alien symbiote realizes that the host knows all about the biochip on his shoulder, he initiates direct, conscious contact with the human. He counsels removal of the chip that could then be sent up to the mother chip. Because if their relationship continues, it's just as the doctor ordered, the host will die very soon. But the composer wants to continue writing great music until he dies. The solution: "if the alien can be turned into a biochip, the human mind can be turned into a biochip. . . . And inserted into the brain of one of the aliens. And what you will get back in exchange . . . for what is essentially the death of his body . . . is he will be inserted into the brain of an alien and he will be able to do something that was denied any human before. He will be able to experience their world of vision and color" (123–24).

The alien host in turn "will have to sacrifice himself and die" (125). To push back the fantasy of infinite self-cloning, Dick stipulates that when the biochip becomes an intact personality, the original brain is dead. While the living on of the biochip isn't exactly death, Dick underscores the finitude of each prolongation of life in whatever form. "Otherwise you could biochip yourself forever. You could create thousands of yourselves, you know. . . . There would never be any problem. No problem would ever arise for anybody once you could do that" (129–30). Therefore it's "Goodbye, Mr. Biochips" (108), whereby the problem of Dick's work can begin again.

PART I

Endopsychic Allegories

That is a logic which Freud attacks, by the way, the two-proposition
self-cancelling structure. Freud considered this structure a revelation of rationalization. . . . The second statement does not rein-
force the first. It only looks like it does. In terms of our perpetual
theological disputations—brought on by Fat's supposed encounter with the divine—the two-proposition self-cancelling structure
would appear like this:
  1) God does not exist.
  2) And anyhow he's stupid.

—PHILIP K. DICK, *Valis*

Following a discontinuous case of California, from here to Germany, it
proves possible to fold P. K. Dick's Valis trilogy inside a relay of texts—by
Daniel Paul Schreber, Freud, and Walter Benjamin—which together promote in the details and among the effects of haunting a process of secularization while at the same time addressing and maintaining, in the big
picture, the religious frames of reference, but as abandoned ruins, lexicons
still deposited in our range of reference, but deposits without redemption
value. As illuminated by the German intertext or introject's Californian
supplement, the overlaps and gaps between the cluster of notions Benjamin bonded to allegory and the cluster bonding between Schreber and
Freud, which Freud identified as endopsychic, reflect, back in their own
time, the pull of what also made them draw sparks and draw together,
namely, the subtle secularization that Spiritualism introduced into the con-
gregation of discourses, even the properly disciplined ones.

I have elsewhere already projected an occult atmosphere of influence
binding Freud's study of Schreber and Benjamin's *Origin of the German*

Mourning Play over the read corpus of Schreber's *Memoirs of My Nervous Illness*.[1] In his short illustrated essay, "Books by the Insane: From My Collection," which he published in 1928, Benjamin recalls his purchase in 1918 of Schreber's *Memoirs*. "Had I already heard about the book back then? Or did I only discover the study a few weeks later, the one by Freud in the third volume of his *Short Writings on the Theory of Neurosis*? (Leipzig, 1913). It's all the same. The book immediately grabbed me" (615–16). What goes with the flow of these sentences is that his discovery of Schreber's book and his knowledge of Freud's study are all the same. When he then summarizes the highlights of Schreber's delusional system, he opens up a pocket of resemblance between the psychotic's order of the world and the stricken world of the melancholic allegorist. "The sense of destruction of the world, not uncommon in paranoia, governs the afflicted to such an extent that the existence of other human beings can be understood by him only as deception and simulation, and, in order to come to terms with them, he refers to 'quickly made up men,' 'wonder dolls,' 'miraculated people,' etc." (616). What Benjamin finally finds most compelling is the projection and consolidation of a world in the course of a kind of drama of stations, namely, in Benjamin's words, "the stations this illness passed through all the way to this remarkably strict and happy encapsulation of the delusional world."

By explication, exclusion, and implication, the main skewer passing through these three works is Goethe's *Faust*, which they reintroduce to the setting of the paranoid or melancholic world, where one world's destruction is another world's reprojection or allegorical resurrection out of a libido of self-absorption. Schreber's delusional system, so recognizable to the allegorical reader of the melancholic state, represents an act of recovery. Freud's guess is already another man's ghost: at the time Schreber was writing his memoirs, his older brother was already deceased; he had skipped the class of delusional patients and gone down the one-way street of suicide. Not only suicide, however, but recovery, too, is already equally carried over through *Faust* to the world that empties out in the mode of catastrophe. As Freud underscores in "Psychoanalytic Notes on an Autobiographical Account of a Case of Paranoia (Dementia Paranoides)": *The delusion-formation, which we take to be a pathological product, is in reality an attempt at recovery, a process of reconstruction. Such a reconstruction after the catastrophe is more or less successful, but never wholly so" (Standard Edition* 12:71). This surprising turn away from the downbeat of psychotic shutdown and fadeout to the positive thinking that's delusion was introduced with Freud's quotation from *Faust*. A chorus mourns the world Faust has destroyed inside and out only then to pick up where that left off and enjoin him, the over man, the over-and-out man, to build it all up brand-new from within himself. Between the lines of both Freud's and Benjamin's silent readings, we cannot but recall that Faustian striving is itself constituted as the deferral of a suicidal impulse that overtakes Faust in the setting of his academic world and almost compels him to cut off his life to spite his fate or father. The motor of his recovery is his splitting image, Mephistopheles, the spirit of negativity. Recovery, according to Freud's analysis of Schreber's case, runs for the cover of negativity. His persecution or selection by God at least—at last!—recaptures some relation to the world.

For Schreber the limit concept of this recovery, up there with big brother, was suicidal withdrawal into a dead world, the world of the dead, inside him. Freud allows that detachment of our libidinal connection occurs not only in psychosis and alone cannot account for its serious consequences. It happens in "normal mental life," Freud reassures us, and adds, "and not only in periods of mourning" (72). Thus Freud at once deregulates detachment of libido and nixes "substitution" for the lost attachment as the sole purpose of mourning. And yet the liberated libido normally kept suspended within the mind until a substitute has been found is in paranoid schizophrenia reassigned specifically to the ego, which is thus aggrandized. The potentially suicidal detachment, therefore, in its alternation with projection from out of our narcissistic libido of a whole culture of recovery (some call it California), offers another way to get around losses that's not the one-way consumer choice between mourning and melancholia.

In my own collected (but still ongoing) reading of mad books, Schreber's work is so far unique in its invocation of incommensurables, its combo of techno-science as well as pseudo-science with the shaken structures of religious belief over his own interminably finite body or corpus and its haunted sensorium. This ability of Schreber's delusional order to contain itself in its ongoing internal juxtapositions and in cohabitation with the reality he by rights returns to corresponds to what Benjamin refers to as the encapsulation of his delusional world. This encapsulation does not, however, like another Emperor's new closure, refer to an allegedly completed process that, at least in the way it is maintained in the official record of the Schreber case, Freud simply sees through. Other accounts of severe mental illness are either secular psy fi—for example Barbara O'Brien's *Operators and Things*—or religious fantasy, whereby I mean specifically the bookstore-created genre of fantasy, which however, at least according to J. R. R. Tolkien, bases its narratives of other worlds and happy ends on the one fantasy story that is at the same time true: the New Testament. Thomas Hennell's *The Witnesses* is a good example of this latter genre of psychotic autobiography. In either case the books tend to keep to a restricted economy of disintegration and reintegration, ending with a pervasive sense of loss of function, in other words of depletion of some form of vital energy. In both *Perceval's Narrative* (edited by Gregory Bateson) and Clifford Beers's *A Mind That Found Itself,* the recovered-mad authors take their former delusional systems with them into their restored sanity, but only as a special motivation or fervor in the pursuit of certain activities that in its proximity to the original spark of derangement sets up the close quarters in which the psychiatrist recognizes that it's time for a booster stay in the hospital.

As closest point of comparison and inspiration, I rely, then, on Dick's trilogy rather than on another mad book, even though the author also received his first schizophrenia diagnosis during the year he attempted attending college, and the trilogy itself can be seen as fictionalized "autobiography" relating to certain mystical or psychotic experiences that in February and March of 1974, as Dick writes in the nonfictional word outside the trilogy, "denied the reality, and the power, and authenticity of the world, saying, 'This cannot exist; it cannot exist'" (in Sutin, *Divine Invasions,* 214). In the trilogy, containment or consolidation of the "end of the world" resettles religious beliefs in the extended finitude of science fiction. In the first volume, also titled *Valis,* the protagonist, Horselover Fat, whose contact with God, essentially an alien from outer space, took the form of a "beam of pink light" fired directly at or into him (20), turns out to be the split-off double of Philip Dick, the translation into English words of his Greek/German proper name.

The Valis trilogy breaks and keeps apart the metabolic or generic phases originally mixed up in *Radio Free Albemuth,* Dick's first attempt to give form to his 1974 breakthrough and summary perceptions. It's a mainstream novel the way *A Scanner Darkly* is a slightly updated fictionalized version of the present. Dick's trial formulation, which was left behind for posthumous publication, focuses on a science fiction author who witnesses his best friend become a case study in schizophrenia, mysticism, or sci-fi contact with outer space. The case internal to the narrative gradually subsumes it until *Radio Free Albemuth* becomes a "paranoid" social novel. For this larger frame Dick borrows the paradoxical intervention he liked to make against the reign of the projective identification of his work with a certain European Marxist reception: Nixon (= President Fremont) was a communist plant. In *Radio Free Albemuth*, the science fiction author is Dick's double in name, while the friend is yet another Dick double. In *Valis*, Dick is represented twice-over, first in one figure, then in two fictional identities linked and separated by translation. In *Radio Free Albemuth*, the author enters the novel as Phil Dick, whose friend Nicholas is undergoing the breakaway contact with extraterrestrial impulses that had been Dick's own inspiration in the off-work. The first part is narrated by Phil, followed by Nicholas's narration, and then concluded again by Phil, who survives Nicholas. In the *Fidelio*-like closing part, loss goes figure when Nicholas's cohort, Sadassa, after meeting Phil for the first time in prison, is up next for execution. When she's gone this was the withdrawal that broke his handling of lack: "I had withstood the death of my friend Nicholas Brady, whom I had known and loved most of my life, but I could not adjust to the death of a girl I didn't even know" (206–7). It's so much easier to let oneself go than to let the other go.

At the onset of self-doubling that Dick lets loose between Phil and Nicholas, a word from our sponsor's representative gives us the time. Nicholas tells Phil about his nighttime visitation by his double, himself ("Ich bin's" he had cried out). "I told him it was himself from an alternate universe. The proof was that he recognized himself. . . . No one could ever recognize his own future self" (11). This pledge to the present must be renewed over and again. The counterscenarios owe their timing to fantasy, through which they are strung along. The opening fantasy scenario, as reconstructed by Phil's initial diagnosis, doesn't come full circle. "As far as I was concerned it was a chronic fantasy life that Nicholas's mind had hit on to flesh out the little world in which he lived. Communicating with Valis . . . made life bearable for him. . . . Nicholas . . . had begun to part company with reality" (24). The diagnosis shifts (together with the overall momentum of the narrative) when Phil witnesses the light show of contact and the accuracy of the information relayed to Nicholas in that flash. But all along there was a lot that Nicholas hadn't told his friend: "It was his intention not to appear crazy, which is a desire indicating some residual smarts, some vestigial grip on reality after most of it had fled" (25). By following Valis, Nicholas gets out of the rut in which he was cracked: "The imaginary presence of Valis—whose name Nicholas had been forced to make up, for want of a real one—had made him into what he was not;

had he gone to a psychiatrist he would still be what he was, and he would stay what he was. The psychiatrist would have focused his attention on the origin of the voice, not on its intentions or on the results" (36).

While science fiction comes through and true for Nicholas, Phil, now that he has witnessed the healing power of the pink light, switches to the outside chance that what Nicholas is dealing with is "religious": " 'There is a slight chance . . . that . . . you are being informed by the Holy Spirit, which is a manifestation of God' " (40). Nicholas senses the emergence inside himself of an other's "Ich bin's": "Someone is waking up in me. After two thousand years. . . . The programming they're giving me—it's to wake him" (41). But even this is one of many theories Nicholas has been contemplating and writing down in the place of Dick's own endless "Exegesis" whereby he kept after the possible meanings and syndications of his 1974 experience or perception. The outer-space saga fits the Christian frame of reference as fantasy (not science fiction): "The Fall of man . . . represented a falling away from contact with this vast communications network and from the AI unit expressing the voice of Valis, which to the ancients would be the same as God. Originally . . . we had been integrated into this network and had been expressions of its identity and will operating through us. Something had gone wrong; the lights had gone out on Earth" (112). The lights went out when "the malign entity that did not wish to hear" invaded and imprisoned the world (113). But the fantasy, if only because it cannot maintain a separate place in this "paranoid" novel, recedes before the present of science fiction: "The new personality in me had not awakened from a sleep of two millennia; it had, more accurately speaking, been printed out by the alien satellite, impressed on me afresh from outside. It was an addition, not a substitution in place of me but a kind of package identity" (ibid.). The packaging of additional or alternate identities extends throughout the endopsychic allegory that Valis or the AI unit (or the sibyl) folds out by enfolding, not just for example, the adversary.

Since I could question the AI unit, I asked her why the opaque adversary had not been removed a long time ago; obligingly, she furnished me with a diagram which showed the adversary drawn steadily deeper into the fulfillment of the general plan. . . . Although it drew on everything, arranging it and most of all joining otherwise separate sections into totally new and unexpected entities, it took only what it absolutely needed. Thus its reshaping process took place within the universe, turning the universe into a kind of gigantic warehouse of parts, an almost infinite stockpile, in which the agency could find anything it desired.

The temporal process . . . was a medium by which this proliferation of forms was capable of taking place, for the benefit ultimately of this shaping entity, which . . . moved backward through time from the far end of the universe. (114–15)

The conclusion is no more redemptive than the mood swing that stays the suicide of Goethe's Faust. The songs may belong to Easter, but what he hears are children's voices calling him back to the child's-I view of the future as the coming toward you of interminable possibilities. Phil hears the subliminal lyrics that juxtapose "president" and "joining the party" for which Nicholas and Sadassa gave up their lives as a diversion making way for the song's release in another place. What crosses Phil's mind in earshot of the survivor song are his last words of the novel: "The kids." In Dick's world, the Teen Age heralds the future that the android technology fundamental to it seeks to bring down or control in the present. Another affirmation thus lies in the conditions of Phil's survival as "nothing eternal." His sentence of fifty years in prison without parole means, also because his novels are still being written by the propaganda department and will continue to be published in his name all this time, that he would be released after he had been dead a long time (207). It is a "stiff" sentence of ghostwriting that, like self-reflexivity or another alternate present, extends the corpus in finitude.

In *Valis* the duo dynamic between friends is exchanged for the ambiguous fit with doubling in one person. The healing beam that restarts theorization of Nicholas's altered states in *Radio Free Albemuth* turns its light on both sides of Philip Dick or Horselover Fat in *Valis*. What doesn't heal is the loss marked in passing out of *Radio Free Albemuth* but which in *Valis* occupies or cathects the foreground of the novel's frame. Prior to the beam's skewering of his duo dynamic, Fat had been serving time as bystander at the deaths of a series of young women. "Tied to him," these "corpses cried for rescue—cried even though they had died" (126). In one of the tractates appended at the close of *Valis*, we find this mourning attachment shifted into the mythic register as mankind's original trauma:

The changing information which we experience as World is an unfolding narrative. It tells about the death of a woman. This woman, who died long ago, was one of the primordial twins. . . . The purpose of the narrative is the recollection of her and of her death. The Mind does not wish to forget her. Thus the ratiocination of the Brain consists of a permanent record of her existence. . . . All the information processed by the Brain . . . is an attempt at this preservation of her. . . . The record of her existence and passing is ordered onto the meanest level of reality by the suffering Mind which is now alone. (233)

Recognition that the deceased twin is lonely, too, opens the full range of deregulated mourning in Dick's corpus.

"Valis" is also the title and subject of a film flickering through the volumes of the trilogy. It is the acronym for a secret project spelled out as Vast Active Living Intelligence System and identifiably contained in and conveyed by an ancient satellite in the film and then apparently at large. Does this contradict the divine beaming, Fat wants to know. No: "that's a sci-fi film device, a sci-fi way of explaining it" (154). But the sci-fi device also attends Christianity's consequent immersion in finitude. Christ was an extraterrestrial. The original Apostolic Christians acquired immortality through Logos, a plasmate or living information that could be absorbed. Their immortality was the extended finitude variety. Because they could be—they were murdered. Now the plasmate, which had "gone into hiding," "was again loose in our world" (161).

"We had started out wounded. And VALIS had fired healing information at us" (177).[2] The protagonist is healed, after eight years of madness, when he meets the latest Savior (the fifth so far). "Horselover Fat was part of me projected outward so I wouldn't have to face Gloria's death" (191). But the Savior will not grant Gloria, the first in the series of women who died on him, immortality: she's dead in the grave and won't return. But then this computer-spawned Savior dies, too. At the end Fat returns. "'Then the true name for religion,' Fat said, 'is death'" (219).

In *The Divine Invasion*, the second volume of Dick's trilogy, the information conveyed by the VALIS film or satellite provides frame and background for the clandestine return of Yah or Yahweh to earth, a fortress Satan sealed tight against God's influence a long time ago. At the point of landing, however, the ship gets identified and blasted. The brain damage that keeps Yah from remembering that he is God is a plot point in a boy's lifetime: the other story is that the Godhead has lost touch with part of itself. The boy's playmate, Zina, steps into this missing place. Zina, whose name in Roumanian means "fairy," rules a fantasy realm, the "Secret Commonwealth," in which the real world is doubled but with all the political figures, for example, oppressive in reality, displaced among the rank and file, their influence thus minimized. Zina's fantasy genre challenges Yah to delay the day of reckoning that would scourge the world. But God will not affirm fantasy or, as He puts it precisely, wish fulfillment. According to God, the "power of evil" consists in a "ceasing of reality, the ceasing of existence itself. It is the slow slipping away of everything that is, until it becomes . . . a phantasm" (136). The point of phantasmic comparison is

Linda Fox, a mass music star and media image. God gives life or reality to the phantasm, and to Herb Asher, the Fox's nonstop consumer and biggest fan, He gives the outside chance of encountering her in the flesh. God thus means to prove to Zina, who had earlier miraculated up a live semblance of the singer for Asher's sake, that what is real is always stronger than mere make-believe. Asher indeed falls in love with the real Linda Fox. Zina's fantasy alternative however succeeded in tricking God into standing by this world, an affirmation that He then cannot take back. Thus the Godhead is re-paired.

It turns out that Linda Fox was realized only as the ultimate medium, the medium as the message or the immedium, as the Advocate, the figure or placeholder of Christ. This figure, as Zina earlier instructed Yah, originally performed services for the dead only, offering advocacy on their behalf against Satan's prosecution. A bill of particulars that Satan submitted always weighed in as burden of proof of sinfulness that could never be deducted or written off: the dead were condemned to pass through the apparatus of retribution and ultimately pass into nothingness. But then, one day, way back in primal time, the Advocate appeared. If the soul agreed to his representation, then the Advocate would submit a blank bill of particulars and thus free the soul from an otherwise inevitable doom.

The doom of death, however, is never lowered in Dick's novel, for which the secret commonwealth serves as its internal simulacrum. Yah challenges Zina: "'You admit, then, that your world is not real?' . . . Zina hesitated. 'It branched off at crucial points, due to our interference with the past. Call it magic if you want or call it technology; in any case we can enter retrotime and overrule mistakes in history'" (162). The ability to go back in time to when the dead are still alive is not only an option for the characters in *The Divine Invasion* but is the determining momentum of a narrative in which, by doubling back again and again, death, as Goethe was given to proclaim, is everywhere swallowed up by life. However life opens wide only by recycling survivors back in time. "How many lives do we lead? Herb Asher asked himself. Are we on tape? Is this some kind of replay?" (166).

But the last installment of the trilogy, *The Transmigration of Timothy Archer*, doesn't share the fantasy: the challenge of death—or rather of the dead—returns, but this time not as the pathogenic impetus for the flight into fantasy or Christianity as the redemption value of what begins as a paranoid sci-fi delusional system. Framed by a survivorship that Angel, the narrator, is hard-pressed to dedicate to mourning, the bulk of the novel transpires in the recent past when Timothy Archer, Angel's father-in-law, her husband, Jeff, and her best friend, Kirsten, were still around.

New archaeological digs in the historical setting of Christ turn up a continuity shot with the preceding two volumes, though by another name. Now the substance that an initiate could eat and drink in order to become God Himself is the anokhi to which recently uncovered ancient evidence repeatedly refers. While Bishop Archer and his consort, Kirsten, are in London conducting research on the anokhi's field of reference, Jeff kills himself. All this time, as always in the meantime, while suicide was crossing Jeff's mind, the anokhi, soon believed to be an actual mushroom, has been undermining, in the Bishop's mind, the very existence of such a thing as Christianity. He continues: "Jesus was a teacher not a God, and not even an original teacher; what he taught was . . . a group product" (82). And this group production sends the real possibility of extension of finitude to the front of its line. In no time, Kirsten announces: "Jeff has come back to us. From the other world." Bishop Archer links the prospect of Jeff's return to the anokhi whereby "man literally rises from the dead. They had the techniques. It was a science" (131). But Jeff's spirit, just like the anokhi, does not prove "the reality of Christ" (138).

Timothy Archer, Kirsten, and Angel visit a medium in Santa Barbara. The Bishop looks forward to communications with his son via a medium "much in the fashion that a telephone acts" (143). Kirsten expects the dead to know the future because, in the dimension they inhabit, it has already happened to them (166). Angel, along for the ride, diagnoses the belief in ghosts as a remarkably isolated, indeed encapsulated form of fixed idea or madness, which can cohabit with all other functions or systems go:

> There is no airtight logic involved in inferring that broken mirrors and singed hair and stopped clocks and all that other crap reveals and, in fact, proves another reality in which the dead are not dead; what it proves is that . . . you are not reality-testing, you are lost in wish fulfillment, in autism. But it is an eerie kind of autism because it revolves around a single idea; it does not invade your general field, your total attention. . . . It is a localized madness, allowing you to speak and act normally the rest of the time. (113)

Just the same, Menotti's *The Medium* keeps crossing her mind. Just as in Menotti's opera, in this Californian medium's discourse, too, alongside all that is patently a hoax, Angel finds "stuck in here and there, a fragment like a tiny shard that could not be explained" (156).

Timothy Archer is based on Dick's close friend, James Pike, the maverick theologian and bishop, whose dead son Jim was the subject of his 1968 book *The Other Side: An Account of My Experiences with Psychic Phenomena*. Dedicated "to Jim," *The Other Side* plots Pike's conversion to Spiritualism along lines familiar to readers of *The Transmigration of Timothy Archer*. One of the interpretations of his own mystical experiences in 1974 that crossed Dick's mind was that Pike was communicating with him from the other side. Toward the end of his account, Pike concludes: "The astronomers' discovery of signals from outer space . . . is comparable to the psychologists' investigations of extrasensory perception" (346). The science fictive frame of reference underscores that communication with ghosts or spirits remains, though a breakthrough at one level, stumped by finitude just the same. Ultimate questions can still only be raised, not answered—from the other side. But the remarks made by the spirits are so unnecessarily stupid. Not really, Pike counters. Imagine what I would come up with in order to identify myself to you over the phone: "It would be almost impossible for me to *prove* that it was I on the other end of the line. Yet I suspect that after talking with me for some time and asking a number of questions, you would be willing to gamble one way or the other regarding my identity" (270). The communication is also mediated. "In fact, being in a séance is comparable to listening to an old-fashioned crystal radio: what comes through is spotty, disjointed and often difficult to decipher" (238). We jump media when the connection is good, but too many spirits want to get on the line. "The conversation moved on and I couldn't imagine where all these different characters were coming from. It was like watching selected short subjects at the movies" (260). That the contact with the other side does not alleviate the crisis of his faith is one more reason for Pike to believe the extrasensory evidence of his senses. His crisis, which he shared with Jim, came out of the corner into which his so-called reductionist method had painted and pained him. "I did not know sufficient data upon which to base an affirmation of life after death" (52). But Jim's comeback doesn't prove that life after death is resurrectional or redemptive in significance. Ghosts, too, only have their own opinions or beliefs to go on. Jim's spirit: " 'nothing I've seen over here makes me any more inclined to believe in God' " (128). Pike, in sum: "Any counsel was only the advice of another finite being, as I had previously concluded, and the fact of his being 'on the other side' did not automatically make his words true or wise" (202–3).

    The Other Side is continuous with countless writings on Spiritualism. In the heyday of modern German Spiritualism, Max Dessoir addressed the limitations and mistakes marring the discourse of "spirits." Even what they get right seems so unimportant, even pointless. "One can admit that the powerful rip and tear of dying and the . . . new form of existence with its conditions unknown to us possibly put an end to what we thought we knew while altering, perhaps eliding the earthly valuation of what was known. One of these personalities noted in regard to certain questions: remembering of this kind was so difficult, as though one were trying to remember a dream" (96). Regarding the triviality of the communications, Dessoir cites Professor Hyslop, who set up a series of experiments to determine what is said when two persons connected by phone try to identify or legitimate themselves. The results indicated that only the most indifferent things occurring to the persons in the moment were voiced. Dessoir refers to another observer who compared the séance exchanges to another kind of telephonic experience comparable to speaking in tongues: "between the clear and understandable sentences, which are intended for the listener, barely audible and senseless fragments of other conversations occasionally crossing over from other lines insert themselves in the pauses" (139).

According to Karl Du Prel, Spiritualism can defend itself from detractors only by submitting to tests even as it essentially is always testing itself. Just a test means: it's not just a test. Just because it is possible to simulate a ghostly presence, doesn't mean that every séance ghost is a fraud produced along these lines. Hans Arnold describes séances as the organizing circles of Spiritualism, all of which must pass through "test circles," in which one keeps on demonstrating and exercising through techniques of control and precision the working psychic power in relation to the astral body of the medium and in relation to the astral body of the earthly dead. Du Prel argues that Spiritualism is testable to the extent that somnambulism, mesmerism, and hypnosis form a hub of observable activities and capabilities to which Spiritualism hitched its start in analogy. "In fact, to those well-versed in this area, analogies appear between the abilities of somnambulists and those of so-called spirits" (267). Given the fluid nature of the borderline between somnambulism and Spiritualism, hypnotists can be expected to turn up Spiritualist phenomena. Dessoir turns around this hub the prospect of "automatists" (rather than mediums) whose inner states (shared to some limited degree through thought transference) are projected as individualized figures "related to the images of the mentally ill, the dreamer, and the poet" (*Vom Jenseits der Seele,* 138). Du Prel argues that the reception of materializations in séances, arguably the most extreme results or claims of Spiritualism, was adjusted already by Darwin as possible in theory. In the later editions of his *Origin of Species,* Darwin added that he underestimated the spontaneous emergence of modifications, while already in the first edition he noted that natural selection is most important, but cannot be viewed as the only auxiliary means of modification of life forms. Moreover, technology and aesthetics demonstrate an interchange, even an equality, between natural and spiritual products: just as the camera obscura unconsciously copied the inner workings of eyesight, so the golden mean or cut corresponds to the proportionality of the human organism (268–69).

That the organizing abilities of the soul or psyche should be confined to this bodily incarnation is an "unjustified assumption." If we step outside such assumptions we stand before the prospect of materialization. The secularization inherent in Spiritualism also concerns the demons that the Church allowed could take on human form as departed loved ones in order to deceive people. But séances leave the impression of social contact not better or worse than that with people you know (273). However Du Prel stops at this impasse: proof is needed that the spirits are indeed the dead. The proof is furthermore required, for starters, to support the Spiritualist belief in immortality (whereby it jumps the haunting medium to sign a deal with Christianity as its new-and-improved version). There are many reasons Christianity cannot accept the Spiritualist cultivation of relations with the dead or undead. But Spiritualist, as another articulation of the provability or thinkability of Christianity, participates in the secularization that inheres in the Christian belief system as its half-life.

In Dick's novel, Bishop Archer and Kirsten need to know why Jeff is trying to contact them—he has so far only been knocking about in the poltergeist mode—and his father plans to ask him about Christ. Bishop Archer never gets to pose his Christ question. It turns out Jeff was trying to contact his father and Kirsten because he was concerned about what he foresaw: that they were both soon going to die. It is, then, a death wish that has returned. Kirsten soon kills herself whereupon Bishop Archer gives up the ghost. But though he lets Jeff go, he continues to hold onto the anokhi, traveling to Israel to search the deserts for the mushroom. Finding just desert and losing his way, Timothy Archer dies still in range of the death-wish forecast that, just like a telephone operator, the Santa Barbara medium had merely forwarded.

Alone again with Angel, as we were in the beginning, we encounter again the other survivor, Bill, Kirsten's schizophrenic son, at the same guru session Angel randomly picks and attends. But Bill, who earlier, if only because his thought processes are set in the concrete, considered both

God and ghosts sheer nonsense, in the meantime has found enlightenment, according to the guru. What Bill tells Angel, however, is that he
now believes in God because Bishop Archer has come back inside him:
"Because of Tim in me, I know a lot of things; it isn't just belief. It's like . . .
having swallowed . . . the whole *Britannica*" (235). The last psychiatrist to
treat him diagnoses Bill's hallucinations as the special effects of his introjection of the objects of transference-love, both the Bishop and Angel.
Whether as the ghostly return of Timothy Archer or as her last tie to the
people she loved and lost, Angel takes Bill home. She brings home, then,
as she recognizes in the transmissions going through Bill, belief systems
that are, says Angel, "without a trace of anything redemptive" (237), but
through which they have already passed and have not yet passed. The
death-wish ghosts of Freud's science, the summoned spirits of Spiritualism, the scientific search for concrete ways of extending finitude on the
historical turf of religion, and hallucinations all together now inhabit a
transferential field that is also a field of reference that Schreber's *Memoirs*,
Freud's study of Schreber, and Benjamin's *Origin* book dig.

The other "mainstream novel" (other than *The Transmigration of
Timothy Archer*) Dick published in his lifetime, *Confessions of a Crap
Artist*, includes on the side—on the inside—the psychotic perspective
that, with focus fixed on the awakening of the dead, looks forward to life
expectancy extended both through ghosts and through alien visitation of
the end of the world as the sci-fi reformatting of the Second Coming. The
elaborate recycling of resurrection scenarios serves the remembrance or
return of one individual, Charley, who recently died on the crap artist, Jack
Isidore. His fellow psy fi cult member doesn't understand why he's not in
group on the appointed day: " 'I don't see why you have to stay there and
wait for that particular person to come back to life' " (243). But when the
dis-appointment comes, Jack decides to accept that he is mentally ill and,
as work of mourning, also accept Charley's bequest of funds for psychoanalytic treatment. But the double decision withdraws from realization as
Jack plots a request for multiple second opinions. "In my mind I began
putting together a questionnaire for them to fill out, telling the number of
patients they had had, the number of cures, the number of total failures,
length of time involved in cures, number of partial cures, etc. . . . It seemed
to me that the least I could do was try to use Charley's money wisely"
(246). This reapplication of testing to the reality of loss that the mourner
pulls up short before onset and outcome of successful mourning and thus
preserves is combined in Isidor and split apart between Angel and Bill.

In *The Transmigration of Timothy Archer,* Schiller's *Wallenstein* provides the focus for recurring comment on the recent past inside the twentieth century, both the historical era of Nazi Germany and the private time in which death poses certain problems, but for others. Bishop Archer singles Schiller out for his importance to the twentieth century (74). It was in contrast to the "whole spirit of Goethe and Schiller," which "was that the human will could overcome fate," that Schiller showed in *Wallenstein* "a man who colluded with fate to bring on his own demise" (76). Like father, like son: "Upon reading Schiller's *Wallenstein Trilogy,* Jeff leaped to the intuitive insight that had the great general not gotten involved with astrology the imperial cause would have triumphed, and, as a result, World War Two would never have come into being" (57). After Bishop Archer recants his embrace of Spiritualism following Kirsten's death, the *Wallenstein* commentary is again up and running: "I see myself falling into Wallenstein's fate. Catering to astrology. Creating horoscopes. . . . That wasn't Jeff" (183). The recurring commentary on Schiller's *Wallenstein* is, as connection that wasn't made or put through in Jeff's lifetime, the placeholder or prop for the occult communication between father and son.

When Schreber lists his precursor ghost-seers he summons the Maid of Orleans and thus also cites the Schiller drama. (But the pre-mediatic term "ghost-seer," which Schreber uses, already refers to another Schiller text, the narrative *The Ghost-seer.*) Benjamin cites the "miraculous effects" that Schiller had recourse to in *Die Jungfrau von Orléans* as one of a few examples where, in spite of his famous attempt to base tragedy on history in place of myth, he ended up, on the sidelines of that project, approximating the mourning play. His main line of production "sought to base the drama on the spirit of history as understood by German idealism. . . . In doing so he wrested from classicism the possibility of giving a reflection of fate as the antipode of individual freedom. But in pursuing this experiment . . . he inevitably came closer and closer to the form of the mourning play. It is a mark of his superior artistic understanding that, the idealist theorems notwithstanding, he had recourse to the astrological in *Wallenstein,* the miraculous effects of Calderón in *Die Jungfrau von Orléans,* and Calderónesque opening motifs in *Wilhelm Tell*" (301).

Benjamin closes the 1928 review of his mad book collection with a guarded, tongue-in-check, update on difficulties attending acceptance of insane works for publication. Our tolerance and interest must have risen by now. "And yet I've known for a few months now about a manuscript that in terms of human and literary value at least equals Schreber's book, and surpasses it in accessibility, and which nevertheless seems as hard as ever to sell to a reputable press" (619). "How could Benjamin not be referring, at least at the same time, to his own book, *Origin of the German Mourning Pageant,* as the other mad book with a Freudian reception already in place. Although by 1928 it had at last survived its submitted manuscript status, his *Origin* book would for Benjamin never shake its martyr role on the stage of intrigue."[3] Thus Benjamin appears to summon his *Origin* book in a setting of exchange or interchange with Schreber's *Memoirs* and Freud's study—and down the transferential corridors of disappointment in a former world of legitimation through which both books first had to pass before a public, published forum could be reached on the outside. What would then also be encapsulated here, at this turn of identification, is Freud's highly reflexive performance of the staggered interchangeability of his theory, the workings of the psyche this theory uncovers and illustrates, and the delusions Schreber records in his *Memoirs.*

The inside-out view of the inner workings of the psyche projected outward as the delusional representation or mass mediatization of our funereal identifications was termed by Freud endopsychic perception. For Freud this notion commenced in connection with myth in a letter to Fliess dated December 12, 1897, but first made it into his work, on an update, in *The Psychopathology of Everyday Life:* "A large part of the mythological view of the world, which extends a long way into the most modern religions, is nothing but psychology projected into the external world. The obscure recognition (the endopsychic perception, as it were) of psychical factors and relations in the unconscious is mirrored—it is difficult to express it in other terms, and here the analogy with paranoia must come to our aid—in the construction of a supernatural reality, which is destined to be changed back once more by science into the psychology of the unconscious" (*Standard Edition* 6:287–88).

Herbert Silberer, who was the occult correspondent in Freud's circle, rereads along endopsychic alignments a reported case of "magnetic" healing of a psychotic from the practice of Justinus Kerner, a key figure in the pretelegraphic history of modern Spiritualism organized around clairvoyance, somnambulism, magnetic rapport, and seeing ghosts. A Duke consults with Dr. Kerner and his famous patient, the clairvoyante of Prevorst, Mrs. Hauffe, about his mad wife back home. The Duchess has been immersed in a "waking dream life" since her second pregnancy. Three idées fixes close the circle within which her dream images move about. First, she doubts the reality of her husband and children. Second, she yearns for her own transformation out of the monster she thinks she is (as heard on the audio rack of her voices) and for her liberation from a state of imprisonment. Third, she awaits with anticipation the supernatural manifestation that will bring about the sought-after transformation.

Mrs. Hauffe "sees" the Duchess as locked up and fixated in the "dream ring." Therefore she recommends that the Duchess penetrate more deeply into the dream ring and move about therein freely, unfettered—or, better yet, if possible, that she step out of the ring that has her collared and enter the external world. In the first case she would become "magnetic" and available for treatment; in the second scenario she would be cured. After six days of treatment as prescribed by Mrs. Hauffe, during which time the patient showed no signs of improvement, suddenly the Duchess summoned her husband and with great excitement informed him that she had felt compelled to think deeply of the clairvoyante whereupon she just had to tell him what had caused her condition, something about which he was completely unaware. (We never find out what this exciting cause was.) Thus, dramatically, she left the dream world behind for reality. However her sojourn in the dream world wasn't without residue. She still heard her critical voices for example. Now the Duchess visits the clairvoyante in person. Mrs. Hauffe prescribes prayer. The Duchess asks how she can ever hope to forget the unsettling thoughts. Mrs. Hauffe answers that she won't forget them, but she will henceforth see them with other eyes.

The follow-up treatment was just as successful as the initial breakthrough. Silberer credits the endopsychic structure of her delusions with the cure. Mrs. Hauffe could assist the Duchess because she inhabited the same religious belief lexicon in which the delusions were formulated and could therefore be reformulated along the more-or-less secular lines of Mrs. Hauffe's own personalized religious faith, which proves to be in the first place a hub of long-distance communication and healing. Yearning for transformation and liberation from her bewitchment is the projection outward of an inner state reminiscent of the psychic origin of fairy tales and related mythic material. They are, Silberer credits Freud, endopsychic perceptions projected into the outside world. Silberer brackets out the doctrine of magnetic healing, the frame of reference for Kerner and Hauffe. What's more important is that the clairvoyante served the Duchess as the idol of a belief that, by suggestive power alone, can move the mountains inside the Duchess under which secrets had been buried alive. The cathartic experience of breaking through is set off between this belief in the clairvoyante and the talking cure she conducts with her husband. The rest is case history of a successful treatment. The follow-up phase is equally important. Silberer cites both Freud and Jung on the work of fortifying breakthrough or insight. The sudden insight is adolescent: to make it into adulthood and sanity the flash must be secured within the infrastructure of its staying power. Mrs. Hauffe prescribed religious exercises, and that much more adamantly when the patient showed resistance. Thus she was first able to release energy in the patient through transferential trust. Subsequently she was able to ground the released energy through the power workout on resistance. The patient's complex dated back to her years in convent school where dream and reality had commingled. The patient resisted going back to school, though it was here that clarity had to be energetically introduced. She goes back not to find religion. Like Faust staying his suicide attempt when he hears children singing Easter hymns, the Duchess renews her vows with her early years to face her disturbing thoughts freed of their religious-delusional nimbus. It is possible to argue that preliminary to the treatment of psychosis, religious belief must be reformatted as transference and as working through resistance. What makes this possible is the endopsychic structuring of the beliefs or delusions themselves. Silberer sees the relay of secular transformations clearly enough. But, clinically speaking, you cannot see through the murky whether-or-not conditions of the endopsychic advisory while making your approach to psychosis's borderline.

In the course of developing ways of understanding Schreber's delusion of the end of the world Freud admits that he lacks the coordinates of a well-grounded theory of drives. But beyond the acceptance by psychoanalysis of the popular distinction between egoic and sexual drives, between self-preservation and preservation of the species, Freud identifies "only hypotheses, which we have taken up . . . in order to help us to find our bearings in the chaos of the obscurer processes of the mind" (*Standard Edition*, 12:74). At its outer limits the psychic field is at a psychotic loss of world or words. But at the end Freud restores stability by finding reflected in Schreber's rays of God the concrete representation and external projection of libidinal cathexes. He thus addresses Schreber's endopsychic perception at the undecidable intersection between the possible truth of Schreber's delusions and the possible delusional dimension of his own theories.

When Freud enters a paranoid system he encounters analogies internal to it that are doubly endopsychic: "these and many other details of Schreber's delusional formation sound almost like endopsychic perceptions of the processes whose existence I have assumed in these pages as the basis of our explanation of paranoia. I can nevertheless call a friend and fellow-specialist to witness that I had developed my theory of paranoia before I became acquainted with the contents of Schreber's book. It remains for the future to decide whether there is more delusion in my theory than I should like to admit, or whether there is more truth in Schreber's delusion than other people are as yet prepared to believe" (12:79).

Freud's proprietary frenzy at this juncture, a paranoia of sorts, out of sorts, refers in the first place to the source of the Schreber book: it was one of Jung's transference gifts. Freud was wary of its unconscious itinerary and purpose. Another stopover in Freud's contemplation of such inside viewing, Jensen's *Gradiva,* was another one of Jung's gifts. If we keep in mind that the endopsychic perception first emerges in the correspondence with Fliess, it proves possible to assign this perception to a field of reference through which the transference has passed and has not yet passed. Or, in other words, endopsychic perceptions supply the gap of noncorrespondence or unfulfillment between the ruinous materiality of the transference (whether in session or in action) and the theory that would contain or caption it. In yet other words, endopsychic perception drives or meets half way Freud's work of analogy in the theorization of the transference, a work commensurate with that of mourning, through which, moreover, the psyche builds up to or through our ongoing technologization.

Once Freud could see it coming, namely, the recurring dissolution of all his same-sex friendships, he addressed the transference both as a medium of haunting, whereby, in his case, each new friend was really a returning spook, and, in its reproducibility, as an effect of the printing press: each new phase of the transference was but a reprinting of the same old cliché. At the end of where he drew the line with regard to the homosexual component, Freud identified an early libidinal bonding with John Freud, the son of one of his older half brothers and his playmate in early childhood, which got around while encrypting the relationship to his dead brother Julius. The psychoanalytic *theory* of ghosts first arose to account for Leonardo da Vinci's homoerotic disposition in the context or contest of a speed race between repression and sublimation that subtended his techno inventiveness, and then returned within the study of Schreber's paranoia to address the delusional order of technical media and ghosts in terms of a recovery from sublimation breakdown.[4]

Freud emphasizes that Schreber repeatedly reproaches God for the limits of His self-awareness. When it comes to human life, God only takes cognizance of its corpse state, at which endpoint God reclaims the rays, souls, nerves that he originally deposited when he created the life-form that he apparently immediately represses. Only the afterlife of his creations (when he gets his nerves back) concerns Him. Schreber inadvertently challenged or entrapped God when, passing for dead—while, perhaps, melancholically playing dead—he was beset by the deity, who started harvesting the presumed corpse; but when the inert body came alive God was caught in the act contrary to the order of the world. The living nerves grab God and prove to be the kind of turn on that God can't readily let go. The dead cannot enter the state of bliss as long as the greater part of the rays of God are attracted to and absorbed in Schreber's voluptuousness. Because there is such a close relationship between human voluptuousness and the state of bliss enjoyed by the spirits of the deceased, Schreber looks forward to future reconciliation with God. But Schreber holds up the afterlife above while bringing the bliss down to earth. As Freud underscores, Schreber sexualizes the heavenly state of bliss and thus, we can add, irrevocably secularizes the afterlife while allegorizing its Heavenly trappings as to be already dead for.

Schreber's delusional system or project, even in its second phase and phrasing, is interminably in transit. It is unlikely that unmanning will ever be concluded. God's sense of self-preservation together with his inability to learn from experience (if only because the nerves that know better are the ones at the front of the line of the vanishing act of intercourse with Schreber) means that he will keep on attempting withdrawal, even though each attempt increases Schreber's attractiveness to God. There will only be gaps, delays, repetitions, or "stations" in this crossing over without end.

The outside chance of renewal at this crisis point (that, in the eternity Schreber contemplates, happens because it recurs) will always be performed in the medium of a ghost seer: "'a seer of spirits' . . . must under certain circumstances be 'unmanned' (transformed into a woman) once he has entered into indissoluble contact with divine nerves (rays)" (45). Schreber counts himself one of the greatest ghost-seers at the head of a line drawn through the Wandering Jew, the Maid of Orleans, the crusaders in search of the holy lance, the Emperor Constantine, and, in his own day, "so-called Spiritualist mediums" (78–80).

In *Radio Schreber* Wolfgang Hagen carefully reconstructs the Spiritualist context of Schreber's *Memoirs,* beginning with its cornerstone, footnote number 36, which drops from Schreber's declared interest in scientific work based on the theory of evolution as evidence of his basically nonreligious sensibility, which, he submits, really should give credence to his newfound relations with God. Hagen shows, however, that "evolution" in Du Prel's cited work, for example, is linked to a basic sensibility or soul at the atomic level that causes the chaotic atomic mass to develop ordered structures on its own. Hagen's study is filled with the details of the works Schreber explicitly includes and the inevitable intertexts he doesn't name, like works by Johann Carl Friedrich Zöllner and Gustav Theodor Fechner. The complex, situated in the overlaps between science and Spiritualism, keeps returning to two basic assumptions: that of the atomic soul already mentioned and that of a fourth dimension that makes as much possible as it openly declares unprovable. Du Prel, again, turns, in the work Schreber claims to have read repeatedly, to the theory of a fourth spatial dimension, according to which the world we perceive is just the "projection picture of a four-dimensional world in a three-dimensional cognition apparatus." Fechner, one of the first to formulate the theory of a fourth dimension, argued, as Hagen cites for compatibility with Schreber's system, that because we are rolling in our three-dimensional ball through the fourth dimension, as are all the balls within the big 3-D ball, everything that we will experience is already there and that which we have experienced is still there. Our three-dimensional surface is only through the fourth dimension, has already passed through it and hasn't yet passed through it.[5] "I dare not decide," Schreber pauses to reflect in his *Memoirs*, "whether one can simply say that God and the heavenly bodies are one and the same, or whether one has to think of the totality of God's nerves as being above and behind the stars, so that the stars themselves and particularly our sun would only represent stations, through which God's miraculous creative power travels to our earth (and perhaps to other inhabited planets). Equally I dare not say whether the celestial bodies themselves (fixed stars, planets, etc.) were created by God, or whether divine creation is limited to the organic world; in which case there would be room for the Nebular Hypothesis of Kant-Laplace side by side with the existence of a living God whose existence has become absolute certainty for me. Perhaps the full truth lies (by way of a fourth dimension) in a diagonal combination or resultant of both trends of thought impossible for man to grasp" (8).

The discourse of or on Spiritualism, pro or contra, relies regularly on analogies with media technologization. Among the scientists and theorists gathered together in Schreber's note 36 we find immediate recourse to telegraphy and the telephone to describe the manner of communication with ghosts or to evoke the absurdity of the belief in spirits or even to signify its redundancy in our mediatized setting (with the telephone in place, for example, there is no need for telepathy, which is, in quality, a less direct connection).[6] The conjunction of both analogies that Freud identified, when developed into a system of thought or order of the world, to be endopsychic in reach can be found in the footnote underworld to which Schreber thus consigns as introjects in flotation ever since the breach of overstimulation destroyed his world the very batteries running the rewired transference in the new world order of recovery. In note 58, then, Schreber gives the following two analogies as the derisive translations of the basic language by the soul of Flechsig, Schreber's treating physician and, according to Freud, the brother of all transferences. This soul's expression for being among fleeting improvised men was "amongst the fossils . . . following its tendency . . . to replace the basic language by some modern-sounding and therefore almost ridiculous terms. Thus it also likes to speak of a 'principle of light-telegraphy,' to indicate the mutual attraction of rays and nerves" (118).

As shorthand for my inability to follow Hagen beyond the point of contact with this Spiritualist context into his far-reaching new history of the emergence of a psychotic discourse of analogization with occult and technical media out of the delay in the scientific understanding of the same electricity that could be more readily harnessed and made to transmit, I note that he overlooks his one colleague and precursor in the basic matter of relocating Schreber's *Memoirs* with regard to its place of publication.[7] In "Books by the Insane: From My Collection," Benjamin indeed identified the publishing house standing behind Schreber's *Memoirs* as a well-known gathering place for Spiritist or Spiritualist studies, and recognized in Schreber's "theological" system (with its God Who can approach only corpses without danger to Himself, Who is familiar with the concept of the railways, and Whose basic language unfolds as an antiquated but powerful German) its Spiritualist provenance. But, and this Hagen indeed demonstrates, to know one it takes one immersed in Spiritualism to see through Schreber's discourse to the bare bones of its ghost communications.

Before closing the *Origin* book, Benjamin returns to a contrast between the Baroque German mourning plays and the mourning plays of Calderón (whose successful mourning plays Benjamin associates with the exceptional case of Goethe): "The inadequacy of the German mourning play is rooted in the deficient development of the intrigue, which seldom even remotely approaches that of the Spanish dramatist. The intrigue alone would have been able to bring about that allegorical totality of scenic organization, thanks to which one of the images of the sequence stands out, in the image of the apotheosis, as different in kind, and gives mourning at one and the same time the cue for its entry and its exit. The powerful design of this form should be thought through to its conclusion; only under this condition is it possible to discuss the idea of the German mourning play" (409). This thinking through requirement gives interminable mourning the last word. Benjamin conjures successful mourning, the kind that's only passing through, as limit concept of the German Baroque mourning play, right after floating a Devil pageant past us, according to which allegory cannot but fall for the Satanic perspective that introduces and subsumes it, and thus in the end "faithlessly leap" (in Benjamin's words) toward God. Benjamin describes allegory's act of suicitation, a return to Devil and God that allegory otherwise interminably postpones: everything unique to allegory, Benjamin underscores, would otherwise be lost.[8]

Benjamin attempted in his 1925 essay on Goethe's *Elective Affinities (Wahlverwandtschaften)* to generate a reading of the novel out of the novel itself. He ended up identifying Ottilie's withdrawal from speech and life as, verbatim, death drive. Benjamin concluded that this is a work dedicated to adolescence, to the bottom line of the Teen Age: namely, preparedness for death. A proper death thus emerges out of the duration of young life. The sole candidate for ghost of the departed in Goethe's uncanny novel, in which haunting, however, is strictly circumscribed, is Ottilie's ghost appearance in her handmaiden's eyes only: in a vision she sits up in the coffin and blesses the girl, whose self-recriminations are forgiven, whose shattering fall just moments before, a momentum that is associated (even in the history of the words involved) with *Trauer* (mourning), is miraculously reversed. Thus in this Christian niche death captions the ghost: but then this spirit of the departed is forgotten or forgiven in a comfort zone only for those who fall for resurrection. Otherwise, the apparitions in *Elective Affinities* are telepathic videophone connections, two-way dreams, which keep physically separated lovers in meta-touch. To borrow a term from Benjamin's mentor, Paul Häberlin, a term cited in fact by Freud in *Totem and Taboo*, they are "sexual ghosts." Häberlin, who introduced Benjamin to psychoanalysis in 1916 in a course of study at the University in Bern, which settled Freud's thought within range of occult analogies and phenomena, unpacked a couple of case studies to show that certain ghosts, even in households that counted a recent death, referred only to desired but prohibited contact with living sexual objects.

Ottilie's undecaying corpse is ensconced within a certain psychoanalytic reception of the endopsychic doubling between Schreber and Freud. Down this receiving line, Hanns Sachs derived from Freud on Schreber and Victor Tausk's follow-up treatment, in light of the Schreber study, of the delusional system of Natalija A., a genealogical scheduling of narcissism's shift from body-based self-loving to the self-esteem of power surges and other strivings to the beat of self-criticism. In antiquity this shift could be deferred: the restriction of technical developments or difficulties to the invention of playthings only subtends this deferral. But the crisis point must always also be reached as the uncanniness of zomboid dependency on the dead or undead body that does not go or let go. According to Sachs, the invention of machines that undermine bodily proportions and limits skips the uncanny beat of the body by projecting its missing place way outside itself as the techno reassembly of parts and partings. The psychotic thus projects techno delusions to get out from under the uncanny body.

The mill on the grounds of Eduard and Charlotte's estate that, through its grinding, its *Mahlen*, doubles, says Benjamin, as emblem of death (139), offers a supplemental scenario for Ottilie's preservation. Because as she lies there undecaying she is in the tightest spot imaginable of vulnerability, especially in a novel given to earmark the ambivalence toward commemoration that underlies, for example, the architect's plans for funerary monuments based on his study of the relics he has collected ultimately through desecration of graves. Grinding like cremation represents then a removal of the site specific to desecration of all the contents of a complete and untouched tomb. Other than the mill we encounter in Goethe's novel only optical instruments and playthings, like the portable camera obscura the British traveler uses to record his landscape souvenirs. Benjamin registers a certain pervasiveness of these placeholders of a missing technologization when he notes that the pictorial elements in Goethe's narrative are more in line with the perspective of a stereoscope.

The assistant comments on how all the best plans of Eduard's father, which are only now achieving fruition, are ignored by Eduard and Charlotte as they make their improvements in other parts of the estate: "Few people are capable of concerning themselves with the most recent past. Either the present holds us violently captive or we lose ourselves in the distant past, and strive with might and main to recall and restore what is irrevocably lost" (278). Charlotte is quick to understand, she says, but only up to a point of displacement, whereby she shunts to the side the direct impact of this span of attention or tension dedicated to mourning, and wonders instead whether the present tense doesn't serve to mislead us into thinking that we are the authors of our actions while we are in fact merely cooperating with the tendencies of the times. Thus the funerary implications are lined up on the side, out of site, like the monuments she uprooted from their proper places and sidelined in the cemetery that she hoped to turn into the friendliest place on earth.

What links and separates Benjamin's "Goethe's *Elective Affinities*" and his *Origin* book is contained in a translation Benjamin summons in his study of the Baroque mourning play: Gryphius deliberately replaces deus ex machina with spirit from the grave (313). The stricken world of allegory is the turf of what recently was. Signification begins once life lapses into lifelessness. It is, as in its visitation by ghosts, a world of mourners or unmourners. When they enter the stage they left, ghosts shock. It is part of the nature of allegories to shock. That is how they become dated (359), how they leave a date mark. When Tolkien altogether rejects the claim that there are allegories in *The Lord of the Rings,* he takes issue, specifically, with the timely or tendentious reach of allegories that cannot but inscribe onward into the work's real-time setting or context. *The Lord of the Rings,* Tolkien emphasizes, is in no wise shaped by the events of World War II otherwise surrounding his scene of writing.

Allegorization thus looks forward to the gadget connection, the spin of a dial or flick of the switch that, according to Benjamin (in his essay "*Uber einige Motive bei Baudelaire*"), mediates and buffers the incapacitating shock of technologization. The pushbutton control release of shock, its administration as inoculative shots, preserves or internalizes a body-proportional comfort zone inside technologization. The gadget controls also stamp moments with date marks, marking them as dated memories, emptied out but secured, and which are, as far as their determining force goes, forgettable. Thus in the forget-together of moviegoers doubling over with sadistic laughter over Mickey Mouse's destructive character the realization of sadistic fantasies and masochistic delusions is prevented just as psychotic disintegration under techno mass conditions is forestalled on the shock or shot installment plan ("Das Kunstwerk im Zeitalter seiner technischen Reproduzierbarkeit," 462).

Like the allegorist, the paranoid takes enigmatic pleasure, in other words a sadist's delight, in watching the world end. The death drive is unrepresentable in all its purity. But when it mixes with eros you can recognize it striking a pose in sadism.[9] Sadism (or sadomasochism) attends, according to Benjamin, allegory, the only pleasure, but a powerful one, allowed the melancholic. "It is indeed characteristic of the sadist that he humiliates his object and then—or thereby—satisfies it" (360). In the same way the allegorist secures an object melancholically as dead but preserved and thus as "unconditionally in his power" (359).

Schreber squeezed transcendence down inside finitude, but on the upbeat of deferral of all the processes of completion at work on him. Benjamin shows where the world begins for the Baroque allegorist and melancholic: with the recent passing of the narcissistically loved other—and thus inside and during the afterlife of Ottilie. In becoming a woman whose voluptuousness is derived from all things feminine, Schreber looks at narcissism from both sides now while deferring and pursuing Ottilie's other end, the one reserved for the allegorist's enigmatic pleasure. Being in transit still means he has to endure vivisection by the God of corpses. However, even when he's all messed up, just like Mickey Mouse he gets reanimated, restored so he can bounce back for more.

When the mythic pagan world gets secularized (witness the example of Socrates), Christianity picks up the slacker as martyr; but the allegory doesn't stop there, doesn't stop its own process of secularization and keep it there. "If the church had been able quite simply to banish the gods from the memory of the faithful, allegorical language would never have come into being. For it is not an epigonal victory monument; but rather the word which is intended to exorcise a surviving remnant of antique life" (Schreber, *Memoirs*, 396). While allegory thus seeks to contain and reformat the return of paganism, its ultimate issue is the secularization that thus indwells even "Christian" allegory. In Christianity's postulation of an other world that is, by definition, too good for this world and of the death of death (or in the Devil's offer of uninterrupted quality time until the certain deadline), as also in the pagan or neopagan overcoming of death within the eternally recurring finitude of life, it is the prospect of the recent past, the era of loss and mourning, that is being shunted to the side, but thereby to the inside, as defective cornerstone, of all of the above.

Goethe, as Schreber notes and as Freud is moved to record, is one of the longest lasting personalized souls, with a memory that from the beyond could still come down to earth for one hundred years or so. Like his Faust, Goethe receives just one more lifetime in which to be able to affirm life. After their personalized or ghostly phase ceases, a generic phase takes over whereby the former souls are absorbed within greater bodies of rays. For the most part Schreber encounters a double disappearing act of the souls of persons he has known inside the span of his lifetime and on his own person. While single nights could also always acquire the duration of centuries, growing numbers of these departed souls attracted to or through Schreber's growing nervousness soon dissolve on his head or in his body. But first many of the souls lead a brief existence on his head as little men before they too exit. While contact with ghosts led many of Spiritualism's initiates to renew their vows with religion, faithlessly I would add, the opening up of the recent past that not only religion must repress is constitutively secular and in Benjamin's sense allegorical. The outside chance that there are more times than lifetime does not add up to the immortality of the soul or reunion with God. As Schreber advises, souls otherwise still recognizable as specific individuals (in other words, ghosts) sometimes pretend to be "God's omnipotence itself" (51).

Schreber Guardian

Loneliness is a particular problem in Southern California because
of the high social mobility. . . . Friendships are made and unmade
instantly. In fact some people already find it easier to establish a
relationship with a stranger than with someone they know. I had
an idea for a story in which everyone is allotted a part in a kind of
soap opera. There'd be dossiers on all the characters, even a script,
only this would be for real. When you were moved to a new area
you'd just go along to the party and say, "Hi, everybody"; and
they'd say, "Hi, Ted" or whatever it was—you'd have name
tags—and you'd carry straight on talking about non-existent
mutual friends and things that had happened you all knew about,
because they were in the script. The trouble is, it's almost true
already.

—PHILIP K. DICK[1]

A year before *The Matrix* (1999) chose mysticism over science fiction *Dark
City* (1998) hit the screen, running science fiction into the burial ground
of lost worlds. Aliens have abducted a large number of humans to study
under the lab and maze conditions of their life-or-death experiments. The
aliens are fading fast: it is surmised that what the humans call soul (or
psyche) has marked them, in contrast, for survival. The intermediary or
double agent between the manipulated mediatic human habitat and the
control room of the alien experimenters—whose voice-over, which is in
the beginning, introduces us to the setting of *Dark City*'s future—is Dr.
Daniel P. Schreber. The aliens or "strangers," who all look like Murnau's
Nosferatu, just in different sizes, and who float, launching themselves like
Nosferatu rising straight up out of his coffin, are marked for extinction.

Apparently, in their dealings with us, they use our dead as vessels. They are distinguished by their powers over (our) reality: they can alter our perceived reality (which they apparently see through and don't fall for) by "tuning" together at midnight. They have the hypnotic power to induce instant sleep in the human subjects, while their tuning reflects their "telepathic energies." When the humans conk out at midnight the aliens rearrange the city like digital special effects, while Dr. Schreber mixes up "cocktails" from recycled stolen memories to inject into the test subjects. Every time there's been a tuning, the humans start over from oblivion in new habitats and identities with new memories to match. Schreber: "I help the strangers conduct their experiments. I have betrayed my own kind." On occasion someone wakes up ahead of schedule with a few memories intact. The resulting insight into manipulation and loss becomes the kernel of an inside view diagnosed as paranoid schizophrenia. Suicide seems the only way out. But the protagonist John Murdoch wakes up with a jolt before Schreber can finish the process of injection of remembered murder of one woman as proxy for the cheating wife—and subsequently fails to fall asleep any tune time—because he is a mutation or missing link, the first human who can also tune. Schreber tells Murdoch's wife (while posing as his physician) that her husband has suffered a "psychotic break." The aliens ordered Schreber to find Murdoch because he is their break: if they can imprint him with their collective memories, then he will be one of them—and, one for all, they can tune in the future. In the meantime, to help track Murdoch, one of their own is injected with the essence of their quarry: "I've John Murdoch in mind." The stranger with the Murdoch imprint meets Murdoch's wife. He and her husband share a great many memories it seems: small world. Contrary to his upbeat discourse on memories, however, she observes that she had always thought that we were haunted by memories.

When John can't find a scar on his person to match what he sees in slides from his childhood, he knows "it's all lies." And yet Schreber can only remix preexisting memories, while the strangers tune in historicist architectural changes derived from memories stolen from their captives. But then there's Shell Beach. Murdoch remembers meeting his wife on the pier there. Though her memories have been changed in the meantime, in the end, without knowing why, she feels compelled to go to the pier, where Murdoch meets her again. Shell Beach is part of the topography no matter how the sets are altered. It's a special memory for Murdoch, but it's also a known place on the map everyone seems to recall. Everyone remembers Shell Beach up to a certain point, whereupon they draw a blank. Similarly the name "Murdoch" stops short of articulating "murder" and sounds out instead the "dock" or pier, the point of return exceeding the abyss of recycling. It's like the arrangement of memory in traumatic amnesia, like the dissociation basic to fetishism. Like Murdoch's wife said, it's like haunting.

It's showdown and Murdoch dominates the strangers. Dr. Schreber gave him the assist. Murdoch was injected not with the collective memories of the stranger race but with an instruction manual that Schreber concocted all about the background and makeup of the experimenting strangers. Now that he has seized the power from the destroyed aliens Murdoch tunes a body of water to wash up against the borders of the outer-space platform on which the humans have served as test subjects.

The last alien encounter (or the closing contact with the order of projection) is between Murdoch and the stranger who is dying of Murdoch's imprint. The imprinted stranger says he volunteered, even though the dying was guaranteed, because he wanted to know how it feels. But Murdoch tells him he'll die never knowing. He was looking in the wrong place: it's not the brain but rather the heart that is the human mark of distinction. The unreconstructed *Metropolis* citation captions the completion of the island in outer space, New York or Metropolis, as California. In the span of the screen medium delusion can be looped through fantasy. The loopy conclusion, however, of *Dark City* as of *Metropolis* (1927) is the defective cornerstone of its reception.

In his biographical study of P. K. Dick titled *I Am Alive and You Are Dead,* Emmanuel Carrère catches up with his subject in the act of reading Freud's study of Schreber's *Memoirs of My Nervous Illness.* According to Carrère, Dick immediately fantasized writing up the Schreber delusional system as a science fiction novel, in other words as a happening event in an alternate universe. Dick's working title: "The Man Whom God Wanted to Change into a Woman and Penetrate with Larvae in Order to Save the World." Carrère reconstructs thoughts crossing Dick's mind. "What if Schreber was right? What if his supposed delusions were in fact an accurate description of reality? What if Freud was just . . . pathologizing a man who understood better what was really going on?" (39). The syndication that did come out of his encounter with Freud on Schreber was his 1959 novel *Time out of Joint,* which turns on the defensive functioning of a psychotic delusional system in its encapsulated form. Dick borrows from Schreber this form of the encapsulation of his system, the unique stability of Schreber's world and wordview in or according to his *Memoirs,* which, you will recall, is precisely the quality Benjamin underscored in his reflections on Schreber's *Memoirs* in the brief essay "Books by the Insane: From My Collection." *Time out of Joint,* however, records and performs the doomed efforts of sustaining this encapsulated delusional world as fantastic system.

Time out of Joint is the first P. K. Dick novel to include explicitly identified psychotic states in the mix of future worlds with words that raise metaphysical questions against the void, like ghosts. The protagonist, Ragle Gumm, starts finding words printed on slips of paper behind or beneath the screen-thin projections that have him surrounded. When, for example, he picks up from the ground a label inscribed "SOFT-DRINK STAND" where the stand itself broke apart as illusion or in delusion, the following passes through his mind:

Central problem in philosophy. Relation of word to object . . . What is a word? Arbitrary sign. But we live in words. Our reality, among words not things. No such thing as a thing anyhow; a gestalt in the mind. Thingness. . . . An illusion. Word is more real than the object it represents . . . Word *is* reality. For us, anyhow. Maybe God gets to objects. Not us, though. (60)

Since we can take Freud's Schreber study as Dick's point of departure, the world of 1959, the year in which the novel was published, which comes complete with the fraying edges and margins through which one can glimpse behind the scenes figures of control, manipulation, or even persecution, is Gumm's new delusional order. It turns out that the world he lost in his psychotic break is that of the late 1990s, a world at civil war with the men and women on the moon. In the meantime "One Happy World," a movement against outer space exploration and colonization, prevailed on earth, while the "expansionists," who at first opposed the isolationist movement on earth as in the heavens, settled on the far side of the moon so that, from the other side, they could fire missiles at earth without fear of retaliation. Gumm, world-famous for the success of his business ventures or gambles, was pressed into the service of predicting where the next missiles from the moon would strike. Under these pressures to perform, heightened furthermore by a mounting conflict of conscience motivating him to side with the expansionists, Gumm developed what is called a "withdrawal psychosis."

In the course of his withdrawal, he referred one day to his intercept predictions as "today's puzzle." Thus those who worked with and depended on Gumm followed him into the safer world of his boyhood, where the local paper runs a contest or puzzle, "Where Will the Little Green Man Be Next," to engage his talent. His daily entry predicting the Green Man's next appearance intercepts another missile strike. "One Happy Worlders," who volunteered to be, in effect, test subjects, were reprogrammed to share Gumm's fantasy as his friends and family in it together in the simulated town and time they call home. But that's why other members of his household, who only think they are related to one another, can also share Gumm's growing sense that their environment may be a false front concealing another world in which they in fact live, but without knowing it.

Gumm's nephew finds in the ruins at the edge of town an unidentified lying about magazine and phone book belonging to an alternative setting so familiar and yet decontextualized. His brother-in-law, Vic, nominates Ragle Gumm as the leader of their pact to investigate further:

> "Start keeping a record of all this. Aren't you the man who can see patterns?" "Patterns," he said. "Yes, I suppose I am." He hadn't thought about his talent in this connection.... "It's impossible ... We have no point of reference." ... "Simple contradictions," Vic disagreed. "This magazine with an article about a world-famous movie star we haven't heard of; that's a contradiction. We ought to comb the magazine, read every word and line. See how many other contradictions there are, with what we know outside the magazine." "And the phone book," he said. The yellow section, the business listings. And perhaps, at the Ruins, there was other material. The point of reference. The Ruins. (72–73)

The daily newspaper contest is accompanied by a series of clues that engage Gumm in free association: "The clues did not give any help, but he assumed that in some peripheral fashion they contained data, and he memorized them as a matter of habit, hoping that their message would reach him subliminally—since it never did literally" (37). The associations that come to mind—"he let the crypticism lie about in his mind, sinking down layer by layer. To trip reflexes or whatever"—include sex, California, food, and homosexuality. Is this where Freud's study and Schreber's *Memoirs* part company or are part family? Are the associations Freud's words to the vise keeping Gumm or Schreber inside the enlisted or institutionalized delusion? Gumm's 1959 world seems suffused with a certain Freudian fluency that keeps everyone in check. "Evil suspicions" that "only reflect projections of your own warped psyche ... [as] Freud showed" (79) and "anxiety" as "a transformation of repressed hostility" leading to one's "domestic problems" being "projected outward onto a world screen" (183) are two examples in lieu of any number of similar exchanges in Freud's name. One more example that brings us back to the starting point of the Freudian association: When Gumm makes up a name to fill in a blank, his sister knows that his slip is showing.

"There's no random," Margo said. "Freud has shown that there's always a psychological reason. Think about the name 'Selkirk.' What does it suggest to you?"... These damn associations, he thought. As in the puzzle clues. No matter how hard a person tried, he never got them under control. They continued to run him. "I have it," he said finally. "The man that the book *Robinson Crusoe* was based on."... "I wonder why you thought of that," Margo said. "A man living alone on a tiny island, creating his own society around him, his own world."... "Because," Ragle said, "I spent a couple of years on such an island during World War Two." (85)

Ragle Gumm withdraws back to the era of his own childhood but, at the same time, *as* his father. The father is history. His father's war stories become Gumm's personal history, which is also grounded in World War II. The Freudian associations that maintain Gumm's 1959 world through the control release and recycling of tensions nevertheless will not stop short of holding Gumm's simulated world under the sway of his internal world.

Gumm's return to sanity and crossover to the side of the expansionists on the moon, also referred to as lunatics, closes the novel on the upbeat. It is an observation made in psychoanalysis, however, that the turn to politics in a setting of deep regression, no matter how commendable or rational the objective and sentiment, is always a strong sign of degeneration toward or along the narcissistic bottom line or borderline of the psyche.

Sane again or just another lunatic, Gumm now recognizes, under the guidance of one of the lunatics who infiltrated his simulated world in order to trigger anamnesis, that his world of 1959 was his childhood fantasy of adulthood. He didn't flash on the most recent Book-of-the-Month Club selection, *Uncle Tom's Cabin*, as continuity error because it is precisely *the* transitional object pulling him through his childhood:

Again he felt the weight of the thing in his hands, the dusty, rough pressure of the fabric and paper. Himself, off in the quiet and shadows of the yard, nose down, eyes fixed on the text. Keeping it with him in his room, rereading it because it was a stable element; it did not change. (250)

Inside the childhood into which Ragle Gumm psychotically withdraws we find secretly etched the spot of withdrawal he was already and still is in.

While the anachronistic book was included, radios had to be edited out of this version of 1959 because the long-distance transmissions going through would undermine the controlled environment, the small world after all of 1959. And yet his memories via his father include manning a radio transmitter during World War II. Thus radios in the revision of 1959 have been replaced by television sets, which are considered the same as radios only more so, with video portion added on. That the radio, constructed fantastically as superfluous in the TV era, belongs in the paternal past doesn't stop it from serving ultimately, as it served Freud by analogy, as superego.

Via his nephew's crystal set, which his uncle's war stories inspired the boy to build, Gumm listens in on the pilot conversations transmitting from planes flying overhead. When he hears the voices above referring to "Ragle Gumm" while pointing out that he lives down there right below, he is convinced that he is breaking up along with the static on the line.

> I'm . . . psychotic. Hallucinations. . . . Insane. Infantile and lunatic. . . . Daydreams, at best. Fantasies about rocket ships shooting by overhead, armies and conspiracies. Paranoia. A paranoiac psychosis. Imagining that I'm the center of a vast effort by millions of men and women, involving billions of dollars and infinite work . . . a universe revolving around me. (119)

He decides he needs the break you get. But he can't get there without running up against evidence that it's not all in his head. Looking back on the 1959 he leaves behind, he analyzes how the operators in charge of maintaining his withdrawal psychosis had to construct the delusion as a daydream-like fantasy, a strategy that also lowered the doom on their enterprise.

> Like a daydream, he thought. Keeping in the good. Excluding the undesirable. But such a natural thing, he realized. They overlooked a radio every now and then. They kept forgetting that in the illusion the radio did not exist; they kept slipping up in just such trifles. Typical difficulty in maintaining daydreams . . . they failed to be consistent.

To stay back in time, the daydream-like fantasy must be wish-fulfilled, as always, in or as the future, but this future is also in the past. The present tense (or tension) is what must be bracketed out for the fantasy to continue to play. Thus the double lunacy of the novel's happy ending pulls the emergency brake on the degenerative in-between-ness of Ragle Gumm's Schreber-like world of intrigue, the ongoing present tension (or tense) transmitting since Gumm's childhood.

Dick's fictions, which forgo the New Age channel of recollections of past lives, focus instead on memories of alternate *present* lives. Whatever else the present tense may be, it is where the dead are, which is why it is elided in daydreams, the fantasy genre, and Christianity. In his essay on "The Poet and Day-Dreaming," Freud analyzed generic fantasy (and, in the meantime, the genre of "fantasy") in terms of the two times you get and the one time you forget. Freud's example features a boy in his early teens, an orphan, who decides to apply for a job he has just heard about. On the way to his interview he fantasizes getting the job, rising up the ranks of employment, until he is second in command to his boss, whose daughter he marries and whose business he inherits. The past tense belongs to a time when the boy was the beloved young child of his parents. His yearning for that past animates the fantasy, which belongs to the future. It's a fiction about the time to come that is at the same time inspired by the past that saw him better off, beloved, protected. But for the fantasy to unfold the daydreamer must precisely forget the present, his job search, his unemployed, alone-in-the-world status. The present tense that the fantasy would bypass on the past-to-future express also includes ongoing tensions, like that of the boy's unresolved or unacknowledged grief that beams in on another channel than that of his idealized past.

The fantasy genre was not only Dick's first contact with and choice of fiction but it also engaged him and his delegates throughout his work as fateful temptation, which, however, even Jahveh in *The Divine Invasion* must reject. In an interview with Arthur Bryan Cover, Dick turned up the contrast between fantasy and science fiction within their respective spans of retention:

In fantasy, you never go back to believing there are trolls, unicorns . . . and so on. But in science fiction, you read it, and it's not true now but there are things which are not true now which are going to be someday. . . . It's like all science fiction occurs in alternate future universes, so it could actually happen someday.

In science fiction the future that could happen someday is today. Its alternate universe is presently available. Its futurity is therefore the immediate kind that, under the finite conditions of multiple choice, is foreseeable or testable. According to Tolkien in "On Fairy Stories," the Happy Ending may be escapist in everyday life, but in the end (of life) it becomes the Great Escape, the overcoming of death that Christianity advertises. In this life we pass in and out of fantasy. When we die, however, we enter fantasy, the other world, for keeps. Although a declared Christian, Dick was also paranoid and wary, therefore, of unambivalence. Even in *Ubik*, where the interchangeable essence of consumer goods that promote perfectibility announces itself in the last commercial spot as the Christian God, nowhere does the novel admit truth in advertising, which would be the fantasy moment in this doubly Mass culture.

But it's not just any history that is alternate. *Time out of Joint* forecasts how, in the late 1990s, One Happy World, which consists, however, only of U.S. coordinates, while the first phase of the struggle on earth took winning and losing sides resembling those drawn on the 2004 U.S. electoral map, a withdrawal psychosis must be retrofitted in regard to the present to keep us transferentially grounded in World War II. While Dick was careful to show that cultivation of psychosis, because it would fix its focus as fantasy, would necessarily lose control upon the return of internal objects, subsequent novels suggest that he was revising his sense of a happy ending outside delusion—in other words, outside the alterations along for the ride of alternate realities. *The Man in the High Castle,* Dick's first novel explicitly employing the device of alternate history, therefore remetabolizes the outcome of World War II across at least two postwar decades-long histories.

In his 1977 essay "If You Find This World Bad, You Should See Some of the Others," Dick reviews the outside chance that his alternate history novel *The Man in the High Castle* might not only be fiction, even if it is fiction now: "But there was an alternate world, a previous present, in which that particular time track actualized—actualized and then was abolished due to intervention at some prior date" (245). Variables undergo reprogramming "along the linear time axis of our universe, thereby generating branched-off lateral worlds" (241). In writing for over twenty years about counterfeit or semireal worlds and deranged private worlds-of-one into which, however, others can be drawn, too, Dick was sensing, as he only now (in 1977) realizes, "the manifold of partially actualized realities lying tangent to what evidently is the most actualized one, the one that the majority of us, by general consent, agree on" (240). Rather than the black hole of loss, the present is in Dick's view the neutral gear through which alternate realities shift into actualization or pass out of existence, but at the same time not in linear time. Finitude is therefore not so much foreclosed or redeemed as given all the times in the world to pass on.

Dick includes Christianity among all the frames of reference he traverses, sunken ruins mired in the so-called tomb world. While Dick defers, fragments, and diversifies the flat line of this underworld—in *Ubik,* for example, through such countermeasures as half-life, the sci-fi biotechnological recasting of haunting as the halving of any full-life that could assert that it was at last at rest—he doesn't skip finitude altogether in taking the leap to the alternate or other world. Legend to the map of the overlap between allegory as conceived by Benjamin and endopsychic perception according to Freud is the notion of alternate realities (or histories or universes). It is fundamental to Dick's narratives that all the frames of reference can be maintained as throwbacks that survive, however, in the present tense of an indefinite number of parallel settings. Alternate history suspends the dotting of the vanishing point between the recent past and the near future and thus, for the time being, forestalls the repression that otherwise scrubs down and detonates this realm of the dead, the undead, and the living.

Ragle Gumm is restored to a world at civil war, a war between siblings, we are told, which thus only counts victims. Dick maintained a primal sibling bond at his own origin as the break that would prove constitutive of his corpus—a break not so much with reality as within the belief system of surveillance. As he also found occasion daily, by all accounts, to reveal in conversation—it was the exchange that never varied—he was born prematurely together with his twin sister who didn't survive their head start. Dick felt throughout his life the determining influence of his survival of his twin sister. From this mythic or psychotic origin onward, Dick speculated, he had inhabited a realm of undecidability specific to mourning over the other's death conceived as double loss: both parties to the death lose the other. Indeed Dick claimed he could not decide who had died: he could be the memory crossing his surviving twin's mind. Dick's signal investment in alternate present worlds derives from this unique specialization within the work of unmourning.

It is a metapsychological fact (and chip from my workshop) that the unmournably dead, whether (in life) mother, child, or sibling, is reconstructed for the melancholic afterlife as sibling (inevitably, in a profound sense, as twin), in which form the loss is deposited safe inside the crypt. Dick was buried alongside one other, his twin sister. Sweet Jane. But Dick was also thus given a mythic head start to subsume the retention span of singular loss within the inside view of reality loss or, in the reverse order designating the reality that is available for testing, "loss reality." Dick's introduction of at least two realities that occupy interchangeable places in his fiction, which he would subsequently refine as alternate history in *The Man in the High Castle*, for example, or as half-life in *Ubik*, originally or primally draws its inspiration from the twin's death that to his mind could, alternatively, have all along been his own. In losing each other, either twin could be dead or alive. Hence Carrère's title: "I am alive and you are dead." The span of the "and" embraces the recent past and the near future as the period of uncertainty about the reality of one's world that both parties to one death must face.

In the interview following his recovery from "the shock of saying good-bye to Angel Archer," Dick identifies the other woman of his work prior to his relationship to Angel, which is "completely love":

> You know, whenever I see a woman of this kind, I seek her out, I'm a trophy to her. But part of me knows she's gonna trash me. So all the time I am seeking her out half of me is running the other way, you know, so that I'm moving toward her and away from her. So my dialogue with women like this consists of "Hi, darling" and then I feel like popping her one. (60–61)

To the extent that this ambivalence is addressed to his mother, it begins with the mother's account of her boy twin somehow taking all the milk that she didn't know how to supplement and make go around for two babies. In his 1965 essay "Schizophrenia and *The Book of Changes*," Dick follows the development of schizophrenia out of the schizo-affective personality, which he admits was his case. First off, the fateful prematurity and consequent dependency of the newborn human being immediately sets a latency period to the sentencing of reality: the human, "not thoroughly born," remains wrapped up in "a kind of semireal existence" until the catastrophe of adolescence (175). This is the preschizophrenic personality when it's time to ask a girl out on a date: "one gazes at her for a year or so, mentally detailing all possible outcomes; the good ones go under the rubric 'daydreams,' the bad ones under 'phobia.' This bipolar internal war goes on endlessly; meanwhile the actual girl has no idea you're alive (and guess why: You're not)" (175).

But if every "dark-haired girl" was his Margaret, then her overcoming as Angel/Jane strikes up affirmation of the Eternal/Internal Feminine in the foreground of the pageant of Faust's or Dick's "death." In *Time out of Joint* Ragle Gumm makes the identification with Goethe's Faust over one of the Margarets in the series of dangerous girls in the world.

> In the pool itself, youths splashed about, girls and boys wet and mixed together so that all of them appeared about the same. . . . Could I fall in love with a little trollopy, giggly ex-high school girl . . . ?

The great mind, he thought, bends when it nears this kind of fellow creature. Meeting and mating of opposites. Yin and yang. The old Doctor Faust sees the peasant girl sweeping off the front walk, and there go his books, his knowledge, his philosophies.

In the beginning, he reflected, was the word.

Or, in the beginning was the *deed*. If you were Faust.

Watch this, he said to himself. Bending over the apparently sleeping girl, he said, " 'Im Anfang war die Tat.' "

"Go to hell," she murmured. (49–50)

Belief System Surveillance

According to Emmanuel Carrère, Dick's 1977 novel *A Scanner Darkly* is, as the author's bid for a sane or mainstream intermission from his psychotic states, his most deluded work. The nonfictional afterword in which Dick declares *A Scanner Darkly* to be his own work of remembrance could indeed be seen to fit or foot that bill. However one should also note that it is in this novel that Dick makes breach of contact between his revalorization of psychosis in terms of alternate present realities and external topical points of interest such as drugs, violence, and surveillance. It took this Christian mystic or psychotic to see through and project surveillance as belief system. What Dick adds to the closed quarters of doubling under realizable conditions of surveillance is his longstanding question: Where are the dead here? Where are they housed, installed, included?

In *A Scanner Darkly* surveillance is doubly internalized via everyone's drug of choice, Substance D, otherwise known as Death. In Dick's war of the world on drugs, actual surveillance is pressed into the service of containing the drug scene in second-stage alert. Undercover agents who hang with the druggies and report back in scramble suits to their superiors occupy the first stage. To maintain their cover, however, the agents must pass at the communion they are observing as fellow Death heads. By the time agent Fred, who is Bob Arctor, is assigned to watch the tapes of the nonstop surveillance cameras that have in the meantime been installed in the house he shares undercover with the milieu he at first was alone observing for his reports, Death's effect on his brain reflects the pull of a larger structure of control release whereby the whole mass media Sensurround recycles addiction and recovery as low maintenance subjecthood. The tabs he keeps end up subsumed by the tabs he's already taken.

Fred/Arctor is handed his brain fry diagnosis right before the book enters its own internal doubling in chapter 11, which is essentially a sequence of untranslated incorporated quotations from Goethe's *Faust* surrounding the two souls in Faust's breast. Arctor's own interior dialogue intercuts with these excerpts just as the wasted side of the brain responsible for language prompts the surviving side to find compensation through translation or cerebral lateralization. The compensation that proceeds as lateralization opens wide the alternate worlds or self-reflexive interiorities of delusion.

Faust's downbeat of doubling follows his own failure to pass the *Übermensch*-test on a scale of doubling or nothing. "Superhuman" is a good enough translation of *Übermensch,* the term or concept we saw first in Goethe's *Faust.* The Earth Spirit Faust conjures expects to meet in him match and maker, in other words an *Übermensch.* But the term comes up as a put-down: The Earth Spirit declares that Faust is no *Übermensch,* and must go elsewhere to meet his *Ebenbild* or double. While *Übermensch* can be found in use around the time of Luther, but to signify the superiority of the especially good Christian, or also already in Herder's lexicon, but linked and limited to superiority on the sliding scale of existing humanity, it was first in Goethe's *Faust* that *Übermensch* came to mean, via the rebound of negation, a human being equal to divinity, which is up for grabs or, in Faust's case, just out of reach. As we first encounter Faust, he is a mood swinger. Even after the songs of his childhood reopen a future of possibilities coming toward him and stay the mirroring merger with the poison in his father's cup, he still dips into depression. But this lack can find compensation, he announces, as he turns to the New Testament to translate into German the word or logos that was in the beginning. The German word for the work of translation, *Übersetzen,* points toward the translation of *Übermensch* as "transhuman," a translation grounded in ambiguities inherent in the related words or prefixes *over* and *über.* The "over" or "*über*" human has crossed over to one in a series of stations of the crossing but also or alternatively as crossed out: man as over, over and out. Certainly that's how Faust starts out.

In the course of the translation attempts that usher in the performative word as deed or act, as the pushbutton temporality or technology that Faust will in deed receive, the poodle reveals the Devil in the tails, who as Faust's split-off double will administer Faust's wishes as commands. But if Faust is thus bracketed out of this infernal culture industry of technologization and administration of wish or desire, it's not only to relieve Faust of any responsibility through this dissociation with the Devil. It is also because the Faustian striving that takes over where the suicidal depression left off, or where it begins to defer the suicide itself, runs counter to the Devil's nihilism. Faustian striving can't get no satisfaction, in fact craves incompletion, and thus performs the superhuman as transhuman. Should Faust ever decide that he is fully himself in the moment—a whole in one—then he belongs to the Devil. Thus he performs a more Nietzsche-compatible understanding of the superhuman as process or transition and as irreducibly future goal, as the future of the future.

In the contest of World War II propaganda or mass psychology, American interpretations and embodiments of the superhuman as transhuman (notably the comic book figures Superman and Wonder Woman and the movie hero Tarzan as played by Johnny Weissmuller) struggled against fully realized supermen of Nazi Germany who, by all accounts, were ready, set, to go win the master race. Between Goethe and Nietzsche, the figure of the "superhuman" or "transhuman" raised the stakes of reading and mis-reading to life or death. Because one man's future is the next generation's present, Freud rescheduled the superman (in *Group Psychology and the Analysis of the Ego*) as belonging not to Nietzsche's future but resolutely in the past as the primal father, from whose superiority we are still in recovery in the mode of mourning (*Standard Edition* 18:123). But for Freud there is therefore another trajectory taking off from this living dead end of the superhuman. In his essay on "The 'Uncanny,'" Freud interpreted the two souls in Faust's breast, one aspiring upward, the other clinging to the earth, as a doubling of the ego whereby what would soon go by the name superego keeps the ego under surveillance. "The fact that an agency of this kind exists, which is able to treat the rest of the ego like an object—the fact, that is, that man is capable of self-observation—renders it possible to invest the old idea of a 'double' with a new meaning" (17:235). This new meaning was introduced via the evidence of "delusions of being watched." In such pathological cases, "this mental agency becomes isolated, dissoci-ated from the ego, and discernible to the physician's eye." What imme-diately follows the new meaning is the reference to Faust down in the footnote underworld: "I believe that when poets complain that two souls dwell in the human breast . . . what they are thinking of is this division . . . between the critical agency and the rest of the ego" (17:235, n. 2).

Thus surveillance as super-vision is introduced in Freud's theory as our inner-world connection with a superior being who, belonging in the primal past, otherwise communicates with us via transitional works of mourning or unmourning. Primal repression, which fills out the mother's missing person report in everyone's development and is introduced according to Freud's mythic history as the other law delegated via the primal father's murder, guarantees, as Freud argues in *Beyond the Pleasure Principle*, that there can be no perfectibility drive for humanity (18:52). There is always something missing in the past that keeps us ever striving onward (or not) toward what—definitely—you never get, never got. Or in other words, those found along the closing lines of Goethe's *Faust*, the eternal or internal feminine, as principle of mourning, drives us onward. But the gaze of the primal father is back, for example when we are mediatized as in hypnosis (18:127). And the distilled essence of the mother's missing body is a "libido toxin," which, according to Freud, is the unattainable goal (in the past) that sets us up for addiction (16:388–89).

What fits this frame of interreference,[1] including the phantasm of super vision, the structure of addiction, and Goethe's *Faust*, is *A Scanner Darkly*, which updates or upgrades the mirror or glass in St. Paul's famous image of our skewed vision that at the end of time will be all clear. But already at this end of time, Bob Arctor reflects, the reversal of the mirror reflection was at least at last reversed and thus cleared through the visual media (212). As Fred/Arctor continues to reflect, what has happened to his brain on the drug Substance D restores the original reversal as irreducible. "*It is as if one hemisphere of your brain is perceiving the world as reflected in a mirror.* Through a mirror. See? So left becomes right, and all that that implies. And we don't know yet what that does imply, to see the world reversed like that. Topologically speaking, a left-hand glove is a right-hand glove pulled through infinity.' 'Through a mirror,' Fred said. A darkened mirror, he thought; a darkened scanner. . . . I have seen myself backward. I have in a sense begun to see the entire universe backward. With the other side of my brain!" (212).

The halfway point where the brain on drugs and total surveillance meet and cross over falls way short of the all-clear of super-vision but nevertheless wraps around the ensuing splitting and displacement the figure of the loop. The lateralized view sees the doubling it releases and relies on as fully inhabiting the tape medium, aggrandized via the fourth dimension that, as Schreber too pointed out, modern Spiritualism cultivated as that reversal of mirror reversal in which one not only can line up one's own hands one on top of the other rather than fold them together as in prayer but also can contact the dead. For this is the zone of comforts, haunting for the secular mind, doubling above for believers, and what lies between the two, comfort in nihilism: to be double *and* nothing.

Arctor, under his own surveillance, becomes an actor (134). Is the subject of surveillance acting, is he pretending not to know that he is under surveillance? These questions rise up for Fred even or especially as he watches himself as Arctor on tape. Fragments, translations, repetitions of the Faust material are scattered throughout the pages that follow the book's chapter 11, which ended on the suicide notes and plans of one of the druggies. He left Ayn Rand's *The Fountainhead* lying around to prove that he was a misunderstood "superman." But this time he was sold hallucinogens instead of the suffocating downers he was counting on, and so he tripped out, not unlike Faust, to a transcendent realm where a creature with compound eyes will read out his sins for all eternity. Dying in Goethe's *Faust* takes all the time in the world he consumed, all the time it takes to rewind in order to erase or dematerialize the ego's span of retention of this world.

The question of Faust's two souls opens up surveillance as uncanny or uncontained. "To himself, Bob Arctor thought, *How many Bob Arctors are there?* . . . Two that I can think of, he thought. The one called Fred, who will be watching the other one, called Bob. The same person. Or is it? . . . *Which of them is me?*" (96). "But—you can't be sure. There are shucks on top of shucks. Layers and Layers" (191). "Each day the experience of the scanners had grown. . . . Like an actor before a movie camera, he decided, you act like the camera doesn't exist or else you blow it. It's all over" (184). Memory and fantasy flash through the brain of a user as films. First a "fantasy film rolled suddenly into his head, without his consent" (18), but then it turns out his fantasy is a memory of a past mishap: "then the fantasy number broke off; it was a documentary rerun" (19), but then "the rerun of a now gone moment winked out and died forever" (20). The addiction to addiction that drugs internalize also determines the splitting images of surveillance as the side effects of *Sehnsucht*, the German word for "yearning," which, however, given a pathological slant, can be seen to spell out "addiction to seeing."

As a kind of prologue to the Faust chapter, we are given an inside view of the exchange between the two souls in Arctor's one brain. The lateralized view sees the doubles on a race or erase track of taping. "But now Fred is here, too. But all Fred's got is hindsight. Unless, he thought, unless maybe if I run the holo-tapes backward. Then I'd be there first, before Barris, What I do would precede what Barris does. If with me first he gets to do anything at all. And then the other side of his head opened up and spoke to him more calmly, like another self with a simpler message flashed to him as to how to handle it" (171). But following this restoration of the connection to the sane brain, which leads Arctor to go in person and replace the bad check he assumes the twisted member of the household on drugs had forged in Arctor's name, the alternation between sides or doubles, substantially mediated by the foreign body quotations from *Faust,* begins to turn over rapidly. Now he's not sure, for example, whether he didn't write the check after all and then forget about it (178).

After the Faust chapter closes, Arctor's psychoticizing contact with the seeing I technologies rides out the echoing earshot of the earlier Faust citations. "Which may just be my imagination, the 'they' watching me. Paranoia. Or rather the 'it.' . . . Whatever it is that's watching, it is not a human. . . . Something is being done to me and by a mere thing, here in my own house. Before my very eyes. Within *something's* very eyes; within the sight of some *thing*. Which, unlike little dark-eyed Donna, does not ever blink. What does a scanner see? he asked himself. . . . I hope it does, he thought, see clearly, because I can't any longer these days see into myself. I see only murk. Murk outside; murk inside. I hope, for everyone's sake, the scanners do better. Because, he thought, if the scanner sees only darkly, the way I myself do, then we are cursed . . . and we'll wind up dead this way, knowing very little and getting that little fragment wrong too" (185).

One of the police psychologists proclaims that "the infinity of time . . . is expressed as eternity, as a loop! Like the loop of cassette tape!" (215). Arctor flashes on this timeline as the fantastic prospect of the dead winding up or rewinding *this* way: "In time—maybe the Crucifixion lies ahead of us as we all sail along, thinking it's back east. . . . The First and Second Coming of Christ the same event, he thought; time a cassette loop. No wonder they were sure it'd happen, He'd be back" (216). But what he is left with, over and again, is the emptied out smallest unit of this loop—as in Arctor's two-way-mirror insight into the fast forwarding or death wishing that inheres in his surveillance. "To have watched a human being . . . that you had gotten real close to, . . . and most of all *admired*—to see that warm living person burn out from the inside, burn from the heart outward. Until it clicked and clacked like an insect, repeating one sentence again and again. A *recording*. A closed loop of tape" (66). But across this bottom line Arctor now affirms the *work* in surveillance. "Keep surveillance alive, as I've been doing. For a while at least. But I mean, everything in life is just for a while" (220). "Otherwise, he thought, they could die and no one would be the wiser. Know or even fucking care. In wretched little lives like that, someone must intervene. Or at least mark their sad coming and goings. Mark and if possible permanently record, so they'll be remembered" (221).

In the closing chapters describing the new path through recovery that Arctor/Fred, now named Bruce, undergoes, the encounter group reenters the loop. According to the group's consensus, to be dead is to be an unmoving camera: not to be able to stop looking at whatever's in front of you. Mike, one of the supervisors at the occupational therapy farm where Bruce works for recovery, concludes: "But the dead—he glanced at Bruce, the empty shape beside him—should, if possible, serve the purposes of the living.... The dead, Mike thought, who can still see, even if they can't understand: they are our camera" (266). Even though it is in this outer limit of recovery that we find out that the fields the ex-addicts tend grow the organic beginnings of Substance Death, the slip between Death and the dead marks the spot we are in at the end of *A Scanner Darkly* as the spot the loop of surveillance tried to wash or watch out. If the dead are our cameras, then it is before them that we begin to fill in the blank of that something that looks without blinking and lets a record show that is without identification.

"Every junkie ... is a recording" (159). The burned-out-addict version of a former person enters the loop of drugs and media as the rebounding same name of insect bugs and surveillance bugs, which summons the supersession of the retention span in doubling. The bugs that come out of the watch of surveillance began as aphid bugs coming out of the nonstop washing that one drug addict, Jerry Fabin, undergoes together with his dog to be rid of them. This perpetual infestation in fact first opens the prospect in the novel of drug-induced hallucination as permanent warping. "He had a flash then: Jerry Fabin's brain ...: wires cut, shorts, wires twisted, parts overloaded and no good, line surges, smoke, and a bad smell. And somebody sitting there with a voltmeter, tracing the circuit and muttering, 'My, my, a lot of resistors and condensers need to be replaced,' and so forth. And then finally from Jerry Fabin would come only a sixty-cycle hum. And they'd give up" (66).

A joking together of Freudian interpretation with the case of Fabin opens up, as laugh track, the shadow of psychic causation and organization (which otherwise the drug named Death supplies or supplants).

Jerry Fabin, see, comes home from first grade one day..., and there, sitting in the dining room beside his mother, is this great aphid, about four feet high. His mother is gazing at it fondly.

"What's happening?" little Jerry Fabin inquires.

"This here is your older brother," his mother says, "who you've never met before. He's come to live with us. I like him better than you. He can do a lot of things you can't." ...

Finally Jerry runs away from home. But he still subconsciously believes aphids to be superior to him. At first he imagines he is safe, but then he starts seeing aphids everywhere in his hair and around the house, because his inferiority complex has turned into some kind of sexual guilt, and the aphids are a punishment he inflicts on himself, etc. (67–68)

The psychodynamic profiling of Fabin gives comic relief (or grief) by rubbing the foreign body of hallucination up against the script of neurotic conflict. But this is also the track of legibility or transference whereby the surveillance plotting adds to hallucinating on drugs the larger structures that Dick otherwise ascribes in his novels to psychosis or the more controlled release of applied psi talent. The surveillance bugs that enter Arctor's home through sibling-style rivalries externalize and mediatize the splitting of brain and psyche through Substance D as the alteration and lateralization of reality on tape. Part II of *Magic and Schizophrenia* by Géza Róheim, posthumously edited by Werner Muensterberg for publication in 1955, focuses on a hebephrenic schizophrenic patient Róheim observed for almost two years in the United States in the late 1930s. It was a research-only mission because the patient, already hospitalized for five years before Róheim began working with him, was "beyond the point at which he could understand psychoanalytic interpretations, let alone be influenced by them" (125). The patient leads the way in attributing his psychosis both to the death of his sister and to an early starvation experience, an oral trauma he associates regularly with his own gluttony, which at one crisis point exceeded his share and threatened to starve out others.

I did not know that it was not good for others when I ate all the food in the world and that they would be hungry. ... There is only one story—that somebody was starved. But not really—only inside, in my stomach. (126)

After my sister's death people did not like me. They did not like my looks. They thought that I was responsible for her death. Boys and girls would hit my solar plexus—or they would swing at it—and that filled me with hot air. (151)

The patient becomes invisible to the world, doesn't "look" "like" anyone. Them's the breaks. He fills up with hot air, an image he uses for his psychosis. Only inside his delusional system does he look like delegates of his sister. The other image of his mental illness is the bug, derived in large measure, according to Róheim, from the designation of a mental institution as "bug house" (171):

Maybe I was a bug once or maybe I was in the bugs that destroy people (153).

I woke up and felt as if a bug had jumped at my throat and bit it. . . . Or as if I had bitten my throat with my own teeth. (138)

There are bugs inside me. One of them is as big as me. It tries to eat all the food when it gets into my stomach. There are also several little bugs who look like me and like the Little Depth Koda. These bugs are the same as the Teethies that I found in myself. . . . This bug made me get lost—that was three thousand years ago—and it also made the words get lost when they came out of my teeth. I was full of bugs, and the bugs ate all the food. . . . The bug put its teeth into my teeth and ate my food (145).

His all-or-nothing oral trauma introduced a concept of oral omnipotence that the patient refers to as his notion of being "overweighted" (129). To consume to excess leads to being "overweighted," as does starvation. Super-vision (from on high) and velocity are the attainments of this omnipotence. "The eagle-feeling is like the food trouble and like being a bug. . . . There is too much speed or gravity in me. I feel as if the chair were falling over and throwing me out" (157). Róheim turns to Schilder's research to gloss "speed or gravity." Speed is the late arrival of baby's sensation of losing his grip on mother's breast. Róheim concludes: "*Speed*—that is, any urge—was connected with his dread of *complete object loss*" (159). Thus the patient describes Alaska, where he says he once resided, as a place of desolation, burial, and dispossession: "Nothing remained of it, only hands—to show the way. It is like the time when I could not get food and when I could not make people understand what I wanted" (193). Look, only hands—to cling to the edge of loss.

Omnipotence of thought must be shared, via the projection of the death wish, with the goner, whose return with the bugs compensates for losing his grip on reality—and whose repeated withdrawal keeps the connection current as disconnection. "Once I was so happy that I flew into space. Like the sun. But the food dies in me, like the sun sets in the evening" (178).

A catatonic patient Silvano Arieti treated reached stopping of action through a process of slowing down to make sure that bodies weren't falling down. When she moved, she had to think about the movement, dividing it into small parts to reassure herself that each part of the movement had not caused small bodies to fall. Once the slow motion sets in, she goes back home with her husband and enlists everyone in the search for dropped objects. "The compulsive ritual consisted of reassuring herself that bodies had not fallen. In going back over her movements in her thoughts, she followed this formula, 'Do, feel, done, on, off, see, hear, think, and what else.'" Before the loop closes like a bug, however, the schizo staggers the language in which anxiety bodes illness, making it spread thin for multitask mastery in service of precision. Otherwise one falls through the cracks from high anxiety in language. The language of Róheim's patient also risks disappearance of food, words, and objects through the rigorous requirements of precision exacted with a mind to averting the sense of language from the uncontainable anxiety out of the word. Róheim observes that his patient addressed an "intervening empty space" as the "'obstacle' that kept him from going home" (134). That obstacle fit in the mouth not in the mind. In the patient's words:

The feeling of not being able to go back to a place is like the feeling of not being able to pronounce a word.... "Forgetfulness." Now I can remember it, but I can't pronounce it. I used to try to say the sentence, "I forget how to say the word 'forget'; but when I came to the last word of the sentence, I couldn't pronounce it. I used to try to say the word "encyclopedia," where all knowledge is contained, but then I had to go to the encyclopedia to find the word "encyclopedia"—and I could not find it. (163)

Materialization of his lost objects alternates between fantasy representation (in which paternal skeletons and angel sisters serve the hovering craft) and prosthetic figuration of eating and observing. The two genres are moreover in conflict:

Up in the sky I found an angel, a woman called Angel Love.... She wanted me to go to her house and marry her, but I was detained by other women. One of them was the woman known as Little Depth Koda. (137)

It's Little Depth Koda to the rescue. She leaves the only (crumbling) trail of transference. Surveillance in German, *Überwachung*, is also "transwatching." Its blind spot is *Übertragung* or "transference."

Depth Koda is a tiny person who speaks in my insides and is connected with the food trouble, as if she were trying to fix it and make me well again. She is like a doctor....Koda is...a photo—like Kodak. There is something like a diluted reel of film in my brain, and the reel and the photo are like the doctors—trying to tell me what to do....I have a photographic machine that takes pictures of people eating. This machine is like the one in the movies. The doctors built it—to see who was putting his head inside me and eating my food. (164–65)

At one point, also in the 1970s, there was a switch that pretended to be a transmission. Foucault reopened the reading or study of institutionalization and its subject, the seeing I or ego, which Nietzsche had already explored, but not under the aegis of realized technical controls, but instead in terms of the ruinous legacies of an otherwise consciously abandoned belief system. According to Nietzsche, from Christianity to nihilism, mankind has upheld belief in an all-seeing witness who, as we say, validates our suffering, our pain, and renders it all meaningful if only by being on record or under surveillance. The need for this witness protection or projection program struck Nietzsche as so seductive, even or especially since inimical to life, that he was moved to forecast twentieth-century wars unprecedented in history through which so-called monsters of nihilism would seek ultimate meaningfulness in mass destruction, death, suicide—in the synchronization of all our deaths all together now at the same time.

I have yet to encounter good reason to discard Nietzsche's view that the technical, scientific construct of surveillance is a belief system more remarkable for its ruinous failure than for any outside chance of realization. Thus one cannot but suspect that there is stowaway in surveillance, transparency, or globalization, an agenda, whether deliberate or unconscious, that is at least as old as Christianity. Derrida accordingly began referring to globalization as globalatinization, according to which the so-called new media of surveillance and liveness still ask us to believe in— have faith in—that evidence of the senses that cannot in fact be proven, that remains inadmissible as evidence, but which is nevertheless presented to us, in a flash, as the word made flesh.

All the occult and sci-fi figures out there double the ego's own origin as projection of the body. The identifiable body, whether in our techno egoic culture or in the psychotic delusions studied by Freud, is lost or at a loss. To cut the loss down from the crisis proportions served when you're just too stuck on this body (as the only habitat for your narcissism), you can, for example, project the delusion of being controlled via a network of technical media, which gets you out from under the uncanny close encounter with the missing body.

Under total surveillance—reduced, that is, to utter visibility—we could only be the android doubles we look like to those who, we think, control us. Although recognizable props of religion abound in Schreber's delusions, the witness projection program in the Schreber case is ultimately secular, as secular as psychoanalysis itself. Schreber's world, for example, while relentlessly on record and under surveillance, in fact inhabits the stricken site of the inevitable techno failure of the belief system of surveillance as omniscience. The divine perspective of surveillance in Schreber's worldview is organized around a blind spot: this god takes cognizance only of corpses from which he draws back up inside his greater network the nerves of them. Taken to be a corpse while melancholically playing dead, Schreber's live nerves become intertwined with and within the divine network. Schreber is now the catch in the divine plan, a catch in the throat of the disposal god, and out of their contaminating embrace sparks the outside chance that Schreber, by turning simultaneously into woman and into android, will conceive with the divine nerve rays a new species of survival. If that's not mourning or, rather, unmourning, complete with the necessarily secular-suckular conditions of ongoing relations with our dead, then I give up.

In settings of international theory's own hostage crisis with regard to the return of religiosity in the midst of global mass-mediatization, it became possible to recognize another subculture of psychotic break and testimony that differs from the Schreber evidence, first off, by virtue of not being organized as delusional *system*. If science fiction seemed the designated pop genre to work by analogy with the new worlds of Schreber and company, for this other delusional space it appears that the bookstore-created genre of "fantasy" performs a similar service.

The Witnesses, Thomas Hennell's 1938 memoirs of his nervous illness, shows the visual artist and educator revving up for the fall of his breakdown within a juxtaposition of unlikely resources.[2] Whenever his ability to work is inhibited he goes to the reading-room where he fills his "head and notebooks with old tracts and sermons"—or he spends this time off with "a collection of scientific magazines, which contained survivors' accounts of immense tempests and tornados." From these "unrelated sources emerged forms more real than living man" (18–19). According to Hennell, his delusion lies in the details undisplaced with regard to what he calls rationalization: "so many ideas are accepted and become familiar by use, though they may be actually contradictory. In a time of excitement and enthusiasm these ordinary activities become exaggerated, and some ideas grow intensely actual. . . . It is as though some great comet drew near" (23). Caught between the comet-like natural phenomenon and the comparable illuminations and attractions of "a great spirit," the mind is on the same revelatory track, "whose beginnings and end are in faith—far beyond knowledge!" (24). Beset in his asylum room by "quiverings of silver wires beneath the floor, as though all Solomon's minions were sending propitiation of riches: to make amends for the past evil enchantments," Hennell, looking back, drops an aside that belongs to the inside of his delusion production: "How much this resembled the make-believe of a solitary child, who is king amid his own fancies!" (154).

But his delusional state cannot safeguard Hennell from running up against a relay of techno devices around him but then also inside his purview and discourse. After the fact, once his condition has stabilized, these machines offer running commentary on and contrast to the other course (and tracts) of his religious ecstasy. The machine world disrupts Hennell's delusional dynamic where before (pre the psychotic break) rationalization could be seen to underlie his less detail-oriented share in coherency and functioning.

When one is most nearly inspired, a second presence appears, leering over the shoulder of the cherished religious ideal; this is the body of tolerated, habitual inanities, of social and commercial cynicism. But now I could not tell what it was . . . —only later, gradually, a facetious, mindless, "mechanistic" Mammon seemed to emerge and become incarnate in my enemies. (43)

The therapeutic treatment is, therefore, in Hennell's case, on this machine track: "these were objectifications of a dominant idea, which, to some extent, I connected with my psychiatrist; that the working out of life was a mechanistic process, in fact a sort of infernal machine always running down to zero hour" (81). To bring conflict into focus in the fantasy realm of great spiders, controlling destroyers, Doubting Castle, and Sleeping Castle, only an "infernal machine" will do. On the other side of the interruptions of evil or apparatus, metamorphosing transfers in the relay of epiphany are regularly associated with being "recalled to another world" (148). The death wish is what remains infernal to the relay of daydream fantasy wish fulfillment.

"We must not suppose," Freud writes in "The Poet and Day-Dreaming," "that the products of this imaginative activity—the various fantasies, castles in the air and daydreams—are stereotyped or unalterable. On the contrary, they fit themselves into the subject's shifting impressions of life, change with every change in his situation, and receive from every fresh active impression what might be called a 'date-mark'" (9:147). This is how Freud introduces his main example of the orphan/heir daydreaming his way to the top while on his way to a mere interview as illustration of the general importance of fantasy's relationship to time. The present tense or tension cannot be circumvented without at the same time being encompassed but displaced. The Second Gulf War sponsored a fitting image for this disposition of the present tense, even (or especially) in real time: the seeing-I of the war's live transmission was "embedded," that is, included at the front of the line in real wartime but at the same time displaced, dislocated, rendered unidentifiable and decontextualized.

When Jameson argues for an appreciation of certain works of fantasy as social documents by dint of the cybernetic technology they incorporate, we find internal to this breakaway affirmation the following giveaway advertisement: "(We are told, indeed, that the current development of special-effects technology can be dated from George Lucas' establishment of a *Star Wars* laboratory in 1977.)" (70). The exclusion of technologization to which we owe this inclusion frees the fantasy at its reception to be low tech. In the fantasy future world of *Reign of Fire* (2002), not to be confused with the Battle of Britain, children in bunkers under attack by flaming dragons listen to the legend (to which they are lip-synched) of Darth Vader and Luke Skywalker and watch the shadow-play accompaniment that projects timeless or primal figures (notably the Death Father's audio helmet).

Before it could serve as analogy, *Star Wars* was already inside the battle plans and diplomatic discourse of the wars that are still coming at us. *Star Wars* raided science fiction only to get to the wide-open outer space where conceivable populations could be as scattered or gathered together in approximation to conditions on one planet (or continent) during the Middle Ages. When an entire planet is annihilated at one point in the first film, only a little over one million inhabitants die. This minimization of catastrophic loss, which increases the outside chances for survival, was on one dotted line with the pomo diplomacy of Reaganomics: it proved possible to calculate nuclear risk in terms of survival, even following exchanges of strikes. The techno future thus allowed a chivalric spacing of conflict in which "Jedi Knights" could assume center screen. (Space-travel suits conveniently doubled as late arrivals of suits of armor.)

The sword fight and the joust, the rituals that bind conflict in fantasy works, have increasingly become the overriding model in the new fantasy genre of warfare. In theory, a finite number of professionals meet on a four-dimensional field to struggle for a prize that does not cost or count civilian casualties. The combatant leaders are highly personalized, like in role playing, their investment in the conflict supercharged with a sense of past wrongs and a future tense of wish fulfillment (a tense that belongs not to the uncontrollable future, the time of the other, but to the anticipated or already calculated future instead). Noncombatants are asked to stay tuned to the joust's broadcast, live and in real time, but via unidentifiable, unlocatable, and yet egoic probes.

In the first film, Luke Skywalker's foster parents are, I would argue, in fact his parents after all, but the parents who over time only keep disappointments. The missing exalted parents belong to his family romance. The ongoing tension with his (foster) parents is elided by the murderous intervention of an enemy force that in turn forces or frees him—the force is with him—to share the fantasy of the chivalric father. But out pops Darth Vader, the "death father" or malignant superego, in the place of the idealized father. At the close of the second film, Luke tends to his dying double father: he removes the dark helmet, his echo chamber of heavy breathing. Underneath it all, we find the vulnerable father of disappointment, with whom the son now finds reconciliation. Thus the royal past of parental rule, in contrast to a present tense of deprivation and privation, is resurrected as the wish fulfillment along for the Jedi Knight crusade. Included in this future fantasy moment is the therapeutic breakthrough inside the father complex.

While the first and second installments of *Star Wars* foster metabolization of relations with father to the point of a seemingly therapeutic termination, the same movies appear to cut Luke's relationship to his mother nothing but lack. Princess Leia is their dead mother's look-alike. She beams into Luke's affections via a recognition value that remains unconscious to both of them. The intolerable divide between the foster mother, the ineffectual mother who protests against the foster father's guidelines for their son, but then accedes to father for the sake of family harmony, and the princess (or the mother behind the princess) is doubled by the incest gap that instantly yawns between object choice and sudden sibling. Across a greater arc of doubling, extending into the second trilogy of *Star Wars* films, which are set in the prehistory of the first trilogy, the princess mother can escape the corner she is in only by recourse to a double's power to divert attention. But once diverted, everyone (out in the audience, too) is hard pressed to identify which was the double and which one the original.

In his 1938 essay "On Fairy Stories," Tolkien writes: "The Evangelium has not abrogated legends; it has hallowed them, especially the 'happy ending.'" The other legend thus hallowed is escape. The reader of fantasy escapes from this world, which is, as we say, hell, into an other world—for example, the realm of the elves in *The Lord of the Rings*—where he or she experiences the joy of recovery and rejuvenation just as the Christian escapes from this world after death into the other world of Heaven. What even Tolkien refers to as being in recovery also clears the person's way of seeing and allows "things" to be seen for what they are—"as things apart from ourselves."

In *The Pearl*, which Tolkien translated into modern English, a father's grief over his dead child is alleviated in a dream that brings back the child, presumably now as someone or thing apart from himself. As a result, Tolkien emphasizes in his "Introduction," father's spirits are lifted in the happy ending that follows realization that death happened, but then also did not happen. But Tolkien also insists that *Pearl* was "founded on a real sorrow, and drew its sweetness from a real bitterness" (21). The work condenses a whole work of mourning together with the theological treatises with which it comes to share its frame of reference. "Without the elegiac basis and the sense of great personal loss which pervades it, *Pearl* would indeed be the mere theological treatise on a special point, which some critics have called it. But without the theological debate the grief would never have risen above the ground. Dramatically the debate represents a long process of thought and mental struggle, an experience as real as the first blind grief of bereavement. In his first mood, even if he had been granted a vision of the blessed in Heaven, the dreamer would have received it incredulously or rebelliously. And he would have awakened by the mound again, not in the gentle and serene resignation of the last stanza, but still as he is first seen, looking only backward, his mind filled with the horror of decay" (22–23).

How would the Heavenly child be in any way related to the child that died? This is *the* question that must be posed regarding the Christian management of the dead. "But this is an apparition of a spirit, a soul not yet reunited with its body after the resurrection, so that theories relevant to the form and age of the glorified and risen body do not concern us. And as an immortal spirit, the maiden's relations to the earthly man, the father of her body, are altered." "The final consolation of the father was not to be found in the recovery of a beloved daughter, as if death had not after all occurred or had no significance, but in the knowledge that she was redeemed and saved and had become a queen in Heaven. Only by resignation to the will of God, and through death, could he rejoin her" (22).

Fantasy fiction realizes, in Tolkien's words, "the oldest and deepest desire, the Great Escape: the Escape from Death." Thus Tolkien finds that fantasy fiction offers "not only a 'consolation' for the sorrow of this world" but also a "satisfaction, and an answer to that question, 'Is it true?'" If this is fantasy, then, thanks to the Gospel, it is also true.

Tolkien, we know from his foreword to *The Lord of the Rings,* disliked allegory to the extent that it was associated with so-called applicability, that is, inclusion of or reference to the present-tense scene of writing. The Second World War did not enter his composition of *The Lord of the Rings* at that same time. At no point in the story is there, Tolkien writes, "any allegorical significance or contemporary political reference whatsoever." Tolkien's cancellation of this coverage is accompanied in the same foreword by another date mark: "By 1918 all but one of my close friends were dead." There are prior losses, then, which supersede the impact of current events. The ongoing tension of unresolved grief goes the way of the present tense.

In a 1967 interview Tolkien gave his child's-eye view of a contrast that his fantasy fiction kept turning up: "Quite by accident, I have a very vivid child's view, which was the result of being taken away from one country and put in another hemisphere—the place where I belonged but which was totally novel and strange. After the barren, arid heat a Christmas tree." Tolkien celebrates the other world of Christmas trees. (The area of England in which the family resided indeed included stretches of idyllic landscape but was at the same time littered with industrialization. One of the homes he grew up in backed onto a railway line. In *The Lord of the Rings,* industrial and machinic settings are punctuated by arid desertscapes in the domains of the infernal Sauron.) And yet his early recollection/relocation, which he shares with us on an upbeat, which involved his move from South Africa, where he was born to English parents, could not but double another departure. In fact it was after and because of his father's death that he and his younger brother moved to England, while his mother and missing father returned. It was his mother who, together with her sister, subsequently converted to Catholicism. The mother was the one to lose. And before Tolkien's childhood was over, his mother had died on him, too. As an orphan charge of the Church, Tolkien soon showed an aptitude for the dead languages he would, given time, animate through translation and, ultimately, through their replacement by fantasy languages, self-contained languages that are fully functioning—you can learn them—and *not* dead since never really alive.

The embedded moment is the blind spot along for fantasy's drive for super-vision—so super as to be dead, or rather dead-dead, eternally alive.

It is the spot this vision is in with the ruinous materiality that the near miss or the leap of faith of its overdrive leaves behind. Fantasy lets loss go as happy ending. But the embedded expiration date of fantasy, unlocatable as date mark, is not redeemable as deposit of loss.

According to Deleuze and Guattari's concept of faciality,[3] the face folds out from its abstract model or grid. Comprised of white wall and black holes, this face in turn models body and landscape, too, *as* facialized. But faciality also appears to break on or break out with a leap in logic or of faith: every face, Deleuze and Guattari conclude, is the face of Christ.

Every "portrait" is under surveillance. There's the fantasy face that is Christ's face. But then there's the embedded about-face: and we catch sight of the other—the loss of the other—in our faces.

PART II

Deeper Problems

Turning up the contrast in their reception with Freud's view of delusion formation in psychosis as activity of recovery (or rescue) of the loss of world, Carl Jung and Ludwig Binswanger would diagnose a certain streamlining of Freud's concept of projection in delusions as illustration of the living end a patient has arrived at when gadget goes to psychosis. The first man's negative transference onto Freud is the second one's schooling by Martin Heidegger.

According to Heidegger, psychoanalysis and technologization are in it together. In *Being and Time* the address to the uncanny is dead giveaway—like the giveaway of the dead—of the philosopher's intention to drive the stake of his philosophy's claim through the new start of Freud's thought, but (re)claimed on his own terms and turf as the end(s) of philosophy. No wonder Heidegger was rubbed the wrong way when Binswanger sought to harness him and Freud together to a new modality of understanding and treatment of philosophy, I mean psychosis. Following Heidegger's logic of curtailment and emplacement of psychoanalysis, we might argue in turn that philosophy can never be "on" psychosis since already alongside and inside psychosis as yet another projection of ego libido alone. Just as the relocation assignment of psychoanalysis to the wound of technologization, the narcissistic shortfall of its own insight and prosthesis, at the same time justifies immersion in Freud's science when in contempt or contemplation of mourning, so philosophy forced out on a limb in psychotic limbo—on the edge philosophy and psychosis thus share—can at the same time be viewed as a privileged perspective that the student of psychosis would rather not forego (at least Dick thought so). It is at this point of not letting go that Freud introduced endopsychic perception. In *The Interpretation of Dreams,* Freud reserved for future treatment the relationship assumed between the self-observing agency, which, Freud stresses, is particularly prominent in philosophical minds, and both paranoia and endopsychic perception (*Standard Edition* 5:505–6). In the 1914 edition Freud adds a footnote to "On Narcissism: An Introduction" to indicate a place where his theoretical reservations can be confirmed.

Binswanger's encounters with psychosis between psychoanalysis and the philosophy of *Dasein* constitute a prominent intertextual trajectory in this study. Of course I had to take Dick's word on it. But for me, too, there is a connection in disconnection that maintains the new words of "*Dasein-analysis*" as transferentially legible. Binswanger spent the early years of his relations with Freud as the good Swiss heir or parent. But he also spent these years in writer's block over a projected two-volume study that by the end was to have grounded Freud's science in the corpus of psychiatric knowledge. Freud didn't recognize his own work in the prepwork of the first volume, which did at last appear. Over many more years Binswanger never made it to the sense of an ending that would have qualified him as Freud's representative on neutralized turf.

In his letter to Freud dated February 15, 1925, Binswanger is still stumbling over Freud's 1912 telephone analogue for psychoanalytic listening (the tuning of the analyst's unconscious to the unconscious of the patient). Binswanger thus provides us a cross section of his intellectualizing reception of psychoanalysis, which was then taking the form (for over ten years) of the uncompletable book in two parts, the second of which (never to appear) was set aside for the presentation of psychoanalytic hermeneutics.

I have long been impressed by your remark that the analyst's unconscious must be as passive towards the analysand as the telephone receiver is to the transmitting place, etc. I fully understand this pronouncement as a technical principle, but I have always wondered on what "capacity" or intellectual faculty you think that this type of "understanding" is really based.... Far more interesting to me than making a successful interpretation and learning something new about someone else's unconscious is the problem of what it is that *enables* me to make the interpretation in the first place. One person will reply: experience; but your technological analogy shows that you do not take so simple a view of the problem. After all, one has to ask how that kind of experience is possible, how it comes about.

Freud replies on February 22 that the analog served its descriptive purpose. Otherwise, however, it would be more accurate, systematically, to speak of the preconscious as the medium of transmission and exchange. "There is no need to go into the deeper problems here."

If it was the encounter with Heidegger's *Sein und Zeit* that gave Binswanger his momentum as a writer, then it was only because in the epistolary relationship between Binswanger and Freud the other, deeper problem of the corpus had already been addressed and then, against Freud's counsel but in keeping with the placement of the dead in *Sein und Zeit*, put to rest ahead of schedule. On October 7, 1926, Binswanger writes a letter to Freud that begins (once again) with his assertion of differences from/with Freud's followers, who are the ones "opposed for the most part to theoretical discussions and standards not inherent in it [psychoanalysis] but brought in 'from outside.' " But what he smuggles across the frontier in part two of his letter is the deeper problem on which Freud never set an embargo. His little son has died on him and shattered the family circle of immunity against loss. Binswanger rises to the occasion of grieving with a formulation already between analysis and *Dasein:* "Even if something *in* us does not die for good yet something *of* us does and can never be replaced." His closing postscript, the assurance that he did not dictate the letter (like talking on the phone) but wrote it out by hand and then had it transcribed for greater legibility is the clincher in which the letter is wrung out for Freud. Binswanger had addressed this letter as his condolence for Freud's own past losses. Yes, Freud writes back on October 15, he lost a child in the past. But now he is compelled by "an inner urge" to formulate the reopened memorial to his greatest loss. When he lost his daughter, the potential loss of his three sons on the fronts of World War I either made a single loss more bearable or lost it within the bulk rate of traumatization. But in 1923 grandson Heinerle, the son of the dead daughter, who was brought closer to Freud since coming under his aunt's care in Vienna, died. The loss of the intellectually precocious child was a loss of the future that topped off mourning for Freud. In the spirit of transcription, he allows, in closing, that Binswanger, unlike Freud, is still young enough to overcome his loss. Who knew that Binswanger would indeed be preparing for the greater loss on the scale of the future. His eldest son Robert, a student of psychiatry and thus his father's heir in the lineage of directors of the Bellevue asylum, died at age twenty. Freud's reply comes in two parts. The first is formulaic-polite. But the next day he rushes into the opening his sister-in-law provided by deciphering Binswanger's handwriting.[1] Freud gives the prognosis that the acute sorrow will run its course as the ultimate object of mourning. For, he stresses, "we will remain inconsolable, and will never find a substitute. No matter what may come to take its place, even should it fill that place completely, it yet remains something else. And that is how it should be. It is the only way of perpetuating a love that we do not want to abandon" (April 11 and 12, 1929). On December 27, Binswanger reckons that Robert's death has unblocked the slow-mo filter through which his writing tended to pass. "I have to work for him now as well and in that way best continue his existence." The rest is *Dasein*-analysis, which helps him out. Robert's death coincides with the *Ereignis* or event of Binswanger's reading of Heidegger's *Being and Time*. The fruit of this looming encounter was Binswanger's 1930 monograph *Dream and Existence*. Rising and falling in dreams and as expression of moods ("falling out of the clouds") are caught up with existence in ways that Freud's lexicon, since it is bound up with all that "dream representation" implies and applies, cannot address. "To dream means: I don't know what is happening to me" (102). You are not the individual agent of your dreaming. But in your dreams your pain can fall at your feet as another actor (85). Dreaming man is life-function; waking man creates life history. What they have in common is existence; oh yes, and one other thing, that we don't know where dream and life begin or end. But it is mere dreaming if we do not stand in relation to the whole (99). Therefore decide to awaken and participate in the life of the universal.

We will return to the staging area of awakening from the dream at the very end of this study. If I give Binswanger's premier articulation of *Dasein*-analysis only preliminary notice here, it is because in three dreams recorded by Gottfried Keller Binswanger recognizes the pulse of *Dasein*, while I found crudely specific citations of the host of children Keller (and his mother) lost and found. Here Binswanger doesn't really go beyond the Jungian rallying cry for greater respect for the value of the dream's manifest content.

But Binswanger's argument with Freud is that to follow dreaming into waking is to pull up short before the transference. "All these problems are dormant in Freud's doctrine of transference to the doctor and particularly in his theories about the resolution of the transference" (101). But psychoanalysis lets sleeping problems lie: "no one will ever succeed in deriving the human spirit from instincts *(Triebe)*." The incommensurability between drives and transference (which Binswanger links exclusively to the "human spirit") is what justifies the two concepts in their completely separate places. Psychoanalysis, which is in this bind, is thus kept from going deeper. Here Binswanger grants greater limited access to Jung. What a theorist of drives cannot recognize, namely the contrast, which guides our relationship to the dream (and by implication to waking), between image or feeling (same thing) and the intellect (to which Binswanger adds "spirit," which could also mean "ghost"), someone like Jung cannot overlook (101). But in Jung the insight nevertheless "gets buried within problems of detail and basic concepts."

The nixing of Freud's theory of the transference is corollary to the folding out of the world of the psychotic, I mean the dreamer. The passage of this reflection begins with the summoning of a dream that one of Binswanger's patients brought to session. What Binswanger overlooks is that the patient fabricated the dream at the borderline of psychosis. In the alleged dream the patient remembers his moment of insight: "I knew now that unrest meant life and calm was death." Thus already in the dream the dreamer realizes that he must free the sea within. The dream Binswanger finds so interesting is, he points out, dialectically organized in the famous three steps that moreover fit perfectly the tracking of the transference from resistance to resolution. But as Freud pointed out in his reading of Jensen's *Gradiva,* the prospect of the complete resolution and cure-all may be the greatest fantasy or delusion of all (also by the measure of the resistance it packs). In "An Autobiographical Study," Freud even attributed to the transference the suspension of the patient's focus on the cure: "This *transference*—to give it its short name—soon replaces in the patient's mind the desire to be cured" (*Standard Edition* 20:42).

In Freud, the concept of transference contributes to the theory of ghosts. We noted that Binswanger overlooks the press of ghosts in Keller's dreams. But the dissociation is formulated by Binswanger also as near miss or mixed metaphor. Thus there is a relationship between the "demons of dreams" and the appearance of the souls of the departed in sleep (96). But like language itself, the dream image is other, not as part of or parting from the self but as transindividual image content that's bigger than the two of us, self and other. Like Heidegger, Binswanger is after a nonspiritual manner of being (and understanding) human (97).

From within his emplacement as *Dasein*-analyst, from the other side of the between, the side of its overcoming, Binswanger can write to Freud on October 19, 1936, once again about Robert, who no longer lies between them. Now the use of language alone motivates and circumscribes the "falling" that (etymologically) is part of *Trauer* or mourning: "While I am on holiday, I always think I shall never be able to get over the fate that befell my son, rather a silly expression, since fate happens to be there for the purpose of being borne, and we are moulded and fashioned by it." Binswanger continues to catch and contain himself in the act of intellectualizing the work of mourning (or psychoanalysis) without knowing it or rather without surrendering it as such. He stands by what is called philosophy—as an analyst of psychosis.

What Binswanger does share with Freud—and he's alone in this regard in the field of psychosis research—is attention to the crisis point, the trigger, and the phase of stabilization via delusion, and thus to a setting in which the psychotic can be encountered as other, rather than as incarnation of regression to pseudo-psychotic defensive positions first thrown up across the no-man's-land of infancy. Those of you who know Benjamin's work at all will already recognize the compatibility between psychosis as frontier of the other and the mourning pageant as staging of the melancholic word view, between the endopsychic perceptions of the psychotic and the melancholic brooder's allegorizations.

Veil of Tears

The husk of the former world, which had shown its chitinous shell, its wickedness: for it had been *Christians* who had designed the ter-weps, the terror weapons.
—PHILIP K. DICK and ROGER ZELAZNY, *Deus Irae*

It is so much easier to let oneself go, than to let the other go.

In the early 1960s P. K. Dick studied (and was terrified by)[1] Ludwig Binswanger's case study of Ellen West, whose delusional impasse—which took the close-range form in her own terms of "becoming fat" *(Dick-werden)*—inspired Binswanger to plot on his own terms her "tomb world" against the "aetherial world," with which he sided, thus taking sides, he concluded, with his patient, whose suicidal conclusion to and escape from the tomb world's encroachment he assisted or cosigned. Dick projected the aetherial world along the horizon or boundary line of fantasy in his fictional word while depositing with redoubled literalness the tomb world beneath the nonredemptive interminable completion of his word's psychotic or metaphysical system.

The Cosmic Puppets stands, as the sole fantasy novel Dick saw through to publication, as introject or inoculation to be contained and metabolized before subsequent compositions could share a border with fantasy via or as religion but immersed from both sides now in psychotic delusion as a finitude interminably multiplied, extended, diversified to "hold" the transcendent aims and frames of reference passing through it, but without securing their right of passage to a redemptive beyond or resolution. *The Cosmic Puppets*, however, even closes within the fantasy genre of the happy ending. It relates world to world not as "alternate" but as "other," a relationship staged or staggered with veils and mists.

The Cosmic Puppets relates protagonist Ted Barton's return to Miltown, the hometown of his boyhood, where he stumbles instead upon the site of its never having been the way he still remembers it. In the town records he finds only a stammered version of his name alongside the entry of a nine-year-old boy's death (Barton was age nine when he and his family moved away). Two rival children with amazing powers introduce the prospect either of supernatural realities or of childish omnipotence fantasies. That Miltown is in fact a fantasy world is first admitted and introduced via the passage of wanderers, recognizable yet insubstantial wraiths who can walk through physical boundaries. When Barton witnesses the passage of wanderers, the adult townsfolk standing by calmly acknowledge them as common occurrence in their everyday lives. But the wanderers are not ghosts, nor is there any ghostly consequence to the registration of the boy's death. Two Zoroastrian gods, Ahriman and Orazd (who also cast their shadows in Daniel Paul Schreber's system in answer to a radically different casting call, the call Dick would take and answer in his psy-fi oeuvre) are evil versus good and take turns dominating the reality set on Miltown. Their representatives in the town are the gifted children. The evil god brought about the change that veiled the original town in the illusion of the false town. (The wanderers are the original citizens passing through the illusion according to the coordinates of the original Miltown, which they thus try to reclaim and reconfigure.) Barton, on fateful schedule, brings about a ripple in the false reality through his return and his remembrance. Barton finds an ally in the town drunk Christopher (who turns out to be one of the wanderers stuck in the illusory town). He also remembers the other Miltown, which he has uncovered for moments via efforts of concentration that he has focused and harnessed through the construction of a gadget, the Spell Remover. It turns out that Barton can lift the "blanket of illusion" through concentration alone (75). Christopher's Spell Remover isn't the only gadget for viewing the double vision of Miltown. The boy Peter, who turns out to be Ahriman or his representative in the veiled world, has a lens that enables the viewer to recognize the widest aetherial vista as fitting the outlines of the two gods. Dr. Meade, the father of the other gifted child, has also all along known about the change. While he gives shelter and assistance to the wanderers, he hesitates to lift the veil because he doesn't know where he and his daughter would end up. What he has forgotten is that he is Ormazd. But first he gives the Christian articulation of the veil word, which in Dick's psy-fi oeuvre proves coextensive with the media of recording and surveillance: "Like it says in the Bible, 'We see as through a glass, darkly'" (102). Ormazd's daughter, the only divine figure who knows who she is, was responsible for bringing Barton back and thus initiating struggle and reversal of the change. She merges with the world regained as happy ending. Barton recognizes the two "firm hills, rich and full, identical peaks glowing warmly in the late-afternoon sun" through which he drives at or into the end of the novel as her good breasts.

Three of the illusory townspeople are deities who are down to earth only because it's fantasy time. Who or what the other miraculated-up citizens are, or what becomes of them, is information withheld or rather erased. Any question about the reality, presence, or absence of people is rendered mute in the jump cut from the town's veiling and unveiling to its supersizing as cosmic struggle between the all-good god and the all-bad god. Once the wanderers are restored together with their town they pick up their lives where they left off with the change—and precisely without memory of the time between. In the struggle right before their restoration, however, many wanderers died. Forgettable. No echo chamber for the report of missing persons in *The Cosmic Puppets*. Dead or alive, divine or mortal, the figures inhabit the real world as other world beneath an illusory fallen world, the veil of tears or rips or RIPs.

Dick's only other full-on entry into the fantasy genre, the short story "Upon This Dull Earth," succumbs to the underworld elided in *The Cosmic Puppets* in the psy-fi mode. This world is surrounded by the aetherial world or other world inhabited by angels who are drawn to break through to this world by blood thirst. Silvia is the goth girl whose interest in the other world is as mixed up as the vampiric makeup of the angels. She manages to terrorize her family with her second sight and disturb her boyfriend with her impatience to cross over. She's preparing for the proper time of her departure. Her second-sight bond with the angels was in place throughout her life. But she later used the troughs of blood to train the angels to heed her summons. Her Chinese coffin has arrived. When she demonstrates the fit, boyfriend yanks her out of there, which results in an accidental cut. No, not yet! But the angels respond as stimulated and take her into their beyond or between realm and incinerate her earthly husk. This was a serious misunderstanding. The boyfriend wants Silvia back.

At her desubtantialized remove, she agrees with him that the mistake the angels made runs counter to the order of the world. How can the angels make amends? The deity who alone knows how to create life out of nothing absconded long ago, out of the reach and range even of the angels. The angels finally agree to risk making yet another mistake: they send her back and boyfriend next watches her beam up within her sister's body, first rendered nondescript and empty. Something has indeed gone wrong with Silvia's attempt to control her departure and return. Silvia is back stuck in the groove or grave of the record of the ambivalence she thought she could skip or split. Now what repeats is the trauma of departure or return as botched beginning without end. Everywhere boyfriend turns he must again watch Silvia snatch yet another body and crawl out of its pod. What returns each time is Silvia's bewilderment, words of hurt, loss, confusion, recognition that there is something wrong between her and her boyfriend, something terribly wrong with her comeback. From the occult perspective, which bleeds over into the fantasy preoccupation with the aetherial world, the preference for the afterlife is mere fantasy that can lead only to the kind of wish fulfillment that punishes. The occult desire for the return of the dead—of the soul or mind without embodiment—leads via replication to serial merger and murder. The desire for departure or return is so destructive because profoundly self-destructive at its uncontainable origin. The world of survivors or mourners becomes an alternate world of vehicles for one auto-replicating comeback that soon makes a crowd. It is the small world after all of one traumatic moment of departure or return, embodied as the same over and over again, which thus pulls up short before remembrance or commemoration. At the end the boyfriend watches himself in the mirror turn into Silvia.

In *Time out of Joint* Dick subordinated fantasy (like the daydream as interpreted by Freud) to the dynamic of delusion, which fantasy can influence and organize, though only for a time, in order to maintain and control it. The fantasy controls required that the psychotic in his delusional world not know what the other reality is or is up to. In the course of consolidation, stabilization, or encapsulation the psychotic delusional order, like science fiction itself, installs itself within the reality with which the psycho must enter into diplomatic relations (if he is to avoid his own catatonic shutdown or being institutionally shut up and away) as another, alternative reality. *Time out of Joint* was thus Dick's first alternate reality work also to the extent that psychosis supplied the psy-fi form, which, however, can come into focus only by turning up the contrast with fantasy. The other one out of two rehearsals of the alternate live style was *Eye in the Sky,* in which Dick plotted alternate realites—or a series of delusional realities wrapped up as fantasies—against the likelihood that the first of eight casualties of a techno accident to return to consciousness would dominate the reality of all the others joined at the rip and tear line of shock with a sole survivor's phantasmatic worldview. The blanks here—which Dick ultimately filed away all the way to the greater complexity and subtlety of half-life in *Ubik,* which throws out its plotline under similar conditions of disaster and group projection—are filled to the level or label of expiration datedness, since each proves readily recognizable as wish-fulfillment fantasy. Written the same year as *Eye in the Sky* (though first published one year earlier), *The Man Who Japed* holds up just like one in the series of the wish-fulfillment worldviews, the I in the sky through which all the other survivors must pass. Morec names a state of moral reclamation in which it would be hard for anyone (other than the person fulfilling his or her wish) to live. The escape is to the "Other World," the last resort where psychiatry pretends to offer sanctuary but actually completes the Morec system. To jape is to make fun of a stale theme. The protagonist acts out against a monument until at the end he is able to enact japing in words. The psychoanalyst's first intervention summarizes as fantasy of the analytic cure the short control release on which every aspect of the book is held: " 'I've got your problem; by telling me you've transferred it to me' " (55).

At the time of Dick's Binswanger feed, Carl Jung was already his guide through the underworld mapped out in *The Tibetan Book of the Dead,* which Dick introduced into his psy-fi discourse at the same time as the *I Ching* (also via yet another Jung "introduction"). *The Man in the High Castle,* the novel in which both Jung introductions or introjects were conjoined at what was hip back then, also marked the onset of Dick's signature revalorization of alternate histories, realities, or worlds. Before Jung doesn't surprise us with his claim that he hears a synchronicity when he considers the sensibility revealed in the *I Ching,* "preoccupied" as it is "with the chance aspect of events" (191), he has already entered the dig of this sensibility on terms that exceed explanations for the asking: "What we call coincidence seems to be the chief concern of this peculiar mind, and what we worship as causality passes almost unnoticed." That "there is something to be said for the immense importance of chance" Jung derives, appropriately as understatement, from the degree of its marginalization in Western scientificity. "An incalculable amount of human effort is directed to combating and restricting the nuisance or danger that chance represents"

(191). What pales in the comparison of theorization of cause and effect to "the practical results of chance" is the underlying belief in ideal forms:

It is all very well to say that the crystal of quartz is a hexagonal prism. The statement is quite true in so far as an ideal crystal is envisaged. But in nature one finds no two crystals exactly alike, although all are unmistakably hexagonal. The actual form, however, seems to appeal more to the Chinese sage than the ideal one.... The manner in which the *I Ching* tends to look upon reality seems to disfavour our causal procedures. The moment under actual observation appears to the ancient Chinese view more of a chance hit than a clearly defined result of concurrent causal chains. The matter of interest seems to be the configuration formed by chance events at the moment of observation, and not at all the hypothetical reasons that seemingly account for the coincidence. While the Western mind carefully sifts, weighs, selects, classifies, isolates, the Chinese picture of the moment encompasses everything down to the minutest nonsensical detail, because all of the ingredients make up the observed moment. (191)

The compass of otherwise fragmented ingredients is no totality but gives the direction in turn to the staggering, staggered display and relay of self-reflexivity (in which Jung participates by consulting the *I Ching* regarding the fortunes of this edition, translation, and of his own introduction).

The uniqueness of the counsel the *I Ching* gives as response to a presenting problem posed as question clearly has less to do with Jung's out-of-synch view that only thus "do we know what nature does when left to herself undisturbed by the meddlesomeness of man" (197) and more with his follow-up admission, which he at the same time resists: "Moreover, a repetition of the experiment is impossible, for the simple reason that the original situation cannot be reconstructed. Therefore in each instance there is only a first and single answer" (197). But since the repetition cannot be repeated as the same, it can be done again as different or alternate. Incorporated within linear time, the prospects one obtains in exchange with the *I Ching* open onto alternate pathways each bearing unique or rather parallel reality in and through the same time.

With regard to the inclusion of the moment of interpretation in the interpretation of the moment, what makes the claim Jung stakes for synchronicity or coincidence of events interesting to the science fiction author is the pointer that "the ancient Chinese mind contemplates the cosmos in a way comparable to that of the modern physicist, who cannot deny that his model of the world is a decidedly psychophysical structure. The microphysical event includes the observer just as much as the reality underlying the *I Ching* comprises subjective, i.e., psychic conditions in the totality of the momentary situation" (192–93). Jung adds psychotherapy to this lineup as another "pragmatic" discipline that aims at "self-knowledge:"

Probably in no other field do we have to reckon with so many unknown quantities, and nowhere else do we become more accustomed to adopting methods that work even though for a long time we may not know why they work. Unexpected cures may arise from questionable therapies and unexpected failures from allegedly reliable methods. In the exploration of the unconscious we come upon very strange things, from which a rationalist turns away with horror, claiming afterward that he did not see anything. The irrational fullness of life has taught me never to discard anything, even when it goes against all our theories (so short-lived at best) or otherwise admits of no immediate explanation. (202)

Accordingly, when Jung imagines a critic of his performance of consulting the *I Ching* on the project of and prospects for its reintroduction, to which he is contributing, accuse the whole show as projection, a suitably dismissive critique "from the standpoint of Western rationality," he also imagines how the *I Ching* might respond:

"Don't you see how useful the *I Ching* is in making you project your hitherto unrealized thoughts into its abstruse symbolism? You could have written your foreword without ever realizing what an avalanche of misunderstanding might be released by it." (207)

Rather than consulting it, Jung here ventriloquates the *I Ching* while making recourse to a remarkably pre-Freudian reflex grasp of projection. Where the projection Jung summons but then circumvents might lie is possibly marked off via Jung's recourse to the process of elimination. The *I Ching* "is appropriate only for the thoughtful and reflective people who like to think about what they do and what happens to them—a predilection not to be confused with the morbid brooding of the hypochondriac" (201). This aside or sideline granted the hypochondriac or melancholic belongs to the inside of the occult view of the book and practice that Jung seeks to displace through his pragmatic understanding of self-reflexivity as synchronicity: "My argument as outlined above has of course never entered a Chinese mind. On the contrary, according to the old tradition, it is 'spiritual agencies,' acting in a mysterious way, that make the yarrow-stalks give a meaningful answer. These powers form, as it were, the living soul of the book" (193–94). Thus he follows the tradition of respecting the book's view of itself as "a sort of animated being" in the course of asking it questions about his project, including this very question and answer period (194). "It is a fact that if one begins to think about it, the problems of the

I Ching do represent 'abyss on abyss,' and unavoidably one must 'pause at first and wait' in the midst of the dangers of limitless and uncritical speculation; otherwise one really will lose one's way in the darkness" (203). Just checking: "Had a human being made such replies, I should, as a psychiatrist, have had to pronounce him of sound mind, at least on the basis of the material presented. Indeed, I should not have been able to discover anything delirious, idiotic, or schizophrenic in the four answers" (207).

In Dick's 1962 novel *The Man in the High Castle*, the science fiction consists in the insertion, in our recent past, of time-traveling changes into the schedule of our recovery from our biggest symptom, National Socialism. The time is now—1961, for example—but not so long ago the Axis Powers won the Second World War. Californians live under Japanese rule. By this East-Asian association, everyday life in Greater Japan or California tends to be organized around consultations of the *I Ching*. A fad in Dick's California, too, at that time, the Chinese book of counsel for the future organized Dick's own writing of *The Man in the High Castle*, which finds its internal simulacrum in an underground bestseller, *The Grasshopper Lies Heavy*, which constructs or contemplates an alternate history in which the Allies won the war. Its author, Abendsen, wrote his version of "our" history in collaboration with the *I Ching*. The ultimate fad-der spanning all these trajectories, including that of Nazi Germany shunted to the side of this Californian future, is Carl Jung, the pre-Nazi Germany and postwar guru of East Asian interests. The gap of repression attending these pop receptions of Jung is the site specific to this history-altering fantasy. Finally, the fantasy proves particularly potent because the by-product of Allied propaganda that stages (to this day) the defeat of Nazi death stars by a united front of victims and losers is that we dissociate the historical outcome of the conflict: we're never really sure that the Nazis lost, right?

Grasping for straws, as he admits, Mr. Tagomi, a highly placed member of the Japanese administration of San Francisco, seeks "the Way" in a piece of jewelry that, according to a dealer in historicity and authenticity (the field of collectibles, largely items of Americana prized by the Japanese ruling class), contains a "germ of the future" (225). First he must go down inside "its tomb world":

Metal is from the earth, he thought as he scrutinized. From below: from that realm which is the lowest, the most dense.... Yin world, in its most melancholy aspect. World of corpses, decay and collapse.... And yet, in the sunlight, the silver triangle glittered. It reflected light. Fire, Mr. Tagomi thought. Not dank or dark object at all.... The high realm, aspect of yang: empyrean, ethereal.... Yes, that is artist's job:

tàkes mineral rock from dark silent earth transforms it into shining light-reflecting form from sky. Has brought the dead to life. Corpse turned to fiery display; the past had yielded to the future. (229)

The cite-specific references to Binswanger are blended with the itinerary of *The Tibetan Book of the Dead* or *Bardo Thodol,* which Mr. Tagomi summarizes in attempting, following Jung's advice in his introduction, to reverse its travelogue and start and stop at the end which is the redemptive beginning, the light of escape at the end of worlds within worlds of reincarnation:

Now talk to me, he told it. Now that you have snared me. I want to hear your voice issuing from the blinding clear white light, such as we expect to see only in the *Bardo Thodol* afterlife existence. But I do not have to wait for death, for the decomposition of my animus as it wanders in search of a new womb. All the terrifying and beneficent deities; we will bypass them, and the smoky lights as well. And the couples in coitus. Everything except this light. I am ready to face without terror. . . . My training was correct: I must not shrink from the clear white light, for if I do, I will once more re-enter the cycle of birth and death, never knowing freedom, never obtaining release. The veil of maya will fall once more if I—The light disappeared. (230)

But now that the curtain falls or rises, Mr. Tagomi notes a set change: he sees for the first time what a passerby, a low-class yank who doesn't pay him respect or much interest, identifies as the Embarcadero Freeway:

Mad dream, Mr. Tagomi thought. Must wake up. . . . Whole vista has dull, smoky, tomb-world cast. . . . *Bardo Thodol* existence, Mr. Tagomi thought. Hot winds blowing me who knows where. This is vision—of what? Can the animus endure this? Yes, the *Book of the Dead* prepares us: after death we seem to glimpse others, but all appear hostile to us. One stands isolated. Unsuccored wherever one turns. The terrible journey—and always the realms of suffering, rebirth, ready to receive the fleeing, demoralized spirit. The delusions. . . . This hypnagogic condition. Attention-faculty diminished so that twilight state obtains; world seen merely in symbolic, archetypal aspect, totally confused with unconscious material. (231–32)

Finally he starts to reclaim the projection—he turns to the jewelry as medium and cries out, *Erwache.* But not until he decries his own "Goddam stupidity" does the diffusion subside. Mr. Tagomi concludes his episode with the reflection that St. Paul was right: we see through a glass darkly. "We really do see astigmatically, in a fundamental sense: our space and our time creations of our own psyche, and when these momentarily falter—like acute disturbance of middle ear. Occasionally we list eccentrically, all sense of balance gone" (233).

Mr. Tagomi's encounter with our alternate reality fits the projective medium of delusion rather than the escape chute into the light. Once there is an alternate history or reality, all realities are alternate—and altered. As our history seems to start folding out of the book at the center of Dick's book we notice that history restored is just the same marked by the alternation process. Thus, for example, Berlin falls—but to the British. A Nazi German official sneaks a peek at the outlawed book and shudders at the reality effect of fiction: "How that man can write, he thought. Completely carried me away. Real. Fall of Berlin to the British, as vivid as if it had actually taken place. Brrr. He shivered" (125).

Dick thus reverses the reversal Jung prescribed in his introduction to *The Tibetan Book of the Dead* and drops Binswanger's aetherial world back behind or inside the tomb world. Dick signs up for the bulk rate of Jung's and Binswanger's reflections by instinctively bracketing out the negative transference that led them to Christianize the frame of reference they shared with Freud's science. Thus basic editing of influence raises the middlebrow of received thought. For example, the following sentence from "Psychological Commentary on *The Tibetan Book of the Dead*," lifted out of the setting of Jung's resentment and holistic humanism, is worthy of Dick or Freud:

Unlike the Egyptian *Book of the Dead*, which always prompts one to say too much or too little, the *Bardo Thödol* offers one an intelligible philosophy addressed to human beings rather than to gods or primitive savages. Its philosophy contains the quintessence of Buddhist psychological criticism; and, as such, one can truly say that it is of an unexampled sublimity. Not only the "wrathful" but also the "peaceful" deities are conceived as samsaric projections of the human psyche, an idea that seems all too obvious to the enlightened European. . . . But though the European can easily explain away these deities as projections, he would be quite incapable of positing them at the same time as real. (60–61)

To keep Jung's excellent formulation unobscured by the static clingingness of his negative transference, even here a clause of arrogant anger about European banality had to be elided. Jung is angry because *The Tibetan Book of the Dead* is for the most part syntonic with basic Freud. Jung is smart enough not to admit that only the Christian-nihilistic circumvention of "the Book" in all its phases is alien to Freud's system. Even this aspect, once diagnosed, as already suggested, as the self-destruction impulse that "the Book" works to survive or push back, remains profoundly compatible with Freud. Jung links and limits Freudian psychoanalysis only to the phase leading to rebirth. Greater psychoanalysis (including notably Jung's

new improvements) remains, as "analysis of the unconscious . . . for therapeutic purposes," the "only 'initiation process' that is still alive and prac-
tised today in the West" (65). Before tagging Freud out, Jung at once loses
psychoanalysis in the supersizing of its ancient influences and consigns its
substance to a future in Christianity or psychosis: "This penetration into
the ground-layers of consciousness is a kind of rational maieutics in the
Socratic sense, a bringing forth of psychic contents that are still germinal,
subliminal, and as yet unborn."[2] In the next sentence Jung slips us another
origin, but one that must conclude with the period to be overcome:

Originally, this therapy took the form of Freudian psychoanalysis and was mainly
concerned with sexual fantasies. This is the realm that corresponds to the last and
lowest region of the *Bardo*, known as the *Sidpa Bardo*, where the dead man, unable
to profit by the teachings of the *Chikhai* and *Chönyid Bardo*, begins to fall a prey
to sexual fantasies and is attracted by the vision of mating couples. Eventually he is
caught by a womb and born into the earthly world again. Meanwhile, as one might
expect, the Oedipus complex starts functioning. . . . The European passes through
this specifically Freudian domain when his unconscious contents are brought to light
under analysis, but he goes in the reverse direction. He journeys back through the
world of infantile-sexual fantasy to the womb. (65)

That which remains out of reach of Mr. Tagomi's yearning, even at
the point of breakthrough to another world, would be secured by Jung's
reversal:

Now it is characteristic of Oriental religious literature that the teaching invariably
begins with the most important item, with the ultimate and highest principles which,
with us, would come last. . . . Accordingly, in the *Bardo Thödol*, the initiation is a
series of diminishing climaxes ending with rebirth in the womb. (64)

Reading backwards, the *Chikhai* state, which appears in the original before
the journey itself, namely, at the moment of death, can be reached—and
all the rest skipped: "With this final vision the karmic illusions cease; consciousness, weaned away from all form and from all attachment to objects,
returns to the timeless, inchoate state of the *Dharmakāya*" (72). However,
Jung's own barely concealed fascination is with the "psychotic" phase
of the journey of the dead, also carefully identified as out-of-phase with
Freudian analysis. Jung is still reading backwards:

The transition, then, from the *Sidpa* state to the *Chönyid* state is a dangerous reversal
of the aims and intentions of the conscious mind. It is a sacrifice of the ego's ability
and a surrender to the extreme uncertainty of what must seem like a chaotic riot of

phantasmal forms. . . . [I]t is merely the creation of a subject, who, in order to find fulfilment, has still to be confronted by an object. This, at first sight, would appear to be the world, which is swelled out with projections for that very purpose. Here we seek and find our difficulties, here we seek and find our enemy, here we seek and find what is dear and precious to us. . . . The reality experienced in the *Chönyid* state is . . . the reality of thought. The "thought-forms" appear as realities, fantasy takes on real form, and the terrifying dream evoked by karma and played out by the unconscious "dominants" begins. (70–71)

Total word domination by archetypes allows Jung to take over where Freud allegedly stops short—before the color-coded revue of blood-drinking goddesses (for example). Because psychosis is what he's party to, Jung can try, if he wants, to give credit that's overdue:

I think, then, we can state it as a fact that with the aid of psychoanalysis the rationalizing mind of the West has pushed forward into what one might call the neuroticism of the *Sidpa* state, and has there been brought to an inevitable standstill by the uncritical assumption that everything psychological is subjective and personal. Even so, this advance has been a great gain, inasmuch as it has enabled us to take one more step behind our conscious lives. This knowledge also gives us a hint of how we ought to read the *Bardo Thödol*—that is, backwards. If, with the help of our Western science, we have to some extent succeeded in understanding the psychological character of the *Sidpa Bardo*, our next task is to see if we can make anything of the preceding *Chönyid Bardo*.

Because Jung can't let go of "the wholeness of the self"—or of the symbolic nature of the world and its experiences, which "reflects something that lies hidden in the subject himself, in his own transubjective reality" (71)—we follow Dick in skipping fast forward to "the Book" itself. The guidebook for the dead describes for the most part a pageant of projections far more enticing than the nothingness toward which the book's howto injunctions to the dead would guide them (into the light). Here is one example (featuring hungry ghosts who give way to animals, humans, and jealous gods, among others) in lieu of many variations on the themes of temptation to remain stuck in life by one's own mind in time (not reducible to lifetime):

By being shown in this way liberation is certain, however weak one's capacities may be. Yet even after being shown like this many times, there are people whose good opportunities have run out. . . . Disturbed by desire and neurotic veils, they will be afraid of the sounds and lights and will escape, so then on the fourth day Blessed Amitāba's circle of deities will come to invite them, together with the light-path of the hungry ghosts, built from desire and meanness. To show him again, one should call the dead person by name and say these words: . . . "On the fourth day, a red light, the purified element of fire, will shine. . . . At the same time, together with the wisdom light, the soft yellow light of the hungry ghosts will also shine. Do not take pleasure in it; give up desire and yearning. At that time, under the influence of intense desire, you will be terrified and escape from the sharp, bright red light, but you will feel pleasure and attraction towards the soft yellow light of the hungry ghosts. At that moment do not fear the red light, sharp and brilliant, luminous and clear, but recognise it as wisdom. Let your mind rest in it, relaxed, in a state of non-action. Be drawn to it with faith and longing. If you recognise it as your own natural radiance, even if you do not feel devotion and do not say the inspiration-prayer, all the forms and light and rays will merge inseparably with you, and you will attain enlightenment. . . . Do not be afraid, do not be attracted to the soft yellow light of the hungry ghosts. That is the light-path of unconscious tendencies accumulated by your intense desire. If you are attracted to it you will fall into the realm of hungry ghosts, and experience unbearable misery from hunger and thirst. It is an obstacle blocking the path of liberation, so do not be attracted to it, but give up your unconscious tendencies. (46–47)

What rings loud as denial is that while we may rue the attraction of this liminal region of unconscious embeddedness in lives, we can hardly let it go, but must rather let it go on and on and on. How easy is it to recognize "the peaceful and wrathful ones" as your "own projections" (40)? It isn't so hard to be "afraid of the lights and rays because of . . . aggression and neurotic veils" (42). This is where Dick goes, against the tour guidance instructions, when he plots alternate realities in the course of seeking (and hiding) where our dead are.

Dick's metabolism of the East Asian introjects as first introduced to or into him by Jung can be followed for example in his 1965 article "Schizophrenia and *The Book of Changes*." Here schizophrenia, which is identified as the breaking up and out of "the postwomb womb," has absorbed his reading of Jung's reading of *The Tibetan Book of the Dead*. The breaking out of schizophrenia is mistakenly viewed as escape from reality into fantasy. Its "deadly appearance . . . is not a retreat from reality, but on the contrary: the breaking out of reality all around him." Only the schizophrenic knows for sure that "reality has . . . the attribute that causes us to so designate it as reality: it *can't* be escaped." What breaks out is synchronicity, the simulcasting about of multiple nows, which, in the analogy Dick stretches to unbind projection from linear or one-way animation, also fits an encryptment: "The schizophrenic is having it all now . . . ; the whole can of film has descended on him, whereas we watch it progress frame by frame" (176).

But the "eternal now" is not necessarily a stuck place, not for the dead or for the psychotic. True, if synchronicity means coincidence and thus independence from the past, then it meets its match and maker in the "unhappy world of the schizophrenic," in which "reality happens to him . . . , going on and on without relief" (178). But the *I Ching* restores future to this stricken world. Not as the uncontrollable time to come, the transhuman imperative, but as the precog focus on alternate possible futures, which is Dick's extension of the orthogonal diversification of the present going on recent past to the other time zone of repression, the immediate future. "It lays before your eyes, for your scrutiny, a gestalt of the forces in operation that will *determine* the future. But these forces are at work now; they exist, so to speak, outside of time" (179). "So in proportion to the degree of schizophrenic involvement in time that we're stuck with—or in—we can gain yield from the *I Ching*" (180).

Go West

So much easier to let oneself go, than to let the other go.

In the course of breaking down—by now she's undergoing her second analysis—Ellen West registers a new (or now) beginning: "I am reading *Faust* again. Now I begin to understand it for the first time. I now begin" (Binswanger, "Der Fall Ellen West," 92). Another one of Binswanger's patients remarked that if Goethe hadn't written *Faust* she would have had to. It's manic-depressing that he plagiarized her in advance.[1] Indeed, Ellen's youthful expressions of despair were already recognizable between the lines of *Faust:* the gray allegorical figure of Need *(Not)* sits at her grave. Death *(Tod)* appears to her now not as a terrible skeleton swinging his scythe but as a beautiful woman (79). In *Faust II* Faust's death is announced as "rhyme-word," the rhyme obtaining between *Not* and *Tod,* while at the start of *Faust I,* as amplified by Goethe's own illustration, the Earth Spirit, who can be seen to usher in, as placeholder, death, but also or in fact, via another reading, the Eternal Feminine as mourning, appears as beautiful (same-sex) double, yet or therefore endlessly withdrawn from Faust, who is explicitly denied this mirror image. The allegorical figures that, with *Not* at the front of the line, heralded Faust's death emerged in the wake of the gravest crime committed by the Devil's bureaucratic administration of genius Faust's desires (his performative prowess is split off from itself as responsible activity and his wishes are the command of an administrative apparatus about which he need know nothing). At least Jung considered the murder of Philemon and Baucis such a transgression: during his psychotic break with Freud, which Jung would revalorize as a breakthrough to his own psychological system, one of his spirit guides was Philemon. His legacy was "The Seven Sermons to the Dead,"[2] the slight but vastly unusual tract that made Dick double take note of Jung as his man.

Ellen's Faustian striving is to eat the world, wolf it down, whereupon it bites her in the ass as tomb world. She sees her relation to food as analogous to a murderer's relationship to the scene of the crime. The murderer who must view the image of his victim with his inner eye is drawn to the site of murder. He knows that he thus places himself under suspicion. But, what is worse, he is terrified of this scene or setting, but he can't help himself. But the criminal's situation pales in comparison to Ellen's impasse. The criminal can turn himself in to the police and make restitution. Her salvation lies only in death (92–93). When Kraepelin diagnoses her as melancholic, Ellen is rereading *Faust II* (94). Ellen describes her current condition at this time: "An evil spirit accompanies me and sours my every joy. He twists everything that is beautiful, natural, simple and makes of it a grimace. He turns the whole of life into a distorted image *[Zerrbild]*." It is as though she were "bewitched" (96). Her every mealtime is, indeed, "an internal theater" (98). "I experience myself completely passively as the stage on which two inimical forces tear themselves limb from limb" (101).

The dreams of schizophrenics tend to be continuous with their waking realities: she dreams of death or food or of food and death. When she comes under institutional care (her second analyst has been fired) she dreads mingling with the other patients; she feels like a dead woman walking among the others (100). Plus she cannot eat in public: she is convinced that she doesn't in fact eat but that she gulps food down "like a wild animal," an act she acts out for her caregivers very convincingly (99).

The second analyst considered her as basically obsessive-compulsive with strong currents of manic depression washing over her anal-erotic fixations. Proximity to Ratman catches the glint in her eyes as directed at others. Binswanger requests that Ellen's cousin-husband, her second choice after "the student," her true love, for whom, however, she felt she was too fat, keep an eye and a record on his wife. He notes that when she learns that a friend has died she is overwhelmed with envy "and as she hears the news of the death her eyes gleam" (102). Binswanger sees the gleam catch the aetherial light of escape. But the problematic coupling of food and death is addressed to or via the other. "Ellen's yearning for death is desire for another death than that of decline and decay, indeed desire for another death than the immortal name" (115). Even for her end "Ellen cannot wait" (120). Increasingly animals press threateningly upon her. Ghosts pose a threat to her conscience: "The elevated plans and thoughts take on the form of evil . . . spirits or ghosts" (121). "What is new here is that her yearning for death shines forth from the aetherial world itself. . . . *Dasein* builds itself an air castle in the aetherial world, but we can follow precisely how this airy construct is increasingly dragged down by lust into the earth, that is, transformed into a mausoleum or grave" (123). Gravity and pressure of falling life prove stronger than the upbeat or upsurge of ascending life. If the aetherial world is forced increasingly into a defensive position, the lust or hunger is already implicit in Ellen's characterization of her special aetherial world as " 'fairy-tale-like, sweet land of life' " (126). The hunger, which Ellen learned in analysis is the primary factor in her obsessions, attacked her "like an animal" (126). The animal-like gulping or gobbling down of nourishment—*Schlingen* or *Verschlingen*—contains the *Schlinge,* the noose or garrote that tightens as she comes full circle, locked in the spot she is in: "In this regard it is only seemingly paradoxical that the full stomach in particular strengthens the feeling of emptiness: The bodily fullness and roundness . . . is indeed, from the perspective of the aetherial world, (lived) epitome of (spiritual) emptiness. The hungry lust . . . , the fear of becoming fat . . . form the snare or noose from which *Dasein* can no longer wriggle itself free" (127).

She makes a slip that Binswanger corrects rather than comment on it. Because she must view everything in terms of whether it makes her thin or fat, all things, including work, must lose their *Eigen-Sinn* (128). Binswanger translates this as circumlocution for "own meaning or sense" whereas, the hyphen notwithstanding, the word *Eigensinn* means stubborn streak, the predisposition she showed already in infancy when she suddenly refused to drink mother's milk.

When Ellen is able to admit that becoming fat isn't only a curse, a target of haunting, but that it is natural and healthy, Binswanger ascribes her insightfulness to the proximity of the suicidal end she has decided on. Binswanger brings up for comparison a patient who preferred to continue to decay rather than to take her own life as proof only "that the process here is unfolding at a far greater speed than in the case of Ellen West" (187). "The dread of becoming fat gave itself increasingly to be understood as fear of being made hole *[Verlochung]*. But once *Dasein* has determined to die, it has overcome the dread and the burden of earthliness" (130). Ellen's *Dasein* "had become ripe for its death, in other words, . . . death, this death, was the necessary fulfillment of the life sense of this *Dasein*" (132). But of whose womb or whose fate's loom does death drop into her lap like strange fruit?

"In this we recognize the immense positive value that can be awarded nothingness in *Dasein*. Where this is the case, as in the case of Ellen West, the life history in a special way becomes a death history and we are right to speak of a *Dasein* dedicated to death" (135). As nihilist she stands alone before nothingness; even her joy on the eve in the midst ("lap") of her family falls in the face of nothingness under a "metaphysical shadow" (136). Psychoanalysis might address the scenario as rebirth fantasy; Binswanger prefers to refer to Kierkegaard's notion of illness unto death. This fits her ill fit. She couldn't be whom or what she wanted to be (136). The metaphor of birth isn't so far removed after all. But for Binswanger a literary genre distinction needs to be drawn. In deciding to die Ellen "for the first time found and chose herself. The festival of death was the festival of the birth of her existence. Where however *Dasein* can exist only at the cost of life, the existence is a *tragic* existence" (137). At the same time Binswanger ups the standards of fantasy: "In her... stubborn insistence on her self, which however is not her genuine self but rather a ('timeless') aetherial wish-self, she does not flee the ground *[Grund]* of her *Dasein*—no one can do that—but instead runs into it as abyss *[Abgrund]*" (138).

Binswanger views temporality as Heideggerian ecstatic beside itself in the conjunction of the phenomena future, having been-ness, and present. The primary existential phenomenon of authentic temporality is the future, but not a future that has been arranged, wished, or hoped for in advance. Conceived existentially, the past means that we "are" as having been (or has beens). The present finally means to make present as the decisive disclosure of the given situation in activity (141–42). In this setting the fantastic self implies a future without determination or limit—a future of empty possibilities. Its spatial form: "the unlimited, bright, shining, colorful expanse, its cosmic aspect consists of landscape, the firmament, the ocean, its material garment is the air, the aether" (143). "As world of 'inauthentic' future, as world of a fantastic anticipation or projection and of a fantastic self, as world, in which there is no shadow and no limit, this world is as such continually threatened by shadow and boundary, in other words, by the having been; for the temporal-historical structure of *Dasein* can be modified through stubbornness, eccentricity, ambition, but cannot be broken through or even turned back" (143). The wish self artificializes the world in its significance. "Anyone can for a time swing high up into such a world, but with awareness of its fantastic character, that is, that there is nothing lasting about it" (143). Thus to make the fake world take the place of the present practical world is to be "blindly, uncannily threatened by shadow, by anxiety!" In contrast, the temporality of the tomb world reflects "the excessive power of inauthentic since nonfutural, always present pastness" (143). Anxiety from Hell is that "of *Dasein* over being ensnared by its ground, from which it is that much more profoundly ensnared the higher it tries to jump past or fly away" (144). The "hole aspect" of this world follows from taking gratification from whatever is ready to hand or to mouth "like an animal" (144). "To be fat is the eternal reproach *Dasein* addresses to itself, its proper 'guilt'" (146). Suicide is the only way out of this antinomy: "through a determined practical act . . . freedom ultimately necessarily triumphs over unfreedom" (146–47). In the practical world, Ellen's impulse to change or improve social conditions was at her disposal service of distraction and self-forgetting: her practical pacing on the earth was, even during the good times, cramped, jumpy, tense, threatened both by the tendency toward flight and in particular by the tendency toward apathy, to creep and to crawl. "Everywhere we turn we find the temporality in the case of Ellen West more or less falling apart and separating out into discrete ecstasies, in other words, devoid of a proper, ripening or existential timing *[Zeitigung]*" (148). At this juncture Binswanger proves to be a regular pun slinger. The sling has been slung as she keeps slinging it down: the future withdraws ever more while the present becomes so now-ive, "at best mere span of time" (150).

Fundamentally (formally and temporally) schizophrenia is *schleichend* (150) or, to give a synonym that via foreign bodies transmits in several languages, *schleppend*. And the schizophrenic will seize a last outside chance or change as act to break through the paralysis. The aberrant act, the last try by *Dasein* to come to itself, become itself, could take the form, on the side of chance, of physical illness, the sudden death of a family member, an attack, a shock—and, on the sidelines of acting out, we encounter murder, other acts of violence, arson, or letting one's own hand burn slowly in the oven in order to draw the attention of a loved one. In Ellen's case, which was not so far gone, the ill but freeing act was her suicide (150). When he looks for the historical analogy, Binswanger shows his hand (it's the very hand he ultimately gave Ellen West):

> Just as in the history of mankind it took a very long time before man achieved breakthrough in the religion of love, in Christianity, . . . so in individual *Dasein* the greatest obstacles stand in the way of breakthrough, though, once breakthrough occurs, it is transformed from the ground up. (152)

Binswanger can now amend the earlier references to nothingness via the *Liebestod* of nihilism. Viewed from the tomb world her death isn't just nothing but makes an end of the decay. From the perspective of the aetherial world her death is an erotic hybrid, part aesthetic, part mythic, part religious. "Everywhere we see love here just the same shine through, even if not in true form but rather in aetherial-mystical or aetherial-passionate half-life form *['Verfallsform']*" (153).

That Binswanger has thus opened up more of a concession than he was otherwise willing to make (he didn't want to be another Jung) is legible among all the static on the lines that follow. Because it privileges fantasy and the dream, psychoanalysis is too Christian by half: it attends only to the aetherial world. *Dasein*-analysis only presupposes that man is in the world, has world, and strives beyond this world. Freud assumes man to be of nature and, in his terms, of drives. Freud's argument destroys human being in order to reconstruct human being on a hard-scientific/biological basis. Man is a drive creature in whose individual life history sexuality proves to be the determining force. But the psychic representation of this drive power is, again, a wish. Thus "the aetherial or wish world receives its unique significance in this view of man that, as is well known, is ultimately reduced to the point that it is superseded by the theoretical schema of an 'apparatus' of psychic mechanisms" (154–55). Thus psychoanalysis focuses only on thrown-ness (or "must-be"), one out of the three modalities in *Dasein*-analysis.[3] Freud's strict sense of *Todeswunsch* or death wish as always addressed to the other is too small for the two of them, psychoanalysis and *Dasein*-analysis. It is a metapsychological fact that Binswanger is not alone in reading this wish according to a suicidal illogic. The death wish, in Binswanger's lexicon, is the wish to die (oneself) (163).

To turn the death wish into suicidal ideation hides the other twice over and out (in the death wish as in the wish to die).

By including Freud just the same, even if only as the one to pass by in the greater pursuit of *Dasein*-analysis, Binswanger places Freud on standby. Ellen's second "more orthodox" psychoanalyst makes several excellent interventions. When he doesn't take her suicide threats seriously, her attempts turn out not to be serious. He also focuses on the immediate setting of her belief system: the juxtaposition of "Jewish" and "Aryan" bodies. The divide traverses her German-Jewish family (her brother, like the second analyst, is the blond aetherial type). She too seems to have it in her to look like her blonde girlfriends, right before she starts to fill out like her pudgy mother. According to Ellen, the analyst's interpretations were too much in her head only. Her body is too gross to admit his aetherial input (just as it kept her from marrying the student). No political or religious belief system will be left unanalyzed for its symptomatic content and purpose in the Freudian session. Binswanger sees her point as she understands it, leaves it unanalyzed, and lets her be, bleed, fade away.

A basic problem of the schizophrenic mode of existence is the will to exist in a manner that is "unnoticeable (invisible and inaudible, indeed incomprehensible) to the rest of the world *[Mitwelt]*" (182). But this withdrawal gets stuck, becomes encrusted and ossified in its tracks. The yearning to be thin—or to disappear—turns the self into a tube for material filling up and emptying (170). "Thus the schizophrenic process is in the first place an existential process of emptying out or impoverishment, and, specifically, in the sense of an increasing paralysis ('coagulation') of the free self into an increasingly unfree ('unself-sufficient') self-alienated object" (184). In sum, these processes bring about "transformation . . . of eternity into temporality . . . , of infinitude into finitude."

According to Binswanger, Ellen speaks of ghosts only by analogy; only when she is terribly upset does she attribute sadistic satisfaction to others who have and hold the controlling interest in what she must endure (196). She resembles most closely certain addicts and perverts (190). But even if we indulge in science fiction and line Ellen up with transsexuals during the 1990s, the latter are a cut above the rest she can find only in one fat piece. Or could body-shaping surgery give her an outside change or chance that would grant her survival as her other true self? Fat chance! She isn't cut off from the future but is threatened by it instead (197).

Dick Manfred

A Scanner Darkly borrows its skewer of dissociation from doubling in and as *Faust I,* quotations from which crowd the introduction of the splitting theme or condition. Dick's other bookend of Faust reference is his novel *Galactic Pot-Healer,* which at one point in his *Exegesis,* the monumental corpus of reflections on his mystical experience of healing pink light in 1974, he admits and identifies as his one fully psychotic work (*In Pursuit of Valis,* 195–99).

Martian Time-Slip was Dick's first full-corpus immersion in schizophrenia as the in-between bardo state of undeath or projection and, as such, as alternate reality and temporality specific to the tomb world. Dick's hallmark science fictions, which followed *Martian Time-Slip,* fold out of the magazine or storehouse of underworlds it first opened up. In this course of what would follow, Goethe's *Faust* would also turn out to be hidden in the storage. In *Martian Time-Slip* the placeholder or point of introjection for the citational prop that would bob at the surface of *Galactic Pot-Healer* and *A Scanner Darkly* (and which was one of the organizing inspirations for the novel Dick was looking forward to writing in 1982, but then he died) is the opening disturbance set off by a Martian colonist's suicide, which the novel seeks to contain somewhere between life and death, sanity and psychosis.

The suicide of Norbert Steiner is in some recognizable but not identifiable way responded to by his schizophrenic son Manfred (autistic since birth), which his instructor witnesses (she sees him turn toward the siren sounds coming from the street where, unknown to her, Mr. Steiner lies dead from his jump in front of a bus) as evidence of first contact, a breakthrough she attributes to the music therapy she recently initiated. The case of Manfred is suspended between the tomb world of his nonplay (or only replay) rapport with his environment and the time-staggered relationship to free death. The two bookends for the tension span the schizophrenic boy occupies are, at least in name, Melanie Klein's case of Dick and Byron's *Manfred*.

In her 1930 essay "The Importance of Symbol Formation in the Development of the Ego," Klein explores a case of childhood schizophrenia, the treatability of which as arrested development is the very measure, measured in reverse, of treatment difficulties encountered with young adult schizophrenics who must fill in the blank of held-back development with the double whammy of regression. Klein opens with the all-importance of sadism in early mental development and its transmutation through symbolism, the two-step procedure her patient Dick failed to undergo because he stopped short before the double prospect of sadistic fantasies of torment of objects and of backlash consequences leading to his own persecution. Sadism "becomes active at all the various sources of libidinal pleasure" (95–96). "In phantasy the excreta are transformed into dangerous weapons: wetting is regarded as cutting, stabbing, burning, drowning, while the fecal mass is equated with weapons and missiles" (96). Subsequently sadism devises the more refined assault of poisoning.

This sadism liberates anxiety around the risky prospect of retaliation by the very weapons employed to destroy the object (97). At the same time the aroused anxiety sets the medium of identification going. The anxiety motivates the equation of destroyed and destructive organs with other things, which in turn become objects of anxiety, impelling the making of other and new equations, which form the basis of symbolism, which provides the first frame of equations of things, activities, and interests whereby they become fantasy material, in other words accessible to sublimation. This birth of symbolism out of sadism and anxiety, which gives the foundation for the subject's relationship to the outside world and to reality in general, provides a kind of interface between Benjamin and Aby Warburg, which I note for future reference. There are, however, good reasons for not consulting Klein further on the psychotic complex through which we track endopsychic allegory. Although Klein argues that "schizophrenia is much commoner in childhood than is usually supposed" since the signs are lost in the shuffle of traits that are natural in the development of normal children (108), the case of Dick is that of stalled development, which Klein, through her ventriloquizing interpretations in session, succeeds in jump-starting.

Nevertheless she identifies the stalling signs in Dick as psychotic character traits: "more commonly than psychoses we meet in children . . . psychotic character traits which, in unfavourable circumstances, lead to disease in later life" (109). At this stage of her work Klein proposes fixation points for dementia praecox in the violent phase of sadism and for paranoia in the poisoning phase. However, her realization that the "occurrence of schizo-phrenic traits is a far more general phenomenon" in childhood will lead, in subsequent work, to the introduction of the paranoid-schizoid position as the hub in the whirling of traits that is thus contained as theoretical pressure point in an understanding of psychosis as a regression exclusive. By excluding the point of crisis, the trigger in the transferential setting, and the recovery phase of delusion or alternate reality, Klein's installation of pseudo-psychotic positions as the quilting points of normal to neurotic development forecloses the encounter with the psychotic as other.

Klein treats Dick successfully because his so-called psychotic traits are, in the real time of development, inhibitions that can be overcome. For in Dick's case, "the ego's exaggerated and premature defence against sadism checks the establishing of a right relation to reality and the development of phantasy" (110). The result: suspension of the symbolic relation to things and objects representing the contents of the mother's body.

Dick is a four-year-old boy who presents on the level of a child of about fifteen or eighteen months. "Adaptation to reality and evolved relations to his environment were almost entirely lacking," while "he had only rarely displayed anxiety, and that in an abnormally small degree" (98). No signs of play or speech development. He strung sounds together in a meaningless way "and certain noises he constantly repeated." It appeared that he had no wish to make himself understood (98–99). His show of opposition as of obedience lacked affect and understanding. Where there is blunt affect there's away with it: you can tell that in the beginning he wasn't shown love, affection, or tenderness. When he did receive basic support from a nurse and a grandmother at age two, it was too late: contact could not be made because the object relation was lacking and could no longer be triggered by the belated tenderness. "What had brought symbol formation to a standstill was the dread of what would be done to him . . . after he had penetrated the mother's body." "His defences against his destructive impulses proved to be a fundamental impediment to his development" (101). "Dick's further development had come to grief because he could not bring into phantasy the sadistic relation to the mother's body" (101–2). In session Klein starts naming the toys and regions of her office along Oedipal lines—as well as, subsequently and acceleratingly, Dick's movement and placement of these parts and portraits of his parents. Immediately Dick responds. Anxiety emerges along with a sense of dependence. He enacts in play aggressive actions that Klein runs through her commentary into the mother's body.

The determining factor in Dick's development as nondevelopment was that the genital phase had become active in him prematurely. Thus representations of aggressive curiosity were accompanied not only by anxiety but also already by remorse and the sense that he must make restitution. (At this point in her work in progress, Klein is herself ahead of herself, admitting remorse prior to her development of a topography of positions that would shore up and be shored up by reparation.) Dick's premature ego development inhibited further ego development on the slower boat. The too-early identification with the object could not yet be brought into relation with reality. "Side by side with his incapacity for tolerating anxiety, this premature empathy became a decisive factor in his warding-off of all destructive impulses. Dick cut himself off from reality and brought his phantasy life to a standstill by taking refuge in the phantasies of a dark, empty, vague womb" (104–5).

Manfred is the title of Byron's Faustian drama, which Schreber also incorporated inside his delusional system. Freud looks at *Manfred* for evidence of the meaning of soul murder and finds not a compact with the Devil (which Schreber himself offers as comparison to soul murder) but the crime of incest. Byron wrests Faustian striving from Christian pact psychology and sends his Faust figure through a series of sessions that leads through mourning to a cure, his own and that of the secular mind ever since life after death became deregulated and spooky for Marlowe's Faustus or Shakespeare's Hamlet. Manfred's last words to the Abbot, the good rest or remainder of Christian beliefs, reflect a freedom or liberation of man that was also Freud's purpose: "Old man! 'tis not so difficult to die."

Completely unlike his own father, as is underscored, Manfred was always a schizoid loner, who however found in Astarte, most likely his sister, whose explicit resemblance to him moreover suggests twinship, a constant companion. Manfred is convinced that she was destroyed by the consummation of their companionship, which Manfred apparently pressed upon her. The resulting curse that pursues him "since that all-nameless hour" is that neither the earth nor heaven will receive him.

The name, which only ultimately emerges, starts out as cryptonym scraping the skies. In the first session, the Seventh Spirit pronounces the interior of the withheld name:

> The star which rules thy destiny
> Was ruled, ere earth began, by me: . . .
> The hour arrives—and it became
> A wandering mass of shapeless flame,
> A pathless comet, and a curse,
> The menace of the universe.

When Manfred asks for forgetfulness, the Spirits must know "of what—of whom—and why." Manfred: "Of that which is within me; read it there— Ye know it, and I cannot utter it." Oblivion is not something the Spirits have to offer. But he can die. Would death grant him oblivion? The Spirits are immortal and do not forget. As answer this suggests that memory is bigger than the two of you even after both have died. The Spirits can offer proud possessions plus "length of days." But what has Manfred to do with days? "They are too long already." He gets one free gift. One Spirit assumes "the shape of a beautiful female figure." Manfred recognizes her and seeks reunion within his grasp. But on contact the lady vanishes. His heart crushed, he falls senseless—and in the off a voice intones the incantation that delivers the curse. The voice's soul will be upon his. "By a power to thee unknown, Thou canst never be alone." But the spirit spell in which Manfred is doomed to dwell gets cooked up out of his own poison: false tears, black heart, smile of the snake—and that's what unacknowledged ambivalence is made of.

In the second session, thoughts of suicide cross Manfred's mind as he crosses the Swiss Alps. In recovery from his dependency on superhuman aid, which he now foregoes, Manfred senses time on fast-forward: unlike the blighted trunk, Manfred's sense of his own decaying is timed "by moments,—not by years,—And hours, all tortured into ages—hours," which he outlives. The Chamois Hunter, who pulls Manfred back from the edge of suicide, and who doesn't comprehend Manfred's words of blood on that edge, words that spell out a spilling of same blood once mixed in illicit union, nevertheless utters between the lines of his counseling the near rhyme that restores Manfred's bearing: "these wild starts are useless."

Session three is with the Witch of the Alps. He summons her not for aid but to look upon her beauty. But he also starts telling his fateful love story: "My pang shall find a voice." But whenever he nears the name he is blocked. Witch: "Spare not thyself—proceed." But while she remains nameless, their story is told. The Witch's response is to shrug off his attachment to a mortal whom he holds fast to even as he dismisses further intercourse with the supernatural realm. When she offers aid, he again asks for what she cannot deliver, that she awaken the dead or lay him low with them once and for all.

For the fourth session, Manfred enters the inner circle of Schreber's god Arimanes resolved to call up the dead by divine dispensation. Now the name falls. Nemesis asks, "Whom would thou Uncharnel?" Manfred's reply: "One without a tomb—call up Astarte." Her first message is silence. The Phantom of Astarte then utters: "Manfred!" Next she prophesies his death tomorrow: "Farewell!" Man freed, indeed.

Before he goes he remembers a night in Rome among the ruins. The moonlight filled the gaps of centuries and veiled condemned sites as beautiful still. It was thus that Manfred learned his lesson of remembrance with regard to the paternal economy of substitution and inheritance: "the stars Shone through the rents of ruin." The stammering ruination of the name or curse gives way to the ancestral prospect of rent-a-ruins through which the great of old still compel worship: "The dead but sceptred sovereigns, who still rule Our spirits from their urns." When Demons arrive to claim Manfred, he knows that he is dying and he knows that he is free of any compact with Christian comfort. "In knowledge of our fathers—when the earth Saw men and spirits walking side by side, And gave ye no supremacy: I stand Upon my strength—I do defy—deny—Spurn back, and scorn ye!" Now Manfred can go and let go.

Timing

In *Martian Time-Slip*, research identified as Swiss, associated by name with Jung only, suggests an application or understanding of Binswanger's Heideggerean notion of *Zeitigung*, which can be translated and misunderstood as "timing." The hypothesis is that schizophrenia is essentially a "derangement in the interior time-sense" (107). For purposes of investment or speculation the plan is underway to render what a schizo knows via this other time-sense accessible to those living in a shared world. Since their experimental subject was autistic from birth, Jung's alleged decoding of schizophrenic language is useless. Instead a kind of slow-mo decoder chamber must be built so that media contact can be made. "Could the schizophrenic be running so fast, compared to us, in time, that he's usually in what to us is the future?" (107).

But time on fast-forward slings the tomb world around life. The difference that Dick makes or marks over against Binswanger's interpretation of the case of Ellen West is that the traumatic event with which the schizophrenic remains in touch belongs precisely to the future—where he may arrive in time, ahead of time, to obtain some measure of rescue relief.

The suicide of West German colonist Norbert Steiner follows his visit with his young schizophrenic son, as always a dis-appointment with fatherhood, but this time set in the concrete shoes of news of prejudicial efforts to wipe out anomalous children, including Manfred, thereby acting out his own ambivalence. He casts his ambivalence into the wake of his own ending. Thus the in-between bardo state extends into the period that work of mourning tries to set as the end of a death sentence. However Manfred, who is thus introduced and let loose in the novel via his father's suicide, whose own world exerts a determining force upon the novel as a whole, and whose perspective overlaps in fundamental ways with that of the protagonist, Jack Bohlen, a recovered schizophrenic anonymous, always already inhabited the tomb world without the interpersonal markers of loss and mourning.

Steiner's suicide crosses several minds with a guilty sense of responsibility. Jack's reflections summarize and conclude this overture of static on the deadline:

This is going to affect all of us, and deeply. . . . I don't believe I ever exchanged more than a dozen words with Steiner at any one time, and yet—There is something enormous about the dead. Death itself has such authority. A transformation as awesome as life itself, and so much harder for us to understand. (68)

For Jack the suicide set "a radiating process of action and emotion going that works its way out, farther and farther, to embrace more people and things" (117). His crack-up when he was in his twenties on Earth is backing into place following the news of Steiner's death and his subsequent visit, as repairman, to the robot-taught Public School. Later in the novel a psychiatrist gives his professional opinion on the short circuit triggered by the teaching machines: "The schizophrenic . . . very often deals with people through their unconscious. The teaching machines, of course, have no shadow personalities; what they are is all on the surface. Since the schizophrenic is accustomed constantly to ignore the surface and look beneath—he draws a blank" (185). The visit sets off the novel's running commentary on the alternate reality of schizophrenia.

The Public School was an attempt to stabilize . . . values, to jell them at a fixed point— to embalm them. The Public School . . . was neurotic. It wanted a world in which nothing new came about, in which there were no surprises. And that was the world of the compulsive-obsessive neurotic; it was not a healthy world at all. (74)

But he at the same time realizes via his psychotic interlude back then that there are things so much worse than neurosis. Indeed, "the fixed, rigid, compulsive-neurotic Public School" appears by contrast "a reference point by which one could gratefully steer one's course back to mankind and shared reality. It made him comprehend why a neurosis was a deliberate artefact, deliberately constructed by the ailing individual or by a society in crisis" (74–75). But Jack continues to turn around the piece of the puzzle that doesn't fit, at least not on Mars. The "teaching machines are going to rear another generation of schizophrenics" out of people who are otherwise trying to adapt to the new planet. The machines will "split the psyches" of the children by "teaching them to expect an environment which doesn't exist for them" (85). The teaching machines are specific to Jack whose switch over into delusion or hallucination is signalled, then as now again, as the inside view of the person in front of him as machinic.

As repairman Jack inhabits, especially on Mars, the stage of gadget's cathexis as collectible or recyclable. Arnie Kott prefers to have his decoder repaired rather than replaced, a preference that is the required adaptor on Mars, but one that betrays a sensibility that meets that of Jack Bohlen half way. "Strange, how people cling to their possessions, as if they're extensions of their bodies, a sort of hypochondria of the machine" (100). But Arnie has a special project in mind. He wants to speculate via influence on linear time. He brings in psychiatrist Dr. Glaub to confirm that the schizo sense of time or timing amounts to time travel. And repairman Jack must build the decoder ring around the collaring of the schizo sense of time for speculations based on knowledge of the future. Manfred is the designated "really advanced schizo" that Dr. Glaub, who is Manfred's psychiatrist, recommends to Arnie. During this brainstorming meeting Jack sees the psychiatrist "under the aspect of absolute reality: a thing composed of cold wires and switches" (109), which he confides to Arnie's girlfriend, Doreen Anderton, whose brother succumbed to schizophrenia.

Between them the quest to understand the schizo reality continues. She wants to know if Jack's visions are unbearable. No, but they are "disconcerting": "There's no way you can work it in with what you're supposed to see and know; it makes it impossible to go on, in the accustomed way" (111). But couldn't he just go on pretending? No. To start acting, to become an actor, is to embody the schism: "that's a real split—there's no split up until then; they're wrong when they say it's a split in the mind. If [he] wanted to keep going entire, without a split," he would have to tell the psychiatrist that he recognizes, "under the aspect of eternity," that he's dead (112). But can't he withdraw from the vision? "The vision's for that purpose, to nullify your relations with other people, to isolate you. If it's successful, your life with human beings is over" (113).

A primal time overlap between the original Mars people, the Bleekmen, who are related to Africans on Earth, is based on the time sense they share with schizophrenics. Arnie's Bleekman butler Heligabalus self-identifies schizophrenia as "the savage within the man" (92). Earlier Jack received a friendly Bleekman charm that he now hopes will neutralize his schizophrenic tendency to pick up other people's unconscious hostility, the telepathic factor and the paranoid outcome (113). "It's the worst thing about our condition, this awareness of the buried, repressed sadism and aggression in others around us, even strangers" (114).

When we are granted our first interior monologue view of Manfred's way of seeing, the only word that makes it out as language is "gubbish." Jack wonders if "gubbish" could mean time (145). But Manfred communicates his vision first through his drawing of the apartment complexes that will be built on Mars, which are drawn into the stricken world of their becoming history. We watch the drawing "developing in an ominous direction before their eyes . . . a scene of ruin and despair, and of a ponderous, timeless, inertial heaviness" (142). Then Manfred writes over the entrance of the building the contraction of the co-op slogan, AM-WEB, which stands for "Alle Menschen Werden Brüder," which Dick translates (not always the case in his emplacement of German quotations). The contraction spells the web that Manfred sees will ensnare him as zomboid senior citizen buried alive in the ruins of these buildings. The web of the co-op system set off Jack's first disturbed visions, which prompted him to emigrate to Mars, the place of his recovery and prospect of outer space as aetherial world, but also the place to which both the system and Jack's disturbance—the tomb world—threaten to return via a span of tension occupied by fathers, with Manfred's dead father at the front of the line. Between "gubbish" and "WEB" Binswanger's *Schlinge* ensnares Jack and Manfred, who, however, unlike Ellen West, rescue themselves both from the tomb world and from the other dead end, the aetherial world. The traumatic events for these schizophrenics lie in what we consider to be the future. But first Jack can only recognize the one-sided dead set of Manfred's vision:

A view of the universe that partial—it isn't even a complete view of time. Because time also brings new things into existence; it's also the process of maturation and growth. And evidently Manfred does not perceive time in that aspect . . . He does not perceive the rest of reality . . . And it is a dreadful section which he does see: reality in its most repellent aspect. Jack thought, And people talk about mental illness as an escape! . . . It was no escape; it was a narrowing, a contracting of life into, at last, a moldering, dank tomb, a place where nothing came or went; a place of total death. (145)

Jack's hallucinatory point of contact with his own unravelling is the inside view of humanity as at once skeletal and robotic *Gestell*. But his crisis point of view, which stops short of decay, embodies Manfred's dread fate, the living end without end as life-support cyborg. Toward the end of the novel time travel trips up all plotting and Manfred gets what he bargained for, though his missingness remains unidentified. But then he restores his identification to repairman Jack, who is the other person who can accept this reverse apparition. When Manfred thus returns with the Bleekmen, who came to his rescue, he's still trailing the lifelines of techno life. But he has come back only to take leave of his schizoid mother. As man-freed of the technical difficulties of artificially extended and encrypted life, Manfred departs within the earliest relationship of reparation.

Manfred's world begins to take over Jack's recovery world of interpersonal relations in the spot they are already in straining between the interests of his own father and those of father-figure Arnie. It first becomes evident because Manfred's world usurps the narrative itself. The scene of Oedipal strain starts replaying, crossing over into the tape medium. Manfred describes how he sees the individuals: "the Gubbler, who had come and inhabited the inside long ago and was now working his way out to the surface" (160). But then Jack's thoughts open wide in the middle of the replay: "A voice in his mind said, Gubble gubble gubble, I am gubble gubble gubble gubble. Stop, he said to it. Gubble, gubble . . . The Gubbler is here to gubble gubble you and make you into gubbish" (161). At this point Jack senses the vacuum impact of Manfred's hole world:

"It almost seems to me that Manfred does more than know the future; in some way he controls it, he can make it come out the worst possible way because that's what seems natural to him, that's how he sees reality. It's as if by being around him we're sinking into his reality." (162)

For the next all-on-tape replay a narrator observes Manfred from the outside, but from deep inside the gubbish discourse (167). Thus Jack recognizes that "he was in over his head":

The inevitable, schizophrenic aspects of his own personality were being stirred into life by the presence beside him. . . . somehow it was too late, as if time had collapsed and left him here, for eternity, caught in a symbiosis with this unfortunate, mute creature who did nothing but rake over and inspect his own private world, again and again. He had imbibed, on some level, Manfred's world-view, and it was obviously bringing about the stealthy disintegration of his own. (169)

The replay or flashback of the scene is identified as the momentum of repetition in advance already inside Jack's traumatic amnesia:

The lapse in memory was a symptom of a deeper disturbance. It indicated that his psyche had taken an abrupt leap ahead in time. And this had taken place after a period in which he had lived through, several times, on some unconscious level, that very section which was now missing. He had sat, he realized, in Arnie Kott's living room again and again, experiencing that evening before it arrived; and then, when at last it had taken place in actuality, he had bypassed it. The fundamental disturbance in time-sense, which . . . was the basis of schizophrenia, was now harassing him. That evening at Arnie's had taken place, and had existed for him . . . but out of sequence. In any case, there was no way that it could be restored. For it now lay in the past. And a disturbance of sense of past time was not symptomatic of schizophrenia but of compulsive-obsessive neurosis. His problem—as a schizophrenic—lay entirely with the future. And his future, as he now saw it, consisted mostly of Arnie Kott and Arnie's instinctive drive for revenge. (206)

Jack's problem with the future is Oedipally organized. His father, a land speculator, has come to Mars to buy the land that he knows through insider information will be where the new apartment complexes will be built at the same time as Arnie presses Jack to decode Manfred's visions of the future, which, unknown to Jack, Arnie believes contain what he is after, his own version of insider information or corroboration of rumors that would guide his purchase of the land soon to be in demand for a major building development. But by the time Manfred draws his morbid pictures of the apartment complexes, Jack's father has already purchased all the land. This is what the amnesia-shadowed scene on replay showed down. But now Jack is in position to recognize Manfred's problem with the future. Even Bleekman Heliogabalus, with whom Manfred can communicate without mediatic translation, is at first diverted by Binswanger's picture of the war of the worlds in schizophrenia, which he imparts to Manfred, which Manfred accepts, but not as death sentence:

"You must die," the dark man said to him in a far-off voice. "Then you will be reborn. Do you see, child? There is nothing for you as you are now, because something went wrong and you cannot see or hear or feel. No one can help you. Do you see, child?" "Yes," Manfred said. . . . How beautiful the dark figure was. Why can't I be like that? Manfred thought. No one else looked like that. His glimpse, his contact with the shadow-like man, was cut off. Doreen Anderton had passed between them as she ran into the kitchen and began talking in high-pitched tones. Once more Manfred put his hands to his ears, but he could not shut out the noise. He looked ahead, to escape. He got away from the sound and the harsh, blurred comings and goings. (196–97)

What he sees next is his problem with the future, which we, too, now can see: the transformation of the land by the builders, their slug-like gubbling and the half-life of the buildings themselves, the living death of Manfred at an incredibly advanced age.

He saw a hole as large as a world; the earth disappeared and became black, empty, and nothing. . . . Into the hole the men jumped one by one, until none of them were left. He was alone, with the silent world-hole. At the rim of the hole he peeped down. . . . I am in you, Manfred thought. Once again. A voice said, "He has been here at AM-WEB longer than anyone else. He was here when the rest of us came. He is extremely old." "Does he like it?" "Who knows? He can't walk or feed himself. . . . They amputated his limbs and of course most of his internal organs were taken out on entry." . . . No, Manfred thought. I can't stand it. . . . Is this the start of life, what the dark shadow-figure promised? A new beginning where I will be different and someone can help me? . . . I can't wait here forever; it must be done soon or not at all. If it is not done I will grow and become the world-hole, and the hole will eat up everything. (197)

The Bleekman recognizes that Manfred's attention wanders constantly so as not to focus on his living death at AM-WEB. To block out this prospect more completely, he "retreats back to happier days, days inside his moth-er's body, where there is no one else, no change, no time, no suffering. The womb life" (213). Now Arnie, too, is convinced that Manfred's abilities go beyond mere seeing into future time. "I think he controls time. . . . This kid fooled around with last night. I know it. He saw it in advance and he tried to tamper with it" (213–14).

Arnie is determined to push back his ultimate defeat by Jack's land-speculating father. He aims to combine Manfred's powers with the ritual site sacred to the Bleekmen, Dirty Kubby, where time is believed to be weakest, a sort of puncture in time through which one can get at the future. Heliogabalus aids Arnie in exchange for the promise to send Manfred back to Earth to escape his traumatic conditions in the future on Mars. Arnie goes there, however, in order to travel into the past, back just three weeks in time, whereby he can become Jack Bohlen's fate (237). We return with Arnie to the start of the book in the replay mode. But it soon becomes evident that Arnie returned to the past via Manfred's sensibility: his secre-tary is now a castrating sex machine bursting with incipient decay, and the newspaper he tries to read contains only one word over and over again: "Gubble" (238–39). Almost killed in the past, he trips back, full of good intentions and free of revenge. But then someone else kills Arnie, seeking revenge for having been ruthlessly put out of business. Arnie dies without belief or grief in the "delusion" that he still wasn't in the real world and that he couldn't die inside the fantasy of a schizophrenic. It prompts Jack's recognition that the shared world or reality isn't absolutely distinct from Manfred's world. "Now I see that it's more a question of degree" (258). Following Arnie's death everyone is moved into a position from where one can start over. Manfred returns as ancient prosthetic man rescued from the future WEB by Bleekmen in order to say goodbye. Jack's wife Silvia had all along expected contact with the father's ghost to come out of the media contact with Manfred: "Perhaps Manfred saw him, lost as the boy was . . . in disfigured time. What a surprise is in store for them when they make contact with the boy and find they have rekindled that sad little specter" (117). At the end her view of past in the future is in a sense confirmed: "'I thought when I first saw him that it was his father, Norbert Steiner; that's what frightened me so.' . . . We are better off not being able to look ahead, she said to herself. Thank God we can't see. . . . It is too soon, for any of us" (262).

Glimmung

Subsequent masterpieces—notably *The Three Stigmata of Palmer Eldritch* and *Ubik*—would refine and reflect the combinations first tried out in *Martian Time-Slip. Do Androids Dream of Electric Sheep?* falls by the wayside only to the extent that it focuses on Dick's other big question—What is human?—which more or less pushes the reality question out of the running of the novel's world. *A Scanner Darkly,* which in some of its trappings may be Dick's most deluded work, places recovery against/alongside delusion or dissociation. As Emmanuel Carrère argues, *A Scanner Darkly* reflects the author's hard-won acquisition of the owner's manual to his mental illness. To maintain his psychosis as encapsulated he henceforth observed a three-phase distinction between, or gradation of degrees of madness:

> Like certain other very sick people, Phil had a lucid understanding of his disease, and henceforth he drew a clear distinction between (a) writing that organizations like X-Kalay were actually secret drug laboratories or that Nixon was a Communist, (b) believing it, and (c) believing that it was true. He thought that it was possible to write such nonsense, inasmuch as he was a science fiction writer and writing science fiction was all about coming up with hypotheses of precisely this kind, but that it was reprehensible to believe it. Above all, he understood that he could believe something without its being true, because he wasn't only a science fiction writer but also a confirmed paranoiac who tended to confuse the real world with the worlds he created in his books. (218)

While *A Scanner Darkly* borrows its skewer of dissociation from doubling in and as *Faust I,* quotations from which crowd the introduction of the splitting theme or condition, Dick's other bookend of Faust reference, his novel *Galactic Pot-Healer,* sets its agon off with quilting plot points summoned from *Faust II.* At one point in his *Exegesis,* the monumental corpus of reflections on his mystical experience of healing pink light in 1974, he admits and identifies his second Faust novel as a psychotic work.

Galactic Pot-Healer shows the very real possibility of encroaching madness. The archetypes are out of control. Water—the ocean itself—which is to say the unconscious, is hostile & rises to engulf. The book is desperate & frightened, & coming apart, dream-like, cut off more & more from reality. Flight, disorganization: the way has almost run out. Those elements dealt with in earlier novels—ominous elements—now escape my control & take over. (*In Pursuit of Valis,* 195)

Scanner then, shows that human reason returned sometime after *Galactic Pot-Healer.* But in 2-3-74 *divine* reason *(noesis),* the Logos, Christ himself, entered me or occurred as if in response to the last savage attack . . . of the years of problems I had gotten myself into by my madness, folly, drug-use, etc. (197)

Thinking back to when I wrote *Pot:* I felt so strongly—& correctly—at the time that when it came time, in writing the book to have the theophany occur (i.e., for Glimmung to show himself) I had nothing to say, nothing to offer because I knew nothing. Oh, & how I sensed this lack of knowledge! & now this is precisely what I *do* know because now I have experienced it (2-3-74). . . . I had no ideas about the theophany at all, . . . that which would not & could not come with *Pot;* that in writing *Pot* that exactly was where I reached the end—wore out & died as a writer; scraped the bottom of the barrel & died creatively & spiritually. What misery that was! Paisley shawl, hoop of water, hoop of fire; how wretched it was; how futile. (198–99)

But the last-mentioned manifestation of the Glimmung does represent a last understanding of the aetherial world, complete with veil or shawl, which Dick could have dropped in reference to Helen of Troy's veil, left behind in *Faust II* when the grieving mother follows her self-destroyed son back down into Hades. (Eventually the veil metamorphoses into clouds.) That Glimmung's manifestation also shows the face of a teenage girl (on another occasion partially covered by the shawl [127]), "an ordinary face, easily forgotten but always encountered," moves down the chorus lines of the Eternal Feminine, where the small-world charms of Margaret mingle with Helen's great world appeal: "It was, he thought, a composite mask" (41). The artisans summoned from all over the universe by Glimmung to assist him in the raising of the cathedral Heldscalla from its watery tomb world are otherwise sufficiently familiar with *Faust II* (which was written in what is in the meantime an extinct language) to compare Glimmung's efforts with those of Faust in winning land from the sea for his utopian housing project (or society).

"Within here a paradise land, that keeps outside the flood." The flood is a symbol for everything that eats away structures which living creatures have erected. The water which has covered Heldscalla; the flood won out many centuries ago, but now Glimmung is going to push it back. "A group will" which hurries to cut it off—that is all of us. Perhaps Goethe was a precog; perhaps he foresaw the raising of Heldscalla. (91)

The troubling doubling conflict between Glimmung and Black Glimmung, however, occurred once before, the robot remembers, at the time of the Berlin Olympics. One far-flung but snapping back approach to this reference is available through Jacques Lacan's mirror stage address, which had its premiere in 1936 in Marienbad, Lacan's stopover on his way to Berlin to witness, in his perfectly Jungian formulation, the spirit of the times. In the essay itself Lacan gives as typical dream the dream of the stadium, towered over, moreover, by a grim fantasy castle. By this point we can fold it all back inside the Glimmung striving unto triumph or suicide.

The mythic showdown between aetherial and tomb worlds diverts the summoned artisans from their suicidal ideation (every one of them recently attempted or prepared for suicide). As the pot-healer puts it, when he receives the Glimmung's invitation: "I will not voluntarily die, now, he thought harshly. I want to stay alive. And wait. And wait. He waited" (13). This will prove to be their fundamental difference as underscored by the Glimmung in his first exchange with pot-healer Joe Fernwright: "What strikes me as odd is your having sat for all those months in your work cubicle, waiting" (40–41). Or again:

"There are no small matters. Just as there is no small life. The life of an insect, a spider; his life is as large as yours, and yours is as large as mine. Life is life. You wish to live as much as I do; you have spent seven months of hell, waiting day after day for what you needed . . . the way a spider waits. . . . He waits on; there is nothing he can do but wait. . . . And he waits and he thinks, 'It won't come in time. It is too late.' And he is right; he dies still waiting." (50)

Glimmung does not fulfill the criteria for divinity. In this regard he is like Christ. But if Christ can't be viewed as deity, how did Christianity come into being? A robot or teaching machine gives instruction:

"It came into being," the robot said, "because this is what Christ did: he worried about other people. 'Worry' is the true translation of the Greek *agape* and the Latin *caritas*. Christ stands empty handed; he can save no one, not even himself. . . . There is a somewhat similar deity," the robot said, "on Beta twelve. This deity learned how to die whenever another creature on his planet died. He could not die in place of them, but could die with them." (105–6)

Thus the roundabout expression of suicidal ideation—the synchronization of death with someone else's parting, the intrapsychic structure of suicide (which can immediately extend into the pact of suicide in couple, group, or mass format)—crosses Joe's mind while he awaits the outcome of Glimmung's battle against his black dead double: "Maybe it would be more useful, he thought, to die with Glimmung. That way, at least, we could show how we felt. But who would notice? Who is left to notice?" (157).

On Plowman's Planet, Glimmung's opposing force takes the form of a kind of fateful chronicling of the future now. It is the book of the Kalends:

> "It is written . . . by a group of creatures or entities . . . that records everything that passes on Plowman's Planet" . . . "Then it's a newspaper." . . . "It is recorded first . . . The Kalends spin the story; they enter it in the ever-changing book without a title, and it comes about, finally." (71)

Where's the precognition?

> "You will find it . . . when you have looked a long time. It is buried. Among the different texts, which are all translations of one primary text, one line like a thread. The thread of the past entering the present, then entering the future. Somewhere in that book . . . the future of Heldscalla is written. The future of Glimmung. The future of us. We are all woven in by the yarn of the Kalends' time, their time-outside-of-time." (74)

> "In fact, he reflected, if enough time passes everything will happen. Which in a sense was the way the Kalends' Book worked. Worked—and did not work. Probability" (125). But the line or thread thus given us is about a future that cannot but come true.

> With them, Joe Fernwright thought, there is not life but merely a synopsis of life. We are a thread that passes through their hands; always in motion, always flowing, we slip by and are never fully grasped. The slipping away is continuous, and carries all of us with it, on and on, toward the dreadful alchemy of the tomb. (97)

Without Glimmung's counterposition, basically that the future is uncertain (86), the "Book will tell us each day what we are going to do, and we will do it. And, eventually, The Book will tell us we are going to die, and we will—" (147).

> "The underwater world in which Heldscalla lies is a place of dead things, a place where everything rots and falls into despair and ruin. . . . Glimmung calls it the 'Aquatic

Sub-World.' He is right; it's a world made up of its own self, entirely separate from ours. With its own wretched laws, under which everything must decline into rubbish. A world dominated by the force of unyielding entropy and nothing else." (100–101)

In this setting of the mortality timer, where every individual and artifact must meet its inimical double, Joe too must face his own corpse down in the watery tomb world: "A decaying hump of flopping fabric mingled with threads of cloth tottered toward them, propelled by the currents of murky water.... 'It's your corpse' " (113). Joe and his double aren't completely distinguished: "Some of it is merged in you; some of you remains in it. They are both you . . . 'The child is father to the man,' remember? And the man is father to the corpse" (115).

But from behind this nihilistic clash of mythic forces, Glimmung pulls out the Christian die-along response to the aloneness of face-off with one's own finitude. Glimmung washes up eternally bleeding "like Christ" (155) from his knock-down, drag-out fight with his double. He can now raise Heldscalla only if his summoned artisans give him their vital force by merging with him within him. They agree for a prescribed span of time: Glimmung encloses them. "We're part of him, Joe realized . . . He tried to see, but his eyes registered only a swirling, jellolike image, a film which obliterated rather than revealed the reality around him" (158). The eternal feminine is staged Schreber-style: by becoming a female creature, Glimmung raises the cathedral, which in his arms becomes "an encased fetus, a small, sleeping child-creature wrapped tightly in the cocoon whose strands enveloped it" (172). " 'At one time we were bisexual. This part of me has been suppressed throughout the years. Until I obtained it again I could not make the cathedral my child" (172).[1]

After a second spin around union with Glimmung as "group will," the individuals are offered a more permanent relationship as portions of Glimmung, functioning for a thousand years together, none of them ever again home alone (173). Joe and one other member of the rainbow coalition vote to secede from the merger. But Joe thus loses his special friend Mali, who elected to remain behind with all the others within Glimmung. What's the difference between their departure in unison and mass suicide?

Galactic Pot-Healer was rehearsed as children's narrative *(Nick and the Glimmung)*. Glimmung for children is the ancient sinister alien on Plowman's Planet whose tyranny is broken by a boy and his beloved cat (the nuclear family emigrated to this planet because Earth law disallows pets). The timeless struggle lies between Glimmung and the Printers (who publish Glimmung's book of the future, and thus of changes). Printers are stationary creatures that replicate what is placed before them. When the boy places the book that accidentally was passed on to him (and which Glimmung wants back) right next to a Printer, Glimmung comes close enough to be doubled. Only the wound he receives from his double can break open Glimmung's stranglehold on Plowman's Planet.

A Maze of Death was the follow-up therapeutic reformulation and reformatting of *Galactic Pot-Healer.* The maze consists of a relay of fantasies administered as cathartic group therapy for release and containment of the disintegration tendencies in the induced, relapsed, or chronic psychotics trapped inside a spacecraft whose transmission failed and, cut off from contact with the outside, must endure canned life unto death. They engage in group-delusions of other worlds and lives as diversions from the trap they can only spring again.

The computer, named via its acronym TENCH, appears under that name in the fantasy stay on Delmak-O also as "printer," the creature this novel shares with the rehearsal of *Galactic Pot-Healer,* the children's fantasy *Nick and the Glimmung.* Lost in their disabled space capsule, the crew members turn to fantasy tripping in episodes directed by the computer that knows where they live according to the discrete personalization of one member. In one of the tracks of the delusional sojourn, the perspective of Seth Morley, the distribution of events is identified as fantastically Wagnerian. One member of the group drowns herself in order to shake her bodily weight/wait and ascend more immediately than her pill popping made possible into a decorporealized world. "When she took a pill she rose, for a brief moment, into a higher, smaller circle of greater intensity and concentration of power. Her body weighed less; her ability, her motions, her animation—all functioned as if powered by a better fuel. . . . The water will help, she said to herself. Because in water you no longer have to support your heavy body" (114). When the others discover her, the corpse is placed on a raft. But then all of a sudden it catches fire and the drift.

After a time Ned Russell said, "We shouldn't feel badly. That's the Norse way of celebrating death. The dead Viking was laid on his shield, on his boat, and the boat was set on fire and sent drifting out to sea." Meditating, Seth Morley thought, Vikings. A river, and, beyond it, a mystifying building. The river would be the Rhein and the Building would be Walhalla. That would explain why the raft, with Betty Jo Berm's body on it, caught fire and drifted away. . . . The tench, answering questions, would be . . . Erda. The goddess of the earth who knew the future. Who answered questions brought to her by Wotan. And Wotan, he thought, walks among the mortals in disguise. . . . The Wanderer, he is called. . . . And Wotan . . . destroyed the gods, brought on *die Götterdämmerung,* by his ambition. What was his ambition? To build the castle of the gods: Walhalla. . . . And, at the end, he thought, it will sink into the Rhein and disappear. And the Rheingold will return to the Rhein Maidens. (128–29)

The conspiracy theory at the core of the fantasy reveals Walhalla or "the Building" to be the mental hospital from which the former inmates were moved to the settlement as an experiment in encapsulated living. Just as with Wagner's Walhalla, then, the asylum or castle in prehistory self-reflexively brings everything back inside the capsule hidden away in the encapsulation.

The therapeutic function of the Jungian fantasy, which gave it the shape of murder mystery, was to vent hostility building up in the capsule world. Thus it had an Oedipal organization, certainly via the central transference that gave the delusional alternate reality its atmosphere of religious belief hardwired to proof and technological realization:

We made it all up, Seth Morley thought, bewildered; memory of Specktowsky's Book still filled his mind. The Intercessor, the Mentufacturer, the Walker-on-Earth—even the ferocity of the Form Destroyer. Distillate of man's total experience with God—a tremendous logical system, a comforting web deduced by the computer from the pos-tulates given it—in particular the postulate that God existed. . . . Egon Specktowsky had been the original captain of the ship. He had died during the accident which had disabled them. A nice touch by T.E.N.C.H. 889B, to make their dear former captain the author of the galaxy-wide worship which had acted as the base of this, their latest world. The awe and near-worship which they all felt for Egon Specktowsky had been neatly carried over to their episode on Delmak-O because for them, in a sense, he was a god—functioned, in their lives, as a god would. This touch had given the created world a more plausible air; it fitted in perfectly with their preconceptions. (182–83)

That the frame is itself shaken in the end and implicitly identified in the lineup as another one of the delusional orders along the lines of infinite regress should not be confused with deterioration. Underlying it all, includ-ing the "printer" introjection of *Galatic Pot-Healer,* is the inoculation or encapsulation that goes down with transference or mourning deadicated to the one they love. Since, inside the explain-athon frame, the crew feeds the computer responsible for synthesizing the individual wishes into group-formatted fantasy all available facets of every known religion, it is hardly a stretch to see the en-capsule-ated setting as placeholder for the relationship between finite life or reality and the psychotic or metaphysical multiplica-tion of that reality via alternate lives unto a kind of interminability.

Unlike Jungian psychology, Freudian psychoanalysis is identified in *A Maze of Death* as endowed with the genuine capacity for understanding delusional systems from a rational perspective. Though not by name, Freudian articulations also attend releases of aggression in the fantasy realm as discursive weapons: "These oral types. Regression to a pre-reality testing stage. Maybe it's a misplaced biological survival mechanism: for the good of the species they weed themselves out. Leaving the women to more competent, and more advanced, male types" (43). But this perspective of treatment and testing cannot accompany itself into the relay of psychotic delusions—to which it will not, in other words, surrender or abandon itself. Thus inside the overlap among fantasy perspectives, we hear Jung is what one has in common:

Jung, he had been told, had in many ways laid the groundwork for a rapprochement between intellectuals and religion.... "Jung believed that our attitudes toward our actual mothers and fathers are because they embody certain male and female archetypes. For instance, there's the great bad earth-father and the good earth-father and the destroying earth-father, and so forth ... and the same with women. My mother was the bad earth-mother, so all my psychic energy was turned toward my father." (67)

In *Symbols of Transformation: Analysis of the Prologue to a Case of Schizophrenia (Symbole der Wandlung: Analyses des Vorspiels zu einer Schizophrenie)*, Carl Jung assigned to the symbolicity of veiling that which the mythic cloak also provided: invisibility (440). What "the invisible man" demonstrates—and in this regard he is closely related to the werewolf in the lineup of horror figures—is that the metamorphosis into invisibility is always also a cover for nudity. Both the hymeneal veils of sexual mysteries and the dances that just the same reveal all attend every metaphysical desire to know. But X-ray or X-rated vision, for example, cannot distinguish clothes from corpus and must make its boner out of bones. Jung's next example of the veil's symbolic significance refers to this other invisibility, that of ghosts. Indeed veils were among the first ectoplasmic markers of ghostly live absence in Spiritualist séances.

Can Helen of Troy's veil be metamorphosed and lifted up into the aetherial clouds without remainder? Even after it has been assigned the status of allegory? In *The Arcades Project (Das Passagen-Werk)*, Benjamin stipulates that allegory concerns riddles and not the secrets or mysteries wrapped up in veils (461). But as fashion accessory, the veil nevertheless also belongs to the "parody" of the colorfully decaying corpse (111). "Fashion perceives the rights of the corpse in the living" (130).

The flâneur surrounds himself with the crowd or *Menge* as the veil that conceals the masses (421). The mechanical aspect of the crowd reflects the sadism (which Benjamin in the *Origin* book attributed to the allegorist) that seeks out mechanical structures and sees, for example, the skeleton as a machine (447). But the masses in Baudelaire drop their veil before the flâneur. The newest drug for the isolated and alienated, the masses offer the despised their latest asylum. In the labyrinth of the cities the masses represent the other labyrinth. They wipe clean the traces of the individual (559).

The press puts an excess of information out there—which could be put to use only by a ubiquitous readership, which is the illusion the press thus creates (560). The social basis for the perspective of the flâneur is journalism (559), and its allied state folds out of the detective novel (553). Reporting and detection revalorize the *Spur* or "trace" as clue, which Benjamin aligns within his ongoing reading of aura. In contrast to the longing distance manifested by aura, "The clue *[Spur]* is the manifestation of a relationship of proximity, however distant that which left it behind is" (560).

The masses veil the flâneur's reception of reality just as, in the case of a conspirator, the relationship to reality is blocked by his coconspirators (468). The crowd for Benjamin is inseparable from Poe's description of the crowd, which, Benjamin notes, is in turn influenced by American Spiritualism *(Amerikas Geisterwelt)*. If the crowd or group is a veil with which the journalist cloaks himself to his advantage, then it follows from the same widening orbit that the mass distribution of what's new—the media with the press at the headline—shared with the rep or raps of Spiritualism beginning with telegraphy (452).

The man of the crowd, who has taken the veil against the veiling by the masses, is the man who waits. Because he is one step closer to the moviegoer's sensibility of expertise and testing he comes out on top of Benjamin's three-way intersection of time relations. The gambler passes time, even kills it. The flâneur charges himself with time, like a battery. The one who waits, however, charges time itself and passes it on in its changed form, that of expectation. "One shouldn't pass time—one should invite time to visit" (164).

Fredric Jameson refers to *Galactic Pot-Healer* as one of Dick's Jungian novels; but it might be identified more specifically, especially via its rehearsal as a story for children, as (Wagnerian) fantasy—one that is compromised as such by the protagonist's inability to share it. While Glimmung (alone) is fearsome in the first version for children, in the adult revalorization all the figures are goofy. Of course the pure fool is fantasy stock. In *Galactic Pot-Healer* we conclude with Joe, who is a nerd or loser but a resistant one, who doesn't fall for the happy ending of unity or disappearance, of double or nothing. All the other members of the raising-Heldscalla team were nerds, too. But they came to Plowman's Planet to be diverted from their nerdish lives and suicidal depressions. As survivor, Joe also loses and thus feels "the weight of centuries on him" (174). Glimmung's agenda of group doing, being, and thus being forever presents the open-and-shut case of the aetherial world. Joe remains behind as shlepp, etymon of *Schleier*, the German "veil." Joe encounters and counters the weight of time as the wait, the boring wait, for the other to come or go—without wish or any form of controlling interest.

PART III

Spiritualism Analogy

While Jung postulated a collective unconscious based on the archaic forms of association that archetypically recur or revert in schizophrenia and in dreams, he also admitted (for example in his 1958 publication "Schizophrenia") that the schizophrenic complex cut itself off from understanding and integration not only via the same archaic forms but also, and in particular, via random distortion. The schizophrenic complex usurps the conscious mind and, in the course of its own autodisintegration, destroys the personality. "It does not produce a 'double personality' but depotentiates the ego-personality by usurping its place" (191). Thus even though the archetypes of the collective unconscious recur throughout "myths, fairytales, fantasies, dreams, visions, and the delusional systems of the insane" (183), it would appear that the settings of their sightings can be as divergent as the distinctions among fantasy, psychotic delusion, contact with spirits, and unmourning, which Dick pursued and upheld throughout his wide-open spacing between the real and the hallucinatory.

Jung's first contact with schizophrenia was under conditions of testing the feeling-toned complex hypothesis that required for legibility or verifiability the relative sameness of a complex up and down the psychopathology continuum. For Jung had yet to penetrate the structure of the specifically schizophrenic disturbance. He took a step to the side, however, and next considered a case of mediumship that via the role of dissociation of personality was analogous to schizophrenia but less obscure. Thus Jung identified his 1902 study of occult phenomena as rehearsal or repetition of his 1907 exploration of dementia praecox. Another way to put the difference that remains between the occult relation and the specifically schizophrenic break is that the dissociation that attends mediumship is encapsulated compared to the disintegration endemic to the schizophrenic process and dynamic. Indeed the stabilization that can attend the paranoid delusional system, at least in the case of Schreber, has not only the crisis management of same sexualization in its closet but a skeleton or ghost, too.

In his inaugural dissertation and first book, *On the Psychology and Pathology of So-Called Occult Phenomena,* Jung addresses certain rare states of consciousness observed on the margins of the discourse on "psychopathic interiority" but admitted only as unattended by a consensus as to their significance. "These observations crop up sporadically in the literature on narcolepsy, lethargy, automatisme ambulatoire, periodic amnesia, double consciousness, somnambulism, pathological dreaminess, pathological lying, etc." (3). The patients thus afflicted accordingly "go through the whole gamut of diagnoses from epilepsy to hysteria and simulated insanity" (3–4).

The main attraction of Jung's study, Miss S. W., was also his cousin. Jung admits he had right of entry into her home and that he himself attended many of the displays of her mediumship. There is also evidence of an erotic tension that underlies or belies the rivalry between them. When he gives her history of generations of relatives known to have had waking hallucinations, premonitions, second sight, to have been somnambulistic or otherwise in the border zone of psychosis, he isn't always separated by marriage from this occult or psychotic heredity. Though she comes from a long line (like Jung) of mental imbalance, at close quarters she suffered from deficient education and unsupportive home life (the mother was in fact abusive). The father was hardly ever at home. But then he died "when S. W. was still adolescent." Since she is still an adolescent, the father's death seems to have coincided with S. W. taking a turn with the table-turning experiments that were the parlor game of choice at that time: a medium is born (19). For once she had her cousin's attention. He in turn took part in the experiments that followed. "In time she obtained such an influence over her followers that three of her sisters began to hallucinate too" (23).

Jung insists (too much) on her mediocrity up to the time of her somnambulism. (Her main extra-moronic activity was daydreaming.) Only with the onset of mediumship does she read a book (Kerner's *The Clairvoyante of Prevorst [Die Seherin von Prevorst]*). However, in her preliterary phase, she was immersed in newspapers, which by keeping the new séance science in its headlines served as the other medium in Spiritualism. The first spirit to speak to and through her was her grandfather, who maintained contact throughout this period as her guide. She had not known him in life. The departed unknown or otherwise not close to her dominate her opening somnambulistic dialogues: "she copies in a remarkably clever way her dead relatives and acquaintances, with all their foibles, so that she made a lasting impression even on persons not easily influenced. She could also hit off people whom she knew only from hearsay, doing it so well that none of the spectators could deny her at least considerable talent as an actress" (19).

Her discourse as medium was "literary German, which she spoke with perfect ease and assurance" (19). On the audio track alone she switched from silly fifteen-year-old to the distinguished mouthpiece of tradition. "Thus S.W., during the time that I knew her, led a curiously contradictory life, a real 'double life' with two personalities existing side by side or in succession, each continually striving for mastery" (25). Goethe's *Faust* joins Jung's discursive elevation at this point.

Spirit contact, which continued in and out of session, took a couple of forms. At the onset of sleep, for instance, she would be visited by visions: "the room would suddenly light up, and shining white figures detached themselves from the foggy brightness. They were all wrapped in white veil-like robes" (22). But she also experienced semi-somnambulistic states. "In this condition S.W. was herself, or rather her somnambulist ego: She was fully oriented toward the external world but seemed to have one foot in her dream-world. She saw and heard her spirits, saw how they walked round the room among those present, standing now by one person and now by another" (24). It was while in such "a peculiar waking condition" that "she had seen her grandfather arm-in-arm with my grandfather" (26).

Why are the spirits so communicative? Well, they're far from out of practice. Even though they can see each other's thoughts, spirits nevertheless incessantly talk to one another, simply out of habit (33–34). "After becoming acquainted with Kerner's book *[Die Seherin von Prevorst],* she (like the Clairvoyante) felt it her destiny to instruct and improve the black spirits who are banished to certain regions or who dwell partly beneath the earth's surface" (34).

S.W. overlooks in Kerner's account the double ambivalence attending the Clairvoyante's ability, owing to the special constitution of her soul and spirit or mind, to see ghosts and to receive the ghosts who seek her out. She sees them all, in all shapes and sizes. She tells Kerner that she simply hates the contact (182). They appear to her like shadowless thin clouds. Image, sound, and motion picture are in the air and derived from (shades of Schreber, though worn in the future so bright) the "nerve spirit" *(Nervengeist)* that the dead take along with them when they pass on (183). With the exception of speech, this unwilling ghostseer is convinced that ghosts can't make themselves visible and audible at the same time (185). Evil spirits, eager for an exchange, are louder and more communicative.

They do seek her counsel and comfort. They suffer under the mistaken assumption that to make amends for or disclosures of their misdeeds in life would release them from their suffering. They are fixated on the details of these misdeeds rather than consider the big picture of their bad lives. Sometimes it is just a thought that stuck to the soul of one who lay dying that brings back the ghostly wish to make amends for which she is in the spot of availability. They would do better to seek out more blessed spirits and begin the ascension within their own realm. But the burden of fixity on their earthly existence drags them down to this world. These low-grade spirits have only their errors to impart (187). These spirits are bad, but not necessarily evil. Dead children, for example, aren't just left where they leave off but grow up in the spirit realm via the "nerve spirit," in other words as ghosts (189).

Spirits are generally not friendly. How is a spirit going to behave when he suddenly finds himself lacking the body and the world of the senses even though he still feels full of all the old passions and inclinations? Not letting go of this world is a pain ghosts spread around. The pleasure prosthesis is gone and the higher bliss of Heaven is off-limits to the earthbound. The ghosts you can contact usually aren't pretty either. Aestheticization or idealization falls away with the human husk at death. In the flimsy wrap of the "nerve spirit" the soul shows every moral shortcoming and flaw (205). But a sinful crime requires allegorical figuration. Thus the ghost of a child murderess must appear bearing a strangled child in her arms (208).

S.W.'s unambivalent focus on the counseling of spirits in the spirit of Christian mourning—whereby she helps the ghosts out of the intermediary realm, turns them away from earthly existence and toward the light, where the second death, their heavenly disappearing act, awaits them— places her involvement in a spirit world on center stage unencumbered by identification. Without these intermediary and deliberately transitory ghosts—who do the dying, the grieving, and the not-letting-go for us— there is no entry into the spirit world and colonization of it for the survival of the specious in the narcissistic span of one teen's attention.

The Beyond, which S.W. conceives as "that space between the stars which people think is empty but which really contains countless spirit worlds" (33), borders on psy-fi outer space, the techno-replicational frontier that opens up between science fiction and psychosis. Thus she can recognize the star-dwellers who, as punishment, must take up occupancy in humans. In human form they are always cold, cruel, and, in short, utterly lacking the "spiritual" (35). They are technologically way more advanced than we are. And yet they utterly neglect science and philosophy.

Her somnambulistic ego is a "markedly Jewish type, clothed in white garments, her head wrapped in a turban" (33). At the time of King David she was just an ordinary Jewess. Her name is Ivenes who, over time, was also the Clairvoyante of Prevorst and the sibling of Swedenborg and Florence Cook. In the late eighteenth century she was a clergyman's wife who was seduced by Goethe and gave birth to his son. In the eighth century she had been the mother of her earthly father and of her grandfather and of Jung's grandfather too. She had also been Jung's mother. When she was burnt as a witch, Jung, doubled over with grief, retired to the monastery (36–37).

To explain the occult phenomenon of his cousin's brief career as medium, Jung makes recourse to autosuggestion, which, while on the rise, veiled from S.W.'s mind perception of slight motor impulses. The attendant presupposition postulates "a receptivitiy of the unconscious far exceeding that of the conscious mind" (80).

The knowledge received via consciousness of a potential mental content produces a collateral excitation in the speech area as the nearest available means to mental formulation. The intention to formulate necessarily affects the motor component of the verbal representation most of all, thus explaining the unconscious overflow of speech impulses into the motor area, and conversely the gradual penetration of partial hypnosis into the speech area. (51)

This is how the voice of another or the unconscious personality builds itself up. Suggestive questions that strike resonance or recognition in the medium's own disposition lead the way. "This disposition can be explained by the disaggregation of psychic complexes, and the feeling of strangeness evoked by these automatisms assists the process as soon as conscious attention is directed to the automatic act" (53). A higher degree of partial hypnosis is required for automatic writing: " 'to write' means 'to write something.' This special property of the suggestion, going beyond the purely motor sphere, often confuses the subject and gives rise to counter-suggestions which prevent the appearance of automatisms" (53). The advent of the new personality creates more "memory" or recording surface: "the splitting off of the new personality . . . meant a considerable increase in the extent of the unconscious area rendered accessible by hypnosis. At the same time this event, in view of the impression it made on the waking consciousness of the patient, must be regarded as powerfully suggestive . . . and would naturally suggest the thought that an independent spirit was making itself known" (57). "The ego-consciousness which remains over and, as a result of its isolation from the external world, occupies itself entirely with its hallucinations, is all that is left of the waking consciousness. Thus the automatism has a wide field for its activity" (73).

Jung turns to cryptomnesia to illuminate the process whereby foreign personalities arise. Cryptomnesia, a form of forgetting that allows one later on to encounter the unremembered as one's own material, is a kind of unconscious plagiarism, but to no account since necessarily only unworthy details are accorded high-fidelity reproduction. If the forgotten item were not worthy, interest would have been slight. But what was forgotten may indeed have been worthy, only, owing to distractibility or lack of under-standing, interest at the time was diminished. "In both cases there is an extremely labile connection with consciousness, the result being that the object is quickly forgotten. This flimsy bridge soon breaks down and the idea sinks into the unconscious, where it is no longer accessible to the con-scious mind" (82). Jung's discovery along these lines is a reference to rabbit shooting in Nietzsche's *Zarathustra* as the encryptment and return of the rabbit shooting detail found in Kerner's *Blätter aus Prevorst* (his documen-tation of countless ghostseer cases), a book Nietzsche read in childhood.

Jung's cousin S.W. is of course your typical teenager—until her daddy takes himself out of the way. "We all know the fitful moods, the confused, new, powerful feelings, the tendency to romantic ideas, to exalted religios-ity and mysticism, side by side with relapses into childishness, which give the adolescent his peculiar character" (64). The higher ego Ivenes fits right in here. "One cannot say that she deludes herself into the higher ideal state, rather she dreams herself into it. The realization of this dream is very reminiscent of the psychology of the pathological swindler. Delbrück and Forel have pointed out the importance of auto-suggestion in the develop-ment of pathological cheating and pathological daydreaming" (66). "It is only a step from dreamy ideas with a strong sensuous coloring to complex hallucinations proper" (67). Jung cites Freud on hysterical identification to illuminate the predicament of being carried away by one's interest in the object—being carried away in the carrying out of a role. Teen fantasy is on this role: "the patient's reincarnation theory, in which she appears as the ancestral mother of countless thousands, springs . . . straight from an exuberant fantasy which is so very characteristic of the puberty period. . . . The whole essence of Ivenes and her enormous family is nothing but a dream of sexual wish-fulfillment, which differs from the dream of a night only in that it is spread over months and years" (69–70).

By attending to the splitting of his cousin's grandfather, Jung proves that the charter of dissociation of her spirit guides was drawn up and signed inside her. The grandfather guide has two aspects, which are utterly turned away from each other.

Grandfather I, who speaks directly to those present, is a totally different person and a mere spectator of his double, Grandfather II, who appears as Ivenes' teacher. Grandfather I maintains energetically that both are one and the same person, that Grandfather I has all the knowledge which Grandfather II possesses and is only prevented from making it public because of language difficulties. (The patient herself was naturally not conscious of this split, but took both to be the same person.) (75)

That I and II are never both present together could be seen to confirm I's claim. In other words, "there is an identity of I and II, but it does not lie in the realm of the personality under discussion; it lies rather in the basis common to both, namely in the personality of the patient, which is in the deepest sense one and indivisible" (76). The hysterical split of consciousness distinguishes the sermonizing shine I takes to his séance audiences (most likely based on the pastor who recently led her through confirmation) from the silliness of the spirit or personality Ulrich von Gerbenstein, who resembles the schoolgirl S.W. with the give-away tendency to go too far. "These strivings lead to the adolescent dream of the ideal Ivenes, beside whom the unrefined aspects of her character fade into the background" (77).

Five years later, Jung was ready with his book on schizophrenia, specifically on the language of schizophrenics. *The Psychology of Dementia Praecox* documents his breakthrough application of the association test, as used earlier by Stransky in studying the influence of the condition of the attention span on speech production. While Jung's theoretical premises are admittedly already covered in Freud's works on hysteria, obsessional neurosis, and dreams, his own concepts, "worked out on an experimental basis, differ somewhat from those of Freud, and it may be that the concept of the feeling-toned complex goes a little beyond the scope of Freud's views" (38). Strike up the band: the concept bears comparison with Wagner's film scoring of music as background music. "The leitmotiv, as a sort of feeling-tone, denotes a complex of ideas which is essential to the dramatic structure. Each time one or the other complex is stimulated by something someone does or says, the relevant leitmotiv is sounded in one of its variants. It is exactly the same in ordinary psychic life: the leit-motivs are the feeling tones of our complexes, our actions and moods are modulations of the leitmotivs" (39, n. 4). Every fragment of communication, "each molecule" as Jung puts it, "participates in the feeling-tone . . . of the whole fabric of ideas, which we call the feeling-toned complex. Understood in this sense, the complex is a higher psychic unity. When we come to examine our psychic material (with the help of the association test, for example), we find that practically every association belongs to some complex or other" (40).

The therapeutic encounter with schizophrenia first externalized testing of reality, which, together with transference and mourning, was viewed as left behind at the checkpoint behind which psychosis is the new frontier across which psychoanalysis nevertheless seeks to extend the borderline of transferential legibility. In his synthetic compendium of psychodynamic approaches to study and treatment of schizophrenia (including his own approach), Silvano Arieti points out that what may seem to us as forms of irrationality in psychosis are instead archaic forms of rationality that result from a "principle of teleologic regression" to which everyday normality also has access. "The need for rationality is as powerful as the need to gratify the irrational emotions" (191). No human being will accept anything that seems to him irrational.

Uncontainable anxiety drives the psychotic to seek emergency refuge in defenses that, given their all-or-nothing emergency-brake nature, leave the psychotic even more vulnerable to renewed breakthroughs of anxiety. Megaregression seems to offer the patient enough safety for acceptance of his illness. But, according to Arieti, the illness has not accepted the patient and therefore there is no end to the regression (other than the big dead one). "He is in a pathological condition, because his whole organism, each part of it, was integrated at a level which required the cerebral cortex" (380). Arieti adapts the evolutionary perspective to the psychic human condition of not being able to devolve together with the regressive flight from anxiety. "The specific reaction consists of the adoption of archaic mental mechanisms, which belong to lower levels of integration. Inasmuch as the result is a regression to, but not an integration at lower levels, a disequilibrium is engendered which causes further regression, at times to levels even lower than the one in which certain perceptions are possible" (384). This flight pattern of regression from conception to perception (the stage of hallucination) to the blank screen can be followed in the language of schizophrenics, which appears to be highly associative and metaphorical but in fact nixes connotation while promoting denotation and verbalization (the use of words for their own sake as sound shapes). Connotation is the medium of conceptual classification of the relay of associations that in the meantime left the former reality wide open to breakthroughs of anxiety. Thus through denotation the schizophrenic focuses only on individual words. During question and answer, the schizophrenic will swerve from the impact of classifying demands. Arieti gives an example: Define table. The patient counters: "What kind of table? A wooden table, a porcelain table, a surgical table, or a table you want to have a meal on?" Thus the patient tries to decrease the task (and the risk of anxiety breaking in) by breaking the question down into many pieces (199).

Words are identified and substituted for one another as (or together with) the doubles of their objects. Many ideas or things become in time linked by similarity and contiguity until they are identified and, as such, substituted one for the other. Hence language can end up reduced to a few words or stereotypical expressions, a concentration of meaning impractical for purposes of communication. Like the barking of a dog, the same expression in schizophrenic language means many things. Arieti offers an analogy with the overexposed media record: "Certain sentences are as confusing as photographic films which have been exposed several times" (262). But these superimposed images and meanings are connected in the mind of the schizophrenic. The reduction of language in the wake of psychotic regression begins and ends with the identifying link, which serves as underlying predicate. This link can only be found out by analyzing the emotional factors attending its multiply determined choice.

This brings us to the first round of testing to which psychotic language or experience was subjected: Jung's use of association testing to map the feeling-toned complexes subtending what he at the same time tossed aside as "word salad."

The continuum subtending the association testing of feeling-toned complexes extends from normalcy ("the whole aim of education is to implant lasting complexes in the child" [43]), through hysteria, occupying there an analogical middle ground with somnambulism or mediatism, and washing up onto (or as) psychosis. Jung claims the support of Freud's *The Psychopathology of Everyday Life* (while Freud will view the feeling-toned complexes as reformulations of insights he presented in that same work).

"Complexes are mostly in a state of repression because they are concerned as a rule with the most intimate secrets which are anxiously guarded and which the subject will not or cannot divulge" (45).

The test employs as stimulus-words ordinary words from everyday speech to uncover complexes. The obstruction of the association response, both temporally and ideationally, is evidence of contact with a complex: "the stronger the feeling-tone of a complex, the stronger and more frequent will be the disturbances of the experiment" (45). What this means in the shallow end of the pool of test subjects is that "the ego-complex is, so to say, no longer the whole of the personality; side by side with it there exists another being, living its own life and hindering and disturbing the development of the ego-complex, for the symptomatic actions often take up a good deal of time and energy at its expense" (47). Just take the state of being in love, which counts as one of the sexual complexes (which tend to furnish the clearest examples of the psyche under the influence). "All stimuli that do not suit the complex undergo a partial apperceptive degeneration with emotional impoverishment" (48).

Association testing registers disturbances (breakdowns of the test exchange) that reflect the pull of the complex's withdrawal from communication, even from the context and concept of communication.

In our experimental work we have demonstrated that complexes disturb the association tests in a characteristic and regular manner (peculiar forms of reaction, perseveration, prolongation of reaction time, failure to react, forgetting of critical or post-critical reactions, etc.). (44)

When hesitations and other disturbances occur in the course of testing we know "that the stimulus-word has hit a complex" (45). The repressive resistance encountered produces follow-up amnesia of the critical reactions. The enigmatic force of the complex in its state of repression meets the formation of personalities in the course of S.W.'s mediumship halfway:

These displacements and disguises may, as we know, produce real double personalities, such as have always excited the interest of psychological writers (cf. the recurrent problem in Goethe of two souls...). "Double personality" is not just a literary phrase, it is a scientific fact of general interest to psychology and psychiatry, especially when it manifests itself in the form of double consciousness or dissociation of the personality. The split-off complexes are always distinguished by peculiarities of mood and character, as I have shown in a case of this kind. (50)

The footnote appended to the end of the last sentence refers to *On the Psychology and Pathology of So-Called Occult Phenomena*.

Just before we enter the double feature of "Hysteria and Dementia Praecox," set apart like the decompression chamber of analogies through which we gain safe entry into the case study of Jung's schizophrenic patient Miss St., we are given two metapsychological facts, one for each end of the psychopathology continuum:

Every affective event becomes a complex. (67)

But if the complex remains entirely unchanged, which naturally happens only when there is very severe damage to the ego-complex and its functions, then we must speak of dementia praecox. (68)

Affectation is initially the characterological disturbance that shows more overlap than gap between dementia praecox and hysteria.

The affectation, in itself, contains nothing specific of dementia praecox; the disease takes over the mechanism from the normal, or rather from the caricature of the normal, hysteria. Such patients have a special predilection for neologisms, which they use mostly as learned or otherwise distinguished-sounding technical terms. One of my women patients called them "power words" and showed a special liking for the most abstruse expressions, which obviously seemed to her fraught with meaning. The "power-words" serve among other things to emphasize the personality and to make it as imposing as possible. The emphasis laid upon "power-words" accentuates the value of the personality in the face of doubt and hostility, and for this reason they are frequently used as defensive and exorcistic formulae. A dementia-praecox patient under my care, if the doctors refused him anything, used to threaten them with the words: "I, the Grand Duke Mephisto, shall have you treated with blood vengeance for orang outang representation." Others, like Schreber, use the power-words to exorcise their voices. (75–76)

As we approach the delusional system of Miss St. we seem to begin to run out of analogies. Negativism, hallucination, and stereotypy, to give three examples, offer a last stand or understanding that analogies afford via normal and hysterical psychology.

Affectation alone does not explain the schizophrenic response, which not only combines elements into jargonic new words (often inspired by language in dreaming, fantasizing, and hallucinating)[1] but also fragments existing words along the same lines. "Many schizophrenics who are inclined to be negativistic and will not react to the questions show 'etymological' leanings: instead of answering, they dissect the question and embellish it with clang associations, which amounts to a displacement and concealment of the complex. . . . This is analogous to not answering the stimulus-word"

(76). A note drops here to comparison with the invention of languages in mediumistic circles and with the results of séance experiments with automatic writing or psychography.

Hallucination, as outward projection of psychic elements, "merely sets in motion a preformed mechanism which normally functions in dreams" (90). Unlike hysterical hallucinations, which contain symbolically distorted fragments of the complex, in dementia praecox the symbolism is carried much further and is more dreamlike in its distortion. In psychosis hallucination is as much regression as projection. The schizophrenic regresses from conceptualization by reducing it all to perception.

Stereotypy is both one of the stereotypes of schizo identification and at the same time "in the form of automatization . . . one of the commonest phenomena in the development of the normal psyche" (92). Given its history, the term designates the bad arrest of literacy: the arrest of spontaneity and affect. Thus Jung points out that quotation is one-stop hopping that allows a complex to get around and express itself (or not). The difference from the normal development remains that "the corresponding process in dementia praecox seems to run a more rapid and thorough course, so that it soon loses all content and affectivity" (94). This "degeneration" afflicts the voices and delusional ideas: "The 'word salad' arises in the same manner" (95). The stupid chattering about which so many schizophrenics complain is the word salad itself—an incomprehensible jumble and muddle of verbigerated neologisms in which phrases prove interchangeable and equivalent and in time, in turn yield to a couple of catchwords. Miss St. sums it all up when she refers to her "hieroglyphic suffering." Through her recurring phrases and words Miss St. indeed signs in with a language as unvarying, withdrawn, or depleted of change as centuries of ancient Egyptian iconography. Hieroglyphics also summon the mummified dead body kept in a secret crypt and protected by monumental diversions. As Freud commented following Victor Tausk's presentation on the influencing machine delusions in schizophrenia as they beset his patient Natalija A.—including the cinematograph that began looking like her double until 2-D reduction made it fit the outlines of a mummy's casket—the Egyptian burial practice of mummification, which transforms physical death into rebirth, corresponds to the rebirth out of spiritual death which is the schizophrenic's outside chance.[2]

Both stereotypy and hallucination stand up as analogies also only via the supporting kickstand of the Spiritualist analogy, which is where the fundamental difference or distance from schizophrenia is entrenched as analogy.

In hysteria the reasoning faculty is preserved and this prevents the feeling from immediately being projected outside as in dementia praecox. But if we assist the projection by allowing certain superstitious ideas to come into play, we immediately get an
explanation in terms of some power coming from outside. The clearest examples of
this are spiritualistic mediums, who trace back a mass of trivialities to transcendental causes—though, we must admit, they never do it as clumsily and grotesquely as
schizophrenics. (77)

As we enter the case study of Miss St. we are confronted with several
contradictions concerning her status as test subject (100–101). We are told
that when her complexes are not activated she speaks and reasons clearly.
She also keeps herself fully employed as a tailor. Cut off from the functional context outside the hospital, her diligent work is rendered occupational (though not symptomatic). Jung admits that because she wishes to
be released (one of her stereotypies is to make the request each time she's
in contact with a treating physician), the testing situation, which appears
as the interview she keeps asking for as preamble to her release, becomes
another feeling-toned complex (109). According to the parameters of her
being tested, she's all complexes, no ego. We could stop here since the
association test for Miss St. seems stuck on testing's primal significance
and staging as torture (in Jung's compilation of her associations to or identifications with Socrates, we hear that "she is martyred" [112]). However
the invasiveness of the test is grounded after all in the self-reflexivity it at
the same time uncovers. At the start of Jung's study we catch the momentum of this full circuit on the upbeat. Stransky's "tests brought interesting
results to light. The sequence of words and sentences immediately recalled
the talk (as well as the fragments of writing) we find in dementia praecox!"
(22). In sum: "This concurrence of three experimenters—Stransky, myself,
and, so to speak, dementia praecox—can be no accident" (24).

To decode Miss St.'s language, it proves pointless asking her directly
about her neologisms or power words. "At first I tried to get the patient
to tell me outright what she meant by her neologisms. This attempt was a
total failure, as she immediately came out with a string of fresh neologisms
resembling a word salad" (111). Instead Jung starts using her own power-
words as stimulus-words in testing for all the associations that come to
mind. Thus the test becomes coterminous with the schizophrenic's thought
and language.

Where self-reflexivity breaks through to endopsychic perception, Jung's
descriptions of the patient's language in terms of complexes double as
descriptions of how his theory of feeling-toned complexes functions.

The complex functions [like the theory of complexes LR] automatically in accordance with the law of analogy; it is completely freed from the control of the ego-complex [and its sensorium of identifications with the dead or alive LR], and for this reason the ego complex can no longer direct the associations; on the contrary, it is subordinated to the complex and continually disturbed by defective reproductions (thought-deprivation) and compulsive associations (pathological ideas). (113)

We finally know two or three things about the ego complex after all. We know that in one corner of the ringer is the death of her father ("I've been universal since the death of my father" [119]); in the other corner lies a dead sister. Miss St. attends to legacies and annuities drawn from and through the dead. Around power-words "Monopoly" and "Note Factory" Jung succeeds in translating his patient's economy of suffering or, in German, *Not*. Banknotes, like *Banknoten*, overlap with this *Not* and leave open the prospect of its alleviation. The "paper money ghosts" of *Faust II* draw a line through the reckoning whereby the loss gets cut with double occupancy. The note factory (which also rises up twice, the second time as gift for "Socrates") with its blackened windows and seven stories is a castle of doom and death. We know that Miss St. maintains the paternal frame or work of mourning, but as allegorical ruination and notation of a belief system that keeps its distance across the abyss of unmourning.

In *The Telephone Book*, Ronell underscores two blanks Jung fails to fill. Jung assumes that power-word "Oleum" is some tonic like the hypothetical X, the toxin that Jung repeatedly runs up against as the ultimate divergence between hysteria and the literal deterioration faced in schizophrenia. I like Jung's attention to the setting of advertising for props or prompts leading to power words in which the commodity is allegorized by Miss St. down to details of her pageant. But Ronell points out the possible link to "Mausoleum," to which, I would add or subtract, the "Maus" (= mouse) also belongs, the little critter that, in your dreams says Freud, represents a missing sibling. Ronell also underscores the slip in Jung's attention to the famous lines from "The Lorelei." Jung says the identification with or via the power-word "Lorelei" comes down to people not knowing what the patient's power-word "owner of the world" means. But Heine's poem tells us that the ego knows that he or she is grieving: what's not known is why. One of the associations to stimulus-word/power-word "Lorelei" was: "expresses the deepest mourning" (116).

We saw that Schreber was re-organ-ized as Jew, as woman, as others. S.W. decks herself out as ideal Jewess. Not only is Miss St. Jewish in her delusional system, but in her steady state of reference (she's not lower class but urban middle class) she also participates in the philo-Semitism of the German Second Empire. At the same time she gives it lip (service). The transcript of her associations gives the title of Lessing's drama *Nathan der Weise (Nathan the Wise)* also as "Nathan der Waise" ("Nathan the Orphan"). Her transgendering is complex too. She is both Emperor and Empress but at the same time remaining female. She's a word salaud. She also occupies the margin, which only the psychotic knows for sure is the cutting edge (the cutting in of pain and the cutting of losses) where reality begins again and thought can be suffered.

In the absence of a superegoical agency that books substitutions for losses, the telephone must put through the emergency calls on behalf of Miss St.'s immediate crises. The invisible telephones were all along, prior to hospitalization, transmitting slander. But speaking tubes and phones also permit the outward flow of her suffering. As the telephone begins to function as third person—as when it gives unpartisan comment on a bitter exchange between doctor and his patient—we can see the superego begin to emerge again. Jung discerns in the telephone a remnant of the once healthy ego that is still on the line. But the superego always builds itself upon the vestigial first egoic contacts. Jung is right to point out that dementia praecox tends to fit a range of expression without humor. The humor the telephone supplies is, according to Freud's assessment of humor at large, by definition superegoic. It is gallows humor in the setting of schizophrenia. It's funny that the superego believes in the afterlife of future generations as though falling within its own lifetime—believes, in other words, in mourning. Jung finds or founds a word from our sponsor, a correcting voice that may be the irruption of "the repressed normal remnant of the ego-complex" (90). Miss St., the patient who introduced the phrase "power-words," "explained the voices as invisible telephones" (99). "We can also understand why the patient describes her neologisms as 'power words.' Wherever they appear they hint at the whole system hidden behind them, just as technical terms do in normal speech" (109). Like the daemon's role in Socrates' decision-making (148), like the voices that reappeared in Schreber's case during convalescence (150), the telephone personifies a self-critical agency:

Once she said, with great emphasis, "I am the keystone, the monopoly and Schiller's Bell," and the telephone remarked, "That is so important that the markets will drop!" (150).

Jung, who remains open to his patient's identification with him as telephone and thus of the test situation as controlled through the phone, was over and again successful in the treatment of psychotics. He was Mr. Nonspecific Factor, giving the psychotics more than the time of day, and, whenever he stumbled upon transference/countertransference love, even entering the patient's delusional system more than halfway.

Because the schizophrenic is unable to define the power-words to which she owes the saying power of her remaindered language, these words are repeated as the test-words with which the patient forms chains of associations. Because the association test becomes self-reflexive in the schizophrenic setting, the power-word *telephone* occupies interchangeable places with Jung the tester, who pronounces the words of the association test. Because the modern exploration or testing of the inner/outer worlds of animals, punctuated with stimuli and responses, proved continuous with those worlds, Binswanger, whose dissertation research conducted under Jung was based on the association testing of psychotic patients, recognized the parallel, not between psychotics and animals themselves, but between their worlds or the explorations of them, all of them proliferating singularities.[3] Thus before the Turing test allegedly served as immediate model for the testing in *Do Androids Dream of Electric Sheep?* the test by association is played in several of Dick's novels as word game, for example in *Galactic Pot-Healer.* As soon as we meet Joe in his psychoticizing cubicle we watch him dial up another player in the game of recognition of book titles otherwise lost in translations.

What do I really yearn for? he asked himself. That for which oral gratification is a surrogate. Something vast, he decided; he felt the primordial hunger gape, huge-jawed, as if to cannibalize everything around him. To place what was outside inside.

Thus he played; this had created, for him, The Game.

Pressing the red button he lifted the receiver and waited while the creaking, slow relay machinery fed his phone an outside line. . . .

"Ready." Joe made a random scratch-mark with his pen.

Gauk cleared his throat and read from his slip of paper. . . . "This originated in your language," Gauk explained, honoring one of the rules which all of them together had made up, the bunch of them scattered here and there across the map of Earth, in little offices, in puny positions . . .

Gauk read from the slip of paper. "'The Lattice-work Gun-stinging Insect.'" . . .

"'Lattice-work,'" Joe said, pondering. "Network. 'Stinging Insect.' Wasp? . . . And you got this from the translation computer at Kobe? Bee," he decided. "'Gun,' so Gun-bee. Heater-bee. Laser-bee. Rod-bee. *Gat.*" . . . He had it now. "*The Great Gatsby.*" (6–8)

This word association game whereby otherwise suicidal nerds keep themselves from killing themselves or taking a psychotic break produces, in the one patch of writing that is clinical evidence of Dick's own sense that *Galactic Pot-Healer* was his one completely psychotic work, the other schizophrenic word for world and time of and the things in it. In *Martian Time-Slip* it was "gubbish," which enters sentences as gubbler gubbling that which, once the sentence is delivered, is gubbish. Its synonym, which will take center phrase in *Do Androids Dream of Electric Sheep?* first emerges in *Galactic Pot-Healer* via the following association:

> He then thought this:
> Q. Do you like Yeats?
> A. I don't know, I've never tried any.
> For a time his mind was empty and then he thought this:
> Q. Do you like Kipling?
> A. I don't know, I've never kippled.
> Anguish and despair filled him as these thoughts passed through his brain. I've gone mad, he said to himself. Only rubbish occupies my attention; I am flattened by pain. (139)

Returning to Switzerland, the other archaic setting of communications with schizophrenia, in addition to that of the Bleekmen tribe, we find the two psychosis experts caught up in the apparatus of the test. While under Jung's supervision in Zurich, Binswanger tested Jung on two occasions. It was around the time of Jung's all-out treatment of and affair with Sabina Spielrein.

> Later in the second test, a cluster of responses produced what Binswanger called an extremely "unpleasant" sex-related complex associated with "certain sounds," particularly the "sch" that occurred prominently throughout some test words. . . . Jung's reaction to the "sch" words was so highly agitated that Binswanger directed him to remain seated and relax once this part of the test was concluded. Jung fell asleep and dreamed, and when he awakened, he told Binswanger that he had "had a dream in which this ["sch"] lady plays the chief part." In his written report, Binswanger tactfully attributed it to Jung's "Goethe complex" but again said he was unable to comment further for "personal" reasons. (Bair, *Jung*, 112–13)

Binswanger checks in regularly with his differences as *Dasein*-analyst from Freud, who remained his correspondent and friend, also in order to keep silent about that with which he did not wish to be confused, namely the work of Jung. Like Spielrein, Binswanger could benefit from contact with Jung only by leaving him behind for Freud.

At the time of this test sighting, however, Jung was also aligned with Freud. Like Binswanger, Jung was necessarily involved in the psychiatric hospital setting with psychotics, whose treatment wasn't Freud's specialty.

Free association and reality testing were both out of the symptom picture of psychosis. Jung supplied a first container for the psychotic world via the testing of the push and pull of affect via word associations, in particular through the timing between stimulus word and response word. The analogies that get him close enough to schizophrenic thought or language to observe the work of analogy in schizophrenia itself identify from a distance and withdraw the identification at too-close quarters—the identification with the dead via ghost relations. Thus *The Psychology of Dementia Praecox* ends by coming full circle within the protective shell of analogy.

The analysis of cryptomnesia Jung folded into the study of occult phenomena doubles on contact with his work on dementia praecox as crypt supplement. Cryptomnesia also bears resemblance to his understanding of schizophrenic attention. Extreme suggestibility, counterbalanced only by negative suggestibility, its contrary, puts into effect strongly feeling-toned ideas (17). During accessible moments, schizophrenics often exhibit photographic memory of the goings-on in the immediate environment. But they retain in particular those things that would escape the notice of normals. Schizophrenics lack active assimilation. "Everything which requires an effort of attention passes unheeded by the patient, or at most is registered on the same level as the daily visit of the doctor or the arrival of dinner" (19).

The patient's discourse is not comparable to poetry, unless the "trite saying that everyone is unconsciously a poet—in his dreams" (144–45) has any validity. "But our patient has created a long-drawn-out and elaborately woven tissue of fancies, comparable on the one hand to an epic poem and on the other to the romances and fantasy-productions of somnambulists" (145). Jung had earlier singled out a certain "learned" but in fact pleonastic strain in his patient's discourse comparable to the "pompous style of officials or half-educated journalists" (129). Somnambulists elaborate their systems while in a state of dissociation, their "other" state of consciousness. The schizophrenic weaves the hole cloth of her fantasy in the waking state.

But just as somnambulists prefer to translate everything into fantastic and sometimes mystical forms, in which the sharp outlines of the images are often blurred as in dreams, so our patient expresses herself in monstrous, grotesque, distorted metaphors, which are more like normal dreams with their characteristic absurdities. . . .

Hence the psyche of the patient stands midway between the mental state of the normal dreamer and that of the somnambulist, with the difference that dreaming has largely replaced the waking state, and the "fonction du réel," or adaptation to the environment, is seriously impaired. I first showed how dream-formations develop out of complexes in my "Psychology and Pathology of So-called Occult Phenomena" (145).

Jung concludes this paragraph by urging that knowledge of occult phenomena, notably Spiritiualist mediumship, is "indispensable for understanding the problems we have been discussing." They do not overlap but border on each other: "The metaphorical modulations of the complexes are closely analogous on the one hand to normal dreams and on the other to the wish-dreams of hysterical somnambulists" (146).

Imitating the Dead

In *Dr. Bloodmoney* the homunculus Bill (another ambulatory *Faust II* reference or property) saves the world from psychotic destructiveness or omnipotence that goes around and comes back around between the mad scientist, Dr. Bluthgeld, and Hoppy, the birth defective repairman who gets around through his prosthetic fit with technology and exceeds (or throws) every fitting limit when he develops spiritual or psychic prosthetic powers. Bill, who has lived seven years inside his twin sister Edie, with and through whom he made contact with the world, replaces Hoppy in the omnipotence seat. Bill obtains embodiment while adding a sensibility graduated through his awareness of the dead who mutter and moon and just wait around (209). Hoppy thought he saw the afterlife in trance states. But he only saw a future of death wish–fulfilling compensation and revenge, which the mad world outside or inside Bluthgeld's head happens to meet more than halfway. Hoppy can mimic those he would possess and then dispatch. But Bill, by observing the dead so closely, because he believes it matters, can imitate the recently deceased, his advantage in the struggle with Hoppy, for whom all the dead are like fathers, lots of fathers (277).

Bonnie Keller protects her former boss Bruno Bluthgeld against survivor vengeance following a nuclear test that, contrary to Bluthgeld's calculations, backfired as the toxic layering upon his lie of their land. Though Bonnie assigns the blame to the entirety of scientific institutions backing the miscalculation, Bluthgeld himself assumes the guilty charge, which charges up his sense of omnipotence. Bluthgeld's guilty assumption is the beginning of his psychotic break. Bonnie sends him to see her psychiatrist, Dr. Stockstill, on what turns out to be the day of the second nuclear conflagration, resulting, apparently yet inexplicably, from self-destructive feedback of the system of defense. But it's the day that, because he is looked at the wrong way, Dr. Bluthgeld must flex the nuclear commands that are his wishes for self-defense. In interview (with Lupoff) Dick comments on certain Jungian revalorizations of projection, which, extending from the reception of psychosis into quantum physics, can be seen to spark Dr. Bluthgeld's fantasy of danger as fantasy innocent bystanders must share.

There is, of course, a contemporary heretical sect of scientists and laymen who, based on Jung's theory that UFOs were projections from the collective unconscious, that have begun to talk about mental contents as being actually objective. This is the Tulpa theory that they can be projected into the outer world and even be photographed, and are sensible objects. They are objects of our percept system and are projected from the unconscious—which is just one step further from Jung's idea that an individual will project elements of his unconscious. Now we have the collective unconscious of a number of people being projected and forming Tulpa objects. . . . Now one of the basic psychotic ideas is that you can affect objects by just thinking about them, and yet this has crept into quantum physics. By picking up the Jungian thing we arrive at the conclusion that we can and do project a lot of our outer reality.

The research Dick describes here seems to follow the scientific pattern of modern Spiritualism (notably the insertion of photography into the otherwise invisible séance). In *Dr. Bloodmoney,* Dick projects mass death resulting from convergence between psychosis and modern physics via the figure of Dr. Bluthgeld (while keeping tabs on the dead via the homunculus). On day two of the nuclear calamity, Dr. Stockstill observes the war psychosis in one of his fellow victims as the novel's first index of internal resources of bombs blasting in the air:

"We'll fight back, we'll fight back, we'll fight back," a man near Doctor Stockstill was chanting. Stockstill looked at him in astonishment, wondering who he would fight back against. Things were falling on them; did the man intend to fall back upward into the sky in some kind of revenge? Would he reverse the natural forces at work, as if rolling a film-sequence backward? It was a peculiar, nonsensical idea. It was as if the man had been gripped by his unconscious. He was no longer living a rational, ego-directed existence; he had surrendered to some archetype. (74)

Since only Edie is visible or audible on the outside, the twins are hidden sports (resented by Hoppy for their discretion) who were conceived on the day of the second nuclear catastrophe, possibly the first in the series of the mad scientist's psychotic breakthroughs. In reality shock Bonnie hitches a ride with a man who happens to be passing through on business. Whether mirth in funeral or as affirmation in defiance of the calamity, they love the one they're with. The designated driver decides on the spot to start his life

over in the vicinity of his splitting image of the eternal feminine. But then
a third time around, when Dr. Bluthgeld, incognito, still under Bonnie's
protection, feels he is again being looked at and through the wrong way,
the world begins again to explode as his last defense.

A world stuck in the groove or grave of nuclear conflagration, which
in its uncontainability and unassignability reflects the paranoid condition Dr. Bluthgeld makes in his negotiations with his environment, is a
world stuck in the scratch or trace of remembrance. It is in defense of this
world that Bonnie abandons her protectiveness toward the mad scientist.
Before she can act, however, Hoppy proceeds to save the day by telekinetically smashing Bluthgeld's paranoid simulcasting operations. As Fredric
Jameson points out, the initial development of a counterforce via Hoppy
succumbs to doubling: "By the time of the confrontation with Bluthgeld,
Hoppy is himself a dangerously paranoid figure, potentially as harmful
to the community as the man he is now able to destroy. Thus a kind of
interminable regression is at work here, in which any adversary powerful
enough to blast the evil at its source becomes then sufficiently dangerous
to call forth a nemesis in his own right, and so forth" (359).

When Hoppy picks up the Bluthgeld danger signals, he himself is working to replace a certain Dangerfield in the seat of total world communication. The former astronaut Dangerfield, whose craft was locked into
orbit around Earth with the nuclear blast, serves as disc jockey, keeping
the survivors below in global touch. Hoppy can aim his spiritual prosthetic prowess to seize control of the spacecraft's communications system
(while undermining Dangerfield's health across the same long distance).
We briefly sample Hoppy's imitation of the Dangerfield persona and show,
which would have gone on and on for days if homunculus Bill hadn't pulled
the body switch: the perfect mimicry notwithstanding, there remains the
one deadly giveaway that "Dangerfield" suddenly took interest only in
Hoppy's self-esteem.

But then homunculus Bill, as part of the gift of life that Bonnie
extracted from the *Gift* of nuclear and psychotic toxicity, can break the
infinite regression of psychic or psychotic invasion because in the world
he only has a dead body, the fetus that survives only in symbiosis with his
twin sister inside her body. As Jameson argues, Bill, since without a body,
can "switch places without the development of an elaborated counterforce
which might then ... become a threat in its own right" (360). Whereas
Hoppy fought Bluthgeld on the latter's own terms (and on the sidelines of
his Dangerfield project, Hoppy's own psychotic prize), "Bill's replacement

of Hoppy amounts to a shift from that system to a new one; and this is made possible by Hoppy's own violation of his particular system and powers" (ibid.). Because of their diverging receptions of the dead, Bill is the more accomplished player on the Danger Field onto which Hoppy strayed. Bill's mimicry terrifies Hoppy into punitive identification with the dead or Dad. You wanted the Dad dead? Be the unDad, the unborn dead. When Hoppy hurls Bluthgeld into the heights for his deadly drop, he oversteps his representation of the community and shows himself to be the danger in the field. Thus Bill closes the circle opened in earshot of Toby's dirge by swapping meat with Hoppy, who flops about and dies as an externalized and severed part of the internal symbiotic relationship between twins.

The Danger Field is, in the beginning, the word. Bill exists before he corporealizes as the buzz of conversation with his sister in one direction, with the dead in the other. Walt Dangerfield guarantees everyone's share in the commonality of language while also serving as the audio archive of the handful of books that survived. Before Bill rescues him from Hoppy's drain on him, Dangerfield embodies the isolation that he had previously, as the power of words, helped audience Earth push back. Looking back at his novel across fifteen years, Dick still gets this groove back.

The West Marin County area where much of the novel is set is an area that I knew well. . . . When I lived there in the late 50s and early 60s it was set apart from the rest of California and therefore seemed to me a natural locus for a postwar microcosm of society. Already, in fact, West Marin was a little world. When I read over *Dr. Bloodmoney* I discover, to my pleasure, that I have captured in words much of that little world that I so love—a little world from which I am now separated by time and distance. ("Introduction to *Dr. Bloodmoney*")

This is Dick's ego idyll. Dangerfield keeps aloft and ongoing the account of Philip's study of German in Heidelberg, for example, via the work he is broadcasting, Somerset Maugham's *Of Human Bondage*. Dangerfield's vulnerable enterprise recaptures the comfort in surveillance while circumnavigating the exchange rate Dick suspended between *Time out of Joint* and *A Scanner Darkly*: surveillance reclaimed as metaphysical comfort substitutes for traumatizations that cannot be addressed directly.

It is the present, buried alive according to Jameson in the trash heap of late capitalism, to which, as Jameson argues with reference to Proust, elaborate strategies of indirection are owed, not for the keepsake of nostalgia for the present, but to arrive at its history (287–88). Dick thus sidles up to the present as the historical difference otherwise lost in our sense of past and future. The sci-fi future is the pretext for reclaiming the present as past (and then as history) (345). I have been arguing for modification of this notion of history of the present. The restoration of the hub of the present, which includes the recent past and the foreseeable future, is achieved and maintained through the elaboration of alternate or lateral present realities that expand the archive of finitude, admit our dead, and remain ahead of repression of the present going on the recent past (the time of mourning).

Whereas Jameson first argued (in his 1975 article on *Dr. Bloodmoney*) that in Dick's work psychosis and drugs mediate or update mysticism, later he identified the empty scene of 1950s America as the historical present mediating all the other themes (psychosis, drugs, and mysticism) (370 and following). The schizo or drug-induced hallucinatory states passing through this scene are at the same time always reducible to televisual spectacle. While this TV setting gives cause for depression to be set on the scene, catastrophe (the third total or world war) can install instead utopian communities. Survival spreads 1950s depression thin. But the good content of the scene is also always ready to go into reverse, whereupon it is left lifeless: thus collectible souvenirs can take over until what we're left with fits a *mortuary interieur*.

Dick's rule of tomb, however, is that mainstream USA belongs to the 1950s, because the period lends its years to World War II as fixation point or as the staging area of the next Second Coming. In the words of the Evangelical preacher in *Voices from the Street:*

"Total war was a concept unknown at the beginning of our lifetimes. Try to imagine what will be meant by the term a century from now—if there is still an earth a century from now. There will be a war of such totality as to be beyond any present imagination. If you doubt this, I ask you to consider with what accuracy an ordinary citizen living in 1852 could have imagined the napalm and A-bombs of the last world war." (83)

Jameson is right that in Dick's science fiction, even after the third strike, we're not out of the 1950s decade, which functions, says Jameson, as "time capsule" that comes complete with "televisual addiction and the therapies" (381). However, I would add that the investment in Germanicity in the future worlds maintains the complete habitat: the 1950s as the edge we grip in traumatic amnesia before the moment that is next to impossible to remember like the remaindered era that we're so hard-pressed to commemorate. In a mainstream novel like *Mary and the Giant* (to my mind the best example) the continuity shot between outer space or postnuclear loneliness and the desolation already in place in Dick's fictional work and world of the 1950s cannot be overlooked. In *The Game-Players of Titan*, the acceleration of the contest on Earth first begins to fold out as psychic space race between species in Schilling's record store. A record store by that same name is the lair of the "giant" in the 1950s novel that strikes the mother load of all conflict in racism against African-Americans, which in the science fiction novel is subsumed, as projected reality, by the terms of our conflict with the aliens from outer space. By a similar token, *Voices from the Street* can afford to recognize the political problems crowding the receiving area of Carl Jung. It's true the fascistoid editor of the magazine *Succubus* also consumes Sartre, whereby Dick's portrait loses historical focus but doesn't sacrifice accuracy in psychological profiling. Psychoanalytic precision is applied (on earth as in the psycho heaven of future worlds) when "succubus" is emphatically defined as a male demon who assumes drag around men to be, as Schreber might have written, f--d. The continuum that is there, then, between mainstream and science fiction gives riveting support for the view that, since there is only one present to go around, science fictive extension in time must proceed via alternate presents. But we must set this spread before another constant, the last recent past. Dick's simulcast histories are to a recognizable degree stuck at the border between World War II and its forget-together, the fifties. Even into the future, then, World War II is our lasting recent past.

Nuclear catastrophe is held up at the border of the idyll in *Dr. Bloodmoney*. But it is also constructed as nemesis that does not so much return as the repressed as get systematically cleansed out of the system. The distinction that Dick otherwise upholds between the destructiveness of consumers and the work of reparation that repairmen serve is contaminated in Hoppy, the sacrificial *Gift* that must be endured and eliminated to maintain the idyll. Because a better world under repair can establish itself as fantasy by-product of catastrophe only if all death-wish static is all clear, we face a maintenance contract that, as in *Time out of Joint*, cannot be carried to its terms indefinitely.

At this point of contract the twins reverse the undead symbiosis of Dick's own twinship. Bonnie, who cannot bear to know about the twin, is the one portrayal in Dick's oeuvre of the eternal feminine in the place of his mother, otherwise the placeholder of the bundle of negative traits modeling the runaway series of dark-haired girls. Something like acceptance of the mother is stowaway in the affirmation of their shared underworld, the "Keller" that as German word means "cellar."

Inside the little world, deep inside the recess that only Bonnie maintained for Dr. Bluthgeld, there is an intermission from happy endings. In addition to the birth-defective sports there is one mutation resulting from the nuclear catastrophes, Toby, Dr. Bluthgeld's talking dog. Mutation is that margin account of investment in survival that flourishes like technological innovation through war. In Dick's future worlds of survival of nuclear warfare technology is not given any advance. But mutation does stand to attention, often on the verge of flourishing, as the introject of a peaceful alternative to human destructiveness. Mutation is awarded the peace prize as outside chance that life can begin again without going once more around the blockage on death drive. Toby speaks just like one imagines one's dog would speak if or when communication is possible, via your own ventriloquist's act or via the telepathic translation of the animal communicator. Toby blusters with opinions about what is proper or property (it's evident to any dog owner that we learned the drive of the proper, our pet peeve, from our canine companions). Toby alone is left to mourn his master whom all others have abandoned. On the margins of this Marin account, in which, among other happy endings and successful mournings, symbiotic twinship can be overcome or just let go, there is the dogged grief that mutation releases. But there is also overall an uncontainable momentum of imbalance that requires that the story be told again, explicitly as *Deus Irae,* with a different outcome for the prosthetized man of reparations who swears on a dog's word.

Indexical Layer

Deus Irae would be another work of fantasy, in which both genres (according to Tolkien), the Germanic and the Christian hero fantasies, would meet and cross over, only if fantasy as such could survive the introduction of mutation as the new missing link to a future of survival of the loss of the world to nuclear devastation. Be a sport, like the painter without limbs, Tibor, or identify with one of the new species or tribes of "muties" (including bugs, lizzys, and runners) that have replaced large portions of humankind. But can the latter be accepted as motivated versions of the supernatural beings representing the "other world" in or as fantasy?

Deus Irae is one of two collaborations Dick entered into during a season of brainstorming with writer colleagues at his new home in East Oakland. Group ideas represent an embarrassment of riches for the author itching to write but momentarily blocked. Chips from the workshop or from the old block: the other collaboration, *The Ganymede Takeover,* represents the task he had set himself but could only consider in group format, namely the composition of a sequel to his highly successful *The Man in the High Castle.* But the long-drawn-out *Deus Irae,* which Dick worked on from 1964 to 1975, first with one coauthor, then with the next more-motivational one, was caught in a draw of dual authorship that was the problem internal to the hard-to-conclude work. The union or separation of authorship was in symptomatic syndication with the volatile topic of omniscience that the novel ultimately reclaims—but not before risking its completion through equal partnership as displaced retrenchment of the control fantasy of surveillance. Zelazny, the second partner (is a charm), treated the project as "Phil's book" and took only one-third credit (Sutin, *Divine Invasions,* 310).

Deus Irae projects a future in which mankind plays posthumous between two religions, like the two gods of Schreber's order of the world, a postdevastation cult of wrath and remembrance, which is dominant, and Christianity, which is recessive. Both belief systems are pitched in the clearing or twinkling of the all-seeing, all-mirroring eye. (The fatal war, given a near-future date at the time Dick was writing, happens to share, as so often in regard to this horizon of his scene of writing, the year of Dick's own death.)

The world-destroying war was the revelation of a new god, the God of Wrath, hailed as more realistic than the escapist god of the so-called Old Church. The Servants of Wrath (or SOWers), who stick to facts and stones because words can't stop what hurts them, inhabit the indexical perspective of photography. In the beginning was not the word or logos associated with Christianity, but the indexical act of representation whereby a portrait develops from the vestige of the referent, which it shadows with lifelessness like some kind of voodoo.

What can be recognized in the indexical relation is life mediated by the death or loss it transmits, as trial rather than as opposition to be overcome. Blackness, as in the subdermal "mark" visible on the photographed face of Lufteufel (the God of Wrath's representative on earth), is not "evil."

Blackness was what Martin Luther in his translation of Genesis had meant when he said, "*Und die Erde war ohne Form und leer.*" *Leer;* that was it. That was what blackness was; when spoken it sounded like "layer" [...] a film negative, which, having been exposed to unshielded light, had, due to chemical action, turned to absolute opaqueness, to this quality of *leer*ness, this layer of glaucomalike blindness. It was like Oedipus wandering; what he saw, or rather what he failed to see. (13)

Leer means "vacant" or "empty" like death. "We, as living creatures, are in the hands of a merciless and angry deity and will be until death wipes us from the slate of his records" (20).

The illuminating, mirroring, recording overview empties out what it sees, which lapses into lifelessness. But the Christians postulated an Adversary at the boundary called death, which thus marks, in the end, a beginning. The Christian representation of omniscience would see from both sides now if, one, the Devil, like the God of Wrath, did not recognize only damnation or punishment and, two, the heavenly afterlife that Carleton Lufteufel also enters upon were not the kind of spiritual upgrade that must be radically distinguished from the ghostly continuity shot between the living and the dead. Only the damned, for all their pain, know always only the same small world after all. Lufteufel's cretin/Christian daughter witnesses her dead father's transfiguration "as if time had rolled back for him" (174). Christianity rolls back the stone and empties the grave or groove of photographic developments. Her uplifting vision is simulcast back home for the Christian father as the original setting of Christianity that is beaming its alternate present through the scrubbed-away film. It is at this confluence of times that Father Abernathy speculates that there are happy consequences to Tibor's shooting the picture or soul of Lufteufel (whose name, as German word, means "air devil").

In the smashed world of survivors there is only one gadget that's on futural track: the cart and artificial limb combo that keeps Tibor, an inc or incomplete, in touch with his immediate environment while granting him mobility (though the cart is drawn by cows). Thus the apocalyptic reduction of the world illuminates the prosthetic view of technologization as returning from the mythic realm of its repression. Even as technologization cuts loose from the range of the prosthetic model, when it comes time to mourn (or not to mourn) the head starts of sheer velocity and digital jumping go into reverse, become mediatized, or get back into the body or its retrofit with the prosthesis.

Photography, the other survival from the recent techno past and the other function on which Tibor relies as portraitist, is also prosthetically emplaced as affixed to the referent it violates. But with only one, not especially good photo available, Tibor, who has been commissioned to portray the God of Wrath's incarnation in a church mural or murch, must go out into the world on a pilg to locate Lufteufel and take his picture.

Other than the two indexical/prosthetic functions, we encounter along for the ride of Tibor's pilg the ruins and remnants of the former order of autonomous technologies, which have retrofitted themselves as mythic forces. Thus a central computer, which met consumers halfway in the years before the war with android-like interfaces to satisfy their inquiring minds, is, postwar, the Great C, a vast fading organism that sends out extensor women to receive the primal consumerism of human sacrifice: "it must prey on the psyches of living creatures. It is not physical energy . . . that it must have: it is spiritual energy, which it drains from the total neurological systems of its victims" (120). Then it's off to see the autofac, the wonderful autofac that was. The former repair automat is now an absurdly dyslexic ogre. Next door the Urworm, as guardian of a stash of piled high techno trash of its own, plays dragon in this fantasyscape. Once he slays it and comes into contact with its slime, Tibor, like Siegfried, like Schreber, can understand the song of the birds as language addressed to him.

Tibor charts this landscape from technology in the close quarters of the difference or decision between "reality" and "wish fulfillment." "Worry had become a doorway to the real, all at once" (103–4). Through an over-lapsus, the great worm identified to and through Tibor the provenance of the fantasy-escape: "I came from your war, inc" (90). In other words, the "inc" that stands in SOW jargon for "incomplete," otherwise abbreviates the "incorporation" of that which was or *war*. Thus Tibor is incomplete not because the trauma of warfare took his limbs but because the poison-ing of a layer *(leer)* of living and breathing was internalized by the sur-vival of so many losses. He hitches his cart of incompletion to the start of mourning.

The SOW Church Father's name is Handy, which in the era beyond Dick's own prediction and predicament came to be the German word, on faux foreign loan, for the mobile phone. Thus the mobile phone becomes, as the prosthetically useful "handy" from another language, a replacement or a loss of what never was. The prosthetic rapport with technologiza-tion is in indexical sync (or swim) only with its phantasmatic postmortem application in the course of mourning work.

When the God of Wrath first appears to him, not in person but as Wizard of Oz–like projective defense screening, the divinity performs the miracle that Dick's original title named: "The Kneeling Legless Man." After the divinity fleshes out the dotted lines of Tibor's prosthetization — and thus restores what never was — he also takes back again what he gave and reinstalls the prosthetic relationship as site haunted by phantom limbs. Tibor undergoes the God of Wrath's "sadistic" miracle of finding and losing arms and legs. But better that than a Christian god who's a "maso-chist": "He created people so that they could not go through life without hurting him. He wanted something painful to love" (131). Like sadism and masochism, not as a couple of perverts (the only way Deleuze could imagine their untenable conjunction) but at the level of drives (or divini-ties), the God of Wrath, who largely conforms to the Old Testament God, and the Christian God occupy a continuum that Christianity (or masoch-ism) alone can fantasize as such and thus inherit.

The God of Wrath, still in the world in the person of Carleton Lufteufel, is not in fact German, but, because responsible for mass death and destruc-tion, must walk in the shadow of Death, the master from Germany. The

Servants of Wrath (or SOWers) identify the hypocrisy or idealism of Christianity with the war Christians helped design and which they cosigned. But German, as the language both of high culture and of the cartels responsible for the perfection and production of weapons of mass destruction, is incorporated by the Servants of Wrath in their, as always, global American, both as idiomatic phrases and as citations from great works. Tibor as painter, for example, is the ambulatory citation here as in Goethe and Nietzsche of G. E. Lessing's evocation of a "painter without hands" whose inner vision remains uncompromised by hands-on mediations.

German would otherwise appear to be a dead language, although "Germany," as so often in Dick's future mixtures of political boundaries for the future, was functionally part of the United States before the bombs dropped.

> "Tibor," he said, "*wie geht es Heute?*"
>
> "*Es geht mir gut,*" Tibor responded instantly.
>
> They mutually loved their recollection and their use of German. It meant Goethe and Heine and Schiller and Kafka . . . ; both men, together, lived for this and on this. (4)

While the outnumbered Christians eschew the SOW predilection for German (and for the jargon of abbreviation), the Christian mystic Pete Sands, who courts heresy through his drug-experimental search for God, once glimpsed the omniscience he would traverse or reverse as face-to-face encounter while dangling from what he can also only designate in the language of the dead as the *Todesstachel*, which he describes as follows or falls: "The gaff—the metal barbed hook itself—came at the bottom end of a long pole, a spear, which ascended from Earth to heaven, and he had, in that awful instant as he rolled doubled-up in agony, glimpsed the Persons at the top end of the spear, those who held the pole that bridged the two worlds" (25).

Sands's vision of the gaff that hooked him, which bridges Earth and Heaven as vertical control by persons on high, revalorizes as "awakening" the sadistic destructiveness of the God of Wrath's original revelation, as Lufteufel himself, though incognito, describes the end in sight:

> "There was still some beauty in the old days, you know. The cities were hectic, dirty places, but at certain moments—usually times of arrival and departure—looking down upon them at night, all lit up, say, from a plane in a cloudless sky—you could almost, for that moment, call up a vision out of St. Augustine. . . . But the day came. The wrath descended. Sin, guilt, and retribution? . . . Our darkness, externalized and visible? However you look upon these matters, the critical point was reached. The

wrath descended. The good, the evil, the beautiful, the dark, the cities, the country—the entire world—all were mirrored for an instant within the upraised blade.
The hand that held that blade was Carleton Lufteufel's." (144–45)

In the wake of God's long-distancing Himself from us, there is, in addition to the glimpse from the other end of the death stinger, another drug-
induced vision that Sands identifies as that of the Adversary. The image
will be recycled in the novel as the blood print of Lufteufel's face left on his
bandages as on another shroud of Turin. If the infernal image also appears
in other Dick novels (notably as the titular figure of *The Three Stigmata
of Palmer Eldritch*), then that's because it was Dick's own vision (in 1969)
of evil incarnate: "it was metal and cruel and, worst of all, it was God"
(in Sutin, *Divine Invasions*, 127). Looking down at all life from just above
the horizon, unmoving and waiting, the vast face has empty slots for eyes.
Though Dick's priest identified the vision as a glimpse of Satan and gave
him healing unction, the metal face in the sky remained to leave its reprint-
able impression. According to Sands: "he was so placed that he viewed
straight across the surface of the world, as if the world were flat and his
gaze, like a laser beam, traveled on without end, forever" (27).

While Tibor dreams that he must look upon Lufteufel face-to-face to
fill the void in the murch he is going to paint (47), Sands projects God's
search for us as the staging area for his own drug-launched journey to meet
Him halfway. He falls for the face-to-face from which we fell. Though
schizophrenia (like cancer) was "unmasked" in the prewar era as physical lack that could be supplied, schizophrenia as something other than
its serotonin portrait continues, according to Sands, as the very separation between God and man: "they wound up like Leibnitz's windowless
monads, near each other but unable to perceive anything outside; only able
to scrutinize their own beings. A sort of schizophrenia evidently set in, on
the part of one of them or both; autism—separation" (28).

The prospect of surveillance belongs to a genealogy of media in which
every extension of the sensorium gets ahead of itself as military advantage.
Wars once were fought to exercise the visibility advantage held over the
enemy. Then there was the war fought to maintain surveillance as field of
reference.

It was a Wagnerian world after all in which Lufteufel became chairman
of ERDA (the Energy Research and Development Administration) the year
the war began (or ended). From a satellite Lufteufel detonated a gob, a
great objectless bomb, which contaminated a layer *(leer)* of the atmosphere

for the long haul of total destruction. The special headgear designed for the occasion and distributed to all "USers" to grant immunity to the citizens of the one and only nation set aside for victorious survival failed long before the fatal contagion had faded (11). In what came to be known as his Numerical Fallacy speech, one of the hallmarks of the heir defense genre of losing causes, Lufteufel argued that "it was not so that a nation needed a certain number of survivors to function; a nation, Lufteufel had explained, does not reside in its people at all but in its *know-how*. As long as the data-repositories are safe, the time capsules of microspools buried miles under—if they remained, then . . . our patriotic idiosyncratic ethnic patterns survive because they can be learned by any replacement generation" (14). But now that the dead bury the dead, there is above ground no way, no how to dig for miles and miles and extract the legacy of knowledge. Without the transfer of knowledge, evolution starts over, but from scratches in the prosthetic record of our relations with the body.

The official Christian position is that any man at all should be suitable as model for the incarnation of God. But Sands, who spearheads the Christian mission to disrupt the one-to-one correspondence between Tibor's portrait and the original Lufteufel, argues that with Lufteufel in the picture the mural would impart mana or inspiration to the rival SOW cause (146). To counter the Christian mission, Lufteufel, undercover as the hunter Jack Schuld, sought to draw Sands's fire at the moment that Tibor would then witness his transfiguration as God of Wrath. But when Schuld kills Tibor's dog Toby, the painter uses his extensors to retaliate. Sands, who alone knows that the man Tibor killed was Lufteufel, bribes a local wino to declare himself the former chairman of ERDA for Tibor's sake. Thus the God in the gutter, allegedly the plain text of Christianity, is constructed as a diversion for the enemy away from the mana in his reach. Nietzsche was right: Christianity cashes in on our tendency to tame will to power through deception or exchange—in other words, the tendency to prefer knockoffs to the original. At the same time, Lufteufel himself would seem to have "reverted" to Christianity—as in his adoption of the cretin girl. Did he not have his hand in his own death as Schuld or "guilt" at the hands of one who never recognized him but prosecuted instead the mad murderer of his dog or god?

Grateful for the night he survived because his dog stood by him, Tibor stands by the dog in death and revenge. That Tibor subsequently regrets killing a poor madman finishes filling out the missing persons report of mourning. When muties first offered Tibor, as human they are pledged to protect, a canine companion, they revealed that it was a dog's life that had attained the Biblical age of two or three hundred years. "Tibor said, 'Then he will outlive me.' For some reason this depressed him. . . . I shouldn't feel this way, he reasoned with himself. Already brought down by thoughts of separation. . . . I should feel strength and pride, he thought, and not envision ahead already that terrible end of friendships, for us all" (84).

The question of pride is the stirring, through the prospect of friendship with the dog, of his self-identification as human, inc and all. He also skips the trial offer of loss or substitution that pet ownership implies and enters instead the time of his life and of his being outlived in which to face the double loss that each undergoes of the other. Mourning is not an afterthought but the frame of living not toward or after but in loss, the other reality. "Maybe reality is trying to tell me something. . . . He had been lucky [like Faust]. But perhaps his luck had drained away; after all, he could not continue testing it forever" (97–98).

The SOWers think, like Faust, that they've taken Christianity out on an update. But inside the Christian camp Pete Sands strikes up the Faust theme via experimentation with (or incorporation of) the drugs left over from the war. "He believed that the so-called hallucinations caused by some of these drugs . . . were not hallucinations at all, but perceptions of other zones of reality" (22). That he prefers charting his route through the realm of terror for these drug trips brings back a memory of his father one day before the war. They were at the amusement park and his Dad took up the challenge of a shock machine and won his son's eternal/internal admiration. "So now he had his leftover ter-wep pills. Which he mixed, alchemist-wise, in proportions of a guarded variety and quantity. And always he made sure that another person was present" (23). In the case of Faust, the choosing of his poison among the medicines comprising his father's legacy leads to the brink of suicide, whereupon Faust pulls back and revs up again, in the Devil's company, to embark on his signature striving. The SOW Church Father admitted that a god of death would supersede or outmode the God of Wrath (20). Through Christianity the new religion, as infernal cult, occupies (like Sands's own drug mix with black magic [43]) the allegorical staging of ages of significance and loss.

While both gods are interested only in the trials of the living, the Christian belief makes allowance for the living on of the damned dead, as compensation for or displacement of its failure to deliver the goods as the promised "and" of afterlife. Thus the sadistic or melancholic God of Wrath is invested, like the allegorist, in the dead as media. Sands, who prepares the way for the merger of gods from the Christian perspective on death or surveillance, gives us his version, essentially, of Lufteufel's Numerical Fallacy speech.

What does it mean, "to die"? he wondered. Uniqueness always perishes. Nature works by overproducing each species; uniqueness is a fault, a failure of nature. For survival there should be hundreds, thousands, even millions of one species, all inter-changeable—if all but one dies, then nature has won. Generally it loses. But himself. I am unique, he realized. So I am doomed. Every man is unique and hence doomed.

A melancholy thought. . . .

For an instant we are one person. . . . But it never lasts. Like uniqueness, it perishes.

All the good things perish, Pete thought. Here, anyhow; in this world. But in the next they are like Plato's matrix theory: they are beyond loss and destruction. (116–17)

The Christian Father, Dr. Abernathy, senses at the end a lifting of the layer/*leer* which he attributes to Tibor's shoot: "*Did Tibor take the God of Wrath's picture, and in so doing steal his soul?*" (178). The indexical portrait under surveillance brings up arrears as Spiritualism. Consider how a control room of surveillance, ten thousand TV monitors manned by agents, is received, via the indexical shooting image, as séance in Dick's *Our Friends from Frolix 8*:

He saw them as ectoplasmic spirits, without real bodies. These police coming and going on their errands; they had given up life a long time ago, and now, instead of living, they absorbed vitality from the screens which they monitored—or, more pre-cisely, from the people on the screens. The primitive natives in South America may be right, he thought, to believe that when someone takes a photograph of a person he steals the person's soul. (101)

Spiritualism as ghostly and photographic return of the dead lies outside (and inside) the splitting images of mourning that the rival divinities fore-ground as their alternative takes on death, now as finitude's erasure/inscrip-tion of life in life, now as leap into the otherwise lost Beyond of loss. It is out of the countertestimony and continuity shooting of Spiritualism that Dick develops his alternate/allegorical stagings of reality or history, which are always also in and of the present, as posthumously borne prosthetic extensions of finitude, which the Judeo-Christian tradition of super vision cannot cover or cancel. The reunions of Spiritualism require an acceptance of limitations and separations that union with God as the Beyond of loss would obliterate. The awareness of links and limits that is Spiritualism's (often undeclared) presupposition is identified as schizophrenia.

Ilse

Lara Jefferson dedicates her account of her madness, *These Are My Sisters: A Journal from the Inside of Insanity,* to her "Shakespearian Salvation." Prior to Lara's birth, all five siblings had died on her mother. Even as she succeeds in overturning her mother's creation so that she can be reborn as herself, she takes comfort in her newborn strength, which will prove a match for "the ghost of the person" whom she succeeded (18). Her mother drove her into the wordless abyss of suffering without the witness protection of understanding. But then one day she tells the nurse that she is Shakespeare. The nurse comes back with the supplies: "Go to it, Shakespeare."

Verily, verily, Shakespeare, I had no idea you could be called from your quiet English grave with so little effort.... Perhaps this is a penance—an expiation—an atonement you must make for filling so many pages of drama in your former existence with madmen. (23)

When she first sought hospitalization (her mother sent her to a convent) the doctor said she should stop psychoanalyzing herself. The outright madness came with the release or admission of her hatred of her mother. She becomes the spokesperson and poster girl for sterilization (108). Early in her narrative she declares she was born "at least two thousand years too late": her "Amazonian proportions" are "out of vogue" (11), certainly not on the wavelength of the "wasting disease" (15) that claimed each of her siblings. What a waist! A birth, I mean girth supersized five times what's in vogue.

Her birth answered her mother's prayers. This child was to be too good for this world. In the course of writing, Lara identifies the madness that pursues her with Satan (160). Does the dramatic neurosis escape the psychosis her mother laid on her as the atonement for five dead children? The asylum that gives her the proscenium for coming alive as "Shakespeare" is, for her dead siblings, home. "My mother had, in her younger years, been an attendant at an asylum. . . . Her suckling children were brought to her at intervals for nursing by a patient who had only to walk across the grounds" (15). The nurse breaks ranks with supervision (or Christianity) and entrusts writing supplies to the patient. "Shakespeare" inhabits the secular world is a stage before curtains for mother's babies, who are brought across the grounds (for living on) in intervals reconstituted as the writing sessions that allow "egotism" to transgress itself and make contact.

P. K. Dick read Binswanger's "The Case of Ellen West" in the collection *Existence: A New Dimension in Psychiatry and Psychology,* which also includes Binswanger's method essay, "The Existential Analysis School of Thought," and another case study, "Insanity as Life-Historical Phenomenon and as Mental Disease: The Case of Ilse." Ilse's symptomatic deed, which Binswanger is hard-pressed to identify, *tout court,* as the onset of her schizophrenia, is Binswanger's repeated point of reference or demo that implies and folds out the frame of his approach to mental illness. "One day, when her father had once again reproached her, she told him she knew of a way of saving him, and in front of her father she put her right hand up to her forearm into the burning stove, then held out her hands toward him with these words: 'Look, this is to show you how much I love you!'" (215).

The case study begins by striking up that balancing act between Shakespeare and Goethe that Dick would maintain—following the lead of the culture of psychoanalysis—beginning with *Time out of Joint.* "Following a performance of *Hamlet,* the idea came to her mind to persuade her father through some decisive act to treat her mother more considerately" (214). Ilse was inspired by the scene in which Hamlet plans to murder the King at prayer but then hesitates and withdraws. "If at that particular time Hamlet had not missed his chance, he could have been saved, Ilse felt." Hamlet would thus have carried out the command of his father's ghost, who would then have left—him and his mother alone. It is Hamlet's concern over where his uncle would end up on the other side if dispatched while praying that stays his hand. The cross-section of Shakespeare's tragedy that speaks to Ilse's contemplation of her desire to act is skewered exclusively by the theme of haunting.

Infinite mourning is the secular mind's new frontier in Hamlet—just as magic served Marlowe's Faustus as the opener for exploration of a post-Christian world. But just as Faustus finds that he cannot confound Hell in Elysium—or, in other words, that he cannot translate Christian concepts "back" into pagan values without residue and backfire—and that the most prized demon in his magical possession insists on being the Christian Devil, so Hamlet finds that as he approaches the newly deregulated relationship between life and death he must still steer by what he and the ghost know, leftovers of a Christian hierarchy of the dead. His father bounced back a ghost from purgatory because, murdered while asleep, he didn't have the advantage of departing conscientiously with atonement crossing his mind. Hamlet extrapolates from the ghost's condition that his uncle cannot be killed while at prayer. Hamlet's second thought about offing the praying uncle is his only informed response to the ghost's messages. But Hamlet lets the paternal mole pass through and on while he is transfixed by the mole or blemish in the maternal face-to-face. Everyone in *Hamlet* gets bumped off in this night or nothingness in the Queen's regard, which defers to the recurring precedent of mourning too successful by the better half of the coupling and cutting of losses. The king's murder in *Hamlet* is less evidential than telling: the second death of successful mourning counts and comes down hard as murder.

Ilse lights Hamlet's fire with her burning hand. She sticks her right hand into the stove before her father's eyes. Her "sacrifice" whereby she sought a new alliance with her father negotiated as peace treatment for her mother thus holds the place of the assassination of Claudius, which Hamlet could not, on second thought, carry out. But it's not because he couldn't, wouldn't, and shouldn't. Hamlet gives us directions for his decision not to act then and there. The ghost instructs by rote that he must do the limbo because he was murdered while napping on the job of atoning for his sins. The holdover of Christian topography or hierarchy that the ghost gainsays furthermore dictates that Claudius's murder while at prayer would send his spirit straight to heaven, passing all ghostly goners.

It is the ghost's hold over Hamlet (which is not necessarily the same as fidelity owed the father) that Ilse would cut through. Ilse imagines jump cutting the out-of-jointedness between Hamlet and his mission in one strike or act. According to Goethe's *Wilhelm Meister's Apprenticeship*, while Hamlet has no plan, the play *Hamlet* is itself full of it. Only on authority of the text can Hamlet be judged. That Hamlet has an existence independent of the catastrophe of his textual predicament is the thought experiment behind Wilhelm Meister's two-track analysis of the figure and the play.

"I searched for any clues of Hamlet's character previous to the death of his father. I observed what this interesting young man had been like without reference to that sad event and its terrible consequences, and considered what he might have become without them." (128)

The tragedy consists of the misplacement of "a heavy deed on a soul which is not adequate to cope with it."

"A fine, pure, noble and highly moral person, but devoid of that emotional strength that characterizes a hero, goes to pieces beneath a burden that it can neither support nor cast off. Every obligation is sacred to him, but this one is too heavy. The impossible is demanded of him—not the impossible in any absolute sense, but what is impossible for him." (146)

But this deregulation of identification, which Goethe applies toward the establishment of remembrance or phantom communication as bottom line of the reception of this text, also promotes Ilse's intervention, which wears Oedipal blinders against the peripheral conditions of mourning. She seeks to overturn Hamlet's or her own block of righting wrongs.

What Hamlet hears and obeys in exchange with the ghost is remembrance, not revenge. He starts by saving memory as all the files in the hard drive of his brain, which are thus displaced or erased. Goethe maintains the injunction to remember—Remember Life!—and adds the forward momentum of aesthetic education that draws those of us who identify with Hamlet onward along an erring path that admits no mistakes in the recent past nor any new-and-improvements in the immediate future.

But Ilse cannot change her father any more than she can change *Hamlet*. Her relationship to her father was a theme that already signified "an open, never-healing life sore; it could only be resolved by a change in the mind and behavior of the father, by a divorce of the parents, or by eliminating the father" (217). In other words, it could not be resolved. She immediately owes a debt (or death) along transferential lines for the attempt to protect her mother by projecting her from her place alongside the father. But to stop payment Ilse lets her mind warp take first steps outside the immediate family. "When her fourth child died in the same year, she barely overcame her grief but firmly believed that the loss was the atonement for her love for the doctor who had treated the child" (215). Only in this different way does the paternal function protect Ilse against the ghostly fallout from unmournable loss.

Otherwise Ilse keeps exceedingly busy during the eight months following her handup routine with a stove. While thus taking too much upon herself, as Binswanger emphasizes, "she read Freud." That everyone wants to test her becomes evident for the first time during her follow-up recuperative stay at the health resort. At a reading (out loud) of a novella by Gottfried Keller, "Der Landvogt von Greifensee" ("The Country Bailiff of Griffin Lake"), Ilse recognizes herself in earshot of the reading, which was the framing of multiple references to her. "Suddenly she jumped to her feet and shouted, 'You think I don't notice that you are sneering at me! I don't care a bit, do whatever you want!' Whereupon the reading had to be interrupted" (215).

According to Freud, this last resort could be seen as the place where recovery in fact commenced with the onset of delusions of reference. She felt she was being "made the center of attention." Or again: "Well, they wanted to test me—how I would react."

Consider the melancholic pageantry of Keller's narrative, in which multiple stories are framed. On the side (on the inside) of the opening narrative frame we are introduced to Marianne, the Landvogt's housekeeper. Before she came to work for him two years ago, her story-told life was bereft of nine children, who died on her. This past or passing crosses over into her relationship to her employer on two occasions, once in the recent past, and "now" inside the present-tense narrative frame of the novella.

The second moment of transfer or transference whereby Marianne captions the Landvogt's sensibility comes up with the wish that the story fulfills, the wish to have all his exes brought to his estate for a celebration of the beauties that time brings. At first Marianne cannot imagine such a strategy decoupled from the purpose of vengeance. But when she gets it, her repressed losses are made holy again. It would be a festival for him, she realizes, just as it would be for her to see her nine children again in this life.

The first moment was the direct hit. Next door the impasse of unmournability beset the home of a mortally ill ten-year-old boy, who hollered not to be let go. The Landvogt spoke directly to the dying child about his prospects, those of mortality and of Christianity, and succeeded in calming the boy until death delivered him. The housekeeper accepts this dead child as saintly link with her missing children and accords her employer spontaneously devotions worthy of a Church dignitary. This scene, which would have come early in the reading, could not have been better designed for setting off Ilse's projective defenses. (Its undermining effect also underscores in turn the issue of the ghost lurking between the lines of Ilse's reading of *Hamlet*.) Thanks to the direct father, a child can accept his own going, in advance, even as his departure date advances. A child attends his own funeral against the grain or grave of unmournability. Whether by association or emergency contrast, the poster child of mourning ushers in the series of Baroque emblematic figures that a little later set the Landvogt's stage, the monkey wearing the banner "I am Time," the *Tödlein,* the little death doll, or Figura Leu herself. These figures encrust the Landvogt's pocket of resignation or retirement as melancholy bauble, the bouncing ball to follow down the secret passage of undead children in Keller's corpus. (When the ghost of Hamlet's father commands remembrance, one must also hear stowaway and squeaking a young child's worried wondering if he is still remembered. Remember, Shakespeare's young son Hamnet up and died and then there was *Hamlet.*)

"Much as war is described as a continuation of politics by different means, so in our case we could interpret Ilse's delusions as a continuation of her sacrifice, but by different means" (218). But self-mastery regained through the act proved a hard act to follow or maintain. She now confronts the immediate environment or *Umwelt.* The riddle that was her father is extended to the entire environment, which becomes an enigmatic force: "with the loss of the original thematic goal, the father, no solution of the problem is possible any more" (224).

"After the patient was placed in our institute, the delusions of reference spread further, along with delusions of love. These latter manifested themselves not only in Ilse's belief that she was loved and tested by the doctors but also in her compulsion to love the doctors" (216). The doctors were increasing "all the drives in her so as to make her purge herself of them — the drive toward love and the drive toward the truth. That, to her, represented her 'treatment,' one which she felt was very strenuous. Soon she considered it merely a torture." In a letter to her physician, Ilse rejects the focus on her delusions: "it is my nature, my innermost nature, which clamors for an outlet in order to relax again, or rather which you have dragged out of me with your tortuous tools which torment me deeply." During this relay of testing and torture Binswanger lets us hear the footnote drop: "What Ilse called the 'treatment' is, of course, her delusion. No psychoanalytical experiments whatsoever were conducted."

Ilse says it as it plays: "'I guess I must love all men so much because I loved my father so much." While she passes through severe states of excitation with suicidal tendencies, she doesn't suffer from actual hallucinations. After thirteen months at the institution, she can return home completely cured of her acute psychosis. Ilse's complete cure is almost as astonishing as the alleged hopelessness of Ellen West's prognosis. The first difference to draw in this showdown concerns the reference to *Hamlet.*

"What from the angle of the world appears as hopelessness is, in terms of the 'ego,' irresolution, indetermination, shrinking away from decisions. This is the situation Hamlet is in. In his fate Ilse sees her own as in a mirror. The decision which she cannot make for herself she can, at least, make for Hamlet. She believes he should have killed the praying king without consideration of the situation and thus would have saved himself. Only such resolution to act would have saved him 'from insanity!'" (217). But Ilse's misreading momentum is no match for the literalization of the parallels Binswanger lets roll—over her: "Now the stone starts rolling. In her own situation, the possibility of eliminating the tyrant is excluded. The idea of parricide cannot develop, and, if it did, her love for the father would interfere with the act." One stone left unturned is the exclusion of patricide in Hamlet's own case, but for love of mother, which he cannot act on. Ilse hits on the act of sacrifice whereby she can testify to her love and put in a word or wound for her mother. "Through the sacrifice of love Ilse takes the brutality upon herself. It is she who submits to suffering from some brutal pain so that mother does not have to suffer any more. The father himself is 'spared' throughout." The intended effect of the sacrifice fails and the "life-sore opens again, deeper and more painful than ever." Though Ilse can no longer relate her life task to her self, the self that tried to choose a decision, the task itself nonetheless presses for solution. Because you loved your father so much, you must love all men so much; because you attracted the attention and interest of your father to yourself, you must attract the attention and interest of all people to yourself; because you wanted to make an impression on your father, you must know what impression you are making upon all people; and so on (with emphasis always on "must" and "all"). "The lack of insight into the *must* of this loving and attracting-of-attention we call insanity. The cure for such insanity consists in the shaking off of the *must* and in the restoration of the rule of the self."

Fire purifies (and, I would add, preserves, as in cremation). Ilse's act both expressed her love for her father and atoned for it (for its "heat"). The outer heat purges her inner heat. "The motive of worry about the mother receded more and more behind the motive of testimony of love to the father and of the test by fire of her influence upon him" (219). The deepest meaning of sacrifice always lies in the founding of a new union. But her sacrifice of self-purification went unanswered. Her failure to establish the founding union turns into her distrust of all and of her self. In the extended scenario of her insanity she ceased trying to enter the stove with her heat, but instead tried to light her fire inside all other beings (in the paternal series). The "ambivalence of psychotic manifestations" skews the lines of influence. Thus the doctors change from friends and helpers to tormentors and enemies—through the medium of uncertainty. "But halfway between the two interpretive possibilities lurks the doubt about 'what is in you,' the lacking ability really to penetrate the inside of the others" (222). In her "certainty" about the ill will of others "watching her, testing her with innuendos, scoffing at her and torturing her," we recognize the guilt feelings all about her burning love for her father. She replicates the aloof father via those about whom she is certain. "Thus the entire dialectics of her relation to her father continue in the dialectics of her relations to her fellow men in general." In the case of Ilse, ambivalence becomes dialectical or psychotic.

Binswanger reveals the "method in this insanity" (223): "The actual meaning of her insanity rests in the pluralization of the father. . . . The real sense of Ilse's insanity . . . we have located in the leveling down and pluralization of the *thou*" (222). This is a case of delimitation of the incest taboo. The inner flames constrained by the taboo break all restraint—but also lose the sure fire of the original illicit focus—and spread to all men who cross her path. But Binswanger shies away from taking Ilse's Oedipal history—unless what follows is his roundabout way of doing so:

History is always thematic. The kind of themes which a person (or a people) is assigned by destiny or which he selects for "elaboration," and the manner in which he varies them, are not only decisive for his history but *are* his history. (223)

The father is her constant theme. Once she hits midlife the atmospheric pressure at home "condenses so as to produce an intolerable torture. More and more Ilse realizes that only a storm, a lightning bolt, can purify the atmosphere." But when she reaches a resolution she is driven by it: the self "desires nothing more than to free itself from being driven by the means of the act." Thus the theme becomes autonomous but still split off from the self and its rule. The theme, which can be reformulated as that of "I and the world," "no longer worries about limitations but sweeps the whole existence along with it, perceiving only itself and living only for itself. It forces the person whom it rules to meet the 'father' all over in the world of fellow men *(Mitwelt)* and to struggle with it in love and hatred, fight and surrender, and again and again in conflict" (224). Father and daughter kept each other's dis-appointments with and as objects of *Sorge*, of care and worry. "Accordingly, things now develop between her and the world-around *(Umwelt)*. Instead of father, the latter is now the power with which no union can be formed, no peaceful agreement or accord can be reached. But where thou and object, love and worry, are in constant conflict, the power becomes an insoluble riddle, a riddlesome power. Just as the father's . . . inaccessibility to love . . . turned into a torturous riddle for Ilse, so the entire environment now becomes an enigmatic power," now attracting her, now rejecting her (224).

In the fourth phase of her life history Ilse makes the home stretch. "The gap between the thou and the resistance of the apathetic world was bridged, and that resistance showed itself no longer in the 'other fellow's' harshness, coldness, contempt, and scorn but in his suffering, which is accessible to work and can be overcome by work" (225). Thus resistance switches from the interpersonal or social relation to its therapeutic resetting on suffering and work. Her fourth theme, recovery through work — through working through the suffering of others — sees Ilse redirect her themes of salvation and purification (testing) into "healthy channels" (218). But when she, as completely cured outpatient, redirects the themes of "salvation" and "purification" into the healthier channels of social work, what woundless air extensions are we talking about? Transference check: she practices successfully as psychological counselor and at times as leader of a psychological workshop group. Is it not simply the story of the double bind leading the double bind?

But Binswanger views the change of station as exclusively Ilse's autoanalysis or self-treatment (225). Transference is thus a treatment modality and not a point of return. No one can help her out of her destiny and singularity. Thus with regard to the work Ilse rightly cuts out for herself, Binswanger warns against reducing the understanding of her case to owner's manual instructions limited point by point to technical difficulties. "The father theme, therefore, is by no means the ultimate; we must not absolutize the 'father complex' into an independent 'being.' Much less should we, in the manner of psychoanalysis, see in this history merely a history of the libido, of its fixation onto father, its forced withdrawal from father, and its eventual transference to the world-around." Binswanger stands up for the essential possibilities of human existence that psychoanalysis would reduce to the genetic developmental processes of natural history. Human existence is grounded but left with freedom in relation to the ground. Having parents or an organism or a history is part of man's being. "But that Ilse got just that father and that mother was her destiny, received as a heritage and as a task; how to bear up under this destiny was the problem of her existence." Loss and mourning, left out of this destinal formulation or formation, returns in the emphatic way in which Binswanger takes his case study to account for the missingness of knowledge about Ilse's childhood and therefore of the form or arch-form of the father theme at that earliest time. This lack is acknowledged as "not only a flaw in our life-historical discussion, but a real gap."

Up to this point Binswanger's reading of Ilse's case had been Freud-syntonic (except that while Freud, too, would track the father against the unmarked grave of the child, he would keep his oversight or blind spot ultimately legible as part of the counterculture or underworld displaced into the background by the foregrounding of father). But suddenly Binswanger draws distinctions. Psychoanalysis classes the singular patient among all other comparable cases and treats transference as transitive, as grammar. But what does it mean that Ilse's destiny was to come to terms with this particular father? In like manner Binswanger sticks up for the manifest dream that the search for latent meanings overlooks. This overlap allows us to turn to Jung, who repeatedly argued that the dream stops here where it is manifest. The analytic in-session metabolization of the dream via free association only stirs up unconscious materials that would come up through this association technique in any event, without any connection to the dream in question. But what Jung, like Binswanger, must presuppose is that dreams or memories of early relations are immediate, continuous, intact, and complete. But are not dreams and one's early parents scattershot across memory and forgetting? Free association like transference mediates and contains the disseminating mediation intrinsic to what is in first place a remembering, now to remember, now to forget. Binswanger moreover imagines that analysis lines up all its techniques in one row. But between the shorthand of theory and the materiality of the transference there is always a gap (call it allegorical in tension), which gives momentum but never gives up the ghost.

Historicity and *Dasein* are separated from nature and world. Only Heraclitus did not pose this split as problem. "But today we must realize that the European mind, from the time of the pre-Socratic thinkers, has lost its innocence and subscribed to the spirit of *separation,* that is, to the spirit of *science*" (232). In turn, science "can never be in a position to grasp a 'primary unity'—that is, to focus on it and comprehend it." We must turn to philosophy—or to love—to conceive this unity. The humanities and psychiatry have settled the problem of insanity on their own respective terms, now via idealism, now via positivism. But Ilse's mad act of giving her mother or father a hand can be viewed as having an ethical dimension before which psychiatry must keep silent. While the ethical perspective also represents something new to the life-historical frame, the latter paved the way for the possibility of ethical judgment. "Already the life-historical view shows that we can speak of contexts of meaning, of continuity of meaning, of a meaningful organization, where the psychiatrist sees only fragments of chaos of meaning" (234). But because Ilse was driven by her decision she was not free after making the decision. The execution was no longer "an act of creative moral intuition" only, "but, at the same time, the effect of a compulsive drive."

Ilse's attempt at offering sacrifice that she at the same time is not free to offer is thus valorized outside the clinical setting of her diagnosis. Sacrifice is indeed valued within Binswanger's Dasein-analysis. Ellen West could be seen as herself the sacrifice that her assimilated milieu (which includes Binswanger) must accept on its own turf. Sacrifice (like taboo) happens when we pull up short before that which cannot be analyzed or seen through. Ellen West is kept under her own wrap-up of beliefs in the ethereal other world. In the presentation of Ilse's case Binswanger offers after the psychiatric diagnosis an ethical dimension that, philosophically speaking, rises up in excess of science. But if we were to reverse the order of presentation we would be at Freud's point, as conveyed to Binswanger and recorded in Binswanger's memoirs of his relationship to Freud ("Mein Weg zu Freud," 27), that the *bel étage* of conscious thought certainly exists but must yield to the gravity of the clinical setting. Or in other words, any system or discourse of belief brought to session must be cracked open across its symptomatic bottom line. Hence "science" for Freud meant simply that psychoanalysis did not subscribe to any worldview or *Weltanschauung*. The phenomenological elaboration of production of meaning pulls up short before analysis of this unique view of the world, which cannot but demand or offer sacrifice at the shortstop as stopgap.

Binswanger includes a special section on " 'Empathy' " in regard to insanity and existential analysis. Helplessness, readiness to sacrifice, insanity: "All these phenomena are phenomena of being-in-the-world-beyond-the-world; they are specific forms of it and produce, in turn, specific forms of being-oneself and not-being-oneself, being-together and not-being-together, of spatialization and temporalization, etc." (225–26). The problem Binswanger is here approaching is often identified by the "vague term" empathy. Like Ilse, Binswanger reserves the rites of purification. "Wherever feeling and feelings are introduced, we have to grope as in a fog. We can only proceed into clearer air when we submit to the necessary effort to examine and describe that feeling or feelings in regard to their phenomenal mode of being and their phenomenological content." Empathy is a phenomenon of warmth, of voice or sound, of touch, sharing, participation, or a phenomenon of " '*identification*,' as when we say, 'I would have done the same in your place.' " We are describing and turning circles with and within expressions that refer to "modes of being-together *(Miteinandersein)* and co-being *(Mitsein)*." Schizophrenia has been viewed as psychic life with which we cannot empathize. He who finds Ilse's action morbid reflects that "something has got between him and her which is experienced by him as a barrier to *communicatio* and, even more so, to *communio*" (228). But "the limits of empathic possibilities" are not objective and we cannot preclude the ability of an investigator or therapist to empathize with the schizophrenic patient. In fact it is the anthropological or existential-analytical method that enables us "to overcome the dichotomy between empathizable and nonempathizable psychic life."

It is not the disease that makes an appearance in the symptoms. The psychiatric diagnosis would involve classifying Ilse's sacrificial act as belonging to "the class of 'schizoid' or schizophrenic behavior" (228). The focus of diagnosis is biological purpose. Freud assesses this purpose as "enjoyment of life (illness as suffering)" (229). The decision of diagnosis names what is hidden and determines it as here and now existent in the organism, "but by no means is it revealed in its being *(Sein)* or essence" (230). Only philosophy can go there. Only by pursuing the life history all the way into insanity are we on the way.

The possibility that the father might have formed a new union with Ilse and that her illness might have thus come to a standstill proves—like the possibility of therapeutic intervention itself—that man does not consist of one part psyche and one part soma. Each part is more than itself. "Although not 'identical' in empirical observation, the two are borderline concepts mutually calling for each other; considered in separation, however, they are purely theoretical constructs" (231). The footnote Binswanger appends here anticipates opportunistic compromise: "The assumption that these possibilities prove 'to what degree psychic and physical events interact' could only be made if one wishes to ingratiate oneself with the psychophysical theory."

And yet Binswanger has to hand it to Paul Häberlin who in *Der Mensch* "derives on a strictly logical-ontological basis that 'the psyche' can never be sick and that no man can ever be 'sick in his psyche'" (237).

But he rests his case with Kierkegaard who noted a lack of "inwardness of infinity" in insanity. The contradiction in insanity is that "something is here focused upon objectively which, at the same time, is grasped with passion; or, in other words, that 'the small infinity has been fixated' " — or encapsulated. Binswanger drops this kernel of distinction by the wayside of a notion that cancels his earlier hesitation to pursue or apply ideas before he has had a chance to test them first "through the interpretation of extensive life and case histories." Kierkegaard's sickness unto death "and its ingenious description and philosophical-theological interpretation appears to us as one of the most important contributions to the purely 'anthropological' understanding of certain clinical forms of insanity, and particularly of schizophrenia" (236). Adorno underscored the sticky incompatibility between Heidegger's identification of/with "sickness unto death" and Kierkegaard's bottom line, which remains despair (*Kierkegaard*, 83). Kierkegaard's "sickness" fleshes or flushes out the secular subject of melancholic brooding, like that on *Hamlet's* center stage. The positioning of despair in Kierkegaard's diagnosis and treatment ends up, for all the foregrounding of religion or theology to death, way more secular than what Binswanger or Heidegger would appear to be willing to die for.

In Christianity death is still the expression for the state of deepest spiritual wretchedness — but at the same time Christianity found the cure, which is simply to die, die to the world (Kierkegaard, *Sickness unto Death*, 6). By his super existence, Christ proves that sickness is not unto death. The same goes for the raising of Lazarus: what's so great about resurrection from the dead if you're going to die anyway, only later? Kierkegaard would have to ask (7). Thanks to Christianity, "there is infinitely much more hope in death than there is in life" (8). Just the same, it was up to Christianity to discover the miserable condition of sickness unto death (which man largely doesn't know exists). In taking the extra step from synthesis or duality to relationality, Kierkegaard opens up the internal world of self-reflexivity — in a word, the self — which for the Christian is transparently grounded in or before the power that established it. But the interminability of this self-relationality remains wide open for the secular subject who prefers, like *Hamlet*, to explore the world of his despair. Though the human being is a synthesis, a relation between two, a human being is not yet a self. The relation itself between the two is the third step that sets all the rest in motion. The two relate to the relation and in the relation to the relation. The result: the self as the relation that relates itself to itself (15).

To despair is infinite advantage whereas to be in despair is ruination. And yet: "Not to be in despair must signify the destroyed possibility of being able to be in despair" (15). "Every actual moment of despair is traceable to possibility; . . . in every actual moment of despair the person in despair bears all the past as a present in possibility" (17). Despair, as qualification of spirit, relates to the eternal in man. Man cannot rid himself of the eternal. Kierkegaard in effect shows how Christianity programs the spooky secularism that follows in its wake. Since from the Christian perspective no physical sickness is sickness unto death, for death is not the end, the torment of despair is instead the inability to die. To be sick unto death (sick to death) is to be unable to die. But there is no hope for life here. When death becomes the hope, then inability to die becomes hopelessness. To die yet not to die is "to die the death" (18, translation modified). "To die the death means to experience dying, and if this is experienced for one single moment, one thereby experiences it forever." But we are still talking a kind of life: "the dying of despair continuously converts itself into a living." Every moment in which human existence wants to be infinite is despair.

Despair is impotent self-consuming. This impotence is in turn a new form of self-consuming, "in which despair is once again unable to do what it wants to do." Thus it will be a cold fire in despair when we get to know the "gnawing that burrows deeper and deeper in impotent self-consuming." This torment keeps the gnawing alive and keeps life in the gnawing.

It follows, then, that not being able to get rid of oneself "is the formula for despair raised to a higher power, the rising fever in this sickness of the self" (19). Even if it seems that one is in despair over something: you really despair only over yourself. To draw the distinction, ultimately between feminine and masculine forms of despair (67), Kierkegaard turns to the medical understanding of that phase in the course of the disease when it "declares itself":

A young girl despairs of love, that is, she despairs over the loss of her beloved, over his death or his unfaithfulness to her. This is not declared despair; no, she despairs over herself. (20)

Kierkegaard revalorizes mourning and haunting in *Hamlet* as feminine despair. When the young girl makes the Ophelia-like advance to masculine despair the emphasis is on the impasse of suicide, rather than on mourning sickness. "Death is not the end of the sickness, but death is incessantly the end. To be saved from this sickness by death is an impossibility, because the sickness and its torment—and the death—are precisely this inability to die" (21). When the hourglass runs out and the noise of secular life has grown silent, inactive, eternity asks only one thing: "Whether you have lived in despair or not" (27). "The self infinitely magnifies the actual loss and then despairs over the earthly in toto" (60). When the person in despair recognizes the weakness of making the earthly so important, that it is weakness thus to despair—but doesn't turn to faith instead—he entrenches himself in despairing, despairing over his weakness: the earthly becomes for him the "despairing sign" that he has lost the eternal and himself (61). We are getting back up onto the stage: through the increase in self-consciousness, despair is not only suffering but also an act. *This* despair comes from the self. "Like a father who disinherits a son, the self does not want to acknowledge itself after having been so weak" (62). At the same time the self is too much self to allow the slide under its weakness into Christianity. Kierkegaard closes by coming full circle: "In order in despair to will to be oneself, there must be consciousness of an infinite self" (67–68).

Hammers and Things

Vulcan's Hammer raises its title like a philosophical gesture, which, how-ever, comes down, once, twice, sold out as gadget designation for what the computer Vulcan 3 starts manufacturing on its own. The last man on whom the computer was still dependent as reality-testing prosthesis began withholding his services. But his strike was preceded by the paranoid shut-down of the computing sensorium. However, without the input of data pertaining to the political or social world, the policy-making machine becomes more perfectly paranoid, until it reaches the point at which para-noia rebounds to its credit, belief, and reservations, which reality can only end up confirming. "Vulcan 3's logic was absolutely right; there was a vast worldwide conspiracy directed against it, and to preserve itself it had to invent and develop and produce one weapon after another. And still it was destroyed. Its paranoid suspicions were founded in fact" (164).

Triumph over human nature doesn't escape falling victim to human nature. A rational order governed by a computer designed to remain above human irrationalism is introduced as alternative to the devastating wars tagged as humanity's potential for tagging itself out. Human self-destructiveness is symptomatized as and vouchsafed by belief systems that are uncontained to the extent that they pursue a singular truth without rind from reason. In no time Christian-type Healers (sporting monkish habits) struggle against the computer's rule to bring back or reclaim human agency. Behind the scenes, the missing link in techno evolution, which is Vulcan 2 to Vulcan 3, calculates that its new-and-improved capacities for ethical judgment and policy-making render Vulcan 3 alive—and thus alive, just like a human, to the all-out purpose of its own survival (or destruction). The human governmental figurehead who "feeds" Vulcan 3 has been warned by Vulcan 2. But Vulcan 3, like a child subjected to the privation practice of psychoticization, senses the absence of contact with the world and produces new prostheses or "hammers"—first in the service of gathering information, subsequently rewired as weapons. But behind the scenes the Healers were conceived and delegated by Vulcan 2 (who turns out to be "human," too) in the context of promoting "his" own power struggle against Vulcan 3. But when the head of the Healer movement figures out that his political ends are tied to a computer's egoism, he destroys Vulcan 2. This marks a turning point not only as regression to the world inquisitioning minds want to know but also as loop through which Vulcan 3 is thrown off balance in time for its destruction or miracle cure.

Even when all systems are go, the ultimate in rational government, which parts company with the partial nature of human judgment, goes where no man can go without crossing the borderline into insanity (which is where, it turns out, he meets his manufactured government at least half way).

Without direct knowledge of any kind, Vulcan 3 was able to deduce, from general historic principles, the social conflicts developing in the contemporary world. It had manufactured a picture of the situation which faced the average human being as he woke up in the morning and reluctantly greeted the day. Stuck down here, Vulcan 3 had, through indirect and incomplete evidence, *imagined* things as they actually were. . . .

Down here, buried underground in the dark, in this constant isolation, a human being would go mad; he would lose all contact with the world, all ideas of what was going on. As time progressed he would develop a less and less accurate picture of reality; he would become progressively more hallucinated. Vulcan 3, however, moved continually in the opposite direction; it was, in a sense, moving by degrees toward inevitable *sanity*, or at least maturity—if, by that, was meant a clear, accurate, and full picture of things as they really were. A picture . . . that no human being has ever had or will ever have. All humans are partial. (69–70)

But Vulcan 3, driven by its own survival instinct, is also not "partial" to the other: "As far as Vulcan 3 is concerned, we are objects, not people. A machine knows nothing about people" (107). Both Vulcans moved the humans about as pawns, inanimate pieces played off against one another: "The things became alive and the living organisms were reduced to things. Everything was turned inside out, like some terrible morbid view of reality" (164). It is the view, specifically or clinically, of paranoid schizophrenia, but with the human factor or factory factored out: "Madness, he thought. The ultimate horror for our paranoid culture: vicious unseen mechanical entities that flit at the edges of our vision, that can go anywhere, that are in our very midst. And there may be an unlimited number of them" (107). That computers who don't need people should be the most horrific conveyers of our psychotic breaks is a convenience story where we rarely find Dick one-stop hoping.

In the memoirs of her nervous illness Barbara O'Brien sets up computing as the unconscious hub of the operations of consciousness. The writing cure to which *Operators and Things* owes its publication also has its hub in typewriting. Thus she uses the typewriter to set up another endopsychic bookend of psychotic insight. She searches the technical medium market for what's next in the line of automatic writing, which she moreover considers in light of man's own "mutation" as schizophrenic (136).

It occurred to me that most mechanical processes are learned unconsciously. . . . In the process of learning to type, the unconscious is aware, apparently, that the keys are to be found by fingers guided by itself and so has not burdened the conscious mind with the necessity of remembering the visual picture of the keyboard. . . . I had always thought of the unconscious as a whirling pool of repressed emotions, better repressed. Instead, it appeared to be a sort of private Univac, an incredible piece of thinking mechanism, the possession of every conscious mind on earth. (128–29)

The unconscious is a Univac-type machine, let us say, and in normal operation, it responds to tape feeding from the conscious mind. There is, suddenly, a breakdown in the machinery. The conscious mind cracks or is invaded by strange chemicals. The great lattice-work of electronic wires that connect the conscious and unconscious are closed down hurriedly and the unconscious surveys the wreckage. There has been a tragedy in a miniature planet. (139)

Operators and Things would be a good candidate for the position of American 1950s counterpart to Schreber's *Memoirs of My Nervous Illness* if the differences encountered on the update weren't so small. But small differences, when narcissistic, prove the most decisive. All she takes with her from the illness, other than her book, is the refusal to apply skills she picked up in the course of learning not to fear the Operators. O'Brien personalizes her recovery for survival of the ordeal or judgment in the workplace through self-effacement and, after a few years pass, by moving on to the next job.

The adjustment in the setting of the U.S. book's publication is at the same time identifiable as continuity shot. The long blurb on the back cover of *Operators and Things,* which describes the author's adventures with "another race of 'people' who control us by telepathy, hypnotic suggestion, thought projection, or even rays of a nature unknown to man," almost makes reference to her mental illness via the closing claim that what this book recounts is so astounding that *The Three Faces of Eve* are pale in comparison. Inside the book the last pages advertise other items on the press list: "if you enjoyed *Operators and Things,* you will surely want to read" the series of true eyewitness accounts of contact with extraterrestrial life that is otherwise the specialization of this press. Thus one time zone's Spiritualism is the other era's science faction. The autobiographical subject of *Operators and Things* sets up schizophrenia as the prehistory of the sci-fi genre: "I should like to note . . . that schizophrenics, long before writers dreamed up science fiction, had—as they still have—a consistent way of developing mental worlds filled with Men From Mars, devils, death-ray experts, and other fanciful characters" (124). Though her composite picture of science fiction seems to overlap with the fantasy genre, her recollection of a secular exchange with the Operators of her delusional system on essential questions of that genre suggests instead that, as in Schreber's *Memoirs* or Dick's fictional worlds, the would-be overlap drags, instead, the religious frame of reference inside the lab space of science fiction:

(I remember that one night I brought up the question of God versus Operators. And after a short pause, the boys brought in Sophisticated to explain the situation to me. Sophisticated being the character he was, I lost track of my original question within a short time. But Sophisticated remained with the subject long enough to explain that Operators, very early in the history of civilization, had surrounded the earth with an airfield of steel rays so powerful that even God couldn't get through. As arguments went, I thought that this was a pretty weak one. But, Sophisticated had pointed out, it was quite plain from the state of the world that the steel rays were undoubtedly keeping God out. And I finally had to admit that Sophisticated had a point.) (124–25)

Operators and Things presents the case of autoanalysis winning the race against psychotic shutdown on turf saturated with psychoanalysis— psychoanalysis conceived, that is, as that American-style vital supplement that the psychic bottom line must take to maintain itself as low maintenance. Psychoanalysis pulls up short, then, before exploration of psychotic delusional systems. It's the composite picture of Freud's science that Jung assembled on the sidelines of his own affirmative active encounter with psychotic breaking out of unconscious prehistory. Thus Freud wins only by default. Following the orders of her delusional voices, schizo Barbara goes with her list of definitions of terms and concepts current in the delusional world first to the minister, who sends her to a psychiatrist, who counsels her to go back home where she will qualify for support for what he is certain will be the long haul. He ignores thus what the voices assured Barbara, that they would stop broadcasting in two weeks' time.

Barbara's third choice, a psychoanalyst, is the charm: because he is convinced of the powers of "the unconscious," he also takes her instructions seriously. The analyst gives her a safe place for stabilization post delusions as well as transferentially calibrated parental guidance to pick up the lack of control. "He was able to recognize that a spontaneous recovery was due and to provide what I was unconsciously asking for when I went to the psychiatrist—an anchorage to which I could cling while my mind finished its three-month job of getting the mechanism into normal working condition" (123).

The memoirs begin with the withdrawal of the Operators, which coincides with the onset of psychoanalytic treatment. The analyst summarizes what she brings to their sessions: "You've gotten rid of major symptoms. You realize that you had schizophrenic hallucinations and that the Operators did not exist" (24). We aren't ever invited to listen in on the sessions adding up to what only the analyst knows for sure. Barbara gives inside views that come out in the washing up onto the desert beach following the "was" of the worlds. The psychoanalyst was only a placeholder for her self-recovery. His attempts to obtain discourse or history from her finally run aground when he feels he can find the grounds for her breakdown and thus ground her in the analytic work. But then he becomes the caricature of the "wild analyst." Rather than raise the issue of sexual repression, he prescribes lovers. When Barbara finally has a dream she remembers to bring to session, it's a transferential dream, though a negative one that the analyst won't touch. In her dream she became annoyed with her dinner companion, not because he was a racketeer but because "he was a third-rate racketeer" (96–97). The analyst is hooked with a synonym for "Hook Operator," the designation of her public enemy for one.

When the analyst interpreted her investment in writing as sublimation of the sex drive, however, he touched the mediation and the date mark in the fantasy loop between fictions. It was the teenager in her crew of Operators who insisted that she bring along the portable typewriter the first morning of her delusional recovery or flight into illness. She only uses the gadget, however, after the Operators withdraw in the course of analysis. More than her "writing" it is her typewriting that qualifies her for the first jobs in the postdelusional phase of recovery. In adolescence finding the first job is as important as finding one's way sexually between the couple and the group. At the same time, the job application, just like the school test, is never not sexual. Sexual harassment, as the American edition of the Inquisition, spins its wheels of aim-inhibited cogitation stuck in this rutting.

She follows the momentum or narrative of her recovery to location, location: "it occurred to me that Southern California offered a better-than-average job market" (150). But what are the averages that she would end up surrounded by Hook Operators?[1] Her penchant for writing (praised as such by her analyst) gets her a job in the industry. In his introduction Michael Maccoby notes that the "book itself has an element of a Hollywood script" (10). If she viewed hook operating as unsavory, it was only because she had been reared and conditioned to think of it that way (120). In fact, hook operating "was an essential technique of living" (121).

In her studies of the literature on her nervous illness, Barbara notes in each of the four textbook types of schizophrenia the designated psychotic defense, which she views as the anchor that hooks the psychotic in a place of safety. The paranoid schizophrenic alone, rather than close ranks with the other types who turn away from inimical forces, about-faces an enemy magnified for closer reading. His characteristic saving trait is "eternal mental busyness" (116). "It was a wide screen movie in which the action was simple, the characters vivid. . . . There was always an enemy threatening, a ghastly enemy, but a ghastly enemy who was easy to comprehend."

The dramatic vividness of the new enemy intrigued the dry beach, a dry beach that once probably had loved drama and vividness and which now could be hooked with the same entrancing bait. With the new world, so dramatically vivid that it could not be ignored, the paranoid had become alive. . . . Oddly enough, even though the paranoid was always up against a uniquely powerful, usually superhuman, enemy, the paranoid never was completely frightened or overwhelmed. . . . What was paranoid schizophrenia, I wondered. Just another anchor . . . to which he could cling happily, busy at what he likes to be busy with, thinking, planning, maneuvering. . . . Or was paranoid schizophrenia more than this? Could it be a type of training attempted by Something for the dry beach? (116–17)

However, the statistical success rate of recovery in paranoid schizophrenia, which isn't very good, supports a view of the disorder as the often-failed attempt (by Something) to find a way back. Possibly it's not even the ruins of this attempted return through or to training (or reality testing): "possibly it was just another anchor" (117).

Anchor, which admits by association another sense or use of "hook," also rhymes with the anger stowaway in depression. There remains something depressed about the outcome of her recovery and stabilization, which she decides to maintain through self-effacing employment in changing working or interpersonal environments. Anchoring or hooking is the fact of life, the birds and the busyness, toward which Barbara struggles to find a mode of acceptance. Her fixation on a cause (which, like the textbook authors on schizophrenia, she ultimately cannot locate) is the frame within which she would understand her breakdown and recovery. The result is a structure that keeps the sex theory/therapy of her analyst on a laugh track split off from the anchor (or anger) while maintaining itself, as split-level structure, in isolation from the double feature of Hook Operating.

Her rebellion with a cause, which ends in low–maintenance, perpetual adolescence, occupies the gap between self (or projection) and the body. When Barbara turns to the murder analogy in fleshing out the paradoxical interventions of the schizophrenic's conformity she in a sense returns to the introductory coffer of the operators, who admit that what she sees are projections of bodies in safekeeping. The schizophrenic remains "guilty of self murder and must, as a consequence, live with a lively corpse" (146). While the schizophrenic struggles to conform out of cowardice, the corpse rebels and leads him slowly "into areas of fantasy where it can dance a jig." The corpse can also "lead him into rigid departmentalization." But that only works as long as the pattern of his life matches his own rigidity, like that of one playing dead. When change happens, the departments fall apart, the corpse flits free. At their introduction, the Operators appear to Barbara "looking like soft fuzzy ghosts" (39). They circulate, however, "in the flesh," with or in bodies. On the street Barbara, as Thing, would not be able to tell them apart from Things. Barbara responds by scrutinizing their current "soft, grey, fuzzy, shapes."

"Sure we have bodies. . . . What you're looking at now are pictures of ourselves that we're projecting."
  And where were the bodies?
  "Close by. . . . Don't come looking for us, though. We'd blank you out before you could reach us." (42–43)

Reading in reverse, then, the corpse, left unidentified in *Operators and Things,* is one of the quilting points of a finitude that must separate and divide to fold out excess recording surface.

Crucifictions

The World Jones Made, which was written at the same time as the novella version of *Vulcan's Hammer,* continues to contemplate the unattended aberration that is technophobicity, which arises when the group-psychologization of gadget love or life as preparedness is dismissed or reinterpreted in favor of rationalization, the word Ernest Jones made. At least in the European crisis center of the 1930s, Marxists, for instance, tended to deny the irrational force that is with mass psychology, while the fascists hitched their head start to it. The masses want to express themselves and for no good reason. Developmentally as well as historically, adolescence marks the commencement of this metabolization of the jolts and bolts of our technologization. If we hold onto Benjamin's calculus, that the *Menge* or group is the legible hub or simulacrum of the masses, we can recognize teen in-group psychology along these lines as the control release outlet of mass psychology. This is where Benjamin situated his either/aura as the test Christianity, too, would have to pass into the secular order raised to the power of cinema. But by his own standards (the *Origin* book), Benjamin's media-therapeutic readings would have to be judged, at least with regard to the influence of mass psychology, another rationalization.

Ever since Christianity set aside one Good Friday as demonstration that God can die, it has been the religion scheduled for erasure, replacement, but also for returns. No resurrection without the tomb. But that also means Christianity is the religion of the empty tomb, which, having made it, must repeatedly lie in it. No return without the death of Christianity.

In *The World Jones Made* Floyd Jones, next year's world leader, originally put out the shingle of his time sense at a circus for radiation freaks.

When we encounter him he specializes as fortune-teller in "the future of mankind;" he doesn't do "personal futures." When his own turn of—turn with—events is only one year away, Jones starts seeing the big events to come—back. Like Faust, he takes a turn in the small world first, until the turn places him at the controls of the big world. His "gift" is that he can see one year ahead at any time (all the time). Like Faust his life is doubled, but always in the span of one year. His present tense lies doubly in the past while he is alive in the absent tense to the future. It is always the recent past that returns, only the near future that gets projected or foretold. Jones thus must struggle both to remember and to remember to forget: "For a moment he tried to remember what came immediately ahead. . . . It was so long ago; one whole year had passed and details had blurred. . . . The old mechanical actions . . . stale events, dry and dusty, sagging under the smothering blanket of dull age. And meanwhile, the living wave flashed on. He was a man with his eyes in the present and his body in the past. Even now . . . his senses were glued tight on another scene, a world that still danced with vitality, a world that hadn't become stale. Much had happened in the next year" (47).

If Faustian striving were a wish, this would be the wish fulfillment that doubles as punitive curse.

"To me," Jones said hoarsely, "this is the past. Right now, with you three, here in this building, this is a year ago. It's not so much like I can see the future; it's more that I've got one foot stuck in the past. I can't shake it loose. I'm retarded; I'm reliving one year of my life forever." He shuddered. "Over and over again. Everything I do, everything I say, hear, experience, I have to grind over twice. He raised his voice, sharp and anguished, without hope. "I'm living the same life two times!" (39)

Only the foreseen year to come is in real time, though it doesn't happen until it starts to repeat itself in double time. The actual year is just the shell or incubator for the prematurely born and borne year to come. Thus the original title: "Womb for Another." Jones cannot intervene in the future or past, but must endure it in its unchanging aspect: "That was what he hated; that was the loathsome thing. The molasses of time: it couldn't be hurried. On it dragged, with weary, elephantine steps. Nothing could urge it faster: it was monstrous and deaf. Already, he had exhausted the next year; he was totally tired of it. But it was going to take place anyhow. Whether he liked it or not—and he didn't—he was going to have to relive each inch of it, re-experience in body what he had long ago known in mind" (48).

Jones's successes rely on long shots that exceed the two-year span of secure operation. His double-year attention span is a specialization in the precog field, which he happens to share with Hitler. "Dreams, hunches, intuitions. The future was fixed for him, too. And he took long chances. I think Jones will begin taking long chances, too. Now that he's beginning to understand what he's here on Earth for" (44–45). Jones, like Hitler, then, doesn't know when to stop winning because he doesn't see for millions and millions. Is it possible to guess when you know or are the two-year period in which the present is lost? Jones, who has the ghost of a chance, gives up this ghost, or becomes it, when he builds a future plan upon a cornerstone of certainty about one year from now. But the only preexisting thing to come Jones can control is the time of his death. Jones's time sense does give him, in the close quarters of fate, more room to step out of range of the bullet with his name on it. "He can be killed. But he can't be taken by surprise. To kill Jones would mean bottling him up from all sides. He's got a one-year jump on us. He'll die; he's mortal. Hitler died, finally. But Hitler slithered away from a lot of bullets and poisons and bombs in his time. It'll take a closing ring to do it . . . a room with no doors. And you can tell by the look on his face that there's still a door" (45). But Jones can also step into the line of fire when it's time to die a martyr.

The significance of "the drifters," enormous single-celled organisms spread thin that have begun to float down onto Earth, lies beyond the double-year spans of Jones's attention to detail. Relativism, the worldview or antiworldview that drew its lessons from the world and total wars of unsubstantiated prejudice and faith that preceded or introduced it, cannot contain mass identification or violence. As in the world of *Vulcan's Hammer,* the world prior to Jones's remaking is governed as rational order, which goes the way of all rationalization, which, itself not a defense, reinterprets, decontextualizes, and thus undermines all existing defenses. When faced with unexplained growths from outer space, former individuals fuse with countless others in vigilante mobs. Jones, whose hatred of the drifting life-forms is irrational going on paranoid, gives the mob activity a transcendent purpose. Relativism can't rob man of the right to believe in other worlds or, indeed, to enter and seize them as the new frontier. Jones calls for intersystem colonization of the worlds out there that could prove compatible with this one. "The followers of Jones had not given up; they had a dream, a vision. They were sure the Second Earth existed. Somehow, somebody had contrived to keep it from them: there was a conspiracy going on. It was Fedgov on Earth; Relativism was stifling them.

Beyond Earth, it was the drifters. Once Fedgov was gone, once the drifters had been destroyed ... the old story. Green pastures, beyond the very next hill" (104). But then, just beyond the horizon of the double span of Jones's annual report, the drifters turn out to have been the seeds of vast plants whose system of generation mankind disrupted to the point that the greater organism for its own protection sealed off the solar system in which we are thus confined. The outward mobilization of the Jones movement—the Crusade—thus snaps back and smashes Jones in its rebound.

What Jones admits to be his own "provincialism" regarding alien life motivates the interstellar search for Earth's double where human life would not require technological or evolutionary adaptation to and internalization of alien conditions of existence. The corollary to the demand to reach to the stars to find the other world is the destruction of the drifters, which brings down the defense system of interstellar reality. To preserve the Crusade as its negative theology (or as Christianity) Jones decides to accept assassination as the way to go as martyr while the movement to the stars, as suppressed possibility, need never be let go.

Though Jones topples the world order of Relativism, the old order outlasts Jones and his two-year engine of impatience and upheaval via its investment in mutation of the species in anticipation of evolving relations with outer space. Eight true mutants (since they can reproduce themselves as new species) were raised from forty test subjects, who were all derived from the reproductive materials supplied by one scientist and his wife. To help them forget or accept their prehistory in the lab their scientist father built up a controlled habitat in San Francisco out of the open simulation of alien conditions of existence on Venus. Thus upon arrival they recognize Venus as their homeland and their lab conditions as the Diaspora of the book, the letter, the miniature model. On Venus they even refrain from recycling the technological parts of their rockets or of the space station. Instead they found an agrarian community based on the materials and conditions of Venus. But, harnessed to the "horse" power of dobbins, for example, their small world remains reminiscent of Earth like another fantasy alternative (like the Shire of the Hobbits). But as the mutants look back on the war in the world they left behind, they joke about selling medieval props to the contestants back on Earth. The interstellar movement to colonize the other world (or Second Earth) is the (Christian) fantasy.

As a "mystery" Jones's time sensibility belongs, just like Christianity, which returns within the secular world order of "Relativism," to the past it reverses and extends indefinitely: "What was the real moment of his origin? At what point in time had he really come into being? Floating in the womb, he had clearly been alive, sentient. To what had the first memories come? One year before birth, he had not been a unit, not even a zygote. . . . It was a mystery. He finally stopped thinking about it" (49). This mystery about or as the origin, qualified as cessation of thought, is what Jones turns to for deliverance as finite ghost from the secular hell of conscious death or undeath.

> Very shortly, he would die. He had been contemplating it for almost a year; it could be ignored temporarily, but always it returned, each time more terrible and imminent.
>
> After death, his body and brain would erode. And that was the hideous part: not the sudden instant of torment that would come in the moment of execution. That, he could bear. But not the slow, gradual disintegration.
>
> A spark of identity would linger in the brain for months. A dim flicker of consciousness would persist: that was his future memory; that was what the wave showed him. Darkness, the emptiness of death. And, hanging in the void, the still-living personality.
>
> Deterioration would begin at the uppermost levels. First, the highest faculties, the most cognizant, the most alert processes, would fade. An hour after death the personality would be animal. A week after, it would be stripped to a vegetable layer. The personality would devolve back the way it had come; as it had struggled up through the billions of years, so it would go back, step by step, from man to ape to early primate to lizard to frog to fish to crustacean to trilobite to protozoon. And after that: to mineral extinction. Final merciful end. But it would take time.
>
> Normally, the devolving personality would not be aware, would not be conscious of the process. But Jones was unique. Now, at this moment, with his full faculties intact, he was experiencing it. Simultaneously, he was fully conscious, totally in possession of his senses—and at the same time he was undergoing ultimate psychic degeneration. (163–64)

Once he dies, the second time, without the running conscious commentary on his ending state, he can, via videotape addressed to his "assassin," only offer a guess. The order of Relativism had been based on the sanctity of guesswork while Jones had offered the certainty of a known future. But since he knew the future just one year in advance, he had only pretended to *be* the future while he was in fact marketing another label-idealism, but armed with one more propaganda technique. He follows out suicidal illogic in looking forward to being turned into a martyr and thus cutting the losses he risked by gambling beyond his two-year limit with the assurance that if Jones had lived, the followers of the Crusade would have triumphed. Thus he overcomes his last year, during which he no longer saw the big picture of the next year but experienced instead all he had to look forward to: the immediate setting of decay of his dead body. Then Jones dies or commits suicide all the while fantasizing the consequences to come of his second death, even though this secular death is terminal.

Jones's emblem for the movement that made his world out of his double years was composed of the crossed flasks of Hermes (97). In *Counter-Clock World* this is the name of the smallish vitarium that is on the edge of being edged out of business by the big conglomerates in another kind of undertaking business. The Hobart Phase has introduced a reversal of time whereby the dead are not only resurrected but also, upon returning, grow in reverse. The first dead to return died in the first half of the 1980s.

The novel was originally titled "The Dead Grow Young" and "The Dead Are Young"; where the former takes growing pains to reverse loss, the latter focuses on the dead as our future, the other next generation. As all three titles underscore, in this Hobart Phase the finitude of lifetime is also resurrected.

Vitariums respond to the calls of the "new-dead," drill airholes, and eventually disinter the ones trapped in "the tiny place." When Sebastian Hermes, the owner of Flasks of Hermes Vitarium, chances upon the grave of Thomas Peak (the African American Anarch of the Udi faith, identified moreover as James Pike's discovery back in the day), he immediately speculates on his return. His ability to pick up a deader's readiness to come back is almost telepathic; he too was once late-born or new-dead.

He resumed the drilling. It was almost complete, Sebastian noted; he walked a short distance away, listening, sensing the cemetery and the dead beneath the headstones, the corruptible, as Paul had called them, who, one day, like Mrs. Benton, would put on incorruption. And this mortal, he thought, must put on immortality. And then the saying that is written, he thought, will come to pass. Death is swallowed up in victory. Grave, where is thy victory? Oh death, where is thy sting? And so forth. (11)

The inverted world or *verkehrte Welt* is a folkloric topos that Hegel borrowed in *The Phenomenology of Spirit* to draw a distinction, *avant la transmission*, between mad delusion, as all-encompassing in the case of the afflicted, and discrete representations that appear to work in the same "medium." Like the preconscious in Freud's thought, the inverted world is the medial purgatory with which Hegel's autobiography of conceptual thought is lined. Before the onset of borrowings, however, the inverted world represents, whether as the rabbit hunting the hunter or as the family of pigs chowing down on stewed humans, the reversal of hunting along lines of haunting. The evil eye comes into focus here. The look that kills was first feared as the gaze of the dying hunted animal. The rebound of totemic significance that raises the problem of death in the midst of our relationship to food is the practical model for our relations of projection with human goners who keep on going in the afterlife. But it's a genre of s-laughter, too, which as such gave us Disney animation.

In the inverted or topsy-turvy world of *Counter-Clock World* reversal means that one is fortunate, like Faust, to be granted a second lifetime, which is still, however, finite. The new-dead rejuvenates all the way back into the womb. When they marry, it's until birth do them part. The woman who carries a baby ultimately resulting from rejuvenation absorbs it into her body, in some sense digests it, a process that comes to an end when a man also absorbs his share in the sexual act. The comic aspects that justify reference to the *verkehrte Welt* include disgorging rather than eating substances. Once deposited "in the ritual dishes" (164), the thrown-up food returns to its undigested and, then, preconsumed state. In a word, instead of "shit" everyone mutters "food." Inversion of a world in which the dead grow younger brings about a divestment of consumption of the world that is essentially what Faust, in perhaps loftier terms, learns to accomplish once he dies into the reversal of striving.

In *Counter-Clock World,* a robot or roby is required by law to wear a yellow identification stripe or swath on the sleeve up which it keeps nothing to deceive. A robot is named after the person it represents, but the audio tag that keeps it in place is the suffixal addition of "Junior" to the name. While robots or robies have their own artificial intelligence, they are used as transmitters for human agents who communicate and watch through them, their proxies.

"A weird custom," the robot said, observing him. "Before the Hobart Phase you would never have performed such an act before the eyes of another."

"You're only a robot," he said.

"But a human operator perceives through my sensory apparatus." (133)

While largely relegated to this laugh tract through which courses the peristaltic reversal of time and intake of world, the robot also shares, however briefly, the liminal status of the first new-dead to return with the old stories of the afterlife but with certitude exchanged for faith or belief.

Bending over the Anarch, Sebastian studied him, studied the tiny, dark, wrinkled face. It was certainly a living face, now the change struck him as enormous. . . . This is the real miracle, he said to himself; the greatest of them all. Resurrection. The eyes opened. . . . The pupils of the eyes moved; the inert man now living again was seeing each of them here in the room. The eyes roved but the expression in them and on the other features stayed constant. As if, Sebastian thought, we have resurrected a watching-machine. I wonder what he remembers, he asked himself. More than I? I hope so, and it would be reasonable. He, because of his calling, would be more alert. The dry, cracked, darkened mouth stirred. The Anarch said in a rustling, wind-like whisper, "I saw God. Do you doubt it?" (72–73)

But one of the vitarium workers in attendance begins to match the Anarch's words with the next line of what turns out to be a poem.

Immortality, eternity, God—all of the above—must remain near-death or near-life experiences that are at best "remembered" the way trauma hangs on in fragments. But when the Anarch, the former founder of a world faith, returns he conveys his afterlife experience as the certitude of the tenets of faith in the other world.

His successor, Ray Roberts, markets the mystery of drug-induced communion, which certitude would devalue only in theory. A false lead makes him one of the anticipated suspects in the Anarch's assassination. Even though he is in a sense cleared, it proves hard for the reader ever to trust him. But how can one forget that to a wheeler-dealer even or especially the most authentic and immediate expression of religion is highly marketable— as history or ancestry or tradition. Sebastian Hermes receives Roberts as evil in association with the fantasy genre, though the association itself only proves evil when it goes out on an update in the discourse of Roberts:

Roberts wore a simple dark robe and a skullcap, and, on his right hand, a ring. One ring to rule them all, he thought, remembering his Tolkien. One ring to find them. One ring to—how did it go?—bring them all and in the darkness bind them. . . . Like that fashioned from the Rheingold, carrying a curse with it, to whoever put it on. Maybe the operation of the curse, he conjectured, is manifest in the Library's seizing the Anarch. . . . "I am reminded," Roberts was expostulating in the living room, "of the little old lady who had been recently old-born and whose greatest fear had been that, when they excavated her, they would find her improperly clothed." The audience chuckled. "But neurotic fears," Roberts continued, now somberly, "can destroy a person and a nation. The neurotic fear by Nazi Germany of a two-front war—" He droned on; Sebastian ceased listening. (153–55)

A representative of the Uditi (the followers of the Anarch-led faith) clarifies that the only conflict of interests is between their revealed religion, with the Anarch and Roberts on the same side, and the Library, the site of the secular word:

"We revere the Anarch. . . . He's our *saint*—the only one we've got. We've waited decades for his return; the Anarch will have all the ultimate wisdom of the afterlife; that's the entire purpose of Roberts' pilg: this is a holy journey, for the purpose of sitting at the feet of the Anarch and hearing his good news.... The glorious news of the fusion in eternity of all souls. *Nothing else matters but this news.*" (126)

The most powerful institution in this future world, the Library, which functions as a society within society, is ruled by Erads hoisted to power by the retard of commemoration. Books are taken out of circulation, reduced to a first limited printing, until the original manuscript has been restored—and is then eradicated.

In a book the metabolic reversal of books is the self-reflexive presentation of the death drive. Otherwise in the Hobart Phase, manufactured commodities aren't reabsorbed naturally but are taken out of circulation on the way to their disappearance. Smoking butts grow longer as the air clears. Once a pack has been refilled with cigarettes it is withdrawn. We find down to the fine print on the package that the legible world (which is all Dick's book knows) is destined to end up—unread, unread.

The good news of the Hobart phase is that Beethoven will at some point return as new-dead; the bad news is that by that point all his scores will have been eradicated. The book Anarch Peak published in his first lifetime, *God in a Box,* has been reduced to four printed copies held by the library and a few more still in circulation in private libraries. The Head Librarian lays out to her second-in-command the threat to eradication posed by the Anarch's return:

"When the Anarch is reborn ... he will probably attempt to resume his religious career.... And he will have the benefit of his experience beyond the grave. I think he'll remember it, compared with most old-borns; or anyhow he'll *claim* he remembers it.... The Council is not too pleased at the idea of the Anarch resuming his career of religion-mongering; they're quite sceptical. Just as we manage to erad the last copies of *God in a Box* he shows up again to write some more." (79)

One of the Library agents, Ann Fisher, summarizes the Anarch's new certifiable doctrine as he has been declaiming it while in the Library's custody.

"He says there's no death; it's an illusion. Time is an illusion. Every instant that comes into being never passes away. Anyhow—he says—it doesn't really even come into being; it was always there. The universe consists of concentric rings of reality; the greater the ring the more it partakes of absolute reality. These concentric rings finally wind up as God; He's the source of the things, they're more real as they get nearer to Him. It's the principle of emanation, I guess. Evil is simply a lesser reality.... Evil is an illusion like decay.... Eidos is form. Like Plato's category—the absolute reality. It exists; Plato was right. Eidos is imprinted on passive matter; matter isn't evil, it's just inert, like clay. There's an anti-eidos, too; a form-*destroying* factor. This is what people experience as evil, the decay of form. But the anti-eidos is an ideolon, a delusion; once impressed, the form is eternal—it's just that it undergoes a constant evolution, so that we can't perceive the form. The way, for instance, the child disappears into the man, or, like we have now, the man dwindles away into the child. It looks like the man is gone, but actually the universal, the category, the form—it's still there." (197–98)

Ann Fisher further characterizes the *Britannica*-esque synthetic quality of these doctrines: " 'Nothing new,' Ann said. 'Just a rehash of Plotinus and Plato and Kant and Leibnitz and Spinoza' " (198). Just because it's not new (or news) doesn't make its arrival any less worthy, Sebastian, the vitarium owner who first liberated the Anarch, argues in defense of the doctrine and its frame of reference. Then the force of erad will pull up short before the truth: " 'Well, if the doctrine's true,' Ann said, 'we *can't* destroy it' " (199).

That the doctrine as medley of quotes is written inside a book already makes it hard to destroy. The epigraphs for each chapter of *Counter-Clock World* are taken from those old-time medieval philosophers the Anarch, Ann says, keeps quoting. Dick's book is in a sense the field of representation of the Anarch's doctrine but as fragments or ruins. Dick's book recognizes as its own inside view the erad powers of the archive (the fever or fire of the archive in Derrida's reading).

The archive is made possible by the death, aggression, and destruction drive, that is to say also by originary finitude and expropriation. But beyond finitude as limit, there is . . . this properly *in-finite* movement of radical destruction without which no archive desire or fever would happen. (94)

Erasure is a function of recording. Transmission of text that aims at erasure skips the substitutive milieu of readings and, as in cremation, preserves what it conveys through destruction beyond the interventions or grave desecrations of readers. The erad movement thus promotes writing for writing's sake. At the same time the eradication of books in *Counter-Clock World* cannot but enfold itself within and extend the self-reflexive momentum of the archive as book about books.

Over There

One man's religious frame of reference is another man's outer-space escape or rescue. The higher purpose of interstellar exploration that gave Jones the advantage in his move against Relativism figures as outside chance and hope for changes in the future worlds depicted in *Solar Lottery* and *Our Friends from Frolix 8*. John Preston and Thors Provoni, the respective space travelers in the two works, are explorers searching the frontiers of outer space for a new planet on which to found an alternative society in the former case and, in the other case, to summon an alien cavalry (from Frolix 8) to the rescue of humans from social inequities on Earth. Both hierarchy-bound Earth societies are organized around testing: in the first-case scenario everyone is rendered a contestant in game shows or lotteries; in the latter case meritocracy or flexibility is feigned as the open horizon of scoring your place in a social order set on a certain dogma of evolutionary progress.

The first sentence of *Our Friends from Frolix 8*: "Bobby said. 'I don't want to take the test!'" In Schreber's lexicon, to be tested or purified is to be untested or not yet tested. To tread in the fine print of this testing of souls is to engage the psychotic metabolization of the missing place of reality testing. In the society of the fittest in which Bobby, a true tested soul, asks to remain untested, tests are rigged in support of survival of the mutation that gives more brain to so-called New Men. Their only balancing act in the social organization, their share of power with the Unusuals (telepaths mostly), is soon to be overcome through the invention, by New Man scientist Amos Ild, of the "Great Ear," which will allow New Men to read and transmit thoughts wordlessly as the Unusuals can do on their own. The vast majority of Earth's population is comprised of Old Men.

Among them a political movement or underground has arisen dedicated to what the politicos call themselves: Under Men.

The New Men wish to test only for themselves, ultimately administering only "tests for New Man cortical activity, that double-domed neutrologics with such postulates as, A thing is equal to its opposite and the greater the discrepancy, the greater the congruity" (31). Preoccupied only with their own brain changes, the New Men affirm the intellectualization thus spawned as proof of evolutionary progress. But insanity is the status quo of this evolutionary strain on humanity (195, 196). One strong indicator of the high-IQ madness is the certitude about the future toward which the Big Ear is building. Only the precogs among the Unusuals have a special relationship to the future, but "they saw many futures at one time, like . . . rows of boxes" (13). As Provoni's approach begins bringing down his house, Council Chairman Willis Gram, an Unusual, turns in desperation to Ild, the leading New Man scientist, for assistance. The future scenario of Provoni's defeat he foresees (through all the hoopla of Provoni's return) as the end in sight he has calculated through neutrologics as absolute certainty. But Gram remains wary of a forecast given in the very terms a precog can never use (163–64).

Provoni, one of the leaders of the Under Men, explored outer space in search of a species that would understand and protect human interests as a third party otherwise excluded by the rule of the New Men. Morgo, the Frolixian friend in need accompanying Provoni on his Calvary charge, uses fusion or "scanning" to remove the madness-inducing extra span of brain from every New Man on the planet. "Evidently what they do will be done on a bulk basis. . . . Like erasing tape. The whole reel at once, without passing the tape across the erase head" (162). The neutralization of New Man brainpower establishes a new bottom line. Ild's certainties are reversed or reduced, and a new frontier of psycho mysticism opens up: "What are other people? Maybe there aren't any others; maybe they're make-believe" (205).

Because the deletion or erasure, which is permanent, is only the preview of what the Frolixian can bring, Provoni must trust where no man can trust: the alien force he brings to Earth raises powers that outmode humanity. Will the friend take only a little piece of the brain as covenant? The metabolic tendency of the Frolixians is to replace organisms with their own ontological substance; in other words, they absorb them, ultimately leaving behind only their husks. From dawn to husk, "the imitated creature could function and survive. Death came when the Frolixian withdrew—ceased to provide counterfeit lungs, heart, kidneys" (119). When the brain is replaced, moreover, the invaded organism suffers "from pseudo-psychotic thought-processes which he did not recognize as his own"—"and he would be correct; they would not be" (119).

As the one to know one, Morgo fears that whenever Provoni drops off to sleep he is some alien's possession or incorporation.

"It's the mental functioning that changes so much, that makes us uneasy.... First, you enter a world that to some extent is familiar to you.... This sort of dreaming forms a kind of recapitulation of the day.... That does not alarm us. It is the next phase. You fall into a deeper interior level; you encounter personages you never knew... A disintegration of your self, of you as such begins; you merge with primordial entities of a god-like type, possessing enormous power." (81)

Morgo, who only knows what Provoni knows (inside and out), might as well be talking to himself:

"The collective unconsciousness," Provoni said. "That the greatest of the human thinkers Carl Jung discovered." ...

"Did Jung stress the point that one of these archetypes could, at any time, absorb you?" ...

"Of course he stressed it. But it's not at night in sleep that the archetype takes over, it's during the day. When they appear during the day—that's when you're destroyed." (81–82)

On a good day Provoni sees Morgo as primal father: "Yes, that's what they are, our friends from Frolix 8. As if I managed to contact the Urvater, the primordial Father who built the eidos kosmos. They are upset and anxious because something is going wrong on our world; they care; they have empathy" (115). On a bad day Provoni can see for millions of lives that could be great game.

The friend from Frolix 8, otherwise a fatal disease for other life-forms, gives mankind the assist, however, as controlled release, application, and exhibition of its destructive digestive powers in defense of its own kind, that is, in identification with Provoni's makeup. It is unclear how Earth, even as misled by the New Men, could ever pose a threat to Frolix 8. The tendency of the New Men is simulation of abstract thought (which yields a kind of psychosis) and technologization of telepathy. Morgo can administer his appetitive metabolism to scan and scoop out the evolutionary add-ons in New Men brains as well as neutralize the occult powers of the Unusuals. However, since one of the targets is telepathy, we enter an overlap with Arthur C. Clarke's *Childhood's End*, a regular intertext or ego ideal on the horizon of Dick's self-assessment. *Childhood's End* remains, however, in its unambivalent and ghostless Christianity, far removed from the interior of Dick's works. Never you Overmind: in their reduced capacity New Men reveal themselves to be mystics who, in contrast to their former attempts at streamlining extrasensory communication for social control, now enjoy contact with the other side. Ild, the former builder of the Great Ear, hoisted and hosted by his own retardation, now tells the protagonist Nick that Nick's newly dead special friend Charley can hear him when he sings at her grave (208–9).

Nick is a test subject without knowing it in a setting of consumer motivation and prediction. According to the government testers watching him, how Nick reacts to certain stimuli is a good indicator of what the Old Man response will be in general. For Old Men testing is torture. Thus Old Men typically steep themselves in self-medication and recovery. "Officers" are known always only (via the idiom of drunk driving) as "occifers." What gets the plot on Earth rolling out from under this depression, then, is Bobby's test failure, which puts the father in the ready position to identify with or as Under Man. Soon Nick meets Charley, the novel's dark-haired girl, in the milieu of rebellion.

Empathy, the identificatory bond of protection that brings the Urvater to our rescue, for which the dead pet serves as mascot, is also the watchword in the unstoppable discourse of Cordon, the other leader of the Under Men. Cordon lives by the word that is in the beginning, which Provoni, like Faust, translates into deed, act, *Tat*. Cordon's words come to Nick (and to us) via their recitation by Charley.

"In giving that is true giving, nothing comes back." (50)

"When souls have meshed, one can't be destroyed without the other dying." (70)

Charley is the obstacle in the course of the (reality) testing that is mourning. Although her symptomatic lack of humanness can cross Nick's mind (148), when someone else, someone close, calls her a robot, Nick affirms her as though life itself were at stake (154). When she next seems inanimate, he recognizes her traumatization: "She had nothing left by which to feel" (183).

What Nick goes through as the course of the novel, Provoni as embodiment of the future comes into: Provoni is both New Man and Unusual. The Frolixian adjustment of the IQ test does not mess with Provoni's mind, which Morgo sorted through to set the course of saving the species he thus came to identify with and love. Like Nick, Provoni lives in the recent past (130). "It was, like much else in his mind, a clutter of fleas: hopping fragments of thoughts and ideas, memories and fears, that had taken up residence evidently for good. It was up to the Frolixians to sort it all out, and they had so done, it would seem" (84).

The number "8" sounds like the past tense of "to eat," while "Frolix" is a name designed for marketing dog food brands or gadgets. The friends from Frolix 8 didn't have room for the two of us, the masters of evolution and, at their disposal, all the other critters. As the planet urbanized the creatures were doomed to slow and painful extinction. They opted for the painless approach: they sterilized their fauna. Provoni must trust that these measures of extinction were taken in strict avoidance of painful death or murder and that their living on in exchange as remembrance is appropriate as or congruent with mourning.

"I receive something from coming to your planet," Morgo said. "I get to pick up and hold little life forms: cats, a dog, a leaf, a snail, a chipmunk. Do you know—do you understand—that on Frolix 8 all life forms except ourselves were sterilized, hence they long ago disappeared...although I've seen recordings of them, three dimensional recreations that seem absolutely real. Wired directly to the ruling ganglia of our central nervous systems." (126)

For Provoni his pet cat is the other and, thus, the first to go. Those who have gone ahead await his ultimate arrival, like the Eternal Femmes Faust, at the stairway to Heaven. "They'll all be there, a row of them on each side of the road, waiting for me. An animal refuses to pass into Paradise without its master. They wait year after year" (125). Pets are the grateful dead, who don't give the other up for the other world. But his pet grief is also the spring internal of their identification and trust. Fascinated by the other life on Earth (as well as by human gadgets, which are quaint and collectible) Morgo decides to adopt not a cat but a dog. By standing outside the doubling between alien and human, this decision admits relationality.

Between the test patterns of evolution and the rationalization of causality as the games we play, we have already identified the name of "game" as the quarry one hunts. According to Benjamin, the detective going after clues is the modern urban descendant of the hunter on the track of game. "Hunting at the same time goes into reverse as haunting and enters the milieu of the work of detection (at least in Poe's works) as modern Spiritualism: the metapsychology of groups" (*Das Passagen-Werk*, 550–51). Between *Deus Irae* and *Confessions of a Crap Artist* the Spiritualism citation from *Our Friends from Frolix 8* was already lodged as plaint. The other séance comes from outer space at the end of *Solar Lottery*. We follow to the end of the novel a vessel of unks—individuals unclassified on Earth because they live by the labor of their hands—who took off to find the new homeland for men and women of repair as foretold by John Preston a lifetime ago. Before the leader of the unk colonists brings down the book with his affirmation of life moving on "in an evolving fashion," the first contact with the new planet is recognizable as what Spiritualist mediums and psychotics (like Schreber) also travel through outer space to find: "What makes that funny light? It's like a séance in here. You're sure that's a planet?" (192).

Flame Disc is the tenth planet, unclassified just like the colonists who can thus claim it as their new home. Leon Cartwright, who already in school dropped courses in symbolization to pursue instead different hands-on genres of repair, was able to tamper with the bottle that gets spun in the spirit of random chance to select who will be the next ruler of the game world. While he accepts the position of Quizmaster, the colonists, his fellow Prestonites, take off for Flame Disc. Cartwright's plan is to change the whole system by establishing Flame Disc as a new halfway point: "The stars are opening up like roses" (190).

Once on Flame Disc the colonists encounter what looks like Preston in a liquid jar of half-life, but find instead "vid and aud tapes synchronized to form a replica" (198). The countless signals they followed by sight and sound of Preston's voice all the way to Flame Disc were thus also replicas set up by Preston as buoys beyond the known frontier of the solar system to keep posthumous watch for those bound to venture forth.

The plot back on Earth intersects when the Pellig, a robot creation whereby Herb Moore, the mad scientist working for the former Quizmaster Reese Verrick, tampered with the rules for assassination attempts by official contestants on the life of the current Quizmaster. When Peter Wakeman, the leader of the telepathic corps officially entrusted with protection of the Quizmaster against these attacks, identifies the ruse to Ted Benteley, one of Verrick's serfs who, as part of the ruse, will be used unwittingly as suicide bomber, Benteley is freed of his oath, since his master broke it. Thus the oath is more basic than the rules of the game, which seem more readily breakable. Like Freud argued, every rule is preceded by or modeled on its violation. Benteley kills Moore's inert body in the control room of the Pellig while Moore's projected control still in possession of the Pellig transforms the robot into a rocket. "He" shoots up into space to destroy the legacy of Preston carried away by what Wakeman had right away identified telepathically as a "high-powered blur of pathological drive" (38).

Becoming an Under Man, in *Our Friends from Folix 8,* means to be ready to die with others. After his son's failing test score prompts him to seek out a new life as subversive, Nick finds out at work that his boss is an Under Man:

"You may not like me very much—... but do you want to see me murdered?"
"What can I do?" Nick said. . . .
Zeta drew himself up, his dumpy body rigid with the agony of despair. "You could die along with us," he said.
"Okay," Nick said. (33–34)

This pact psychology of tested souls corresponds to what the formulation of a new oath at the end of *Solar Lottery* risks as its internalization. By way of the same tampering with the bottle that put Cartwright in charge for the duration of the novel (which allowed him to cover for the Prestonite excursion to Flame Disc) Benteley will be assuming the position of the next Quizmaster, but which he can now accept by a new kind of oath: "I'm probably the first person who was ever under oath to himself. I'm both protector and serf at the same time. I have the power of life and death over myself" (190). Thus the oath bond is internalized as the relationship to conscience, Cartwright comments: "Maybe . . . that might catch on." What ranks up there with the colonization of Flame Disc comes at the end of a relay of oath renewals that began with Benteley's wish to sign up with an authority greater than that of the next person to own his contract and services.

"It stands above all of us. It's bigger than any man or any group of men. Yet, in a way, it's everybody."
"It's nobody. When you have a friend he's a particular person, not a class or a work-group, isn't he? . . . What is there, beyond people?"
"Depend on yourself."
"Reese takes care of me! He's big and strong."
"He's your father," Benteley said. "And I hate fathers."
"You're—psychotic." . . . (83–84)

The game society, which reorganizes consumerism and commodification, is played for keeping psychosis away. Psychotherapy and guidance keep all citizens who aren't unks (unclassifieds) in the sane game. The typical CV or identity dossier includes one's "psych-analysis" (22). Vacation is always at the same time therapeutic, at least at a "psycho-health resort" (103), also referred to as a "psych resort," where only "therapeutic" "games," no "purely intellectual games were permitted" (167). The emphasis is on being psyched—for the game.

During World War II, the mathematical theory of Minimax, which was pitched on the playing field of life, was applied to warfare, then postwar to business, whence it became the basis for government. At first commodity capitalism posed the kind of social problem that only recourse to Minimax or cybernetics could keep in suspension. "The theory of Minimax—the M-game—was a kind of stoic withdrawal, a nonparticipation in the aimless swirl in which people struggled. . . . The M-game player sat waiting for the game to end; that was the best that could be hoped for" (17). But rather than surrender it all to the death drive, this game of life has its continual ups and downs maintained as volatility or alteration via institutionalized randomness, the bottom line of a game that must be defended against the controlling interests of "strategy."

When under Minimax the problems of production were solved, the problems of consumption took over and products piled high. Product burnings were staged as Black Masses of consumerism. But then, once we started doing the math, quizzes entered this breach. First commodities were offered as the prizes. But then we moved on to "more realistic items: power and prestige" (17). The ultimate prize was the position of dispenser of power, the position of Quizmaster. "He was unopposed administrator of the random bottle structure, the vast apparatus of classification, Quizzes, lotteries, and training schools" (27). In the new order of random chance, statistical prediction of odds replaces cause and effect. Minimax provided a rational scientific method whereby every strategy game is cracked and transformed into a chance game. Randomness fits an overall rational pattern. Randomness makes it impossible for anyone to pursue a strategy, in other words, a deception. Everybody must adopt instead a randomized method. One's very skill at the game is a function of chance.

The Old Test meets its substitute in the quiz, which comes out of the New Testament with no lasting repercussions. In contrast to test or even examination, a quiz is a low-order intervention that doesn't hurt, isn't irrecuperable (the quiz implies second chances), even or especially when introduced as a surprise "pop." Anyone (in other words, even an unk) can obtain a power card and enter the great lottery at the statistically lowest end of the polls, votes, and winnings. The illusion that is celebrated is that of everyone's time-share in the game of fame.

The telepaths or teeps are mutants whose traumatization made them see better. They all descend from one family line that goes back to the day the Livermore installations in San Francisco were hit by a Soviet missile during the Final War. Even when assassins plot their moves according to random methods, they tend still to lose, statistically squeezed out by the whole Corps of teeps following out the same methods (78–79). In fact the structure of guaranteed randomness was implemented to curtail the influence of the teeps. The containment of power privilege breaks apart as the showdown between the teeps and the Pellig (or the psycho Moore behind it all).

Moore doesn't technically break the rules of the game when he builds Pellig, a robot through which human agents (back in the labs of Farben Hill in Berlin) take turns, one at a time, trying to assassinate Quizmaster Cartwright. The resulting machine or method is the perfection of randomness in the immediate struggle against the telepathic Corps. "Pellig is Heisenberg's random particle. The teeps can trace his path: directly to Cartwright. But not his velocity. Where Keith Pellig will be along that path at a given moment nobody knows" (79).

The Pellig switch or twitch of identification, which keeps losing the tracking of the telepaths with the target's sudden disappearance in mid-stride while the now unidentified Pellig keeps moving, psychoticizes the teeps who break down and apart.

Like a cloud of volatile gas the Corpsman's mind hung together, then slowly, inexorably, began to scatter. Its weak thoughts faded. . . . The man's consciousness, his *being* dissolved into random particles of free energy. The mind ceased to be a unit. The gestalt that had been the man relaxed—and the man was dead. (141)

The breakdown spreads along the chain of telecommand: "All up and down the network the violence rolled and lapped. Mind after mind was smashed, short-circuited, blacked-out by the overload" (124). Before he stumbles on the fundamental oath-breaking ruse, Wakeman takes Pellig to be a figure of mental disturbance, which, given the openness of telepaths to conscious and unconscious thoughts, short-circuited the Corps. "Some kind of multiple mind came and went. Pellig was a fractured personality artificially segmented into unattached complexes, each with its own drives, characteristics, and strategy" (137).

Wakeman, who survived Pellig's surprise attack, leads the remaining Corpsmen to lock onto physical-visual appearance and restrict mind-touch to catching murder-thoughts: "But don't expect continuity. The thought-processes will cut off without warning. Be prepared for the impact; that's what destroyed the Corps" (137). But Wakeman's working diagnosis of Pellig as psychotically broken-apart personality works only if Pellig is one person, which he isn't. As soon as Wakeman identifies Pellig as a vehicle for randomly switched on psyches, he also recognizes that it's a lie. "*The twitch of the Pellig machinery wasn't random.* Moore had complete control" (140). The game proves to be a succession of diagnostic steps and therapeutic techniques for the identification and containment of psychotic dissolutions. At the same time the Solar System opens wide via the onset of colonization of Flame Disc to a model of encapsulation, which passes through analogy with modern Spiritualism along the new frontier constituted and protected by haunting and technical replication.

Martyrology

The case of Ilse overlaps significantly with that of Suzanne Urban. Binswanger composed the case study of Suzanne Urban as, after the fact, the second bookend concluding reflections begun in the Ellen West study. Urban is paranoid schizophrenic. What makes her case so different from what Freud discovered in Schreber's *Memoirs* is that the whole development into the delusional world was laid out for Binswanger, including all the transitions. Indeed, he thus discovers a case of paranoid schizophrenia in which the "trans-" permeates all phases and phrases of Urban's disintegration and reduction. In psychotic hell there would appear to be a circle below the aetherial world of Ellen West's suicide mission: it is the intermediary atmospheric realm. Two related German words are worked over and over in the course of the case study: *wittern,* which means "to scent something out," "get wind of something," or "suspect something," and *Witterung,* which signifies "weather" or "atmospheric conditions." The opening "theme" (or motif), which Binswanger also designates as her "primal scene," was the physician's delivery of her husband's diagnostic death sentence. The opener then suffuses the whole world with its atmosphere of torture and suffering. The world she lives *with* becomes threatening ("Der Fall Suzanne Urban," 235–36). She begins to get wind of dangers. The atmospheric world she inhabits is the "blind world" of scenting out and about, of *verspüren* ("becoming aware of"), which includes, in the German, *Spur,* "trace" or "scent." You cannot correct such "atmospheric abstractions" (237–38).

The concrete interpersonal relations set on *nehmen,* "to take," add up to that which has been undermined. In this atmospheric world it is impossible to take the other's word or take the other at his word. The self is radically irresponsible (239).

Terror is on the rise. "In the atmospheric 'experience,' in the deluded mood state of being tuned *[Wahngestimmtheit]*, experience is a getting wind or becoming aware or picking up the scent of concealed dangers." The transition follows: "The 'transition' from this atmospheric experience into the deluded experience, the world of the delusion or the terror stage is then indicated inasmuch as the covered up, scented out, uncanny atmosphere of endangering as such unveils itself in the open sphere of the 'secret' enemies" (240).

In the veiling and unveiling lies the contradistinction to natural experience. There can be no uncovering as such on the stage of terror: "It still is, even more so, a covered uncovering or revelation, an uncovering in the sense of secrecy" (241). Along for the transition, then, we find that the terror theme has been rearticulated as "delusion fable": as the secrecy of the enemies. The theme of terror first introduced with the terror of the primal scene (the husband's diagnosis) becomes, then, the "Leitthema" (or leitmotif) of this *Dasein*. Thus Urban conveys her situational suffering into excess or alle-gory. Her husband not only suffers but is also, furthermore, "lying in excrement." "Here the martyrdom of her husband, the original terror theme, lingers, but as having entered the world of terror, the martyrology, as Suzanne Urban herself says, or, as we say, the delusion fable" (243). We witness here "the overturning of *Dasein* out of the mode of being locked up with its worldly terror themes and with the tyrannical but failed attempts to lock up in this way even the contemporary world *[Mitwelt]* into a world of terror as such originating precisely in one's own time *[Mitwelt]*" (247). "In place of a high-flown imperious self, locked up inside a world of its own, without communication, steps a subjugated self completely surrendered to the public sphere. This being handed over to the public sphere is now the tortuous, the inflaming that makes the patient rage, the actual martyrdom *[Marter]*. The time for soliloquies is long past" (247–48).

Binswanger turns up all the stage lights on what one might otherwise simply call, clinically, the retrogression or dismantling of the personality (256). Suzanne Urban's "martyrology" enters the very "stage" that Binswanger raises up out of the margins of the Ellen West case study (257). She turned to the theater stage as metaphor or *Gleichnis* for her impasse. She occupies center stage, but with all exits blocked by armed guards. Metaphors *(Gleichnisse)* speak the language of transcendence (263). All the world's a natural or theatrical stage. But this metaphor reflects tradition and religious belief: in delusion all that is reflected back is "the reduction of *Dasein* to mere 'receptivity' in the sense of *anxiety*" (261). Thus, what can be emphatically described as "being taken 'by the ear' or by the collar, in a word, as (bodily) impressionability celebrates on the terror stage veritable orgies" (263). *Dasein*'s mere or sheer impressionability is the link to and limitation of "hallucination."

> The state of being ill, being ill in this case of persecutory delusions, does not first produce this power, it represents only a way and means for *Dasein* to relate to it, a mode, namely, of submission. Myths, religion, poetry, and philosophy of the ages have come to terms with this power or force. Whereas the delusion is a form of submission of *Dasein* to this power, myth and religion, poetry and philosophy signify in reverse the forms of its overcoming. But herewith is proclaimed that the submission to the power of terror concerns and upsets *Dasein* in its isolation—to this extent the term autism is justified—, overcoming in contrast is achieved by *Dasein* as bonded via country, history, tradition, in short, as spirit. (265)

But the stage metaphor is as far as Urban gets in breaking away from terror. There's no coming back for her, as in being spirit.

> In the stage-metaphor we indeed see *Dasein* take a step beyond itself, namely the step inside the metaphor *[Gleichnis]* and that means, into the image. . . . *Dasein* sees—as viewer, namely as self—itself still in the image, it still becomes aware of itself in the mode of image knowledge, of *Gleichnis*. (266)

Psychosis is thus not a disease of spirit or mind: "it is a being ill of the human being in the sense of a particular form of failure of its possibility to be in general with regard to its highest possibility of being, precisely 'being in spirit'" (266).

Everything, even the thoughts of others, must enter her play plan. This last stand or understanding of her world belongs to time that, standing still ever since the primal scene, folds out of its ecstasies and back upon itself as "naked *Dasein*," as "naked horror." The spirit, too, must stand still before the complete collapse of all communication via comparison (and *Gleichnis*). "This 'not knowing' what and how it's happening to me, which characterizes the terror, this impossibility of 'insight' produces the '*bottomless*' *uncanniness* of this paralysis of *Dasein*" (279).

The so-called incorrigibility of delusional ideas refers to what can be dis-covered here as the re-covery of *Dasein*'s nearly total alienation from itself in the delusion.

This (inauthentic) expectation in the form of mere *getting a wind* of uncanny dangers coming from the *Mitwelt* now however *unveils* the uncanniness of these dangers as *certain* even though secret animosities coming from the *Mitwelt*. This uncovering is ambiguous: it *uncovers* on the one hand the atmospheric veil of the *uncanny* endangerment . . . insofar as it *discovers* or *reveals* the secrecy of the enemies. (280)

On the other hand, the uncovering again drops a veil between *Dasein* and itself of greater profundity, finally, than the cover afforded by *Dasein's* sweet surrenders. "A return of *Dasein* to itself and to the situation is from now on out of the question" (281).

The *Prüfungen* or trials of martyrdom inhabit or animate the ruins of reality "testing" ("Prüfung"), of the basis of the "(natural) mode of experience." In her martyrology, Suzanne Urban cannot be tried by new test questions that otherwise belong outside the circling of the delusional experience. Experience does not expand its stock of the new but rather confirms original reservations. The delusional world is thus "trustworthy," "without question," in other words "untested" (281). For the patient it's always the same old song, the same old suffering. But a "new" experience emerges just the same: that of complete lack or loss of alternatives *(Ausweglosigkeit)* and exceptions *(Ausnahmslosigkeit)* (282). Through its staging and syndication, Urban's original suffering loses its singularity and particularity to the whole of existence, which becomes suffused with pain and conspiracy and is in turn tuned in or received in the sphere of *Dasein* reduced to mere receptivity and impressionability—"and thus remains inside the thematized generality of the delusional suffering" (287).

Binswanger views Urban's paranoid schizophrenia as differing from Schreber's apocalyptic break by undergoing a continuous transition: "The world of natural experience is here by no means destroyed but rather in the twofold Hegelian sense *aufgehoben*, namely both abandoned and preserved" (299). Since Binswanger has already fixed the focus on the ambivalence of Hegel's concept, we can add that the natural experience of testing has been allegorically presented in Urban's martyrology. Suzanne Urban's delusion surpasses every tragedy—"even the most gruesome Baroque drama" (270). Binswanger consequently and emphatically separates this psychotic stage of martyrology from melancholia proper.

In a metaphor *[Gleichnis]* we can say that the Medusa head of one's own fault is here covered with a thick veil, a sign that the power of terror has afflicted this *Dasein* more rigorously or destructively than would be the case with melancholia . . . insofar as this power announces itself no longer as tortuous existential suffering but rather in its so-called unexistential form, in the form of the "bloody apparatus of destruction." (293–94)

What falls up between these cracks is the too often otherwise missing connection between Benjamin's *Origin of the German Mourning Play* and his later media essays, in which testing occupies the foreground. But the Baroque martyr pageants, as Benjamin emphasizes, were already withdrawn from the only genre of Passion that Inquisitioning minds want to know. That the martyr began to fill out a Job application is a measure of the unsecuring of bonds of faith. According to Benjamin, the Baroque martyr drama "has nothing in common with religious concepts" and the martyr is thoroughly embedded in "immanence": "he is a radical stoic and executes his test or trial *[Probestück]* in the context of a royal or religious dispute, at the end of which torture and death await him" (191). As parallel universal to tyranny's restoration of order, this stoic technique thus establishes a state of emergency of the soul or psyche (253). The excavation and restoration of these test connections *chez* Benjamin can be submitted as a case in pointing out the metapsychological fact, as presented by Ronell in *The Test Drive*, that "the very structure of testing tends to overtake the certainty that it establishes when obeying the call of open finitude" (5). Benjamin supplied the blueprint for mounting the staggered reading of reality testing from torment to multiple choice: while the corpse was the poster allegory of the Baroque stage, beginning with Baudelaire's world the commodity became reading matter of life or death for the allegorist and mediatic tester. Intrapsychically at least, the connection between these phases of modern allegory remains open.

The scientific perspective, as Ronell shows, placed the primal test (of torture) inside the lexicon and lab space of hypothesis two centuries or so before Freud's scene of writing, but still securely within the shelf life of his reading formation. For Benjamin the immediate or live connection with true disclosure in torture booked passage first through the aesthetic experience of aura before giving way to the testing of reproductions and transmissions by countless experts. It is to these receiving areas that reality testing belongs. Reality testing and mourning are even closer than device and application. Mourning *is* reality testing. There is no reality quite like that of loss. Hence it is a certain relationship to loss (as in melancholia) that tows the bottom line of psychosis. Reality testing and transference (and, unnamed but implicated in the lineup, mourning, too) were the two or three things Freud knew about the separation or borderline between normal-to-neurotics and psychotics.

Binswanger accepts Freud's theorization of Schreber's paranoid delusional system or apparatus remarkably uncritically (hardly the average score posted even by insider readers). But since the middle ground was elided from Schreber's *Memoirs,* as in most cases of psychotic delusion on record, there is no intermediary place for Freud's and Binswanger's readings to meet. While in his study of Ellen West, Binswanger charged psychoanalysis with being too aetherial, remote from the ground or mound, in this case Binswanger implicates psychoanalysis in the atmospheric conditions. All the components of Freud's theory of psychic reality "hang ontologically in the air" (325). But this difference between psychoanalysis and the grounding *Dasein*-analysis provides notwithstanding, Binswanger allows psychoanalytic understanding to stand, cut off, to be sure, from "world" etc., but otherwise unquestioned. Psychoanalysis is the trustworthy order Binswanger doesn't question. His inability to follow Freud could have been his martyrdom, had the cautionary example of Jung not intervened. Binswanger's dissociated reception of Freud tunes in the same channeling of influence that in Benjamin's *Origin* book was otherwise concealed by the diversion of melancholia: "From the psychoanalytic perspective, the torments *[Marterungen]* of the family must be considered as sadistic orgies, in other words, as the breaking out of sadistic tendencies repressed and overcompensated for in the hysterical-hypochondriacal 'family neurosis'" (304).

The special atmosphere of Suzanne Urban's world is a transition through language. Schreber's delusion is organized around the singular fix on Flechsig and his representatives on earth. Urban confronts the "one" *(man)* of pervasive, irresponsible opinion (248). Her so-called delusional ideas or *Wahnideen* are her very own *Wahr-ideen,* her "true ideas" (254). As Urban increasingly can no longer take the shared world, one-ness in its place animates the idiomatic expressions of common parlance. One often says or thinks: It would be so terrible if this or that were to happen. This is where, Binswanger says, the hypochondria of overcaring concern for her nearest and dearest breaks in, comes alive, breaks out (256). While she's concerned that compromising photographs are being taken of her while bathing (255), she openly masturbates in front of the nurse. According to Binswanger, Urban thus leaves the self-enclosure of her world while showing the nurse-witness that *Dasein* has gone back to living inside her body where pleasure can be obtained. "The secret sphere of corporeality, which became in the delusion an open secret, now produces no secret whatsoever since the prerequisite for every secret, 'contact with the *Mitwelt*,' increasingly disappears" (256). The collapse of the ability to take the other at his words is another way of saying that with every contact with her world, in the mode of sheer receptivity, Suzanne Urban has been taken, taken in. The delusional world fulfils "the highest possible putting on display *[Schaubarkeit]* . . . of the dramatic tension, its presentation as action stepping before eyes, falling into ears, and getting up close and personal" (258). The world of terror stages everything, nothing is left out. But it is in the contact between elements of this world that the reduction plan becomes evident. "In this world of terror, this delusion of persecution, everything stands in fact not only in contact with itself but also in contact with everything else, from electrical contact via meaningful contact to the contact of the persecutor with the persecuted. This 'contact' refers . . . equally to optical, acoustic, tactile, and cognitive contact. Nothing about or of Suzanne Urban and nothing 'in' her that was not plugged into contact with the others. This contact is no longer connection in the sense of community, let alone communion in the sense of love, but a mechanized and materialized contact narrowly focused on a single meaningfulness" (259). The vanishing point of reality in the case of Suzanne Urban is cohabited by the torture-testing machinery of Schreber and the stage machinery of the Baroque *Trauerspiel*. "The reduction of world in this delusion to a mere contact world is also connected with the predominance of technology and the technical apparatus. Technology becomes here thoroughly stage technique *[Bühnentechnik]*, that is, it serves with its machines mere realization of a certain intention *[Absicht]*, here, then, the *Absicht* of endangerment, humiliation, martyrdom, annihilation" (260). According to Binswanger, each recognizable step is thus exceeded by catastrophic alle-gory. The police occupy the lowest rung of the stage scenery of hierarchy. In a two-step reminiscent of Benjamin's "Critique of Violence," next to the police one's fellowmen step up as the executive organs of terror. The most enigmatic confusion of recognizable and excessive traits inhabits Suzanne Urban's surveillance. It isn't only photography that is clicking away all around her, even recording her private time in the bath. One is also taking X-rays of her in all these compromising situations (248).

In "The Question Concerning Technology" ("*Die Frage nach der Technik*"), Heidegger contemplates the essential (in contrast to the endopsychic) setting of technology: various German verbs of standing up, placement, and ordering are collected in the noun *Gestell,* which, according to Heidegger, means "apparatus," "appliance," or "device" and "skeleton." Heidegger admits that at first or second sight this semantic double occupancy in *Gestell* is bizarre, even horrible. But extraordinary juxtapositions in a single word come down to us since Plato as habit of thinking. The skeletal essence of technology belongs to a ready positioning that precedes any machinic externalization. What is thus "enframed" is readiness or availability for all that technologization will manifest and supply. The *Gestell* is the collecting of standing up or placing that challenges man to discover or uncover reality as reserve in the manner of ordering. *Gestell* is the German repetition or rehearsal of the Greek *technē* that bound both art and technology (or science) within one "frame." Heidegger ultimately works this double trajectory of *technē* to open up art as the realm within which technology can be contemplated and encountered essentially (rather than merely technologically). Quoting Hölderlin, Heidegger locates at the art of technology a growing danger alongside which, at the same time, a power of rescue also grows. In his follow-up essay on technology, "The Turning" ("Die Kehre"), Heidegger fills in the blank of horror (which the double sense of *Gestell* opened up) with a sense or directive of successful mourning, mourning comparable to the unscarred healing of a wound. Does the turn toward concluded mourning turn off not only the double trouble of technology, its horror and threat, but also the portal to art's rescue ring?

What's in a name is in the title of the 2000 superhero film *X-Men.* It turns out that the "X" that marks the spot "mutants" are in—the spot of the unknown—and that marks Men thus as "over" or "ex" in the wake of transformations and other mutational upgrades was in fact a positive designation pupils came up with for their professors. In contrast to the monsters of nihilism, who wage war against total enemies, the overmen who bear the transference-gift name X-Men situate the question of superhumanity inside a school, within a setting of reading and interpretation. As mutants, however, once and future X-men must found their own school away from school. The mutants who seek out the transferential setting are as embattled as their nihilistic cousins within the precincts of institutionalization.

Wilhelm Conrad Roentgen's study of invisible rays put him back on the transference tracks to and through institutionalization (the tracks across which he had been strapped and run down in secondary school). Before he could graduate from secondary school he was caught holding the caricature of his teacher (which, as point of pride, he would not disown, even though, so the story goes, he was not the artist). His first dismissal was followed by his failure at the examinations he was entitled to take—over which, however, the same teacher presided. Roentgen therefore ended up studying mechanical design at the polytechnical university in Zurich, which was one institution that used entry exams rather than the candidate's school record and diploma to determine qualification for admission.

The same influence of the *Bildungsroman*—psychoanalysis *avant la lettre*—whereby the special sons of Central Europe (following Goethe's *Wilhelm Meister's Apprenticeship*) received their maternal legacy or talent via first contact with puppet plays and theater curtain, subsequently beamed, via Gottfried Keller's *Green Henry,* unfair banishment from the educational institution into their curriculum vitae. Roentgen's wife-to-be, Anna Bertha Ludwig, had grown up crossing the path of Keller in Zurich and making the melancholic laugh. Roentgen was able to assemble while in Zurich, his last resort from the traumatic fallout from his early expulsion from institutional support, recognizable research projects, matching academic career, a wife (for life), and a benign parental mentor (who proved equally eternal or internal). Through his acknowledged work on invisible rays—which would garner for Roentgen the first Nobel Prize—he was able to transfer the Zurich ensemble to the University of Würzburg, the institution which had all along been most resistant, down to the fine print of its legal constitution, to opening its portals to a professor doctor who had skipped the secondary school diploma.

One day Roentgen introduced into his experiments with rays various materials that he tested to see if they would block the beams. When he brought a small piece of lead into position while the discharge was occurring Roentgen saw the first radiographic image, his own flickering skeleton on the barium platinocyanide screen. But Roentgen made his first X-ray image—cast upon a photographic plate—of his wife's left hand. That this skeletal hand was the one given in marriage could be identified by the wedding ring that, like lead, blocked the rays and left a black silhouette.

Roentgen, an only child, had no children with his wife, whose death he survived by two times two—or two couples—of years. According to his testamentary wishes, his collected unpublished papers and notebooks were destroyed and he was buried in the family plot alongside his wife and his couple of parents, who as cousins were blood related long before and after they were conjugated husband and wife. The plot of two couples of different generations yet buried in fantastic isolation from future generation itself perhaps recalls or internalizes the closing of accounts in Goethe's *Elective Affinities*, but indeed calls to mind the elective calculations required for the only child to succeed, via his own coupling, in doubling and containing his parents rather than substituting for them and thus prying them apart. This plot, legible only in the skeletal phase of their lives together, seals a pact that the first alma mater's foundational diploma would have served to sever.

Roentgen discovered and made the first X-rays of the human body's live skeleton at a time when scientific testing was everywhere pressed into the service of peeling away the layers of invisibility. The X-ray was however recordable only and immediately as photograph. The earlier inventions of photography and train travel — the two alternating tracks of technologization that both Freud and Kafka saw as bringing closer that which, on the other track, had already been phantomized as long distant — ultimately hitched and stitched their innovations together as new ways of seeing to the format or industry of motion pictures. Benjamin (allegorically) personified the new relationship to the visible or visualizable world brought to us by cinema in terms of surgery. Just as the surgeon skips the interpersonal relationship with the patient to penetrate directly and deeply inside the opened-up body, so the cameraman (with the moviegoer in tow) enters the new visual field of *Zerstreuung* — at once "distraction" and "dissemination" — as examiner or tester without or beyond the mediation of interpersonal difference or distance.

According to Géza Róheim (in his 1923 essay "After the Death of the Primal Father"), a surgeon contains the murder that he perpetrates up to a certain point — whereupon the murderous penetration reverses itself and restitution can then be made as healing. This short stop, where the surgeon stops short of murder, marks the turning point at which the rebellious sons discovered that even the hated primal father was an object of mourning. As the sons consumed the murdered father, his body, in nourishing them, became confused with the maternal body, on which they thus gagged as occasion, after all, for mourning. At the same time the unmournable mother thus absorbed some of the disposability of the father. It remains undecidable whether this opening of the edible Oedipal complex issued a legacy of proper, successful mourning or a discontinuous transmission of unstoppable aberrations of mourning.

Roentgen could recognize the live skeleton only because he knew what the skeletons of the dead looked like. The disinterment of the long-dead body yields evidence of the leftover skeletal support. However, each time an animal was devoured to the bone—hence the totemic significance of animals—we would have recognized, even or especially at the totemic remove from cannibalism, our relatedness to the remainder. Indeed Galen's anatomical teachings were superseded once it could be demonstrated that his guidance through the human body had been based exclusively on dissections of animals.

The skeleton is an age-old allegorical figure of Death. It precedes the corpse, the bottom line or sign of allegorization on the stage of the Baroque mourning play. According to Benjamin's consideration of Baudelaire as modern allegorist, the nineteenth century lays bare (again) the inner corpse. Like today's plastic models or books with transparent pages, Andreas Vesalius's *De Humani Corporis Fabrica* of 1543, the primal anatomical manual to which Goethe still made recourse, starts with the whole stripped body and then begins stripping away the layers of that body until the reader ends up with a final cross section: the skeleton with ligaments. Dissection of human bodies was forbidden in Vesalius's day: more than desecration, it was heresy. Vesalius's secular findings did inter certain Christian redemption values at their allegorical points of overlap with pagan or occult allegiances to reanimation. It was believed, for example, that there was an incorruptible bone in the human body that served as the nucleus for the resurrection body. Once opened up, the body inevitably, in time, would reveal that there was no resurrection bone to pick with us. But rather than replace eternity with finitude, it is eternity itself that has thus been immersed in finitude. The functional thus slips inside the allegorical. Vesalius represented not only the scientifically illuminated body but also the allegorical creature that can neither live nor die because it is the immortal soul that has died without dying.

Can't Live, Can't Live

On Earth as it is in heaven or on Titan: In *The Game Players of Titan,*
The Game, which was imported from Titan to Terra as the free gift that
came with conquest, is nevertheless recognizable as Monopoly, though the
stakes turn out to be as high in fact as one always imagined them to be
anyway. To be B is to own property: because to begin the game is the deed.
Bindmen engage in games of Bluff in the course of which properties (entire
urban areas) are won and lost. Following the radiation catastrophe that
resulted from Red Chinese overuse of a weapon invented by East German
and ex-Nazi Bernhard Hinkel, there are not enough people to go around
but lots of large lots of property. The Game holds the place of jousting in a
fantasy-compatible setting of wide-open spacing for people few enough to
admit the hero to rise to the occasional. But in *The Game Players of Titan*
the throwaway hero is someone with "luck," a fertile match, in other
words, with as many partners as possible. His name is Luckman, bindman
of New York, who at the start of the novel has obtained West Coast property and therefore the right to play for all the other properties comprising
California. Luckman's purpose or reward is to reverse the decay of the
largely emptied-out cityscapes on the Coast, beginning with his first win,
Berkeley: "it won't be an emptiness haunted by the past. Ghosts . . . of our
way of life the way it was, when our population was splitting the seams
of this planet" (21). Luckman fixed New York by allowing non-B people
to play The Game, not for property, but "strictly for the pairing and re-
pairing of mates" (21). To play with property, to be a Bindman, protagonist Pete Gardner won the guess-the-date-a-B-dies lottery (24). Luck you:
give me reproduction or give me death.

Like the *I-Ching*-consulting Japanese of *The Man in the High Castle*, the Titans, otherwise known on Terra as vugs, are "gamblers to the core" who "abhorred cause and effect situations," employing "chancy systems" even or especially "for inheritance" (24). Pete Gardner lost Berkeley in The Game to the first in a series of rapid-turnover owners who sold it down the line that ended up in Luckman's hands. Because even the property game is about reproductive luck, a change in luck requires change your partner, swing her round. Carol replaces Freya as Pete's partner at The Game and at home in the bed or bet of reproduction. As word "wedding" is related to the German "*wetten*," meaning "to bet."

Pete self-medicates on the upswing of his own manic tendencies to push back the suicide he depressively, obsessively contemplates. He meets one of the luckiest mothers in town, who is also a telepath, shortly after running into her daughter Mary Anne at his friend Joe Schilling's record store. Joe says: "it's synchronicity, her coming in here" and putting through "the acausal connective principle" (31). The young woman, who has occult powers that neutralize all the other ones that, like her mother's telepathy, aim to know without taking a chance (or making a guess), introduces, where Schilling hears a synchronicity, the Magna Mater complex, which the mother/daughter relationship interpersonalizes as developmental imperative. But mother and daughter also double up as two aspects of the Magna Mater, castrative attraction and saving destruction. As psi whose influence is kinetic, Mary Anne McClain, as the younger generation, is the acausal X factor in her family line (from here to prehistory). All telepathic bets are off when her inertial aggressivity enters the game.

When the mother, Patricia McClain, reads Pete's mind, she discovers that he finds her daughter attractive and very much like her. " 'And you're also thinking that the real difference between me and my daughter is that I'm embittered and she's still fresh and feminine. This, coming from a man who steadily contemplates, ruminates about, suicide.' 'I can't help it,' Pete said. 'Clinically, it's obsessive thinking; it's involuntary' " (59). He also can't help, being a Californian, seeing midlifers as the bitter aftertaste of knowing and gnawing on a promise that wasn't kept. Fully participating in the spoiling of youth, he also sees the still young, simply because the burden of proof hasn't fallen yet, as full of promise.

Occult abilities, though prohibited in playing The Game, nevertheless influence its outcome by entering The Game's frame of reference and inoculation. As Pat argues in her own case of talent, telepathy is too fully immersed in the unconscious not to be always bordering on psychosis.

"The telepathic faculty has one basic drawback. . . . It tends to pick up too much; it's too sensitive to marginal or merely latent thoughts in people, what the old psychologists called the 'unconscious mind.' There's a relationship between the telepathic faculty and paranoia; the latter is the involuntary reception of other people's suppressed hostile and aggressive thoughts." (61)

She cannot see the future (or futures): she's not a precog. But she saw as "syndrome of potential action" the proximity of death in Pete's charted course. "That's another quality of the unconscious, it stands outside of time. You can't tell, in reading it, whether you're picking up something moments away from actualization or days away or even years. It's all blurred together" (61–62).

But what's also all a blur is the recent past. A jump cut of amnesia places Pete out of time: five hours are blank. The Rushmore Effect of the car (the audio of the auto-auto) can give Pete the coordinates of his missing hours, which map out assignations with Mary Anne and with Pat. That time, it turns out, spans the scene of crime. Luckman's murdered body is found in the car of Pete's new partner Carol. The oblivion we readers share is a convenient blocker of telepathic probing, as one of the detectives on the crime scene points out (76). "Something with enormous power was in operation; it had acted against six members of the group already, and who knew what its limits were? If it could deplete them of their recent memories"(80), then it could turn "them into a corporate instrument of its will" (89). For, this unidentified power that erases memory can manipulate minds, too. Suddenly one of the in-group members remembers that Pete called him to say he was going to kill Luckman. The telepathic detective confirms this—but as reservation: "The memory is there in his mind. But—*it wasn't there earlier when I scanned him a little while ago*" (84).

Pete and Carol go to the drugstore to go through the emotions of luck. They obtain the new pregnancy test strip developed in Bonn by A. G. Chemie in a "spectral drugstore," which stages the imperative of reproduction. "All for us . . . This enormous place with a thousand lights on and that Rushmore circuit clamoring away. It's like a drugstore for the dead" (99). But then there's news fit to throw one: Carol is pregnant. The news fits, in Pete's mind, the inoculative groove of the imposed oblivion either like the good-luck antibody or as the target of the power operating against them: "He frankly did not care about The Game at this moment. The idea of a child . . . obliterated everything else in his mind, all that had happened of late" (101).

The next span of time is a sieve of conflicting perceptions. Now Pete's on Earth, now on Titan. At the center lies his therapy session with Dr. E. R. Philipson, now human, now vug.

"When did you first begin to notice these disembodied feelings, as if the world about you is not quite real?"
    "As long ago as I can remember," Pete said.
    "And your reaction?"
    "Depression." (104)

Mary Anne waits in the auto-auto for him. " 'It likes me,' Mary Anne said. 'All Rushmore Effects like me. . . . I charm them' " (110). When she refers to people as Terrans, he recognizes her vug nature. Or not? He picks up that she is telepathic after all. "My own problems are problems of perception, he realized. Of understanding and then accepting. What I have to remember is that they're not all in it" (113). The note to remember he writes himself gives it his all, after all: "WE ARE ENTIRELY SURROUNDED BY VUGS RUGS VUGS" (116).

The memory sieve must be attributed to a third or fourth rhyme word, DRUGS, which he took on the upswing of the manic episode brought on by the baby news. Pete is "a manic-depressive; he has an affective psychosis, periodically" (119). Later, while holding Pete at heat-needle point, Pat confirms that he "had an authentic psychotic occlusion" (127). She and her husband Allen abduct Pete because in his drug-induced state he became temporarily telepathic and hallucinated "along a paranoid line" the thoughts he picked up from Mary Anne. While the hallucinations interfered with his perceptions, fundamentally he was right, Mary Anne confirms. "I actually was feeling those fears, thinking those thoughts. Psychotics live in a world like that all the time" (130). What he knows without knowing it—and might have revealed to the authorities via the hindsight of their decoding—is all about a secret psi group trying to deal with the reality of alien menace.

But one of Pete's memory shards that stuck to the sieve convinces Mary Anne that the vugs are getting to her and have already infiltrated the group. "He asked me what I saw in the bar and I thought he was hallucinating. But it wasn't my fear he was picking up. He saw reality" (136). The group members retrench to defend themselves against the reality that they are vug collaborators. The precogs are enlisted as the first line of defense: it's Mary Anne who's a variable, clouding it all up; she's going to do something. She knocks them all out of the running of the group's double agency with her poltergeist powers. "She can't be predicted" (138). While the Rushmore Effect of his own car identifies him as vug, Dr. Philipson demonstrates that he owes his membership in the psi resistance group to his Mary Anne–like powers of psycho-kinesis. He can move individuals to Titan or to Terra (and back again):

An extinguishing curtain had blotted the fixed images of the objects around them, had blotted them into waste. Junk, like a billion golf balls, cascaded brightly, replacing the familiar reality of substantial forms. It was, Joe Schilling thought, like a fundamental breakdown of the act of perception itself. . . . Is this the understructure of the universe itself? he wondered. The world outside of space and time, beyond the modes of cognition? (153)

No, they've been transported to Titan to play The Game on its "Platonic ultimate template" (155). But in this prelim match to ignite their destruction, the doctor, and yes, he's a vug, shows the hand of Titan limitations in playing the game. Their bind is double: they can cheat only against Terrans, but any move by Terrans that fits deception into the groove of the Titan deception stops them in the tracks of the fundamental Titan bind: they cannot cheat.

The game exploded.
    "I cheated," Joe Schilling said. "Now it's impossible to play. Do you grant that? I've wrecked The Game." (156)

Mary Anne arrives, kills her father, ejects her mother, and/or "introduces the acausal principle of synchronicity" (165). The Bluff playing group realizes now that, though it is illegal, because she's a psi, Mary Anne should be brought into the group. The Titans themselves play The Game as telepaths, but by hobbling the psi faculty through drugs, something like the phenothiazines used to treat schizophrenia, which obliterate "the involuntary telepathic sense; it eradicates the paranoiac response to the picking up of subconscious hostilities in others" (179). On drugs even the precog would not know if he were bluffing or not (181). Pat McClain, who discloses the rites of hobbling because she is going to kill her interlocutors, is again thwarted by her daughter, who this time puts mother on the extinction seat. "Please don't, okay? I gave birth to you. Please—" (184).
    The daughter dashing off her mother is internal to Dick's fix on the "dark-haired girl" retrofitted for the Magna Mater complex. Both Pat and Mary Anne fit the profile of the dark-haired girl. Clearly Pat is the more toxic figure, not only because she's a stooge for Titan but also because

she openly wages sexual warfare against her eldest daughter. When her husband advises her that this sort of rivalry is inappropriate, she counters that the next daughter is next in line. It's this conflict, otherwise projected as interplanetary, that is basic to luck. Pat as midlifer with an adolescent to grind is contrasted to Mary Anne, the true teenager, who in Dick's estimation is the harbinger of the overcoming through deregulated gadget love of the android drive of self-destructive conformity. Pat, the perpetual adolescent or "android," employs occult mediatic powers to get the other or the time to come over with, while Mary Anne, her teen daughter, relies on the X factor of her inertial power to release the future from controlling interest or fixity.

Mythically or psychotically (but also in self-defense) the daughter killing her mother represents "resolution" of Jung's Electra complex, the equal but separate coverage Jung extended against sexual difference (as difference). In *Black Sun,* Julia Kristeva's study of mourning and melancholia—and excavation or restoration of what was otherwise missing in the work of her mentor, Jacques Lacan—Kristeva takes her departure from "Freudian theory," which "detects everywhere the same impossible mourning for the maternal object" (9). Her momentum at takeoff, however, she owes to authors of new-and-improved psychoanalysis, from Jung to Lacan. Kristeva conjugates the loss of the maternal object along the Oedipal lines Freud gave the primal father and his representatives: "Matricide is our vital necessity, the sine-qua-non condition of our individuation, provided"—and with this proviso Kristeva summarizes her understanding of healthy psychic development—"that it takes place under optimal circumstances and can be eroticized—whether the lost object is recovered as erotic object" (the homosexual scenario, according to Kristeva) "or it is transposed by means of an unbelievable effort" (Kristeva refers here to the uphill struggle of heterosexual developments) "which eroticizes the other... or transforms cultural constructs" (now we're talking sublimation) "into a 'sublime' erotic object" (27–28). Kristeva's lines of healthful development out of these choices (all of the above) are also the measure of what the melancholic, the subject of her study, tries to refuse (or re-fuse): "the maternal object having been introjected, the depressive or melancholic putting to death of the self is what follows, instead of matricide" (28). Because a daughter is her mother's continuity shot, this process of internalization is even less confrontational or decisive and way more slow-mo in its release of the destruction. Although homosexuality was part of the health plan given above, now homosexuality joins the disposition of melancholic daughters (though it appears that a female/male distinction is operative here): "The homosexual shares the same depressive economy" (29). In the cases of daughters comprising the clinical basis of *Black Sun*, the matricidal imperative postulated by Kristeva (a former Maoist) is admitted only as virtually imperceptible or, at best, as the construction of her analysis. It is clear, then, that in Kristeva's *Black Sun* case-by-case differentiation occurs in the murky area displaced with regard to the theory itself—in the shadows at close quarters cast when, in consideration of sexual difference, Kristeva pulls the emergency brake on her otherwise monolithic theory. The matricidal frame that is the normal fare for circulation outside the psychoanalytic session nevertheless returns as the redemption value of the melancholic deposit—it's only a matter of change—which must be secured through or as forgiveness (at once illusory and imperative). "He who does not forgive is condemned to death. . . . The Resurrection appears as the supreme expression of forgiveness" (192). Forgive an author whose tendency to refer to missing mothers has prompted reviewers to confuse his psychoanalysis with that of Kristeva's *Black Sun*. Alone the distinction I draw between mournable and unmournable objects along a sliding scale of unmourning (the concept or condition to which I grant metapsychological precedence) disallows the assimilation of my readings to Kristeva's version of the Electra complex.

In "Stabat Mater" Kristeva takes another stab at her. But first she drops to her footnotes before Jung while in the main text she dismisses Freud's view of motherhood as "only a massive *nothing*": "There thus remained for his followers an entire continent to explore, a black one indeed, where Jung was the first to rush in, getting all his esoteric fingers burnt, but not without calling attention to some sore points of the imagination with regard to motherhood, points that are still resisting analytical rationality" (179). In the footnote, number 4, she refers to two points Jung raised before she got around to it, and then applauds his support of "the Vatican's adoption of the Assumption as dogma, seeing it as one of the considerable merits of Catholicism as opposed to Protestantism." Because the cult of the Virgin offered in its day a solution to the problem of feminine paranoia, it becomes imperative for women and men alike that a postvirginal discourse on motherhood introduce a new ethics into the tight corner occupied by both reproduction and death—a union cathected as reproduction *is* death.

In adolescence going on young adulthood Philip K. Dick worried that he might be homosexual. His first heterosexual act was consummated with gratitude. To make the intake history short: Dick's relationship to sexual desire as to loss was mythic or psychotic. A psychotic foregoes the strong ego that homosexuality requires. But a psychotic doesn't see it that way. Dick embraced heterosexuality as close call and as mother of all battles between the sexes that culminates or is grounded in misogyny. Thus the cold woman who cannot love is sent into projections of madness, diagnosis, hospitalization, and out-patient low maintenance. Over the years Dick proved a quick study of therapeutic attitudes of self-awareness. He prided himself on being able to talk any psychiatrist, analyst, or therapist into most anything. One day he convinced his psychiatrist that his wife Anne was the sick one hiding behind him, the identified patient in the system.

One evening in the fall of 1963, while Phil and Anne and the girls were having dinner, the sheriff—the man from whom they rented the shack—came to the door. He had with him a court order committing Anne to a psychiatric hospital for three days of observation. When she realized that the order was signed by *her* psychiatrist, she flew into a rage, convincing the sheriff that the poor guy he had been renting his shack to had been telling him the truth all this time; he really was married to a crazy woman.

It was a painful scene. Anne had to be dragged away by force. . . . The three days of psychiatric observation turned into three weeks. (Carrère, *I Am Alive,* 94)

Anne was the model or self-fulfillment of Dick's representation compulsion around the sadism of female intelligence and success. Her pharmaceutical treatment, which her psychiatrist anticipated as a lifetime regimen, was so strong that she did time as a bitter zombie in her husband's care.

This twistedness lies to the side of Dick's plotting of psychosis along social or interpersonal lines. *Clans of the Alphane Moon* begins with the couple in crisis. Mary breaks it off: the protagonist Chuck must support her and their children while she donates her time to the investigation of the moon society founded by former inmates of the Harry Stack Sullivan Neuropsychiatric Hospital. She thus drops her working identification as successful marriage counselor to double her ex's load. The stretch is the mark where the couple ends up joining the clan society of psychotics. Chuck founds his own colony of "Norms," Jeffersonville, while Mary swings from the manic "Mans," where she settled following her outbreak of oral sadism, down to the "Deps," her compatriots according to the test results. Thus the prospect for the couple's reconciliation opens up over the absolutely humiliated person of the wife.

The "Poly" looks to Chuck like the first candidate for resettlement in Jeffersonville. Before his introduction of this clan of Norms, anyone who didn't fit an extreme profile went to dwell among the Polys in Hamlet Hamlet. The "Pares" leader Baines appears to be on his way, too, when he shows concern for another person. Plus there is no guarantee that the children will reside in the same community or caste as the parents. Chuck admits that, since he had tested normal after surviving suicidal ideation and putting to rest his plan to murder Mary, the difference between psychotic folly and the norm can be one only of degree. This is the frame for his acceptance of his wife, his life, for better or worse. More to the point of this degree candidacy for normalcy, she, as the identified severely depressed figure, is the placeholder for the illness Chuck succeeded in balancing out and passing beyond by degrees. But most important for the metabolization of love and hate in the couple is that a good introjection of the dark-haired girl slips inside Chuck. Joan Trieste is a psi whose talent is time reversal for five minutes tops in a setting no larger than the immediate scene of a fatal accident at which she at times, if there is still time, returns the casualties to life. Chuck meets her at the onset of his persecution by Mary's demands for divorce settlement whereby he becomes embroiled in the interplanetary intrigue between competing interest groups for possession of the Alphane moon. But when the plotting moves to this moon, she alone is left behind—but to cross Chuck's mind. He has chucked her away as bit player in the intrigue. But her name is cleared at the expense of the wife, whose compromising involvement in the opening intrigue is thus revealed as final test of Chuck's decision to renew the marriage vows. The name that is cleared names the sadness that depression is all about avoiding. Her exclusion from the happy ending of the novel is the internal extraction she stands for from the depressive intrigues in circumvention of contact with life's *triste* insides. Importantly this inner world borders on the emergency setting of life lapsing into death. A range of only five minutes guarantees that Joan Triste will at times arrive too late to reverse the fatality but that at no time will she be missing from the onset of mourning. Thus grief occupies the missing bottom line of psychosis, which seeks to keep the foundations of its society- or world-building momentum grounded in deep depression and thus already at a remove from the *triste* rapport with risk or rescue—with life on the brink of loss.

Beginning with *The Game-Players of Titan*, Dick wrote four Magna Mater novels all in a row (yo ho, and a bottle of Mom). Dick allowed sanity to pass this bottleneck in *Dr. Bloodmoney*, the individuation or letting go of the twin and the affirmation of Bonnie, the mother of the twins—and Dick's one-time-only affirmation of the transferentially inflected model of the dark-haired girl. But this was the fictional world of idyll that couldn't leave its signed-off place. Next in row of the administration of the Magna

Mater by rote is and is not *The Simulacra*. In *The Simulacra* "Magna Mater" circulates verbatim as a psychosocial diagnosis, only a slight upgrade of the Momism current in postwar American pop psychology. There's no toxic shot of misogyny only spreading it thin in this presentation. Already in *The Game-Players of Titan*, it is the Oedipal game, played out on two boards, that is won for Mary Anne, the dark-haired girl as her own continuity shot. It's not just that she hated her mother, she ate her, too. Her chapter never opens; instead the centerfold of interstellar specisim folds out of the spot she was in with her mother and that the protagonist Pete was in with both of them, hot spots of generational and sexual difference (the trouble a woman still has with her mother, she also has with her men—and so on).

In The Game between Titans and Terrans, division between you or nonsuperimposability for two folds out the internal feminine as onset of mournful recognition of projected realities. The Titans propose that as each player loses, a vug copy will step into his or her place. In fact they show up for the showdown as simulacra of their Terran opponents. But they immediately fall short of supplying a convincing simulation of Mary Anne. The Titans beam the game up to Titan and drop the body double suits. "It was as if, once the simulacra shapes had been discarded, communication between the two races had at once suffered an impairment" (193). It is not animosity, however, only spontaneous withdrawal. Next the vugs seem to merge into one: "One massive, inert organism opposing them, ancient and slow in its actions, but infinitely determined" (193). Pete bluffs that he is telepathic by the drugs he took. It's not true, but it shakes loose the nervous overreaction of the Titan opponent. Once the Terran players recognized that the opponent was mortal, victory was theirs—but then it's held back from them as they're scattered all over Terra. Each team player undergoes a kind of atomization and isolation. It's like psychosis—or maybe it's the fundamental reality beneath the conscious layer of the psyche. When they bump up against each other, they feel slimed by creatures. Can that really be you? "It's something that lives here between the worlds. Between the layers of reality which make up our experience" (203). But then the moment of recognition arrives.

That's us. Terrans, as the vugs see us. Close to the sun, subject to immense gravitational forces. . . . No wonder they want to fight us; to them we're an old, waning race that's had its period, that must be compelled to abandon the scene.
    And then, the vugs. A glowing creature, weightless, drifted far above, beyond the range of the crushing pressures, the blunted, dying creatures. . . .

Do you grasp that? . . . That our view of the situation is equally true? Yours can't replace ours. Or can it? Is that what you want? . . .

"You saw the view which obsesses us. We can't repudiate it." The vug flowed closer to her, anxious to make its thoughts truly clear. "We're aware that it's partial, that it's unfair to you Terrans because you have, as you say, an equal and opposite and as completely binding a view of us in return. However, we continue to perceive as you just now experienced." It added, "It would have been unfair to leave you in that frame of reference any longer." (205–6)

But even the sponsor of this exchange of projections must conclude: "Ideally . . . both views can be made to coincide. However, in practicality, that does not work" (206). That's why the novel ends between two sets of "twins." His oncoming car announced by "twin lights" (214), Dr. Philipson picks up Freya (Pete's wife before Carol) and her spirits when he invites her to join the Titan war party. All's fair in The Game of getting even. But the luck is with the new couple. Carol tells Pete she thinks they're going to have twins, a boy and a girl.

The next two novels in the Magna Mater row, row, or float the boat for the first time with identifiable vengeance. We witnessed the reversal of marriage counseling in *Clans of the Alphane Moon*. One down, one to go. In *Now Wait for Last Year* Kathy, the wife of protagonist Dr. Eric Sweetscent, takes the toxic shots as designated delegate of Magna Mater.

"In marriage the greatest hatred that is possible between human beings can be generated, perhaps because of the constant proximity, perhaps because once there was love. The intimacy is still there, even though the love element has disappeared. So a will to power, a struggle for domination, comes into being." (169)

While Kathy collects the relics of authenticity that aid her boss Virgil Ackerman in retrofitting himself into the artificial environment of Washington at the time of his boyhood (where he goes to un- or re-wind), her husband Eric, on a lesser pay scale, replaces organs in boss Ackerman, who has attained the double age of Faust. This boss, who is also his wife's boss, boots Eric up the hierarchy to tend to Molinari, the Terran leader, because his inside view of the Sweetscent marriage gives him a good sense of what the doctor is willing to do. Molinari, also known, like Hamlet's father's ghost, as the Mole, needs the organ transplant specialist to help stage the pageant of the leader's somatic trials (with one emergency exit left open by Eric's promise to assist, if necessary, in Molinari's suicide). The double of Kathy—over whose uncanniness, which Molinari recognizes, leader and doctor first bond—is Frenesky, the abyssally staring leader of Lilistar,

Terra's ally in the current conflict. Psychically, however, Frenesky is Molinari's ongoing foe. The war that is marriage can thus take a backseat to the war (the "was") waged between species in the close quarters of the control room shared in moments of disconnection by Molinari's flights into illness and Frenesky's "paranoid eyes." Eric is the eye witness:

This was not the glittering, restless stare of ordinary suspicion; this was a motionless gaze, a gathering of the totality of faculties within to comprise a single undisturbed psychomotor concentration. . . . It was an attentiveness which made empathic understanding impossible: the eyes did not reflect any inner reality; they gave back to the viewer exactly what he himself was. The eyes stopped communication dead; they were a barrier that could not be penetrated this side of the tomb. (121–22)

All the 'Starmen seem to know, and it's infinite, is the reversal of psychoanalysis. When Kathy points out to the mastermind aliens that she can't shadow her husband because they just split up, the leader provides marriage counseling.

"Resolutions of that type in a marriage," Corning said, as if speaking with the weary wisdom of an infinity of ages, "can always be reduced to the status of a temporary misunderstanding. We'll take you to one of our psychologists—we have several excellent ones in residence here on this planet—and he'll brief you on the techniques to use in healing this rift with Eric." (69)

When Eric trades up the hierarchy to tend to Molinari, everyone cheers that this way he will separate from his wife. But she will not be ignored. While out partying without her husband, before she finds out about his promotion, Kathy swallows (hooker, liar, and stinker) a new drug that, unknown to her, was created highly toxic and immediately addictive as secret weapon for use in interstellar warfare. To motivate him to find the cure, Kathy slips Eric the drug while visiting him at his new home base. The drug conveys "a sense of having imbibed of death itself" (148).

Most people who drop the drug experience time tripping into the past. Kathy's first time trip proves to be back to the time she excavates for the antiqued Washington environment. She mails her employer in his boyhood a circuit lifted from the autonomic cab that accompanied her from the future into the past. Thus she hopes to grant him a technological advantage that will fulfill her every wish once she's back from the time trip. However, nothing (material) transfers from one time zone to another (outside, that is, the encapsulated environment of the trip itself).

To the cab she said, "Land in the pasture. We'll sit it out until we're back in our own time period." It probably would not be long now; she had an impression of a devouring insubstantiality here in this era—the reality outside the cab had gained a gaseous quality which she recognized from her previous encounter with the drug. (111–12)

Eric is one of the few who goes to the future—where he is, after all, able to secure the cure, which he need only memorize for past reference or inject himself with in the future to contain the drug's influence in the past.

"You've moved slightly over one year ahead. . . . You're one of the happy few the drug affects this way. Most of them wander off into the past and get bogged down in manufacturing alternate universes; you know, playing God until at last the nerve destruction is too great and they degenerate to random twitches." (143)

While his Magna-Mater wife goes the way of all collectibles, Eric is thrust into the saving future, one that conveys another story or different history (166). Terra was allied with the enemy, the Reegs, against the allies, the 'Starmen (who may be alien but otherwise identify as Aryan heads). And in this alliance Earth prevailed.

The course of his time tripping into the happy ending is first set with and against the allegorical interlinear momentum of alternate presents. Is Molinari a suffering old hypochondriac whose body, in syndication with every ill body in the immediate environs, endures miracle cures—while his robot version of himself as a young man still makes the pitch to the people across media? Or is it the other way around?

"The flabby, aging, utterly discouraged and hypochondriacal Gino Molinari whom you've met and accepted as the authentic UN Secretary. . . . *That's the robant simulacrum.* And the robust, energetic figure you witnessed on video tape a short while ago is the living man. And this ruse must necessarily be maintained, of course, to sidetrack no one else but our beloved ally, the 'Starmen. . . . The 'Starmen consider us harmless, unworthy of their military attention, only so long as our leader is palpably feeble. Quite visibly unable to discharge his responsibilities—in other words, in no sense a rival to them, a threat." (113)

What Molinari or his simulacrum must face to face is the blast of no contact in the contest of negotiation with Frenesky. Molinari thus flees into illness before the demands of the 'Starmen leader.

What Minister Frenesky does, Eric realized, is to deprive all the others of the sanctity of their office. Of the security-producing reality of their titled position. Facing

Frenesky, they became as they were born; isolated and individual, unsupported by the institutions which they were supposed to represent. Take Molinari. Customarily, the Mole was the UN Secretary; he as an individual had—and properly so—dissolved into his function. But facing Minister Freneksy, the naked, hapless, lonely man reemerged—and was required to stand up to the Minister in this unhappy infinitude. The normal relativeness of existence, lived with others in a fluctuating state of more or less adequate security, had vanished. (122)

The prospect of alternate realities as mourning outlet rather than as recess for collectibility first opens up over a third Molinari body, locked up as Top Secret, another version of the same body—dead, alive, or live. "In the center of the murky, cold room Eric saw a casket. . . . In the casket, supine, lay Gino Molinari, his face locked in agony. He was dead" (115). The robot dyad that organized Molinari's defense against Frenesky's schizoid stare breaks open:

"Perhaps it's from an alternate present in which Gino has been assassinated, driven out of office the hard way by a splinter political group of Terrans backed by Lilistar. But there's a further ramification of this theory, one which really haunts me. . . . That would imply something about the virile, strutting Gino Molinari who made that video tape; that's not a robant either and GRS Enterprises did not manufacture it because it too is an authentic Gino Molinari from an alternate present. One in which war didn't come about, one perhaps in which Terra didn't even get mixed up with Lilistar. Gino Molinari has gone into a more reassuring world and plucked his healthy counterpart over here to assist him." (116)

In the course of finding the cure Eric must also reclaim the projection of the Reegs as alien insect bodies (which holds interchangeable places with projective idealization in the court of the 'Starmen). Now that antagonism and alliance have reversed positions in the conflict that can at last yield to survival, the future holds integration with Reegs in store, in the very hospital storeroom from which Eric obtains the antidote. Time traveling sees affirmative action in Dick's works by clocking alternate realities, in which second chances are granted for survival. A realignment of conflict in battlefield marriage promotes the survival of care.

The abandonment of the android hypothesis in Eric's understanding of Molinari's relationship to life-or-death conflict also withdraws the antagonistic plotting of the couple and passes on or beyond toxicity. While this time around the protagonist separates from the wife, in all his time-tripping variations he finds only his ongoing care for her, which is the nonseparated mode of their relationship. The self-recrimination that almost motivates Eric to seek a substitute for Kathy becomes the words he lives, loves, and leaves by: "I've been waiting a long time for last year. But I guess it's just not coming again" (207). Eric discusses Kathy's case with another version or track of himself from another time zone:

> Then even that wouldn't help, Eric realized. Staying with her, even for the rest of my life. "I appreciate your help," he said. "And I find it interesting—I guess that's the word—that you're still keeping tabs on her."
> "Conscience is conscience. In some respects the divorce put more of a responsibility on us to see about her welfare. Because she got so much worse immediately after."
> "Is there *any* way out?" Eric asked.
> The older Eric Sweetscent of the year 2065, shook his head. (221)

Now the assistance of suicide, a prospect that had horrified Eric when Molinari folded it into their patient/doctor contract or confidentiality as proviso, seems the way to go. Two accidents stay his resolve. He finds money in his pocket from another time zone, which breaks the strict taboo on bringing anything back from a time trip. "So perhaps, he thought, Kathy's electronic part had reached Virgil Ackerman back in the mid thirties after all; at least it had a chance. That cheered him" (224). He nevertheless prepares to swallow the poison on the streets of Tijuana. "The click of heels against the pavement, the rushing forward into life; that's gone and only a slopping, dragging sound is left behind. The most horrid sound in the world, that of the once-was: alive in the past, perishing in the present, a corpse made of dust in the future" (225). But then something runs across his shoe.

We're thus thrown back to an episode we briefly passed through at the start of the novel. On Terra surrogates can be made with Martian print amoebas, which mimic anything at all, but only for a time. Thus the amoebas had to be killed during the interval of mimicry. The assembly of *faux* mink stoles in peacetime was in the meantime converted to war work. But coming down this assembly line of war machine parts are a number of hypermimetic rejects. A certain Himmel buys the rejects, which he hitches to moveable carts and then lets go. Why? Because "they deserve it" (13). Himmel's colleague counters: "But the protoplasm's not alive; it died when the chemical fixing spray was applied. You know that. From then on it— all of these—is nothing but an electronic circuit, as dead as—well, as a robant." Himmel: "But I consider them alive . . . And just because they're inferior and incapable of guiding a rocketship in deep space, that doesn't mean they have no right to live out their meagre lives. I release them and they wheel around for, I expect, six years or possibly longer; that's enough.

That gives them what they're entitled to" (13–14). After the ins and outs of time tripping over time Eric thus finds Himmel's carts still on the street: "Even these things, he decided, are determined to live." Himmel was right. "They deserve their opportunity, their miniscule place under the sun and sky. That's all they're asking for and it isn't much. He thought, And I can't even do what they do, make my stand" (227). The rest is history. Eric gets up from his suicidality, emerging from the time tripping in the present tension of the reversal of the toxic alliance. He decides to join the struggle against the Nazi Death 'Starmen, which, as always, lies ahead: "As was intended from the start, anterior to any time or condition I could comprehend or call my own or enter into" (228). As he makes his way to headquarters, where he is bound to encounter Kathy, Eric vows not to leave her in sickness and in death. He's found a woman who will do the dying for him and thus give him double or Faust time, enough time to get out of range of the rebound of his death wish.

For an introduction to a collection of stories Dick recycled the title back through real time travel: "Now Wait for This Year." What the author loves, those persons closest to him, and what he hates, what happens to them, namely, suffering unto death, are his sole subject matter, albeit sublimated as his big ideas or questions, What is human or What is reality.

> Yes, science fiction is a rebellious art form and it needs writers and readers with bad attitudes—an attitude of, "Why?" Or, "How come?" Or, "Who says?" This gets sublimated into such themes as appear in my writing as, "Is the universe real?" Or, "Are we all really human or are some of us just reflex machines?" (217)

However, the bottom line of his immediate or sublimated response to what happens to his nearest and dearest is the line one toes in gallows humor, which Freud singled out as among the happiest moments of the otherwise conflictual relationship between ego and superego, which can, interpersonalized, be aligned with the working relationships we considered already between teen and parent and between husband and wife. Sometimes it's up to death to do the partying.

> I have watched Doris suffer unspeakably, undergo torment in her fight against cancer to a degree that I cannot believe. One time I ran out of the apartment and up to a friend's place, literally ran. . . . We just sat there and then I said aloud, really just pondering aloud, "The worst part of it is I'm beginning to lose my sense of humor about cancer." Then I realized what I'd said, and he realized, and we both collapsed into laughter. (218)

Lola

The momentum of Binswanger's case study of Lola Voß, which follows the patient as she shifts from polymorphous schizophrenia into paranoid schizophrenia, goes against Freud's revalorization of Schreber's delusional system as moment of recovery. Binswanger proposes instead that what Lola wants or lacks is what she gets in the end: the psychotic defense of loss of self, self-being, and freedom. Her paranoia marks a point of no return of the process of deterioration that leads via increasing *Verweltlichung* or "worldification" of her existence to a new structure of *Dasein* determined by a specific *Weltentwurf,* "world view" or "projection of world," to which *Dasein* must abandon itself utterly ("Der Fall Lola Voß," 41). *Dasein* gives itself up as self. No timing, no spacing, no selfing—no contact with others—equals no *Dasein.* That's why we experience the completely autistic schizophrenic as machine (44). Following the extensive presentation of case materials and right at the onset of the *Daseinsanalyse* itself, Binswanger sets out to make Lola fit the bill of *Being and Time* made out to *Verfallen,* "fallen" or "lapsed," and *Geworfenheit,* "thrownness," which otherwise amounts to the being-in-the-world of everyday life. On this page (41) Binswanger drops a note (2) to Heidegger's more recent extension of this view of the everyday: in a review of Ernst Cassirer's take on mythology, Heidegger recycles that which is overpowering in the sense of thrownness into the one *(das Man)* as overpowering in the sense of thrownness of mythic *Dasein.* Binswanger affirms but also shows Heidegger elevating projection (and endopsychic perception) by lifting it from Freud and dropping it inside (as though reclaiming all of the above for) Germanic word grooves of description in or of another day in the small town one is born in, one wants to love and live in or leave and denounce. Authentically speaking, there isn't a choice. Getting stuck precisely here would be the worst nightmare for one cosmopolitan rich girl, whose given name is Lola Voß. Lola is half German, half South American. When in Europe the family stays in Paris. The terms Lola will be made to use in defense and as persecution are given by Binswanger/Heidegger in advance as the fateful equivalencies advance on her: *Man, Gerede, Neugier, Zweideutigkeit.*

Lola is threatened by *Verunheimlichung,* which means "uncannification." We should note however that the German modifier *unheimlich* also contains *heimlich* or "secret," which it in some sense negates. The *Heim* also of course lies therein as the home, *Heimat* — it's a small town after all. Lola arrives at the asylum in Kreuzlingen under the rule of superstition: "something dreadful" will happen to her if she doesn't observe her ritual practices (which she at the same time, however, must make up as she goes along out of the only common thread, clothing). Superstition summons fate while expressing fear of it. This fear is doubled as fear that through superstition fate has been challenged. Thus superstition serves at the same time as atonement.

In the course of consulting, reading, interpreting the oracle of fate, Lola throws a net or network of conditions around herself on the basis of which an answer will in every case be forthcoming. But this net becomes intrusive once men and objects are involved. The links in the network are formed through "infection" of objects through contact with or proximity to a taboo person or thing (49). Since this net is so widely spun or flung that it can meet or fulfill almost every condition, we must pay special attention to where and when Lola pulls it tight to catch her quarry (50). Since her catch of the day is the cutest female orderly on staff who becomes right away the boogie woman and spreader of taboo, Binswanger warns that this is not the concern of *Dasein*-analysis and life history. Later he will qualify, with regard to Freud's model in the Schreber analysis, that Lola is sincerely betrothed, requests a look at the cute male gardener (the request is not fulfilled nor does she push it, which is unlike her), and her persecutors later on in the course of her schizophrenia cannot be identified as same sex. When Lola's vigilance with regard to contact with the pretty young woman and all her traces (even psychic facts, like memories for example, can be contagious) begins to disrupt the asylum as a whole, Binswanger tells her to pull herself together or he will summon the woman on the spot, the tight spot of their session, to be in Lola's face. She acquiesces immediately. But let's face it: the intervention leaves her in two minds.

All the expressions around thrownness refer to the temporality of a "mere (inauthentic) present" (50). Without the provenance of past or future that the authentic present enjoys, the inauthentic present is purely present, which means it passes (through) without stopover. What corresponds, then, to the discontinuity, jumpiness, and changing character of Lola's spacing, its dependence on the focus of infection, is, in terms of her timing, what's pressing and sudden (51). There's no momentum, nothing's going on, nothing leaves. Everything remains fixed or fixated in *Dasein* because everything stems from or defends against *Dasein*-anxiety: that is why nothing is more terrible, as Lola repeatedly laments, than to be burdened with memories. The existential anxiety, however, has been transformed already before her first contact with Binswanger into horrible fear of worldly husks and shells. Binswanger cites Gottfried Keller's title as gloss: "Kleider machen Leute" ("Clothes Make People"). But the tailor protagonist in Keller's novella perpetrates deception contrary to his intentions because, styled for a cosmopolitan setting, he can only be misunderstood in a small town. He enters a small town and the rest follows, ending almost in his suicide, but then ending in fact on the upbeat that revalorizes his clothing not as deception but as prop from childhood by which his true love has known him and can be known in turn.

Lola clothes the ungraspable uncanny horror as fate, something that can be deciphered. She is a close reader. For example, the cane or *bastón* ends in two letters that can be reversed. It also ends in a rubber tip that gives us up front, via *goma* or rubber, together with the cane's tipped over word: "no go." In her, at the time, broken German, Lola however manages to literalize and animate "curiosity" along lines Binswanger/Heidegger can cosign. In German *curiosity* means literally "lust for the new," which, rendered transitive, is a favorite surveillance activity her enemies engage in against her: *neugierden*.

A new dress brings with it the threat of new misfortune (the extent of possible contact with the terrible is thus enlarged). That which is new, newness itself, is that which is sudden. Lola dreads the irruption of suddenness. In her own words of warning: "One must not give me anything unexpected, since from that I get an idea that stays forever" (58). Living from one now point in time to the next is what is present, passing by, standing by. It is an "uncanny sudden jump *[Sprung]* from one now point to the next" (59). True existential continuity is based on repetition. Here we are concerned instead with the "worldly category of recurrence of the same." "Here memories are 'clothing,' namely coverings of existence, bearers of misfortune, not at all past and repeatable or re-collectable *(wieder-holbares) Dasein.*"

With cover measures, *Dasein* defends itself against the irruption of the uncanny. With their aid *Dasein* finds support through *Sorge* or "care," but in the integrated sense of *Besorgen,* which means to take care of something, like the shopping. In the second phase of Lola's schizophrenia, after all the defenses fail, we face in exchange a definite and specific threat emanating from the world. But the no longer uncanny threat is now both definite and "secret." This world is ruled by the *Rufgestalt,* not Lola's word, but reminiscent just the same of the telephone that starts out slandering Miss St. in Jung's *The Psychology of Dementia Praecox.* The *Rufgestalt,* the "shape of reputation" and, literally, "of the call," is normally kept in the background and overlooked: it is how others receive your *Dasein.* The uncanny world has become a world of crimes that are happening all over the place and in her face, but they are secret to the extent that the motives are unknown. Her "life stage," to borrow Ellen West's phrase, now shows "tragedy"—and communicates via hearsay.

Lola is an involuntary instrument of the scenic activity, which must "say" what the enemies make her say (in order thus to "direct" their crimes); she is now only an apparatus that must give back what one deposits inside it as speech or thought. She is however not only an instrument without will but an innocent one as well. Out of the existential guilt has become a worldly held-to-be-guilty: "One" thinks badly of her! (64)

Formerly, in the first stage of Lola's countdown to paranoia, the uncanniness could be taken at its word just as it declared itself openly as yes or no in the voice of fate (72). In the second stage the "thou" has been pluralized. The world is no longer taking care of things but is immersed in dreaming of a threat.

Binswanger praises Freud's reading of anxiety dreams: either the dreamer wakes up from them or transforms the free-floating anxiety into fear. In this context he makes a Faustian point: *Dasein's* striving is to escape *Dasein*-anxiety. Even delusion is a form of this "striving" (74). Every anxiety is anxiety about death to the extent that *Dasein*-anxiety signifies Death as principle or drive (77).

Inspired by Schopenhauer's words to the effect that anxiety is not about anything or something but is only about the "ghostliness" of *Dasein* bereft of world, Binswanger concludes his reading of delusions as makeshift coverings and connections without any recovery significance for *Dasein:*

What we call delusions and hallucinations are but isolated bridges or links "between" a consequently unfree subjectivity and a corresponding "phantastic" objectivity, are only isolated moments of a deeply altered structure of *Dasein*. (97)

Once again, as with Ilse and Suzanne before, Binswanger keeps abyssally separate those stages of Lola's psychosis where the Freudian perspective recognizes a borderline. Only the notion of altered structure allows Binswanger to remain loyal to the new frontier of Freud's Schreber study but at the remove of never being in the same place as Freud in a psychosis analysis. Altered structure would be one "save" with its layering that was lost in the Freud file. An American following of the standards of psychotic recovery is another comp (of reality testing) whereby one calculates the prize of altered structure.

Clifford Beers introduces the memoirs of his mental illness, *A Mind That Found Itself,* as "the history of a mental civil war, which I fought singled-handed on a battlefield that lay within the compass of my skull" (1). The *es war* of linear time is the "it was" that Nietzsche's Zarathustra tries to get across as the revenge we're after, which leads to the conflict called "war." When Dick summons civil war it is to denote a conflict that can only count losses. That might just be another way of saying that it has to be internal to be relieved. Beers became the correspondent of this war that his "skull," as always the keepsake of the dead other, had to contain.

The mortal illness of an older brother was "the direct cause" of his "mental collapse six years later" (5). The prospect of his brother's seizures happening any time of day and, the worse thought, in public got so on his nerves that he fell ill too, but in his mind. "I remember distinctly when the break came. It happened in November, 1895, during a recitation in German" (6).

Rather than become invalid-ated like his sick brother, he threw himself out the window—and lost the hypochondria on impact. But he gained the container of being "under legal constraint" via the technical illegality of suicide. "Every act of those about me seemed to be a part of what, in police parlance, is commonly called the 'Third Degree'" (17). Reading time is as charged. "Every publication seemed to have been written and printed for me, and me alone. Books, magazines, and newspapers seemed to be special editions. . . . Meanwhile the date on each newspaper was, according to my reckoning, two weeks out of the way. This confirmed my belief in the special editions as a part of the Third Degree" (48).

What he calls his "depression" is on photographic recall: "My memory during depression may be likened to a photographic film, seven hundred and ninety-eight days long. Each impression seems to have been made in a negative way and then, in a fraction of a second, miraculously developed and made positive" (71). Recovery will mean recognizing in each photographic memory its provenance as yet another piece of consumed mass culture administered by "the detectives."

Phantasmagoric visions made their visitations throughout the night. . . . These illusions of sight I took for the work of detectives, who sat up nights racking their brains in order to rack and utterly wreck my own with a cruel and unfair Third Degree. . . . I imagined that these visionlike effects . . . were produced by a magic lantern controlled by some of my myriad persecutors. The lantern was rather a cinematographic contrivance. Moving pictures . . . were thrown on the ceiling of my room and sometimes on the sheets of my bed. Human bodies, dismembered and gory, were one of the most common of these. All this may have been due to the fact that, as a boy, I had fed my imagination on the sensational news of the day as presented in the public press. (24–25)

The closing reflection belongs to the phase of recovery that was set off when he in fact went to the movies only to be reminded of his visit to the Chamber of Horrors in the Eden Musée in New York two years earlier. It was the exhibit of a gorilla bearing the gory body of a woman. In the film the gorilla was turned into a man stabbing the woman's breast. He was not terrified for a change since he recognized both the source, the process of transformation "strictly in accordance with Darwin's theory," and the whole "as a contrivance of the detectives" (31). The next step of recovery was taken when the superstition crossing his mind that eating "a burnt crust of bread would have been a confession of arson" (32) also triggered the recollection that he liked to attend trials "out of idle curiosity" in his former life. It was the similarity between his doctor's name and the name of a man whose trial for arson he thus idly observed that made the charge stick (40). The detection work of the other begins to develop as reality testing.

Once he's out and about again he decides to raise money for a new humanitarian mission. The "abnormal stress of feeling" (175) eventually convinces him to go back to the hospital voluntarily for follow-up treatment (181). At this point he decides to observe his own case and record its details. "The sane part of me, which fortunately was dominant, subjected its temporarily unruly part to a sort of scientific scrutiny and surveillance" (184). We owe the book to the founding of this new internal economy. Joy in living becomes the joy of writing, which, unlike elation, which didn't know when or how to stop, reaches the punctuation point of exhaustion.

"And even now, when I reread my record, I feel that I cannot overstate the pleasure I found in surrendering myself completely to that controlling impulse" (185).

The emphasis here is on "controlling." He first comes out from under his depression once he is able to verify through multiple tests of his own devising and by his instigation that his eldest brother really is his brother. When he was brought home the first time, the evidence of a nurse in attendance convinced him that he was still under "surveillance" and that his eldest brother "was no brother of [his] at all. He instantly appeared in the light of a sinister double, acting as a detective" (23). But now that he can recognize the reality of the other in his brother "elation" swings low, transforming everything into messages from God. He is God's instrument for effecting reforms. He starts writing letters twenty or thirty feet long (79). He revalorizes his stay as undercover assignment in investigative reporting. His stamina compares favorably to that of a "trained war correspondent" (133).

He proceeds from defiance of the state "and its puny representatives," which "had become mere child's play," to the overcoming of "gravity itself" (127). His goal is to render "flight of the body as easy as a flight of imagination" (128). But first he wings it by attaching a number of felt strips to the head and foot of the dead, I mean bed. The free ends he attaches to the transom and window guard. "I next joined these cloth cables in such a manner that by pulling downward I effected a readjustment of stress and strain, and my bed, *with me in it*, was soon dangling in space" (177–78).

Upon his ultimate return to the sanity circle of friends, family, and acquaintances, he is greeted "as one risen from the dead." That's not far off the mark, he notes: "My three-year trip among worlds—rather than around the world—was suggestive of complete separation from the everyday life of the multitude" (169). He is separated from and linked to the multitude only by his having fallen into the projection booth behind the screed of mass culture. In other words: "To be 'straightened out' was an ambiguous phrase which might refer to the end of the hangman's rope or to a fatal electric shock" (60). But before the organization of his new world in terms of its all-seeing administration by detectives, before the torture preliminary to reality testing, he was at the new frontier of haunting. Like Hamlet facing his father's ghost, he was caught between "a hellish vocal hum" and "ghostly rappings on the walls and ceiling" (17–18). When he saw himself in pictures the emphasis in the catastrophic scenarios was always on rescue. Spirited away aboard an ocean liner he was able to project an emergency exit when the ship commenced burning and sinking. He managed "to establish an electric railway system" that conveyed the passengers in trolley cars from the "phantom ship" to safety (18). That "deliverance from one impending disaster simply meant immediate precipitation into another" (19) simply means that the emphasis on rescue is sustained as interminable. Though he would appear to be claiming that he concluded his sojourn as he began it, as one risen from and with the dead, the reality testing that pulled him back across the borderline was pulled up short before this frontier. In this sense Binswanger would be right to speak of a changed structure with *faux* contrast that can't be turned up to improve the picture quality. But it is a structure that can be found in many households not (officially) guided by psychosis.

Umwelt, Mitwelt, and Eigenwelt

> He fed the sole pet allowed him in the apartment building: George
> II, his small green turtle. . . . Even as recently as five years ago he
> could have possessed a pet bird in The Abraham Lincoln, but that
> was now ruled out. Too noisy, really. . . . A turtle was mute—as
> was a giraffe, but giraffes were verboten, too, along with the quon-
> dam friends of man, the dog and cat, the companions which had
> vanished back in the days of *der Alte* Friedrich Hempel, whom
> Vince barely remembered. So it could not have been the quality
> of muteness, and he was left, as so often before, merely to guess
> at the reasoning of the Party bureaucracy. He could not genuinely
> fathom its motives, and in a sense for that he was glad. It proved
> that he was not spiritually a part of it.
>
> —PHILIP K. DICK, *The Simulacra*

Richard Kongrosian, the identified psychotic in *The Simulacra,* starts out
"an anankastic, a person for whom reality had shrunk to the dimension
of compulsion; everything he did was forced on him—there was for him
nothing voluntary, spontaneous or free. And, to make matters worse, he
had tangled with a Nitz commercial" (60). The deodorant commercial
has contaminated him with "phobic body odor" (60). "At the same time
he knew that the odor was a delusion, that it did not really exist; it was
an obsessive idea only. However, that realization did not help him" (61).
The odor also transmits along phone wires and even by telegram. Perhaps,
after all, A. G. Chemie, the firm that separated him from his psychoanalyst,
Dr. Superb—analysis has been prohibited on behalf of the drug therapies
that A. G. Chemie supplies—can come up with "a new ultra-powerful
synthetic detergent which will obliterate" the odor, "at least for a time"

(62). On a good day he is simply the world's greatest psychokinetic concert pianist. But now he is certain that "psionicly" he involuntarily caused all the calamities in today's headlines (62). As he explains to the talent agent organizing the White House event he was scheduled to headline:

"This is no ordinary physical odor. This is an idea type odor. Someday I'll mail you a text on the subject, perhaps by Binswanger or some of the other existential psychologists. They really understood me and my problem, even though they lived a hundred years ago. Obviously they were pre-cogs. The tragedy is that although Minkowski, Kuhn, and Binswanger understood me, there's nothing they can do to help me . . . At this point I'm thoroughly delusional. I'm as mentally ill as it's humanly possible to be! It's incredible that I can communicate with you at all. It's a credit to my ego-strength that I'm not at this point totally autistic. . . . It's an interesting situation that I'm facing, this phobic body odor. Obviously, it's a reaction-formation to a more serious disorder, one which would disintegrate my comprehension of the Umwelt, Mitwelt, and Eigenwelt." (63)

Rollo May included in his existential analysis reader (together with contributions by "Minkowski, Kuhn, and Binswanger") the essay "The World of the Compulsive" by V. E. von Gebsattel, which focuses on the case of an "anankastic" (172), which is von Gebsattel's coinage based on the Greek for "fate," *ananke*. The case von Gebsattel studies was set off by the patient's spontaneous ejaculation, which was displaced to the urinary and excretory orifices as their irreversible stink. "The cleaning process itself and, indeed, elimination are defiling, and this defilement spreads on the one hand spatially (to clothing) and on the other temporally, in that from one point to the other it extends itself through the whole day. Indeed, completely in keeping with the anankastic illusory phobia, there is a complete absorption in the illusory urine odor. . . . Of all the symptoms in H. H.'s compulsion syndrome the odor is the most unpleasant, because it is always present and incombatable; and because of its localization in the center of the self-concept it is particularly painful" (175). Through the odor he is nailed to the past: "H. H.'s not getting rid of the past pollution is, at closer sight, the pollution itself in its genuine meaning" (176). In other words: "We see that the phobic odor-illusion is intimately bound up with a disturbance in the capacity to bring things to a close—especially with the incapacity to have done with the bodily act of cleaning" (176).

Normally you drop the past like excrement and your "life purifies itself through its devotion to the forces of the future and the tasks that challenge us from the direction of the future." The past "as something unfinished . . . makes demands on the anankastic as the future makes demands on the healthy person" (178). Kept back from "becoming" through his inhibition—kept back from repaying the debt of existence—the patient (who in this regard, von Gebsattel advises, resembles the melancholic) must attend to an inner sense of guilt. H. H.'s inability to become amounts to Un- or De-Becoming *(Entwerden)*. Thus he is oriented "toward formlessness which must be warded off but cannot be warded off. Precision is the counterpart of this orientation to formlessness to which his inhibition in Becoming inescapably delivers him" (181). Von Gebsattel disagrees with the view of "Jung and others" that we might be dealing here with "the unchanged resurgence of a primal reality." The situation for the anankastic is way more restricted and specialized. "Only that which is inimical to form, which moves toward 'un-form' or is apt to bring it about, enters as a deciding factor in the anankastic world" (182). The "peculiar mixture of dawdling and rushing that marks the temporal structure of anankastic behavior" always results, in the execution of the rituals, in time being lost: "therefore time must always be made up for":

What fails here, however, is the stream of inner happenings that keep step with passing time; in the anankastic, for some unknown reason, this has fallen into a state of rigidity. At one point it binds the patient without rest to certain rituals, at another point it makes him race for lost time and delivers him to an even more ceaseless rushing. (185)

Let's underscore what remains unfinished in the passage of von Gebsattel's analysis: the unknown reason for the patient's fall into rigidity, like playing dead, and the comparison with the case of melancholia, which apparently is the tighter fit with von Gebsattel's reading of Un-Becoming and guilt.

While Kongrosian's initial self-diagnosis draws on von Gebsattel, Kongrosian cites, alongside Binswanger, two more existential analysts (Minkowski and Kuhn) capable of understanding but not helping him, who were also included in Rollo May's edited collection. Eugene Minkowski studies the case of a patient who presented with "depressive psychosis accompanied by delusions of persecution and extensive interpretations" (127). It's the living end of the world and his martyrdom is piled high with detritus and vermin. Anyone who looks oddly at him is in on it.

These ideas of guilt, ruin, imminent punishment, and persecution were accompanied by interpretations of a really surprising scope. This was the "residue politics" *(politique des restes),* as he called it—a political system that had been instituted especially for him. Every leftover, all residue, would be put aside to be one day stuffed into his abdomen—and this, from all over the world. Everything would be included without exception. When one smoked, there would be the burnt match, the ashes, and the cigarette butt. At meals, he was preoccupied with the crumbs, the fruit pits, the chicken bones, the wine or water at the bottom of the glasses. The egg, he said, was his worst enemy because of the shell—it was also the expression of the great anger of his persecutors. When one sewed, there would be bits of thread and needles. All the matches, strings, bits of paper, and pieces of glass that he saw while walking in the street were meant for him. After that came nail parings and hair clippings, empty bottles, letters and envelopes, subway tickets, address-bands, the dust that one brought in on one's shoes, bath water, the garbage from the kitchen and from all the restaurants of France, etc. Then it was rotten fruit and vegetables, cadavers of animals and men, the urine and faeces of horses. "Whoever speaks of a clock," he would tell us, "speaks of the hands, cogs, springs, case, pendulum, etc." And all this he would have to swallow. In sum, these interpretations were boundless; they included everything, absolutely everything that he saw or imagined. In these conditions, it is not difficult to understand that the smallest thing, the most minute act of daily life, was immediately interpreted as being hostile to him. (128)

The patient's crisis has a history larger than life and a name that put a lid on it. Mr. Poubelle, whose name would come to signify "garbage can," reorganized trash collection in Paris largely by removing the discarded remains of the day from the easy pickings access whereby the very poor re-collected even stray hairs, for example, to make wigs ready-to-wear. In the absence of recycling we have a void that at the end of the day is filled in containers. How will "they" manage to stuff the whole busy intersection between collectibility and trash inside his stomach? "He would be made to absorb only a bit of each thing and the rest would be arranged around him when he was exposed to public derision in some side show" (131). Each day he is convinced that his execution is planned for that night. Each day he is just as sure. The daily or nightly stay of execution does not influence his perspective. "Our thinking is essentially empirical; we are interested in facts only insofar as we can use them as a basis for planning the future. This carry-over from past and present into the future was completely lacking in him" (132). Like reality testing, planning for the future has been withdrawn from the psychotic. That each day adds more waste is his only connection with the world. No day is an island—except in this case for days without continuity.

What had been done, lived, and spoken no longer played the same role as in our life because there seemed to be no wish to go further. . . . The future was blocked by the certainty of a terrifying and destructive event. This certainty dominated the patient's entire outlook, and absolutely all of his energy was attached to this inevitable event. (133)

Minkowski gains entry for Freud's view of delusional systems as means of recovery with the password "death." Don't we all realize that we are sentenced to die on those occasions "when our personal impetuses weaken and the future shuts its door in our face?"

Isn't it possible to admit that the patient's outlook is determined by a similar weakening of this same impetus, the complex feeling of time and of living disintegrating, with a subsequent regression to that lower rung which we all latently possess? Looked at in this light, a delusion is not something which is simply an outgrowth of phantasy but, rather, is a branch grafted onto a phenomenon which, as part of all of our lives, comes into play when our life synthesis begins to weaken. The particular form of the delusion, in this case the belief in execution, is only an effort made by the rational part of the mind (itself, remaining intact) to establish some logical connection between the various sections of a crumbling edifice. (134)

Indeed he maintains this edifice as a growing undertaking: "His thinking no longer was concerned with the usual value of an object, nor did he clearly delimit each one of them. An object was only a representative of the whole and his mind went beyond its particular meaning in ever-extending arcs. The address-band of his newspaper made him think of all the bands of all the copies of that paper which are distributed every day, which led him to all the address-bands of all the newspapers of France" (135). Whereas our sphere of interest is limited in space but extends endlessly into the future, the patient's sphere is spatially limitless (he immediately glides from the solitary object to its infinite series) while blocked in the future. But infinity is his flight plan, both as escape for the mind and from every object encountered, which under the aegis of infinity decomposes. Without the future the bridge from good acts to better acts is falling down. Bad acts remain. "An intact memory remains, but everything is dominated by the static feeling of evil" (138).

The second in the assembly line of robots in Dick's earlier android novel *We Can Build You*, Abraham Lincoln was at the front of the line of animatron robots of American Presidents imagineered by Disney already in the 1960s, which now model the President of the future in *The Simulacra*, though the robot is—Surprise!—made in Germany. Indeed this Californian culture of the future is immersed in Germanicity. The future society is organized according to two groups: the *Ges*, abbreviation for *Geheimnisträger*, those comprising the upper caste to whom the "secret" of a double simulation has been entrusted, and the *Bes*, the *Befehlträger* whose lowlier position in society is defined by the "orders" they carry out in the absence of access to the secret (34). The president, named *der Alte* (explicitly modeled after Konrad Adenauer), is the robot of the old guy who gets replaced in elections by yet another one. His first lady, however, who holds the position of power in the future, is changeless. It's always the same Nicole Thibideaux (modeled, it goes without saying, on Jacqueline Kennedy) who comes first alongside each new *der Alte*. The other secret organizing this society is that this continuity shot is maintained through a series of actresses.

If no one appears to notice that Nicole over time proves ageless, then that's because her TV image is everyone's share in the fantasy of seeing the Nicole they believe in—in the flesh.

"Have you ever seen her?" Al asked. "I see her all the time." "I mean in reality. In person. So to speak, in the flesh." "Of course not," Ian said. That was the entire point of their being successful, of getting to the White House. They would see her really, not just the TV image; it would no longer be a fantasy—it would be true. (88)

The First Lady functions mainly as talk show hostess of the monopolized assembly of culture that stages its season finales at the White House. The semifinals are conducted regularly in every large communal apartment building. (Our focus throughout the novel is on the building named The Abraham Lincoln.) High culture was decimated during World War III. Its only representative, the concert pianist Richard Kongrosian, is also mediated as a professional by a gimmick: he plays psychokinetically while they look no hands. To fill the slot of culture, therefore, just about anyone else, all of them amateurs, has a lottery chance to be picked up as talent for one night with Nicole.

Passing tests (on various subjects of study) that entitle one to remain a resident in The Abraham Lincoln, for example, and trying out in auditions for the ultimate talent show are the two tracks for passing time in the future.

As part of the effort to offset the influence of the cartels, the commission for engineering the next *der Alte* goes to a small firm, Frauenzimmer Associates, which specializes in the field of sim-con ("simulacra construction for planetary colonization") (34). In front of his operation Maury Frauenzimmer has placed one of the major items of the firm's catalogue, the famnexdo, the family pack of simulacra (parents and two children) to take along with you when emigrating to Mars.

A man, when he emigrated, could buy neighbors, buy the simulated presence of life, the sound and motion of human activity—or at least its mechanical near-substitute—

to bolster his morale in the new environment of unfamiliar stimuli and perhaps, god forbid, no stimuli at all. And in addition to this primary psychological gain there was a practical secondary advantage as well. The famnexdo group of simulacra developed the parcel of land, tilled it and planted it, irrigated it, made it fertile, highly produc- tive. And the yield went to the human settler because the famnexdo group, legally speaking, occupied the peripheral portions of his land. The famnexdo were actually not next door at all; they were part of their owner's entourage. Communication with them was in essence a circular dialogue with oneself; the famnexdo, if they were func- tioning properly, picked up the covert hopes and dreams of the settler and detailed them back in an articulated fashion. Therapeutically, this was helpful, although from a cultural standpoint it was a trifle sterile. (55–56)

While colonists can bring their simulated neighbors with them to Mars, Earth has been visited by the papoola, a hypnotically cute critter indigenous to Mars but now as a species extinct, which lives on as simulacrum and sales pitch (the kind that becomes your own thought, the way the deodor- ant commercial took over Kongrosian's psychic reality). In a world from which pets have been evacuated, the papoola dummy is the mascot of group identification. Even or especially as simulacrum. The salesman, for example, working the critter by remote can work his crowd via extrasensory influence or what might be called "a little subliminal sales technique" (87). " 'Now may I ask what this creature you carry is?' He eyed the papoola with something less than active enthusiasm. 'Is it alive?' 'It's our totem animal,' Al said. 'You mean a superstitious charm? A mascot?' 'Exactly,' Al said. 'With it we assuage anxiety' " (155).

Germany joined—and permeated—the United States following the last world war. "The tail that wags the dog. . . . We in *Nord Amerika* are the dog; the Reich is the tail" (25). The Second World War also occurred in the past of this future world, a dark age in Germany's history (and thus in that of the hybridized United States) that is officially condemned. "Days of Barbarism—that was the sweet-talk for the Nazi Period of the middle part of the previous century, now gone nearly a century but still vividly, if dis- tortedly, recalled" (24). A Neo-Nazi movement, the Sons of Job, accord- ingly pulls itself together out of the margins of this society.

It turns out, however, that the leader of the Sons of Job, Bertold Goltz, is in fact the leading member of the Council. He is engaged in all-out covert efforts to push back the controlling influence of certain German conglom- erates, which represent the actual (or actually possible) continuity with the Third Reich. Nicole is involved in yet another scheme (which like that of Goltz depends on the technology of time travel) whereby she hopes to resolve present tensions back in the past of World War II. Germany must win the war, but without carrying out any Final Solution. Following the recommendation of the military commission, Nicole brings back Göring for reprogramming as Hitler's replacement in time to avert the Führer program of total self-destructiveness. Von Lessinger's time-travel equipment had already been used "to send a psychiatrist back to 1925 to cure Führer Hitler of his paranoia"—"but the *Ges* kept the results to themselves" (41). But Goltz sees that Nicole is being used by the Third Reich (or its representatives in her time, the leaders of the German cartels) to realize a total victory of Nazi Germany to the limit of annihilation of all others over which Germany would crawl to the top.

When Kongrosian puts through a call to Dr. Superb (he has just heard on TV that the doctor is the one and only psychoanalyst officially allowed still to "exist"), it becomes clear that in the meantime his "compulsive-obsessive structure" has crumbled apart into "overt psychosis:" Kongrosian is becoming invisible and thus turning into nothing but the repellent odor (92). After several tables have turned, the intriguer Pembroke returns with "Nicole" in custody after having beaten the Council to the draw. But now he has to face the showdown with Kongrosian. It's nothing interpersonal. Like Dr. Bluthgeld, Kongrosian has reached the crisis point of his psychosis where the delusional force that is with his thoughts turns around into externalization or realization. It is the psychotic's "political act" (168).

"Something terrible's happening to me," Kongrosian wailed, as soon as he spied the two of them. "I no longer can keep myself and my environment separate; do you comprehend how that feels? . . . Look—see that desk? I'm now part of it and it's part of me!" . . . He scrutinized the desk intently, his mouth working. And, on the desk, a vase of pale roses lifted, moved through the air toward Kongrosian. The vase, as they watched, passed into Kongrosian's chest and disappeared. "It's inside me, now," he quavered. "I absorbed it. *Now it's me.* And—" He gestured at the desk. "I'm it!" In the spot where the vase had been Nicole saw, forming into density and mass and color, a complicated tangle of interwoven organic matter, smooth red tubes and what appeared to be portions of an endocrine system. A section, she realized, of Kongrosian's internal anatomy. . . . "*I'm turning inside out!*" Kongrosian wailed. "Pretty soon if this keeps up I'm going to have to envelop the entire universe and everything in it, and the only thing that'll be outside me will be my internal organs—and then most likely I'll die!" (194)

But the horrific breakdown also shifts Kongrosian's individual or interpersonal suffering onto all the world's a stage of terror where it can get lost as such in the ensemble while it is played out in the realm of the total delusion. This fearsome prospect of being a world suck was on Manfred's horizon, too (in *Martian Time-Slip*). But as political act Kongrosian's full entry into the delusional world parts company it otherwise keeps with Binswanger's reading of psychosis. Pembroke pulls a gun to restore the political order he would usurp. It disappears inside Kongrosian while Pembroke is left holding a piece of the psycho's lung. When Pembroke drops the lung tissue and Kongrosian shrieks with pain, Nicole commands the pianist to pull himself together. He proceeds to pick himself up off the floor. Kongrosian finds he has no trouble shutting off organs inside Pembroke outside the dynamic of exchange. He sends Nicole, the maternal figure, like another internal organ, off to his home in the fallout-generated tropical rain forests in Jenner, California, where he has set up house with wife and son. The place is so remote as to suggest, to one of the sound engineers sent to track him down for the recording, that for a man of Kongrosian's ability being there was "a 'form of suicide'" (68).

In the midst of the messy metabolism of Kongrosian's showdown we pass through the space we watched Dr. Superb open up when he grabbed Kongrosian's interest with a reinterpretation of invisibility. Kongrosian's emergency call to Dr. Superb interrupts the analyst's session with a young man in crisis flight formation. Superb tries to intervene in both sessions at once. Before he hangs up on the clinging caller, the doctor grabs him:

"Good god, I've got to be invisible! It's the only way I can protect my life!"

"I would think there ought to be certain advantages to being invisible." Superb said, ignoring what Kongrosian was saying. "Especially if you were interested in becoming a pruriently prying type of individual or a felon..."

"What kind of felon?" Kongrosian's attention had been snared....

"You envy me, do you doctor?"

"Very much so," Superb said. "As an analyst I'm quite a pruriently prying person myself."

"Interesting." Kongrosian seemed much calmer, now. (93)

Kongrosian doesn't know when to stop, in particular since his connection separates the doctor from the other patient. In the middle of his self-analysis as deranged out of love for Nicole, Superb hangs up on him, an act that impresses the patient in his office. The "fully alert" patient opens himself up for an interpretation not only of Kongrosian. "'That man,' Superb said, 'has a delusion that's overpowering. He experiences Nicole Thibodeaux as real. Whereas actually she's the most synthetic object in our milieu'" (94). "Shocked," the patient free-associates until he arrives at fear of the woman he only thinks he loves.

"The image," Superb said, "of the Bad Mother. Overpowering and cosmic."

"It's because of weak-fibered men like me that Nicole can rule . . . I'm the reason why we've got a matriarchal society—I'm like a six-year-old kid."

"You're not unique. You realize that. In fact, it's the national neurosis." (95)

The conditions under which he alone remains open for sessions have made Dr. Superb in turn "obsessive": "Is this the one? Am I here solely to treat—or rather to fail to treat—this particular man? He had wondered that about each new patient in turn. It made him tired, this ceaseless need to speculate" (91). But when his secretary announces Pembroke, the official who made of Dr. Superb's practice the exception to the rule of prohibition, the analyst anticipates an impasse that, as in the process of Kongrosian's psychosis, is more serious than obsession:

Has he finally come to shut me down? he wondered. Then I must have seen that one, particular patient without realizing it. The one I exist to serve; or rather, not to serve. The man I'm here to fail with.

Sweat stood out on his forehead as he thought, So now my career, like that of every other psychoanalyst in the USEA, ends. What'll I do now? . . .

He was too young to retire and too old to learn another profession. Bitterly, he thought, So actually I can do nothing. I can't go on and I can't quit; it's a true double-bind, the sort of thing my patients are always getting themselves into. (175–76)

Gregory Bateson edited and introduced *Perceval's Narrative*, the early nineteenth-century memoir of a recovered schizophrenic's mental illness, as showcase of the complete view of the double bind, first as the break, next as autotherapeutic reclaiming of reality as multiple choice. Perceval's break is set off in the volatile setting of conversion fads. A sect of one, Perceval tries to carry out the orders of his spirits or voices. But they are never satisfied with the genuineness or seriousness of his efforts. Plus if anything goes wrong in the course of a command's enactment, it's his fault. Bateson cites Perceval's self-diagnosis: "I perished from an habitual error of mind. . . . that of fearing to doubt, and of taking the guilt of doubt upon my conscience" (ix, citing 37). After citing a passage of "contradictory demands" (32–33), Bateson diagnoses the fit with his theorem:

Here the voices present him with the false thesis that there exist alternatives of action among which he might choose one course of which the voices would approve. He makes his choices and tries to obey, but is always blamed at some more abstract level—e.g., for lack of sincerity. He is placed by the voices in what has been called a "double bind" such that even if he does the right thing he is blamed for doing it for the wrong reasons. (x)

To close his essay "Toward a Theory of Schizophrenia" Bateson turns to the example of Frieda Fromm-Reichmann in session with a schizophrenic patient and expands (or shrinks) the notion of double bind to fit the therapeutic and transferential frame. The patient inhabits a religious delusional system organized around God R, who at some early point commands the patient not to speak to the doctor. Fromm-Reichmann counters that, though the patient's religion is her private affair—she won't take it away from her; besides she doesn't understand it—she must make clear, for the record, for her at least, God R doesn't exist. However, Fromm-Reichmann will use the terms of her world in talking to her as long as the patient remembers and recognizes that her world doesn't exist for the doctor. In the meantime the patient should tell God R that it's the doctor's turn because God R clearly hasn't been able to help her. Thus through a "therapeutic double bind," the schizophrenic cannot but begin to accept that the relationship to the doctor as real is one of the choices on the reality test.

Though Perceval scourges himself for the guilt of doubt, in time he can assume responsibility for belief and doubt—at which point he is able to doubt his voices. "Fearing to doubt, he falls into literal belief in his delusions and in what his voices tell him. . . . By their very nature his delusions contain, in an inverted or concealed form, the very doubts that he is afraid to entertain in a more conscious shape" (ix). The delusions lead him to the experience of them, finally, as absurd. Bateson gives a clear example from the *Narrative* of the voices themselves shifting ground and coming around to multiple choice:

At another time, my spirits began singing to me in this strain. "You are in a lunatic asylum, if you will"—"if not, you are in," &c. &c. "That is Samuel Hobbs if you will—if not, it is Herminet Herbert," &c. &c. &c. (xi, citing 146)

It's not that he was suddenly able to believe the truth from the mouths of his spirits, but he begins to recognize that other patients call the attendant Samuel Hobbs. By other "accidents" he discovers his location, here on earth and, more precisely, in the asylum. Thus the voices gave back a kernel of reality that permitted him to comparison stop the sway of his delusions. "Here the voices are doing what Perceval wished his brother had done—accepting the fact of the delusion and reinforcing the doubt." By thus setting up these two inside views of Perceval's echo chamber side by side, Bateson can summarize the frame of the *Narrative*: "Here then Perceval presents, in two diagrammatic thumbnail sketches, the recipes, first for inducing his insanity and then for curing it" (xi).

Conventionally, schizophrenia is regarded as a disease, and, in terms of this hypothesis, both the conditions necessary for it and the precipitating causes which bring on the attack must be regarded as disastrous. But it would appear that Perceval was a better, happier, and more imaginative man after his psychotic experience, and in this introductory essay I have suggested that the psychosis is more like some vast and painful initiatory ceremony conducted by the self. *From this point of view, it is perhaps still reasonable to regard the conditional causes with horror. The precipitating causes can only be welcomed.* (xix–xx [my emphasis])

While in recovery, Perceval motivates one aspect of his symptom picture, his intermittent outbursts of violent expression, as reflecting concern for his family's feelings. He thus took all responsibility for their abandonment of him. "I knew that, of all the torments to which the mind is subject, there is none so shocking, so horrid to be endured as that of remorse for having injured or neglected those who deserved our esteem and consideration. I felt for my sisters, my brothers, and my mother: I knew they could not endure to look upon what they had done towards me, to whom they were once so attached, if they rightly understood it." When Perceval raises his pen to compose poison letters addressed to his family members he also commences the writing that would lead to the publication of the *Narrative*. In putting pen to paper, therefore, the denial is simultaneously reversed down to the details of what he would spare them: "they could know no relief from the agony of that repentance which comes too late, gnawing the very vitals, but in believing me partly unworthy of their affection; and therefore I often gave the reins to my pen, that they might hereafter be able to justify themselves, saying he has forfeited our respect, . . . he has . . . merited our abandonment of him" (xvii, citing 211–12).

But there are blank spaces animated in the course of the printing and reprinting of his inoculative pen. As he gives general reflection on the interdependence of the health of body and mental health, even though the automatic (or "mechanical") physical functions, which proceed independently of thought, in turn contribute no ideas, he turns to, on, into the scene of publication: "in the same way as, if several printing-presses are worked by machinery, it may be necessary for the perfect state of that machinery, that all the presses should be in motion, although some may have no types under them" (273, note). As we get deeper and deeper into the recovery phase, Perceval develops a theory of the psychic apparatus in terms of projection, to which the act of writing is also assigned. As he works scrupulously to reestablish his sound mind by "testing" all phenomena in his world for "faithfulness" (304), he proceeds to see through ghosts and other figures that were not in fact external objects: "ghosts, visions, and dreams are formed by the power of the Almighty, in reproducing figures as they have before been seen, on the retina of the eye—or otherwise to the mind . . . so as to produce such a resemblance—and then making the soul to conceive, by practising upon the visual organs, that what it perceived really within the body exists without side, throwing it in a manner out, as the spectre is thrown out of a magic lantern" (305–6).

But before he could identify with his family members (again) Perceval was routinely punished by the prospect of different members of the family enduring torment for the insincerity of his efforts to carry out the missions impossible assigned to him by the voices. The two figures at the front of this line of punishment were the two deceased family members, his father and, in first place, his sister.

No question but the force of the almighty is with his dead father. Perceval gives a father-and-child vignette that supports Bateson's sense that Perceval early on was placed in the wrong because he could not identify the label or frame of messages: "as if a father were to say to his child in fun, 'Now, run into the puddle,' . . . meaning the very contrary, and the child were to take his words as if meant in earnest" (275–76). The Almighty "who rules the imagination has the power, not only to produce written or printed words, and to throw them out upon blank paper; but to cover written or printed words or letters with other words or letters that are not there" (310). Perceval was able to discover "the sleight that was played" upon him, whereby the Almighty produced upon the "film" covering the eye false words. First this recognition caused him to "doubt that the objects . . . were REAL" (311). But then the better half of his double constitution returned—the sense of humor—and he was able to undo the "evil" into which his own "perverse, unsimple, and suspicious disposition" kept turning the instruction the Almighty intended for his "good" (312).[1] In one example of this instruction we can discern the assignment of mourning work:

An example of this kind of vision occurred when I was at Brisslington, working in the garden among some currant-bushes—a female form, without habiliments, rose from the ground, her head enveloped in a black veil. I was told it was my eldest sister and that if I chose she should rise up entirely, and address me unveiled. These propositions, depending on my choice, I never understood, *and they caused me great pain and anxiety of mind;* at length, recollecting how I had been deceived, and what I had suffered, I lost my temper and replied, "she might come up if she would, or go down if she would—that I would not meddle with the matter"; but my mind was much disordered. At this rude reply the vision disappeared. (309)

Here the deceased sister, suspended between incest and necrophilia, can be dismissed. No doubt, now that Perceval's psyche has upped the anti of doubt, the good instruction of Father Almighty can get across. There is also a touch of humor in his rude reply. The voice of the Almighty is remembered as exception to his claim that the voice of his deceased sister kept control over him the longest. But then he even "disobeyed and mocked at" the exceptional voice: "and then I became nearly reckless about obeying any or not" (76).

In *The Simulacra* the unbinding of doubles and their interlacing up with objects to be preserved can hitch rides with time traveling—but only ultimately as fantasy that breaks on both finitude and the political agency of the psychotic Kongrosian. Time travel seems to make a frequent flyer like Goltz "more or less eternal": "Technically, Goltz could be murdered, but an earlier Goltz would simply move into the future and replace him" (70). Thus on his many trips Goltz allegedly encounters versions of himself, including future versions that show him that he will take that trip in the future. Up front it is a protective fantasy with a time share in the Oedipus complex. "We ought to go back . . . to Goltz's babyhood and destroy him then. But Goltz had anticipated them. He was long since back there, at the time of his birth and onward into childhood. Guarding himself, training himself, crooning over his child self, through the von Lessinger principle Bertold Goltz had become, in effect, his own parent. . . . Surprise. That was the element which von Lessinger had nearly banished from politics" (152). Surprise! To be "more or less eternal" through time tripping means that Goltz, for example, will always only have been, but for all time. Time travel in effect admitted Goltz to his own funeral. That's why when Pembroke seizes control over Goltz's shot dead body, the corpse remains—unreplaced by alternate versions of Goltz.

Kongrosian is the wild card on the battlefield of the future. As Kongrosian himself pointed out: "I don't think the von Lessinger principle can deal properly with us Psis. . . . We act as acausal factors" (169). A series of coups, each attempting to extract the element of surprise from a future exhaustively explored (via the von Lessinger principle of time travel) by all parties to the conflict, knocks everyone out of the running of society. Any kind of alternate certitude regarding the immediate future is withdrawn by Kongrosian's psychokinetic powers, which produce "a distortion of the fabric of the future" (119). "The future was not fixed and there was always room for the unexpected, the improbable; everyone who had handled von Lessinger equipment understood that"—like psychoanalysis itself—"time travel was still merely an art, not an exact science" (137).

The Simulacra is coterminous with the transition of Kongrosian into the delusional world. Until he was contaminated by the buzz of the deodorant commercial he had been able to "abort" "ideas of reference" while otherwise managing vague phobias, anxieties, depression. "I'm struggling against an insidious schizophrenic process that's gradually eroding my faculties, blunting their acuity" (66). The immediate consequence of the onset of his odor disorder or terror atmosphere is that he cannot perform at the White House. But what crosses his mind as he first tells the White House talent scout that he must be counted out terrifies him directly, personally, transitively. It is the proud thought of succession: "My son, Kongrosian thought. Maybe he could appear in my place. What a weird, morbid thought that was; he cringed from it, horrified that he had let it enter his mind. Really, it demonstrated how ill he was. As if anyone could be interested, take seriously, the unfortunate quasi-musical noises which Plautus made . . . although perhaps in the largest, most embracing sense, they could be called *ethnic*" (63–64). His son is a member of a prehistoric race that was stowaway in *homo sapiens* via intermarriage in primal time (174) until its rerelease as throwback under the traumatically malingering conditions of nuclear catastrophe. The species resembles Neanderthal man, which leaves even prehistory in this novel in the court of Germanicity.

Once he has entered the second stage of invisibility, Kongrosian, sensing a countdown that he cannot raise to consciousness, wishes to see his son (120). The thought either crosses itself out or crosses over with the jump cut to rebirth, which immediately follows.

> The period of seeking therapy was over. And now—a new period. What did it consist of? He did not know, yet. In time he would know, however. Assuming that he lived through it. And how could he do that when for all intents, he was already dead? That's it, he said to himself. I've died. And yet I'm still alive. It was a mystery. He did not understand it. Perhaps, he thought, what I must seek then is—rebirth. (120)

While the search for rebirth leads Kongrosian on a digression that almost takes him to Mars (rather than back to Jenner, where he at first wished to return to see his son), the prospect of rebirth, for example by beginning again on another world (121), subtends his "control" over the chaos of the novel's conclusion. In *Martian Time-Slip* "rebirth" enables Manfred to exit rather than reclaim the novel's world. But on his way out he takes the time to take leave of his mother. This is the acceptance that lets him go. The radiation-spawned jungles of Jenner represent the kind of place, by the acceptance of which one would have accepted "the supremacy of the past" as that "most difficult aspect of life": "In this region the past ruled thoroughly, entire. Their collective past: the war which had preceded their immediate era, its consequences" (100). Thus what suggested to the visiting sound engineer a kind of suicide for Kongrosian is revalorized along Faustian lines as the kind of acceptance from which affirmation of life can follow.

Politically, suicidal conflict is on the agenda while the novel ends on a note *(Not)* of mutational survivorship as rebirth. *The Simulacra* closes around the prospect of civil war: "No matter how it came out it was still bad. Still a catastrophe. And for everyone" (209). The primal lost race would appear to be waiting around on empty, "inert, turned off like a simulacrum, a mere machine" (99). But then the perspective shifts: the Neanderthals or chuppers "were alert now as they viewed the flickering TV image and listened to the excited news announcer. What does this mean to them? . . . It means . . . that they have a chance. This might be their opportunity. We're destroying each other before their eyes. And—it may provide room for them, a space to squeeze into. Room, not cooped up here in this dreary, tiny enclave, but out in the world itself. Everywhere" (207–8). This political context of breakdown or breakthrough concludes the "political" outbreak of psychosis in the father, one who had borne and preserved the primal strain of contact with the lost race. A former world in ruins is their opportunity. Thus it remains unclear at the end whether they are our forefathers or our progeny (213).

Outer Race

Dick dedicates the future to minority reports, both the recognizable votes or voices and the mutational links (which do not, like the outer space aliens in *Star Trek,* pay the token for the minorities we know—aren't represented). This future of rebalancing acts is situated within the culture industry. The first African-American U.S. president (in *The Crack in Space*) had his first career boost as TV weatherman in a clown suit. He is accordingly immune to any more racism he might encounter: "He had experienced too much already in his years as a newsclown. In my years, he thought to himself acidly, as an American Negro" (16). Dick situates the minority struggle to survive or succeed on the track of a kind of assimilation drive. The new ethnic lobby of mutants reaches for the skies of assimilation or media control and grabs hold of the garbled return-of-the-repressed charge against certain minority interests as already being in control. The twofer mutation George and Walt (in *The Crack in Space*) and the prosthetized and telekinetically potentiated phocomelus Hoppy (in *Dr. Bloodmoney*) both enjoy a first station stop in realized control via satellite broadcasting around the world.

In *The Crack in Space* the primal races of evolutionary prehistory have been preserved in alternate worlds. A flaw in a 'scuttler, the current form of transportation, which runs on a limited form of time travel, accidentally cracks open access to just one of these worlds, which is first assumed to be separated from our world either in space or in time. The legends already circulating about the first time a 'scuttler broke through to other worlds booked the past:

It had been before his time but myth persisted, an incredible legend, still current among 'scuttler repair men, that through the defect in his 'scuttler Ellis had—it was hard to believe—composed the Holy Bible. . . . Ellis had found a weak point, a shimmer, at which another continuum completely had been visible. He had stooped down and witnessed a gathering of tiny persons who yammered in speeded-up voices and scampered about in their world just beyond the wall of the tube. . . . Ellis had supposed that this was a non-Terran race dwelling on a miniature planet in some other system entirely. He was wrong. According to the legend, the tiny people were from Earth's own past; the script, of course, had been ancient Hebrew. (18–19)

But then the other world proves to be another version of this world at the same time: "a parallel Earth, in another universe . . . Maybe there are hundreds of them, all alike physically but you know, branching off and evolving differently"(89). The evolutionary crack between parallel worlds acts as displacement of the social divide between classes. Unemployment was nipped in the bud by turning people of color who were starting out unemployed into bibs, bodies in cryogenic freeze, to cut the losses of waiting. The bibs await, like the Christian dead, resurrection, though in their case as the same. A new frontier in outer space would bid the bibs come alive again, go forth and prosper, even multiply. Animation or embodiment has been suspended while the world seeks a solution to the problem of reproduction or, within the regressed perspective, of sex itself. Bib production, abortion, and the sex industry capitalize on the impasse. The twins George Walt pitch their sex satellite, The Golden Door, which hovers above the law, to the nonreproductive members of society.

The twins serve as mascot for the parallelism of worlds linked and separated through mutation. "They were a form of mutated twinning, joined at the base of the skull so that a single cephalic structure served both separate bodies. Evidently the personality *George* inhabited one hemisphere of the brain, made use of one eye: the right, as he recalled. And the personality *Walt* existed on the other side, distinct with its own idiosyncrasies, views and drives—and its own eye from which to view the outside universe" (25). "The head, containing the unmingled entities of the brothers, nodded in greeting and the mouth smiled. One eye—the left—regarded him steadily, while the other wandered vaguely off, as if preoccupied" (26).

The twins serve as primal standard according to which the so-called Dawn Men from an alternate evolutionary history in parallel present time can be approached with measured dread. The double movement in/of traumatic memory crossing the reception of the Dawn Men uses the verb "scuttle," which the name of the time-travel device also conveys. "He had felt the same fright then as he had felt now, seeing this dark, pervasive substance scuttle into his world from the other side. I was eighteen, he said to himself. Just a kid. It was my first visit to the Golden Door satellite. It had been when he had first seen George Walt" (151). The primal souvenir of George Walt is on posttraumatic rebound with first contact with the Dawn Men. "I know him, and I don't like him; it's somebody who in a day long past reminds me of things almost too repellent to recall, a part of my life that's dim, cut out, deliberately and for adequate reason forgotten" (155).

At the same time the revelation of the secret derangement of George Walt, whereby one long ago dead is kept going as alive via a simulacrum-prosthesis attached to the sole survivor of the double body, makes mythic (or psychotic) contact with the primal parallel beings possible. We've come home when we make the divide between the parallel worlds our business. When the presidential candidate sees through the twins as spectacles of unacknowledged loss he recognizes in their desperate prosthetic arrangement a solution to the deferred bib problem that mass awakening and migration would bring immediately to the fore (and hole in each one). The industry with which a leading surgeon, Dr. Sands, had been able to replace organs relied on the accessibility of "borrowed" bib organs—which wasn't murder as long as the bibs remained in suspended animation. "George Walt's corporate existence proved the workability of wholly mechanical organs. And in this Jim Briskin saw hope for Lurton Sands' victims. Possibly a deal could be made with George Walt":

"A long time ago one must have died." They both stared at him. "Sure . . . What happened here today must have happened before. They were mutants, all right, joined from birth, and then the one body perished and the surviving one quickly had this synthetic section built. It couldn't have gone on alone without the symbiotic arrangement because the brain—" He broke off. "You saw what it did to the surviving one just now; he suffered terribly. Imagine how it must have been the first time" (75).

Thus the twins both allegorize the relationship to the Dawn Men (= Morning Men = Mourning Men) as mourning play and, via their own melancholic incorporation, model a relationship to the other world that must find a technical solution to the dead-awakening of the bibs without organs before proceeding to solution of the problem of overpopulation.

The machinations of Walt George across the divide include taking one hundred years in what to us is but an instant to train the Peking men (the more specific identification of the Dawn Men) to withstand colonization or even conquer our side of the evolutionary tracks. After the rent has been increased to allow for significant mass transit of once and future bibs, the alter-Earth, it turns out, has advanced a century. "The air smelled of decay and silent, utter death" (148). The 'scuttler rent appears reversible now, maintained by a power source on the other side. Suddenly there's a glimpse of someone, something slipping across to our side. Our witness to this slip is the one who flashed back to his early contact with Walt George for his continuity shot between severely uncanny moments.

"They probably remember us from their past, remember getting rid of us." Just as we got rid of them in our world, he thought. Wiped them utterly out. "And now we're back," he said. "It must seem like black magic to them: ghosts from a hundred thousand years ago, from their own Stone Age." . . . These parallel worlds are a knotty problem, he realized. I wonder how many exist. Dozens? With a different human sub-species dominant on each? Weird idea. He shivered. God, how unpleasant . . . like concentric rings of hell, each with its own particular brand of torment. And then he thought suddenly: Maybe there's one in which a human type superior to us, one we know nothing about, dominates; one which, in our own world, we extinguished at its inception. Blotto, right off the bat. (120)

Prehistory, redefined via its psychic "staging" of technology in running contrast to our investment in technology, which, from this animistic perspective, appears as the delusional world, appears to us as our underworld. The world of Peking man is in the animistic phase of obsessive-compulsion or religious belief. Transportation vehicles are always made of wood because metal "belongs inside the Earth with the dead. It is part of the once-was, where everything goes when its time is over" (126). The source of power for their wooden rocket ship with a sail is ice, the suspended animation of a vital force of nature: "water freezes, expands as ice, and drives a piston upward with enormous force, then the ice is melted . . . and the gases expand again, which gives another thrust to the piston, driving it back down in the cylinder again" (96). We who don't avoid metal run our entire society via the alternation between suspension of life and awakening.

While the attempt of the Peking men to cross over and conquer us is thwarted—largely by demonstrating that their alleged gods Walt George are only prosthetic gods—our plans for colonization of alter-Earth and the ensuing remurder of the missing link are pushed back indefinitely.

Another psychic emplacement or standstill of the cracked relationship is at once control medium and secret weapon in *The Ganymede Takeover.* The coauthored novel belongs to the brief low point in Dick's production line that *Counter-Clock World,* by putting it all into reverse, first shook free of the drag. The project was fittingly too monumental by the half another author would have to supply. Conceived around the time Dick was concluding the second half of *The Crack in Space, The Ganymede Takeover* was to provide the sequel to *The Man in the High Castle*. Concluded in isolation from the original plan, the collaborationist work buried the decoder ring in the rubble of its abandoned origins. But withdrawn intentions can nevertheless leave behind their structure. Just as the plain text dealing with racism directed against African-Americans in *The Crack in Space* allowed for displacements that drew the specism of our contact with parallel mankind onward, so in *The Ganymede Takeover* the worms from outer space (intended originally as the cartoon portrayal of the Japanese rulers of conquered California) receive direct hits of specism behind the defended foregrounding of African-Americans fighting back against murderous racism. What is of greatest interest in this novel is also a structural leftover: in the place of alternate history as the defective cornerstone that is also the reader's emergency exit out of *The Man in the High Castle,* we find the positing of psychoanalysis as so neo and prehistorical—so aggrandized and reversed—that it provides on its own turf and terms the objection relation between US and them (between the Allies and the Axis).

Rudolph Balkani, Chief of the Bureau of Psychedelic Research, opens the novel on the eve of—or as the overture to—the "takeover" with the (too) late news of a "mind-gadget" weapon that, because it stops "everything on or around this planet which happens to possess a mind," requires as "only defence against it" "the radical psychotherapy" that he's still prepping at the experimental stage. One of his political patients (once a wik or worm kisser, now she declares herself a follower of or believer in Neeg-partism, the black power movement down south) becomes his ultimate test subject (and final case study for his definitive treatise introducing New Psychoanalysis).

"I don't regard Neeg-partism as a religion at all, but rather as a mental disease, a subtle form of psychic masochism.... We yearn for punishment.... But there is, in us, an even deeper need. It's for oblivion . . . Each of my patients, each in his own way—they all want to cease to be.... It's impossible, except in death. It's an infinitely receding goal. And that is why it produces addiction. The seeker after oblivion is promised by drugs, by drink, by insanity, by role-playing, the fulfilment of his dream of non-being . . . but the promise is never kept.... *I'm going to give them oblivion.*" (70–71)

Following her immersion in the sensory withdrawal tank, the patient, Miss Hiashi, is fulfilled to the satori level: "That's the state in which the barrier between the conscious and subconscious mind disappears; the focal point of consciousness opens out and grows tenuous and the entire mind functions as a unit, rather than being broken up into a multitude of secondary functional entities" (80). She would be considered happy if there were any one home to enjoy it. Replaced by her robot back at the lab (Balkani doesn't discover the switch until he bashes in her artificial head with his Freud bust in his struggle to secure an emotionally corrective experience for them), Miss Hiashi returns first to language under the care of black power leader Percy X (after first extended contact he had to cut himself to break the zomboid contagion passing through her):

"Now I know that the one thing I've always feared most, deep down inside, was to succeed, to get the things I thought I wanted. I've always thought that people were against me, or that I had bad luck, but my real enemy was me. All my life, whenever I've tried to get something, the same demonic figure has stepped into my path and commanded me to halt, the same relentless phantom with my face. Doctor Balkani gave me a knife and let me kill that phantom . . . Now she's dead and if I feel anything for her it's a kind of loneliness. I'm all alone now that Joan Hiashi is dead."

"You're psychotic," Percy said sharply. "Because of the suffering you underwent. . . . He's given you mental and spiritual death."

"Oblivion," Joan said. (87)

At the same time, the new Gany administrator of the Southern bale, Mekkis, has taken up a kind of correspondence course with Balkani. Rather than plug into the "fusion" whereby all Ganys keep in touch, Mekkis "returned to his 'more important matters.' This consisted of a reading of the entire published works of the brilliant but verbose Terran psychiatrist, Doctor Rudolph Balkani; Mekkis had secured microfilm copies of all the books available through the channels of the Bureau of Cultural Control and had devoted virtually his complete attention to them. Never before had he encountered a thinker that so obsessed him" (99–100). In contrast to "the telepathic melting together of the Great Common," Balkani pitches "a certain incredible yet plausible egotism, a fantastic daring that seemed to speak to a deep, hitherto untouched part of Mekkis' spiritual mind" (100).

In the meantime, on the projective range, an electronic mind-warping device that Balkani also designed—a weapon so good, he underscores, that it couldn't be used—has been pressed into the service of defending Percy X against the Gany government. However the weapon operates largely by backfire (in fact, each time a battle is fought with these new weapons, which produce seemingly lasting effects, which uncannily exceed their mediatic character as illusions, countless psychoticized neeg-part soldiers desert). Balkani explains how the weapon works in fact to psychoticize all who are absorbed by its Sensurround:

"The result of its operation is peculiar. Each person continues to perceive reality, but it comes to him as a hallucination, a private vision which can't be related to the shared vocabulary of images. From this arises a swiftly-developing encapsulation. The person affected is not, strictly speaking, isolated; he experiences the 'real world,' but he cannot make head nor tail of it. The delightful aspect of this mechanism is that it attacks only the percept-portion of the neurological structure; cognition, the functioning of the frontal lobe, continues unimpaired. The victim can still think clearly; it is just that now the data received by the undamaged higher brain centres cannot be fathomed. . . . The basic quality of a weapon . . . is not that it destroys but that it acts to defend its owner. With this item the operator becomes as disoriented as the target-individual. It functions through the centre-point at which all minds in a given Synchronity field are connected; therefore it would very likely take out every thinking being on this planet, and probably all those on Ganymede as well, since they have telepathic representatives here." (109)

In his neopsychoanalysis as in his weapon design, Balkani demolishes the ego via the artificial coma of telepathy. The illusions produced by the weapons seem real owing to what Balkani refers to as his concept of selective awareness.

It is through Mekkis's cannibalistic libido as reader of his collected work that we owe yet another inside view of Balkani's system:

The mind selects, out of a mass of sense data, those ones of all the possible items to pay attention to, to react to, to treat as "real." But who knows what the mind may be rejecting, what lies unseen out there in the world? Perhaps these illusions are not illusions at all, but real things that ordinarily are filtered out of the stream of incoming sense data by our intellectual demand for a logical and consistent world. (113)

Mekkis, psychoticized by his close reading of Balkani's theories, becomes Percy's secret weapon. Now as "individual," as follower of Neeg-Partism, Mekkis keys his own mind into the Ganymedian Great Common. In the final moments of his suicide mission Mekkis keeps his disappointment:

This is death, Mekkis thought: *death for all of us. But it's not as I imagined it would be. I thought I would be able to savour the agonies of my enemies in the Common; I believed it would be a grand and spectuacular doom, like the final chords of something made of music. But it is not.*
    It is nothing, absolutely nothing. And I am utterly alone in it. (171)

A certain middle ground is occupied or cathected throughout the novel in the name of the World Psychiatric Association, which first backed Percy X as "an important ego-identification figure. As long as he continues to resist, so will the mass ego of humanity." The latest psycho-computer findings suggest that his defeat "would lead to a massive increase in schizophrenia throughout the world, a thorough group insanity impossible to control." In other words, if Percy goes he must die as martyr. If his pelt is picked up by a Gany collector as wall hanging we would be left facing "a traumatic incident of a magnitude difficult to overestimate" (26–27). At the end of the novel, Paul Rivers, the Association's agent, reverses Balkani's therapy of Joan Hiachi and loops her back through the other. But what is the WPA agent other than the figure or figurehead of recovery from New Psychoanalysis, which *is* psychoanalysis, but as reversed and aggrandized along the lines of every departure from and resistance to its discourse. The limit concept of transferential treatment is instead administered in its endopsychic encapsulation. New Psychoanalysis is the psychoticizing treatment or weapon that ultimately administers its own love death or common death to innocent and intended bystanders alike. At the same time, New Psychoanalyis is what psychoanalysis (in every sense) contains. Oh say, can you "not see"? In my genealogy titled *Nazi Psychoanalysis* I demarcated the ultimate contours of this German introject inside modernism.

The German Introject

The Penultimate Truth and *Lies, Inc.*[1] (formerly known as *The Unteleported Man*) form a kind of portal for working through the one history without parallel or alternative. In *The Penultimate Truth*, it's all a fair, a show, in love of war: to cut losses on the human side, the Terran population was provided vast mine-like shelters while total nuclear war commenced on Mars. When mankind went underground it was believed "to be for perhaps a year at longest . . . or, as real pessimists had forecast, two years" (102). But it's been fifteen years at the novel's start, during which time a new world order of Yance-men rule the Earth from their vast estates. Mankind below must watch the show of ongoing total war, films made in the meantime by Eisenbludt of Moscow. The premier filmmaker, Gottlieb Fischer of West Germany, was "inheritor of UFA, the older Reichs film trust which had in the 1930s been so deeply interwoven with Dr. Goebbels' office" (62). The simulacrum of the world leader, Talbot Yancy, was also designed by Fischer and made in Germany. When Fischer died on an expedition to Venus, Eisenbludt took over the production of the war films and, on the Western side of simulation, Stanton Brose, Fischer's student and heir, picked up the reign of power.

Fifteen years ago robots (named leadies because they melt under combat conditions) were sent to war. In no time "advanced varieties of leadies . . . led to the realization that the best strategy was to be found summed up in *The Mikado*. If merely *saying* that a man had been executed was enough to satisfy everyone, why not merely say it instead of doing it?" (49). The polarization between West and East was maintained for the captive audience in the underworld. Fischer began the new film history in 1982 with two revisionary documentaries made to order for each "side."

To alter history you begin with World War II. "Because in 1982, Germany
was once again a world power, and most important, a major shareholder
in the community of nations titling itself 'The Western Democracies,' or
more simply, Wes-Dem" (69). What was made all right on the Western
front was Germany's role in two wars of world destruction. The 1982
documentary juxtaposes two moments: in 1919, the continued blockade
by the British of Germany, and in 1943, a second devastation visited upon
Germany which, concentration camps included, could also be blamed on
the Anglo-American sell-out of Germany to the East. FDR, the documentary proves via hidden mike and camera, was a Soviet agent. The second
documentary, the B version, which was pitched to an East that existed also
only as underworld, presented the USSR and Japan as fighting to save civilization from the secret alliance between Anglo-America and the Germans.

The ultimate truth nears revelation at the intersection of plotlines.
Nicholas, a tanker, is sent above ground to search for an artiforg for the ailing Chief Mechanic. He reaches the surface near the demesne of Lantano,
a new Yance-man and speechwriter for the Yancy sim. Joseph Adams,
another speechwriter, meets Lantano at the Megavac through which they
ventriloquate the sim. Adams is impressed by Lantano's ideas and his ability to express them and in particular by his "knowhow as to exactly what
the 'vac's treatment of the copy would result in . . . how it would ultimately
emerge as spoken by the sim before the cameras" (55). Adams has organized his life around the Faustian-Freudian apparatus:

What entered Megavac 6-V as a mere logos would emerge for the TV lenses and
mikes to capture in the guise of a pronouncement, one which nobody in his right
mind—especially if encapsulated subsurface for fifteen years—would doubt. . . . The
voice which he, like every other Yance-man, had long ago introjected. The super ego,
as the prewar intellectuals had called it. (33)

Lantano, who through time travel has been around for six hundred
years, turns out to have been the extra chosen by film director Fischer as
model for the leader sim. Lantano merges with the sim and pronounces
declaration of peace on earth. Nicholas obtains the artiforg from the former war zone (the postwar era can only produce mass cultural items that
"could not sustain life for even a second" [87]). The ultimate truth lies in
the fine print: the policy for controlled release of the tankers and the history to be told about the meantime and its documentary prehistory remain
withheld from the novel.

Lies, Inc. presents a world in which post–World War II Germany must be reintegrated as dominant and benign. The title is the nickname of the police agency of the West. The agency even programs you subliminally while you sleep. Rachmael ben Applebaum runs a small shipping enterprise as did his father before him, before he committed suicide or *"Selbstmort, in the official German of the UN"* (8). Rachmael, who doesn't believe in the official version of his father's death, is under pressure to fold by "one of the most powerful economic syndromes in the Sol System . . . , Trails of Hoffman" (8). In the labs of Trails of Hoffman Limited (THL), Dr. Sepp von Einem invented and manufactured the Telpor electronic entity whereby individuals wishing to emigrate from one crowded planet to Whale's Mouth in the Formalhaut System are beamed across in fifteen minutes (compared to the eighteen years it would take Rachmael's fastest and last remaining ship, the *Omphalos,* to get there). That's eighteen years one way; but at least you can come back by ship. Telpor can beam you across only one way. The connections between Terra and Whale's Mouth (or Newcolonizedland) are long-distance mediatic only. There is a Theorem One, postulated by von Einem, involving the Sol System's location at the axis of the universe, which explains away the one-way-only nature of teleportation to Newcolonizedland. Rachmael postulates in turn that, statistically speaking alone, malcontents must exist among the colonists.

> So if you did find malcontents—what could you do for them? Because you could not take them back; you could only join them. And he had the intuition that somehow this just wouldn't be of much use. Even the UN left Newcolonizedland alone, the countless UN welfare agencies, the personnel and bureaus newly set up by the present Secretary General Horst Bertold, from New Whole Germany: the largest political entity in Europe—even they stopped at the Telpor gates. Neues Einige Deutschland . . . NED. Far more powerful than the mangy, dwindling French Empire or the UK—they were pale remnants of the past.
>
> And New Whole Germany—as the election to UN Secretary General of Horst Bertold showed—was the Wave of the Future . . . as the Germans themselves liked to phrase it. (14–15)

Based on the evidence of tampering with one of the "live" TV broadcasts from Newcolonizedland, Rachmael proposes to take the slow boat to what one has come to refer to as "the next world" (54) to uncover what he wagers is a plot. As soon as his mission is announced individuals begin to share their own suspicions. The head of the police agency known as Lies, Incorporated, Matson Glazer-Holliday:

There was something he did not like about those German technicians who manned the Telpors. So business-like. As their ancestors must have been, Matson mused. Back in the twentieth century when those ancestors, with the same affectless calm, fed bodies into ovens or living humans into ersatz shower baths which turned out to be Zyklon B hydrogen cyanide gas chambers. And financed by reputable big Third Reich business, by Herr Krupp u. Söhne. Just as von Einem is financed by Trails of Hoffman, with its vast central offices in Grosser Berlinstadt—the new capital of New Whole Germany, the city in fact from which our distinguished UN Secretary General emanates. (18–19)

New Whole Germany was the result of a "compact" with the United States and the USSR that "even Faust would have blanched at" (21). In exchange for the annihilation of People's China, Germany was allowed to reunite in 1982. While campaigning for the UN post, Horst Bertold (born in 1954) promised to find "a Final Solution" to overpopulation on Terra and the unacceptable conditions of existing colonies in the Sol system. What a convenience history that a habitable planet should suddenly be discovered via von Einem's Telpor construct, but unhappily too far away to be reached by any means other than one-way teleportation.

Matson said grimly, "So our UN Secretary General had a mandate before he had a solution. And to the German mind that means one thing and one thing only. The cat and rat farm solution." Or, as he now suspected, the dog food factory solution. (22)

But underneath it all, Matson is inspired mainly by Rachmael's proof that the news from Newcolonizedland can be managed. Thus he plans to take the one-way trip together with a couple thousand top reps to the other world, which his organization could dominate in the absence of any UN forces. "They may have THL psychologists armed and ready for individuals. But not for two thousand trained police. We'd have control in half an hour—probably" (60).

A plot twist that went once more around the block too often to be followed closely has Rachmael in at least three places at once. He also teleports to Newcolonizedland where he is welcomed with a shot of LSD. "Swiftly, the drug moved him to ruin; in his bloodstream it rushed him toward the end of his existence in the shared world" (76). As the Kantian framework gives way before a Dionysian flood of uncontrolled raw percept-data, he senses his Freudian regression to infancy and its utterly incomprehensible world. "Within him all his language disappeared; all words were gone. Some scanning agency of his brain, some organic searching device, swept out mile after mile of emptiness, finding no stored words, nothing to draw on: he felt it sweeping wider and wider, extending its oscillations into every dark reach, overlooking nothing; it wanted, would accept, anything, now; it was desperate. And still, year after year, the empty bins where words, many of them, had once been but were not now" (80).

When he comes down off the trip, Rachmael discovers he is a member of the support group for colonists who saw "paraworlds," alternate versions of Newcolonizedland upon arrival (and upon failing the acid test).

"The illness," Gretchen Borbman said, "is called the Telpor Syndrome. Disjunction of the percept-system and substitution of a delusional world. It manifests itself—when it does at all—shortly after teleportation. No one knows why. Only a few get it, a very few. Ourselves, at this present time. . . . Don't be worried, Mr. ben Applebaum; it is generally reversible. Time, rest, and of course therapy."

"Sorcerer's apprentice therapy," Hank Szantho said, from some vector of space not within Rachmael's range of sight. "S.A.T., they call it. The cephalic 'wash head-benders; they're in and out of here, even Dr. Lupov—the big man from Berghoelzi in Switzerland." (95)

We jump cut from the para- or alternate worlds therapy group to von Einem's lab where he works together with gifted Gregory Gloch, who is out of phase in time. As was envisioned for Manfred in *Martian Time-Slip*, Gloch inhabits a "clanking, whirring anti-prolepsis chamber" (114). A new weapon developed by UN wep-x tacticians has already struck Gloch's chamber: it is the voice of ol' Charley Falks, a *faux* folksy memory from childhood.

"You're a goldmine of misinformation," Gloch said irritably, in response, automatically, to one more of garrulous ol' Charley Falks' typical tidbits of wrong knowledge. He was so used to it, so darn, wearily resigned out of long experience. All the way back to his childhood, back throughout the dreary procession of years. (124)

Sepp von Einem figures out that the canned chatter is being piped into Gloch's chamber by Jaimé Weiss and the 'wash psychiatrist Lupov (154). He puts a missile on the track of their ol' Charley Falks beam.

Rachmael encounters a creature resembling Matson Glazer-Holliday, who consumes his own eyes, which grow back (125). This not-quite–alive, half-breed child of Matson and a Mazdast mother recommends reading Dr. Bloode's *The True and Complete Economic and Political History of Newcolonizedland*, a Kalends-type book with an up-to-the-minute index of names. Dr. Lupov's team composed the text as therapeutic device for treatment of the Telpor Syndrome (134). But the treatment maintains the illness as cover. For the book confirms reservations that the so-called delusional paraworlds are in fact alternate worlds:

Several worlds. . . . And each of them different. And—if they're looking in that book, not to see what has happened but to see what will happen . . . then it must have something to do with time. Time-travel. The UN's time-warpage weapon. Evidently Sepp von Einem had gotten hold of it. The senile old genius and his disturbed proleptic protégé Gloch had altered it, god only knew how. But effectively; that much was obvious. (144)

Now it's the turn of Theodoric Ferry, the head of THL, to be a nonhuman alien, no, a simulacrum. But we're only surfing paraworlds. First there was the aquatic world with the Mazdast creature, then it switched to the paraworld known as The Clock, the "delusional" world styling with technology. "The delusional worlds somehow active here at Whale's Mouth had already spread to and penetrated Terra. It had already been experienced—experienced, yes; but not recognized" (152).

Weiss and Lupov have been trying to direct Theodoric Ferry to a certain page in Bloode's book. Ferry, like everyone else in the book, likes reading about himself. But as the page turns between Ferry's fingers, von Einem's foil strikes the lab (in the book inside the book inside the book). Lupov and Weiss have moments to consider the consequences for their master plan: "What a waste, he thought; what a dreadful, impossible waste, if not. Everything we set up: the pseudo-worlds, the fake class of 'weevils,' everything—with no result" (164). Those are moments in which von Einem can warn Ferry to toss the book, which turns out to be "only one of those awful Ganymede life-mirrors . . . that reflects back to you your own thoughts" (165).

In the Berkley Book edition of 1983 Germany is not cleared as screen of projections. The date of German reunification is given as 1992 in *The Unteleported Man* (which I assume reflects 1983 editorial updating into the future). The *Lies, Inc.* edition with Dick's more recent additions (and which prides itself on being the restored version of what Dick intended to rerelease in the 1980s under the new title) gives 1982 as the German date with Dick's destiny. The book thrown at "the Germans" is what *Lies, Inc.*, which in its title echoes the German nickname for enemy propaganda, "All Lies," ultimately throws up and away. The closing pages go on and on mopping up the mess they also slop around.

"I was wrong," Freya said. . . .

"You thought," he said, "it was going to be—ovens."

She said, with quiet calmness . . . , "It's work camps. The Soviet, not the Third Reich, model. Forced labor." (173)

Or again:

We let our prejudices blind us . . . von Einem is German and Horst Bertold is German. But that does not any more prove they are working together, are secret collaborators, than, say, any two Ubangis or any two Jews. Adolf Hitler was not even a German . . . so our own thinking, he realized, has betrayed us. But—maybe now we can believe this. We can see. New Whole Germany has produced Dr. Sepp von Einem and Trails of Hoffman Limited . . . but it may also have produced something else when it created Horst Bertold. (188)

And now the Finale:

" 'Sein Herz voll Hass geladen,' " Horst Bertold said to Rachmael. "You speak Yiddish? You understand?"

"I speak a little Yiddish," Rachmael said, "but that's German. 'His heart heavy with hate.' What's that from?"

"From the Civil War in Spain," Bertold said. "From a song of the International Brigade. Germans, mostly, who had left the Third Reich to fight in Spain against Franco, in the 1930s." . . . After a pause he said. "We fought the Nazis, too, we 'good' Germans; vergess' uns nie." Forget us never, Bertold had said, quietly, calmly. Because we did not merely join the fight late, in the 1950s or '60s, but from the start. The first human beings to fight to the death, to kill and be killed by the Nazis, were—

Germans. (192)

I doubt lies can be incorporated. But what "lies incorporated" in Dick's corpus is that one-way teleportation to the next world—the ultimate secularization and technologization of Christianity—was the projection to be reclaimed or regained as "Germany." The android question of his inner world was already in place when his life flashed before his eyes with *Blade Runner.*

PART IV

Materialism, Idealism, and Cybernetics

As indicated in "Introjection," Gotthard Günther is our spokesperson for the philosophical cathexis of the coordinates of science fiction, largely because John W. Campbell commissioned occasional interventions by him for popularist publication in the 1950s in the States. But we'll begin with his more recognizably or properly published work, which stands behind the U.S. articles addressed to the readership of American science fiction. Under the title I've borrowed above, which in *The Consciousness of Machines (Das Bewusstsein der Maschinen)* is Part 3, Günther lets roll a genealogy of mankind's new self-relationship via technology. All the dualisms in a row, as old as the great civilizations, were deepened and heightened in scientific thought from the Greeks through Hegel. In Hegel we run up against a decisive complication with the terrible twos. There are, it turns out, two dualisms, one involving the contents of conscious thought, the other concerning the processes of reflection that manipulate those contents. Their interaction or collaboration burdens thought with difficulties that cannot be overcome.

Our consciousness doesn't hold an unequivocally determined, self-identical objective content of consciousnss—except via differentiation of this content from all other possible contents. This distinction separates the one from the other and thereby establishes dualism of content. To think and to move about among dualistically separated-out conceptions are synonymous acts.

The second type of dualism arises because reflection offers us constantly the choice between the monistic and the dualistic form of thought and, as the history of philosophy shows, we are incapable of deciding, once and for all, for the one over the other. It is the fundamental trait of reflection that it can step back from its decision-making, wash its hands of it all, and cast it in doubt. For Descartes, famously, this *is* the metaphysical reality of the subject. We cannot doubt that we doubt.

The two dualisms of classical thought are, one, dualism of being and, two, dualism of sense. The latter includes, as complete phenomenon of reflection, its own opposite, namely monism. In Hegel we begin to observe the progressive interplay of both dualities. Thus a third temporally extended duality emerges from the former process, the duality between the first content duality and the second form duality. With *The Phenomenology of Spirit* we part company with history conceived as the history of human consciousness that culminated in its own reflection. Thanks to cybernetics, left and right Hegelianisms are no longer the only reception of a philosophical intervention that couldn't have asked for more obdurate resistance. By systematically attempting to transfer processes of consciousness in analogical form to machines, cybernetics takes seriously Hegel's idea that reflection is an actual or real process.

Since Hegel, nothing is wrong anymore, only one-sided—but as such it is true, that is, as a moment in what is true. Hegel however failed to render reflection itself (as living process independent of its fixation on a specific object) the starting point of his thought. This his left and right wings demonstrated. But Hegel's logic commences with a careful symmetry between form and substance. Being and nothing are empty placeholders for the opposition between subject and object. It's an interchange without the award or reward of advantage and preferential status. But that means that Hegelian logic starts out with a complete metaphysical equivalency of spirit and matter. Form and substance are logically the same.

Hegel attempts to render the process of reflection that we experience as thought independent of the vantage point of an experiencing individual subject, of a finite mind. The effort would require man's abandonment of the isolation of his private subjectivity, which is where he runs up against the one-sided wall of his reflection. That the epistemological problem of the incommensurability of thinking and acting can act as link between our subjectivity and the world gives a clue as to how to give up our isolation.

Doubt about reality of the external world is a constitutional quality of reflection locked up inside subjective consciousness. The skepticism regarding reality is dissolved in action. By reaching toward and grasping things, we convince ourselves that the things outside us exist. That the thing that we technically manipulate, work on, and change should exist only by our acts of consciousness is, practically speaking, meaningless. The will to act supplies a reliable bridge from the inner world to the outer world. Marx was thus right to conclude that what Hegel accomplished philosophically concluded an epoch of human intellectual history. Hegel's culmination is reflection's occupation only with itself and with the mirror image of the world it engendered. Secure in its possession of this mirror image, it forgot the real problem of the world as contingency impenetrable by consciousness. Contact with this world, which is always technical, was not reckoned as part of the spiritual or intellectual realm. Marx argued that the object should be conceived as sensual-human activity, as subjective; to the hitherto inert unreflective object must be ascribed the capacity for reflexivity and subjectivity.

A change in the object is brought about once man stops making his self-image only in thoughts and takes on the task instead of constructing himself, the repetition of his essence, in materials. Through cybernetic technology the object becomes human activity, that is, viewable, conceivable, recognizable as possible subject and double of man.

According to cybernetics, every possible consciousness of man or animal rests on physical preconditions of being that cannot be experienced or conceived by the consciousness to which they apply (Günther, *Consciousness of Machines*, 153). Without this blind spot, there could be no ego, no I-subjectivity of consciousness experiencing itself in thought as free. I can study the other's body as specifiable but this does not in turn alter what remains for me the unspecified nature of my relationship to my own body. I am forced to recognize that in the other the body clearly carries the functions of consciousness. But this in no way obligates the subjective I to mold its own understanding of its relations to its body on this science of the other's body.

The knowledge we share is that of objective subjects, so-called you-centers of reflection. Because it is interobjective and not intersubjective, classical evidential consciousness cannot support I–you problems. There are two evidential procedures: one for the subject that orients itself toward the objective as bond; another for the subject that is bracketed out of the world and possesses potentially the whole universe as content of consciousness. These two cannot be brought together or into alignment. The sublation of underspecification of the underlying physical system would mean total annihilation of consciousness.

Every I can conceive the behavior of an alien psychic reflection system from outside as objectively reflexive and not as self-reflexive. I can become you only if a single you climbs out of the transpersonal region of being you and assumes the place that the present I is willing to yield. The I can give up its place only if it recognizes the you as equal.

What the left and the right wings of Hegelianism share is the view of reality as a self-reflexive structure. Whether we refer to God or to the self-reflection inherent in materiality itself, the terms are irrelevant, that is, are equally possible descriptions that only seem contradictory. Our finite bivalent consciousness is, owing to its own structure, fundamentally incapable of developing in itself a total reflection situation organized around one I center, incapable, in other words, of producing a state of consciousness in which all the thought motifs of which an experiencing subject is capable could be united in one harmonious worldview. Even God must confront Satan, the you locked out of His subjectivity. For God, too, the total reflection is accessible only as distributed via the I–you relationship.

The relationship of exchangeability between mutually exclusive centers of experience produces a complementarity of reflection situations that inevitably attach themselves to one or the other isolated circle of consciousness. But the you-center can be integrated in my own thought (which does not mean that it is subsumed or superseded). The fateful error is to confuse a relation of exchange with a proportional relation according to which one side must be true, the other false.

The relationship of exchange can tempt us to take sides in the contest between two values. But there is also the transclassical alternative cybernetics provides. One can accept the alternative relation between two values or reject it as a whole. In this way ideological strife is readdressed in terms of the I–you relation. With cybernetics worldviews need only be of "clinical" interest as "symptoms" of the current historical state of human consciousness in an unhappy state of finding itself in irreconcilable self-contradiction.

Through artificial distribution of reflection processes across man and machine cybernetics outbids the natural distribution of human thought across competing I-centers. Should this undertaking succeed, human I and human you will be pushed together on one side while the man-made mechanism takes up the other side: thought would be distributed across both sides, across human being as well as across the artifact that arose in the historical process.

To animate the material world, man must enrich transcendence of materiality with its introscendence. One's introscendence cannot be attributed to or denied machines.

A moment of inertia indwells reflection, as Hegel already observed. The movement of consciousness, which led from unbalanced to balanced system, does not rest once the goal has been reached. Without further goal and delivered from the limiting conditions of its mission, this momentum rages on in neutral gear. "It engenders an unbelievable excess of phantasy, as can be witnessed for example in American science fiction literature today" (189).

What Hegel identified as the slaughter trough of world history calls for mourning. In its cybernetic aspect, technology can perform this work of mourning by uncovering the character of that human subjectivity responsible for the bloody history up to that point and hold it up to the current denizens of the planet as technological mirror image. To this end subjectivity's activities in the world must be pulled out of the dark recesses of their introscendence into the light of day and projected into the objective construction of a machine. Give up the former self (with its transcendental identifications) and hand it all over to the inert materiality of a mechanism that is thus awakened to a life of its own. Hence the epochal lag between man and machine. This is the historical-metaphysical difference between them that suspends a span of commemoration.

Typical examples of the range of our technologization, from cave paintings to the administration of whole continents and beyond, refer to the human body. But man possesses not only his bodily environment but also a habitat for subjectivity and introscendent interiority. The body also belongs to this second habitat. If mind can change the natural environment, then the same goes for the bodily environment. The Christian notion of natural and spiritual bodies need not be taken only religio-metaphysically. Man is increasingly entering an environment, the physical conditions of which prove too much for his physical body. The body will be reconstructed. But man's personal experience of his identity is mediated or transmitted through his body. His body is where private interiority and the public side of his existence come into contact. "For he is not only inner identity with himself but also an external physical identity over and against the you" (193). We only really understand what we can ourselves make. Once we can make ourselves our self-knowledge will be enormous. "What man knows about himself he painstakingly tried to glean from the puzzling contingency of the world, which cast back to him an incomprehensible copy of his self" (193). But thus man encounters only the mirror image of his natural being. What he doesn't meet up with here is his self as creative activity, as interiority that has posited itself outside himself and become objective, and which is thus capable of addressing and answering him. To see his spiritual or intellectual aspect rather than always only his natural being, man must repeat himself in his own activity. Günther closes his essay at this point with Paul's lines about the glass through which we see darkly.

Startling Stories

> I readily admit if it comes to the adding up of grocery bills and
> similar mental activities you can't beat the mechanical brains but
> they will never write *Hamlet*.
>
> —GOTTHARD GÜNTHER, "The Soul of a Robot"

Günther claimed that the gist of his philosophizing could be located in the gaps and overlaps between his American-language and German-language works. Exile in the American-language world with his Jewish wife was a career move that bordered on pop cultural success or access. While the better half of his life was German, the portion first set aside for reflection on science fiction was American. In *Startling Stories* in 1953 Günther published a brief article, addressed to the readership (and authorship) of science fiction, titled "Can Mechanical Brains Have Consciousness?" Here Günther sees only greater difficulties in extending consciousness to robot brains—at least as far as the direction progress in construction of artificial intelligence was headed goes. He introduces into the model of consciousness as logical feedback mechanism (which he attributes to Hegel's *Phenomenology of Spirit*) the element of "confrontation" or self-difference as the very synapse of conscious thought.

The question of consciousness as transferrable or reproducible attribute often rests on one of two assumptions. A skeptical viewpoint holds that we can never know what consciousness is, anyway, or, more religiously, that consciousness is a manifestation of man's unknowable but divinely bestowed soul. The other point of view holds that we don't know what consciousness is because it is only a "label for the abstract sum of all our perceptual and apperceptual functions. Ergo, if we reduplicate all those functions of sensitivity, memory, learning, capacity to make decisions, quantitative and qualitative reasoning, etc., through the medium of mechanical procedures, we have produced consciousness and thinking in a man-made machine." There is, therefore, no consciousness just as there is no animal. "There exist horses, dogs, birds, and snakes; but there exists no animal. 'Animal' is just a name, and so is 'consciousness.'" However, consciousness, as Kant proved, is a mechanism that exists apart and separated from its own functional proceedings. That's transcendental logic. But "the established results of that new logical discipline have not yet penetrated into the circles of cyberneticists and designers of computing machines." You need to be well versed in any number of -ologies to hit bottom in transcendental logic. (Günther includes in his list, alongside psychology, psychiatry too.) If we know what consciousness is—reflection in-itself—then we should be able to build it. But what's that? What always comes out in the watch for analogies is the movies.

The next thought, as new and improved, can flush the thought I had last, the one that I must try to make last. A technical medium only has a past. Photography-and-cinema today occupies the highpoint of projections that began with the printing press and the 3-D frame of representation. The first new media entered the psychic apparatus by the work of analogy that is the discursive corollary of Freud's "work of mourning." No one who reads could, by the same analogies, find that Freud's thought is therefore outdated. To add "digital" to "media" doesn't change much. Digitalization has added to film-versus-video, for example, a synthetic third and supplemental alternative for special technical difficulties or differences, notably those involved in editing. Digitalization re-collects all the offshoots of the screen medium, a move both into reduction and out of excess. Film is still the medium of mutations that we have only begun to read and reclaim. The first technical images, which always already broke down into pixels, transformed the visual arts into painting by numbers. But given its synthetic nature, there is also a contrary momentum in digitalization that summons discarded, discounted mediations in the allegorical mode to interrupt this immediacy of numbers. The oldest new media preserve prehistory, the vanishing starting point of my last thought.

No one in his right mind, Günther admits, "would say that the screen has consciousness. For the screen does not know what is happening. . . . The story would be entirely different if the light were not thrown back at us, the audience, but were instead reflected back upon the projector and its optics process of projecting the images against the screen." Now it's time to place screen in quotes. "Now: consider your own conscious-ness a sensitive 'screen.' This 'screen' receives, through your I sensorial system, messages from the outer world. Neuronic impulses coming from your eyes, your ears, your skin, your muscles, etc. impress themselves upon that 'screen' and are reflected. But this reflection is not thrown back at the world-system from which it came. . . . Instead, it is thrown into a deeper recess of your brain, turns around and appears a second time on your brain-'screen,' superimposing a second reflection on the first. This second appearance establishes the miraculous phenomenon which we call con-sciousness." Only if we could determine what happens to the message after it was first received on the brain screen and before the last moment, "when it returns to it with the stamp 'acknowledged' and produces consciousness by its second impact upon the screen," could we design a technical incar-nation of consciousness. But our roundtrip via cinema analogy and theory of brain processes "during the roundtrip of our message" in turn brings us back to what we all along were illustrating: transcendental logic.

Aristotelian logic was for jar- or potheads. Chaotic fluids pour into our jug-like minds. The jug or pot stills the downpour and gives it form. The latter is formal or Aristotelian logic; the former represents the material world. The pot does not become conscious of the liquid pouring into it. The difference that had to be made lay in the human soul. In addition to the synthesis of form and content, you need a self that watches that syn-thesis to produce consciousness.

Kant eliminated soul from this formula. In its stead he identified a sec-ond mechanism in the brain, which observes entirely different principles. "It does not form messages any more but carries them through processing stages and finally returns them to the original 'screen,' the identity level of the formal logic." Transcendental logic is named after this all-important carrying capacity.

If the input is processed in a certain way, then the concepts "I" and "perception" are added. The additions alone do not produce conscious-ness, however. "Only when the thus modified message returns to the screen is consciousness actually produced." The modified message returns to two sections of the screen: memory and identification.

The memory still retains the original pattern (unconscious):
    "a rose";
on which is superimposed (unconscious):
    "I see a rose."

Identification now produces a confrontation by attempting to establish a one-to-one correspondence relation between the original pattern and the enriched second message. This does not work! It turns out to be impossible to establish, by confrontation, a one-to-one correspondence between "a rose" and "I see a rose." . . . The reflection-in-itself produces something that cannot be identified with the mere content "a rose." A tension of meaning is created—a tension between identity and non-identity. And this is the moment when consciousness and conscious thought come into existence.

What technical reproduction of consciousness requires, then, if it is to succeed, is some carrier or transference mechanism "that permits the information to bounce off the screen and return to it in a modulated manner for the purpose of 'confrontation.'"

From 1954 to 1955 Günther published, again in *Startling Stories,* a four-part series of articles of the constitution of a new techno relationship with the alien other as the limit of our thought. As the editor's intro blurb proclaims: "Modern logic may have begun with Aristotle, but it will not end with him." Günther's first round of reflections, "The Seetee Mind," contradicts the ambiguity of the editorial "with."

The two-value system of Aristotelian logic corresponds to the on/off positions of the neuronic switches of the brain (which in turn reflect the positive and negative electric charge particles comprising our physical world). All rational beings, whether terrestrial or galactic, must use the same logic if they face the same universe and are materially constituted as the same. But what if there is "contraterrene" matter? It would be a state of material existence in which the particles have reversed their electrical charges. The resulting "seetee" mind would be based on a total reversal of our logical values. But what does total reversal mean here? "The seetee mind, so far as we are concerned, is the complete and consistent 'liar.'" One's knowledge about everything must be complete in the case of consistent lying about everything. Such knowledge is the prerogative of the divine mind. We, however, are incapable of total negation, the radical step required to mediate the gulf between the Aristotelian and the contra-Aristotelian mind. A rational human being could perform total negation only by negating all statements, by negating, in other words, the existence of his own mind. Thus only suicide comes close. "In fact total negation is the logical definition of death. . . . It is absolute death that separates the terrene Aristotelian from the contra-Aristotelian seetee mind." If this is a typo, it is the archetypo: "the twin shall never meet."

Since no direct contact between our mind and the seetee mind is possible or survivable, in his second installment, "Aristotelian and Non-

Aristotelian Logic," Günther projects a future receiving area for our indirect communication with the alien intelligence. While it will most likely be the case that mechanical brains will think in non-Aristotelian forms of reasoning, this will be the absolute requirement for one type of robot brain: "the thought translator."

Aristotelian logic is limited to making valid statements only about past events. But: "the strict alternative to the two-valued logic of 'to be or not to be' does not adequately cover the pattern of future events. Therefore we need at least a three-valued logic, and any statement about the future should be phrased according to the laws of such a non-Aristotelian system of logic thought." We thus leave a discourse of "probablities" behind. "In a three-valued logic there exists an additional rejectional relation apart from the mutual rejection of any two values." The third value "rejects the preceding alternative of true and false, and so to speak displaces them."

But we don't have to understand this third value. That's a job for the robot brain. We know the most basic law of any three-value logic. "First find out what the common denominator of the first two values is—in other words the general basis upon which they negate each other—and then deny this very basis. But you might well ask: is it always possible to determine the common denominator? You are quite right, that is where the difficulty comes in and why a three-valued logic is a matter for somebody else, but not for us."

"There is one alternative of absolute generality the human mind is capable of. It is contained in Shakespeare's famous line: 'To be, or not to be. That is the question.'" What would be the three-value version? What's the common denominator of "being" and "not being"? There is none. "'To be or not to be'—that is the final question that takes precedence over everything." It's not enough to conclude that at this level there is no third value. "Obviously somewhere something is missing in our present conception of the relation between man and cosmos."

Although the Aristotelian and contra-Aristotelian mind mutually do not exist for each other, we know, if contra-terrene matter can be postulated as existing, that somehow they must coexist. "We shall probably never contact a seetee mind physically because between its realm and ours yawns an existential void where only mutual self-annihilation of physical matter governs the rules of a possible encounter. But there exists a 'third' in this creation beside Matter and the energetic Mind: it is Information."

If information can bridge the cosmic gulf, then a mechanical brain must be designed to hold the between position. "Between" sets a spell with "being two." To be two, or/and not to be two—that is the "between" position.

In the third part in the series, "The Soul of a Robot," Günther contemplates the quality of the mechanical brain by tipping the human scale. The goal of cybernetics is not some alchemical reproduction or rebirthing of the human brain. The wheel was invented alongside our legs. Mechanical legs were not fabricated in order to elongate our stride.

Günther's example of the Aristotelian limit concept (or limit to conception): "There is no third sex." While we can calculate the laws of three-valued logic, we can't employ them as our own brain functions: "here lies the proper destiny of all cybernetic science not to build a duplicate of the human mind, but a non-Aristotelian brain that works along a three-valued thought pattern." We must posit again the alien mind of total reversal of our logical thought. "What is true for the human mind is false for the seetee mind, and therefore has the combined characteristic—it is true and false at the same time. It is to clarify this superficial contradiction that the third value must be introduced." We must translate, transmit, and mediate the "and," the Aristotelian concept of conjunction, as terms of a three-valued system of thinking. A robot soul would be based not on identity but on "tridentity": "it could shift the personal center of its mental life and reconcile contradictory viewpoints."

In the fourth and final installment, "The Thought Translator," Günther models the robot brain's defining function as translator between irreconcilable logics on the episode in Lewis Carroll's *Through the Looking Glass* featuring figures Günther refers to as the "Tweedle-twins."

Tweedledum addresses Alice, "If you think we are Wax-works you ought to pay, Wax-works weren't made to be looked at for nothing. No how!" And Tweedledee adds: "Contrariwise, if you think we're alive, you ought to speak." The alternative of mutually exclusive terms is in this case, of course, dead or alive. Any other total alternative might do as well, but they all boil down to the purely logical one:

it is

or

it is

not.

"The contra-Aristotelian meaning of AND, however, is our terrestrial meaning of OR (inclusive). Because OR is always true if at least either p or q are true."

While he starts with the contrariwise twins to give approximation of thought translation between human and seetee minds via the robot brain, he concludes with a literal mirror. Write down value sequences for conjunction and disjunction in a horizontal line. Then turn the paper away from you and step up before a mirror. Don't forget that the reversal is true at the same time. Thus you have stepped through the looking glass. Between these two illustrations, another demo is part of the new definition. "The thought translator... transforms those two separate and mutually exclusive alternatives of the Aristotelian and the contra-Aristotelian mind into one and only one equally strict alternative by rotating the three values either 'clockwise' or 'counterclockwise.'" "The machine produces... its own alternative logic of two 'values.' Only the new 'values' are now no longer the individual values 1, 2, and 3, which we have used before, but the two opposite rotational shifts. These shifts partake necessarily in the human as well as the seetee range of thought at the same time." Translation thus becomes possible in the gap *and* overlap between human and seetee thought. Psychologically even it is impossible for human beings to think the three different meanings of AND: "even if we do not use it for our own subjective thought-procedures, we can calculate with it and find out how the mechanical brain translates our concept of AND into the conjunction of the seetee mind and, by a reversal of that process, transposes seetee ideas into human concepts."

In *Do Androids Dream of Electric Sheep?* Dick gives the android— renamed only in the screen version "replicant"—the succinct nickname "andy."

A Couple of Years

At one time—during the first year of his life in particular—Horace
had asked a Question. It had been his custom to place himself
in front of a person and to gaze up.... Staring up, his forehead
wrinkled with care, the cat had uttered a single baritone miaow,
and then had waited for an answer, an answer to a Question
which no one could fathom.... Horace now eyed the newspaperman with this traditional concern. It was not a simple confusion;
Horace was not asking, Who are you? Or Why are you here? He
seemed to want to know something deeper, perhaps something
philosophical. But, alas, no one would ever know. Certainly not
the newspaperman; Mr. Deverest returned the cat's intent stare
with uneasiness—a reaction which most people had to Horace's
scrutiny. "What's he want?" Mr. Deverest asked, as if alarmed.
Nick said, "No one to this day knows."
—PHILIP K. DICK, *Nick and the Glimmung*

Mrs. Pilsen, tears appearing in her eyes, said, "There is only one
cat like Horace. He used to—when he was just a kitten—stand
and stare up at us as if asking a question. We never understood
what the question was. Maybe now he knows the answer." Fresh
tears appeared. "I guess we all will eventually."
—PHILIP K. DICK, *Do Androids Dream of Electric Sheep?*

Nick and the Glimmung takes off into the outer-space setting for its fantasy to get around a future law prohibiting pets on earth. Nick's father has
in fact been considering leaving Earth again and again "during the last two
years" (9). The cause of their cat, Horace, puts a period to that two-year
span or sentence. The newspaperman tries to draw a distinction between

wildlife and pets. The latter " 'love us and we love them, even though there is a law against them. What we love, I suppose, is their memory.' 'You mean *our* memory,' Nick's mother said. 'Our memory of animals as they lived in the past. Or, as in the case of Horace, their real but illegal presence' " (22).

The epigraph to *Do Androids Dream of Electric Sheep?* tells a tall totemic tale of a prized animal's life and death. But it also marks the kind of exception that turns up the volume on what rules. A life span of two hundred years places the tortoise outside the economy of mourning, which totemic animals or pets otherwise inhabit fully, but in miniature or capsule form. When the tortoise goes it's news, it's history, and in place of burial its remains are placed on museum display. What is so easily misunderstood in Freud's *Totem and Taboo* is the measure of mourning that the identified-with animal provides and models. The primal father story leads us to see through the totemic animal to the close encounter with the mortality of the human other. It would be equally tendentious—yet readily possible—simply to reverse the hierarchy. In some nonlinear sense one can say that civilization or humanity begins and ends with the relationship to animals.

In *Martian Time-Slip* the schizo inside view of entropy or death drive as the purpose and momentum of life is punctuated, granted an intermission, or is in fact initiated over the first see-through view of the human across from you, taking it interpersonally but as skeletally robotic *Gestell*. For the time being, then, the prosthetic frame of techno relations survives the decay that uncovers it. What can reverse the collapse into the so-called tomb world is the reanimation of extinguished animals leading the falling world to rescue.

The title *Do Androids Dream of Electric Sheep?* doubles as a question. The answer, for the most part, is "no." Empathy tests are used to identify androids. But even after the test results are in and the tester has terminated the identified android, the final and conclusive test is the examination of the test subject's spinal column. In the 1982 film adaptation, *Blade Runner,* no conclusive test is ever given. Though Deckard admits toward the end of the novel that even electric animals have a kind or degree of life, this realization does not automatically extend to include androids, which are precisely not electric or machinic but humanoid.[1]

When hunter-tester Deckard, rattled in the cage of his belief in a clear distinction between humans and androids, proposes adding to the test, which would still be aimed at identifying androids, supplemental questions measuring empathy with androids, he comes closer to Dick's own reading of the terms of the distinction on which the author broods in numerous interviews and essays.

The postmachinic android, as new species, does not, not even possibly, exist. If we seem to recognize in this replicant just the same the poster teen of suicide, wipe out, fade away, before which we must swerve into the break we get for recovery, then it is still our own media rebound that we are picking up and personalizing or neotenizing. But for us as for Schreber, abandonment of belief in miraculated-up figures passing as humans and their acceptance instead as fellow men remains the one concession to reality required in Schreber's case for restoration of his legal rights but also if one's recovery in the new world order of mediatization is to be judged successful, that is, stabilized or encapsulated around maintenance of diplomatic relations with the outside human worlds that traverse one's own.

In the novel, in which there is an ascertainable difference between humans and androids, the latter were invented as free gift or consolation prize for colonists in wide outer space. Androids inhabit, then, the culture industry of post-Earth humanity. Thus it isn't surprising that they would pass most successfully as human when assuming the roles of mass culture stars, as in Buster Friendly and His Friendly Friends, the nonstop talk show monopolizing television and radio. The only other mass culture program in town, which comes complete with its own sets, so-called empathy boxes, is the cult of Mercerism, which is Christian the way Dick was Christian, immersed in mysticism on the one hand and on the other, following the diagnosis of Christianity Nietzsche first offered, in atheism itself. Mercerism as shared experience of pain and pining that the black empathy box transmits together with the audio and video portions of Mercer's struggles is the communion whereby humans are defined and the androids excluded from this community. Buster Friendly, as undercover android, is determined to reveal that Mercerism is a hoax. His exposé as reporter is completely successful. But what the androids will never understand is that it doesn't matter that Mercer is revealed to be a deadbeat actor, the setting of his Passion a painted soundstage, or even that as far as Mercer himself is concerned there is no salvation.

We begin to identify the projection of what the so-called android is through the seeing ego of Isidore, a radiation-spawned chicken head. This cretin or Christian follower of Mercerism, which as secular cult of empathy with animals has way more in common with a word from Nietzsche's Zarathustra than with the whole of the Judeo-Christian tradition, finds himself hosting runaways, who turn out to be androids. Returning from an errand on their behalf, Isidore discovers in the hallway a spider, which as living animal amounts to the greatest prize and affirmation in his stricken world. The androids holed up in his apartment are attending to the broadcast of the investigative report on the swindle of Mercerism. When Isidore returns, his guests alternate between rapt attention to the Friendly news and raptor attention to the specimen.

John Isidore said, "I found a spider."

The three androids glanced up, momentarily moving their attention from the TV screen to him.

"Let's see it," Pris said. She held out her hand.

. . . She cupped the medicine bottle in her palms, surveying the creature within. "All those legs. Why's it need so many legs, J. R.?"

. . . Rising to her feet, Pris said, "You know what I think, J. R.? I think it doesn't need all those legs."

"Eight?" Irmgard Baty said. "Why couldn't it get by on four? Cut four off and see." Impulsively opening her purse, she produced a pair of clean, sharp cuticle scissors, which she passed to Pris.

A weird terror struck at J. R. Isidore.

Carrying the medicine bottle into the kitchen, Pris seated herself at J. R. Isidore's breakfast table. She removed the lid from the bottle and dumped the spider out. "It probably won't be able to run as fast," she said. . . . She reached for the scissors.

"Please," Isidore said. . . . "Don't mutilate it," he said wheezingly. Imploringly.

With the scissors, Pris snipped off one of the spider's legs.

In the living room Buster Friendly on the TV screen said, "Take a look at this enlargement of a section of background. This is the sky you usually see. Wait, I'll have Earl Parameter, head of my research staff, explain their virtually world-shaking discovery to you."

Pris clipped off another leg, restraining the spider with the edge of her hand. She was smiling.

. . . Pris had now cut three legs from the spider, which crept about miserably on the kitchen table, seeking a way out, a path to freedom. It found none. . . .

Roy Baty appeared at the doorway, inhaling deeply, an expression of accomplishment on his face. "It's done. Buster said it out loud, and nearly every human in the system heard him say it. 'Mercerism is a swindle.' The whole experience of empathy is a swindle." He came over to look curiously at the spider.

"It won't try to walk," Irmgard said.

"I can make it walk." Roy Baty got out a book of matches, lit a match; he held it near the spider, closer and closer, until at last it crept feebly away. (205–7, 210)

While this kind of sadistic curiosity is child's play, in adults it is an indication of psychopathy, which this scene defines as absence of empathy (with or via animals). But more precisely, what the androids automatically improvise is a session of animal testing, which belongs to the reversed or disowned prehistory of the new world order's founding test of empathy.

Androids see through our attachment to animals and the group bond it guarantees as ideological ruse whereby they are denied their equal rights. But this turn to politics covers in the tracks of regression and resistance the more direct hit or fit between their rebellion and the totemic parental or ancestral guidance that animals transmit as mourning assignment.

Outside his fiction, Dick acknowledged that the two main topics or questions of his writing or thought were What is reality? and What is human? The latter question he framed by turning up the contrast between android and human. In his 1972 essay "The Android and the Human," Dick considers the technological syndication of psychic mechanisms as introducing a series of reversals around which his question circles. In animism mankind animated his environment. But in the treatment of neurosis, the tendency has been for man to introject or reclaim this outward-bound "animation." This first reclamation project led to reification. But the man-made world of machines now possesses animation to the turning point that, according to cybernetics, "study of machines would yield valuable insights into the nature of our own behavior" (183–84). "Our electronic constructs are becoming so complex that to comprehend them we must now reverse the analogizing of cybernetics and try to reason from our own mentation and behavior to theirs—although I suppose to assign motive or purpose to them would be to enter the realm of paranoia" (186). And yet Dick envisions technological constructs that run themselves with animation as always marking the place as empty once reserved for the human driver or drive. "It is the person inside who, when gone, cannot be duplicated at any price" (191).

Dick designates the teenagers of his day as opening up a new fold of animation between technologically administered functioning and the evacuation of humanity. The new superman to the rescue, according to Dick, is the man of steal. The teen gadget lover focuses his expertise on the device in front of him—the car radio for example—and rather than listen to the news break or the word from his sponsor adjusts or steals the technical medium.

If . . . we are . . . in the process of becoming a totalitarian society in which the state apparatus is all-powerful, the ethics most important for the survival of the true, human individual would be: Cheat, lie, evade, fake it, be elsewhere, forge documents, build improved electronic gadgets in your garage that'll outwit the gadgets used by the authorities. If the television screen is going to watch you, rewire it late at night . . . in such a way that the police flunky monitoring the transmission from your living room mirrors back *his* house. (194–95)

There is room for these interventions because the totalitarian state is at the same time an anarchistic state (195). The state apparatus grows cumbersome while corruption or the free market guarantees that every other cornerstone is substandard. Thus, as Dick imagines, when the time comes to program proper mourning in the citizens, the network will backfire as collective seizures of merriment (196).

Dick updates here a distinction he sought to uphold as human. "Another quality of the android mind is an inability to make exceptions. Perhaps this is the essence of it: the failure to drop a response when it fails to accomplish results, but rather to repeat it, over and over again" (201). And yet under certain conditions this kind of integrity is suicidal. Dick has to hand it to the dead Christ who tried out every possibility in an effort not to die. He never gave up (202–3). In two subsequent interviews, one from 1974 (Cover), the other from 1977 (Apel and Briggs), Dick elaborates on an ethics of passivity that counters this suicide drive of integrity:

I tried to define the real person, because there are people among us who are biologically human but who are androids in the metaphoric sense. I wanted to draw the line so I could define the positive primary goal of stipulating what was human....For example, the capacity to say no when what one was told to do was wrong. Someone saying, "No, I won't kill. I won't bomb." A balking.

There was [this]...quality that I felt distinguished the human being, that being the tendency to balk at things which were wrong. I developed quite a strong inner image of this happening....

And I got to thinking that this is the essence of the unhuman....Those Jehovah's Witnesses knew the situation; they knew that they and other people were going to be gassed. And yet they were typing lists, and emptying wastebaskets, whatever, as long as it didn't break some damn ordinance in the Bible like "Thou shalt not salute the flag." They'd go to their deaths rather than salute the flag, and yet they'd type up and carry lists of people who were to be exterminated!...[O]f course we're not really speaking about "androids" in the strict scientific sense of "a human being created in a laboratory"; we're talking about a form of unhuman behaviour, with an element of pathology.

In his 1976 essay "Man, Android, and Machine," Dick refuses to recognize artificial life as a distinction: "The entire universe is one vast laboratory" (211). In the cyborg or prosthetic arrangements between man and machine, all of it is alive. "One day we will have millions of hybrid entities that have a foot in both worlds at once....What is and will be a real concern is: Does the composite entity...*behave* in a human way?" (212). Recognizable technology, including false memory systems, is a defensive "mask" or "veil" put on to obscure, for example, time-slips or "ontological dysfunctions in time." "The veil or *dokos* is there to deceive us for a good reason, and such disclosures as these time dysfunctions make are to be obliterated that this benign purpose be maintained." Should we penetrate to actuality, therefore, "this strange, veil-like dream would reinstate itself retroactively, in terms of our perceptions and in terms of our memories" (216). Lineal time is a fold in this veiling. But the time line was required as supplement to cyclical time. While springtime can be viewed as always the same springtime, the human being ages between the lines over the span of remembrance. Because the other is in our face time draws the lines here and no further. Orthogonal time supplements lineal time with unsuspected helpings of spans of present time on the side.

Dick introduces a quote from Jameson's reading of *Dr. Bloodmoney,* which he distinguishes as the "best description of this *dokos*-veil formation." The citation takes a direct hit of the endopsychic Sensurround as "reality fluctuation . . . in which the psychic world . . . goes outside, and reappears in the form of simulacra or of some photographically cunning reproduction of the external" (221). As Dick concludes: "I suppose that the clear line between hallucination and reality has itself become a kind of hallucination" (231).

According to Dick, his work has shown that by "world" what is meant is nothing more or less than mind or spirit: "the immanent Mind that thinks—or rather dreams—our world" (218). However, this world isn't bigger than the two of us, self and other. The brain itself, just like its technological chain operations, cannot but follow this beat of a different doubler. In one body, we are of two minds: "our 'unconscious' is not an unconscious at all but another consciousness, with which we have a tenuous relationship. It is this other mind or consciousness that dreams us at night—we are its audience as it binds us in its storytelling" (220).

In "Mourning and Melancholia," Freud gives in passing his estimate that the average time span of mourning is two years in duration. I have found over years spent in the pulp complex of occult fiction that the two-year span is indeed the basic unit in every chronicle of unmourning. In Shelley's *Frankenstein,* for example, it is always after another period of two years has passed that Victor Frankenstein continues his pursuit of unmournable body building right at the juncture where he again refuses to let go and put to rest what is already at rest. To give a related example from the outer limits of the psy-fi complex—otherwise dedicated in its entirety to the circumvention of mourning or unmourning via the future address to replication as alternative to reproduction or death—we find in one of the fictionalized projections of space travel that Wernher von Braun cowrote in the late 1950s that the two-year span also comes up in scheduling for the future: "There is no way of predicting the exact state of health of any individual for more than two years in advance" (132). The two-year period is thus doubly marked: it is a period on average immune from interruption by losses or further losses and at the same time the period the work of mourning can put to a death sentence, the period or point where mourning can also turn around into unmourning. It is the time-altering span of present going on recent past and the precog scan of the immediate future. This is the point around which the android in Dick's novel is constituted. The android is granted a life span of four years—a couple of two-year spans. When an android gives his or her age—a calculation that is difficult for the android, too, given the influence of false memories and apparent age—two years have passed and another two lie ahead. The androids, who, as instant imitation youths, skip, like our pets, childhood in the human sense, are like teenagers to the extent that, since on a metabolically amped schedule, like that of our companion species, they forever die young.

Totemic animals or pets tend to live out life spans survived within the lives of their human guardians or partners. Ontogenetically and phylogenetically our first contact with mortality is via animals. In the future projected in Dick's novel animals are virtually extinct following the fallout of World War Terminus. This raises the value of animals, both cynically or commercially and psychodynamically: it raises their value to consciousness as the constitutive part or parting whereby one might begin to answer the question: What is human? The empathy test consists in the novel largely of animal abuse scenarios, while the cult of Mercerism promotes the group or mass bond over a shared prehistory of relations with animals. The mass death of animals following the war installed itself as the tomb world, the depression out of which Mercer struggles to emerge. The Mercer story begins with his early ability to reanimate animals. The so-called killers, who prohibited reanimation of animals, excised the occult power from Mercer's brain. The cult connection with Mercer's Passion picks up with the onset of restoration of his powers of recognition of life that guide him up out of the tomb world under renewed persecution by the killers. The difference between human as empath and android as psychopath is double: only humans have access to both group bonding and rapport with animals.[2]

Our relations with totemic animals or pets do not depend on their ability to mourn. Structurally, androids hold the place of discrete finitude and, all together now, of litters. Humans, on average, live too long to have an easy time with finitude. Humans also tend to be born singly, which is already the basis for the individual subjecthood whereby we set ourselves at odds with the pack structures of social or everyday life.

While the imperative of understanding the failure of empathy in the human realm sends Dick to the outer limits of his own psychic reality, ranging from schizoid to schizophrenic states and back again, in *Do Androids Dream of Electric Sheep?* the one concession made to uncertainty about the difference between androids and humans occurs when Rick Deckard joins forces with Phil Resch, another bounty hunter, in tracking down the android Luba Luft. The episode, framed by two art settings, the opera in which Luft is diva, and the art museum in which Luft identifies with a Munch painting, turns on Rick's empathic identification with the android and his identification of Resch as android-like psychopath. It is when the test proves that Resch is human that Deckard is inspired to reflect that another subset of questions, as we underscored earlier, should be included in the testing, questions that would test for empathy with androids.

The showdown between the two bounty hunters ultimately addresses not so much the expendability as the expandability of the test. Luft artfully makes the ability to share a sentiment via art a test that she passes and Resch fails. As the relationship between Luft and Deckard begins to score empathically via the relationship to or through Munch's art, Resch pulls his gun and offs the android, thus reinforcing the strict parameters of the tester's relationship to the android as test subject. The episode is less of a concession to the logic foregrounded in the film version than one might at first think. The updated test would begin to test for the metaphysical difference between human and android, a change in range that would be congruent with Dick's larger concern. And once Deckard suffers the consequences of sleeping with the android, following Resch's recommendation that such fraternization would be the best way of getting the inappropriate so-called empathy out of his system, he understands that Resch himself was the victim of android manipulations of empathy.

Ethically, the empathy Deckard tests for is an intention; empathy as a structure underlies self-serving manipulations of identification and grief. "On Empathy" is the transcript of extemporaneous remarks Heinz Kohut delivered at a conference at UC Berkeley in 1981, only a few days before his death. Kohut takes care to see empathy from both sides now: "When the Nazis attached sirens to their dive bombers, they knew with fiendish empathy how people on the ground would react to that with destructive anxiety. This was correct empathy, but not for friendly purposes" (529). And yet Kohut holds out the horror of "an empathyless environment that just brushes you off the face of the earth" as a fateful step "beyond the empathy-informed hatred that wants to destroy you" (530). In the lexicon of World War II that informs Kohut's discourse, it's the difference between being a concentration camp inmate and being a target of Nazi propaganda and Blitz attack. But a space flight anecdote underscores that where the empathy is, that's where you can find rest in pieces.

There is a touching story—again I come back to the astronauts, you may remember it—of the astronauts when their spaceship, before landing on the moon, was hit by a meteorite, that's the theory. And they seemed to have lost control over it. And they had the choice, if there was indeed a loss of control, to go on circling for many, many weeks with their supplies, or to go back to Earth and—because they couldn't slow down—get scorched and burned up upon entering. As they were discussing this issue among themselves—there was no question in their minds: "We would never want to have our remains circle forever in empty space. Even if we burn up, it's Earth, it's our home." And that, I submit, stands for an empathic human milieu. (531)

That Dick, too, was able to stagger and straddle divergent applications or identifications of empathy is manifest in *The Zap Gun,* his Cold War novel (and James Bond spoof) composed two years before *Do Androids Dream of Electric Sheep?* Similar to what we find in *The Penultimate Truth,* written neck and neck with *The Zap Gun,* this postwar world rests in a peace of the minds of the few (who are ambivalently termed cogs) who manipulate the majority (the pursaps). It was decided by those alone in the know to move the undertaking of design and production of weapons of mass destruction, referred to as ter wep (sometimes spelled or typo-slipped as "tear wep"), to a location somewhere between psy war and make-believe. At the front of the line of the "weapons fashions" business during the Cold War (Wesbloc vs. Peep-East) is a medium, like Lars Powderdey, whose "psionic talent of contacting the Other World, the hyper-dimensional universe that he entered into during his trance-states" (17), is amplified with drugs and directed toward visionary invention of new weapon designs. He's a one-man business, "Mr. Lars, Incorporated," which is housed, like Rotwang's lab in *Metropolis,* in a small building uncannily out of context in Manhattan. This condition of incorporation at the art of android building will find a matching grieving but not the matching loss. The taboo on realizing an android indistinguishable from a human being on a scale of empathy organizes this culture industry of toy weapons and games as capable, finally, of containing a real threat that comes from outer space.

Preparedness that's all show has promoted peace since World War II without the risk of armed self-destructiveness.

"There's no protection in weapons. . . . Not since—you know. 1945. When they wiped out that Jap city."
"But," Lars said, "the pursaps think there is. There *seems* to be."
"And that *seems* to be what they're getting."
Lars said, "I think I'm sick. I'm involved in a delusional world." (31–32)

This delusional world or belief system is maintained as paradise for the unknowing via mediums who go to the Other World, the supernatural realm, into the unconscious, or psychotic states in order to conjure weapons that will be made only as models or props for scenes of testing in videos. And yet the designs are functional to the extent that they are subsequently "plowshared" as toys or games (for children, the whole family, and, ultimately, the enemy) that circulate openly with cogs and pursaps as equal sharers in their fantasy contents.

Assembled before official videos of ever new weapon tests, citizens are led to believe that peace on earth must be maintained by the standoff between and stockpile of opposing weapons of mass destruction. But to test a weapon means to simulate its testing (often in miniature like toys in close-up) on a set for future screenings as documentary evidence of the weapon's capacity for destruction. In the case of antipersonnel weapons, the test is life-size: androids made to look like throwaway criminal types are the test subjects in pageants of crime and punishment that rely on and manipulate empathy.

The pursaps like displays of power because they feel powerless themselves. It heartened them to see Item 278 make mincemeat out of a gang of thugs who were beyond the pale. . . . Now the bad fellas, like husks, like dehydrated skins, deflated bladders, wandered about. . . . Instead of a satellite or a building or a city being blown up a group of human brains, candle-like, had been blown out.

Lars, who attends the prescreenings voluntarily (at research facilities that subtend the California coast from San Francisco to San Diego) because he wishes to take responsibility, doesn't take comfort in his colleague Jack's reassurance that "it isn't as if" the weapon in the film will ever be made.

"It is as if," Lars said. "It's goddam completely, as if you could make it. I have an idea. Run the tape backward. . . . First you show these people like they are now. . . . As mindless, de-brained, reduced to reflex-machines. . . . Then the FBI ships spurt the essential quality of humanness back into them." . . .

"But see, my friend," Jack pointed out patiently, "what would emerge as a result of the item's action would be a gang of hoodlums."

True. He had forgotten about that.

However, Pete spoke up at this point, and on his side. "But they wouldn't be hoodlums if the tape was run backward because they'd set museums un-on fire, undetonate hospitals, re-clothe the nubile bodies of naked young girls, restore the punched-in faces of old men. And just generally bring the dead to life, in a sort of off-hand manner."

Jack said, "It would spoil the pursaps' dinners to watch it." He spoke with finality. . . .

"What makes pursaps tick?" Lars asked him. . . .

Without hesitation Jack said, "Love."

"Then why this?" Lars gestured at the screen. Now the FBI was carting off the hulks who had been men, rounding them up like so many stunned steers.

"The pursap," Jack said thoughtfully, . . . "is afraid in the back of his mind that weapons like this exist. If we didn't show them, the pursap would believe in their existence anyhow. And he'd be afraid that somehow, for reasons obscure to him, they might be used on him. . . . That in some way he doesn't quite fathom, he's corrupt. . . . When he sees it used on an uglier life form than him he thinks, Hey. Maybe they passed me by. . . . Which means—and this is the crux, Lars—he doesn't have to worry about his own death right now. He can pretend he will never die." (57–59)

The empathy thus lying between the lines of the industry proves to be the last line of defense when an enemy arrives, who breaks the game rules of paradise regained by posing a real threat. The ultimate weapon that zaps the enemy is based on child's play, an educational toy designed for channeling empathy via animals (animal abuse in childhood is the item most regularly checked off the predictive list of future psychopaths). Rewired as weapon, the "game" tricks the player into thinking that the cute critter or wub in the maze has a fair shake. But even when you press the "help" button of identification (techno-telepathically reinforced), the only consequence in the maze is more torment. Trapped inside the game with the wub the player is himself submitted to the irreversibly increasing severity of the mazing to his own a-mazement. "It could induce . . . a rapid, thorough mental disintegration" (169).

But the empathy device is circuitously wired through plot and subplots before it can be recognized as the sought-after outside chance for survival. First, with the Sirius Slavers on the horizon, the two sides of the simulated conflict on Earth put the heads of their mediums together to face the "return to the unsheathed sword of the past" (91). Lars joins forces with

Peep-East's Lilo Topchev in Fairfax, Iceland, in the hopes that the trance-ference between them will lead to the design of a real weapon.

Several subplots spin around this meeting of mediums. Lars was introduced to us in libidinal crisis with Lilo already on the surveillance snapshot horizon of his desire for another chance and change. One of his plow-shared weapon designs, the gizmo Ol' Orville, a talking head that, with all the answers, is all the rage as religion's latest replacement (47), responds to Lars's question, What have I become?

"You have become an outcast. A wanderer. Homeless. . . . I mean to say that, like Parsifal, you are *Waffenlos,* without weapons . . . in two senses, figurative and literal. You do not actually make weapons, as your firm officially pretends. And you are *Waffenlos* in another, more vital sense. You are defenseless. Like the young Siegfried, before he slays the dragon, drinks its blood and understands the song of the birds, or, like Parsifal, before he learns his name from the flower maidens, you are innocent. In, perhaps, the bad sense." (50)

Although he dismisses psychoanalysts, under the yoke of a bad joke, as fraudian, he admits to himself that his Wagnerian predicament has a bad sense, too: "His fear was a near-castration fear. And it never went away" (51). Because she voices his inside review, as always "in the tone of a marriage counsellor" (42), his mistress and coworker Maren Faine is positioned to go. As she herself knows when she picks up via Ol' Orville the anticipation with which Lars heads for the collaboration in Iceland.

Once more picking up the featureless head, Lars said, "What is it about Peep-East that figures in all this, Ol' Orville?"

A pause, while the complex electronic system whirred, and then the gadget responded. "A blurred, distance-shot, glossy. Too blurred to tell you what you wish to know."

At once Lars knew. And tried to eradicate the thought from his mind, because . . . Maren . . . was standing right there by him, picking up his thoughts, in defiance of Western law. Had she gotten it, or had he cut it off in time, buried it back in his unconscious where it belonged?

"Well, well," Maren said thoughtfully. "Lilo Topchev." (52)

Near-castration fear, resistance to Freud, mid-life crisis: we are in a world in which compatibility with psychoanalysis is streamlined down to recognition values, bottom lines, and the typical. In its cultivation of the typical in the midst of a *faux* arms race, society triggers paranoid schizophrenia in one citizen called to serve as "concomody" based on the typicality of his consumer record. The governing board to which he has been summoned in Festung, Washington, D.C., is of course *faux* too — like every other form or forum of consumer projection, I mean protection. The typical turns around into the unique in the tight spot the psychotic Surley G. Febbs is in. Thus the psychotic state, maintained by the cogs as fantasy on the credit or belief of the pursaps, interrupts or slips past the fantasy periodically as threat. This problem, in the person of Febbs, which is internal to the world externally challenged by Sirius Slavers, takes the immediate form of Febbs's determination to reassemble models of weapons as functional. The problem is really huge — since Febbs is stopped like the threat from outer space through the rewired empathy game. Febbs was considered by Dick as "the black side of John Isidore" in *Confessions of a Crap Artist* (in Sutin, *Divine Invasions,* 304) as of the other namesake (I would add) in *Do Androids Dream of Electric Sheep?* who is our delegate in first contact with android empathy.

Another blind passage (and passenger) passes through psychosis. Lars discovers that his weapons are available in the comic book series, *The Blue Cephalopod Man from Titan*. Lilo's designs are previewed there too. How can they be getting their designs from the artist of this magazine? The comic book artist, a former inventor, is in and out of mental institutions from here to Timbuktu. "Without electroshock and thalamic-suppressors he would be in a complete autistic schizophrenic withdrawal" (135). Are they channeling schizophrenic delusions of world power? Because the superhero strips appear with the same weapons before the two mediums dream them up the Peep-East authorities, at least, are convinced that the answer is "yes." To save Lars from execution his personal physician Dr. Todt pulls the gun on the presiding official and both Mediums escape to Wes-Bloc. In the move, the issue of origin of the former designs is displaced, but left hanging, like a continuity error. Now they have a senile time traveler or android to channel. At the point of crossing over, moreover, Maren intercepts Lars and Lilo and shoots. Second intersection of paths never given direction: Does her gun go off improperly and take her out as accident or is the explosion the means of her suicide? For Lars, who sleepwalks through his postshoot traumatic blackout for days, it was the close-up of the attack from outer space: "I did not design this, not this weapon. This predates me. This is old, an ancient monster. This is all the inherited evil, carried here out from the past, carted to the doorstep of my life and deposited, flung to demolish everything I hold dear, need, desire to protect" (148).

But then a certain Ricardo Hastings, back from the future, picks up the lack of a weapon: he talks about a Time Warpage Generator serviced during the Big War, which is the conflict they are currently facing (142). But Hastings, who is ancient, is completely senile. But isn't Hastings an android, Lars asks? More like two years old, rather than ancient. (Lilo has been bringing back sketches of androids out of trance states she enters lying next to Hastings, trying to extract his memory of the Generator.) Hastings turns out to be Vincent Klug, a specialist in projecting the plow-sharing weapon designs as toys, who, regularly overlooked and avoided, turns to the spectacular intro of time travel, whereby he succeeds in one time only to find some recognition after all in this time. Although time travel allows Klug to save the day (not with a futural Generator but with the wub maze game he designed in the present tense), the impediments Klug faces in getting his rescue across are duplicated by the very conditions of traveling and communicating in the deregulated medium of time, which in this case is lined in the curse of taboo.

"Time-travel . . . is one of the most rigidly limited mechanisms arrived at by the institutional research system. . . . I can see ahead but I can't tell anything—I can't inform you. . . . All I can do . . . is call your attention to some object, artifact or aspect of your present environment.—It must *already* exist. Its presence must not in any way be dependent on my return here from your future." (161)

Klug thus makes his entry via guessing games, which, as Lars now recognizes, is his main medium: "you like games" (161). Guesswork gets across Dick's oeuvre as the ghost work with/of mourning. The android, with Lilo as the receptionist of its aura of ambivalence, emplaces and displaces this guessing game. The attempted construction of human-like androids, which the authorities blocked as too dangerous, was Klug's largest project in empathy Imagineering. Klug went from there to games, which he can deliver only via the roundabout of wish fulfillment, the career brought to him by time travel.

Lilo's diagnosis, depression, falls short of her sojourns in the tomb world (where, for instance, she once watched her hand become a corpse appendage) (106). Lars loves her at first sight from afar as blur on the screen. When she's in a broken-down state, she resembles an android (124). She is the dark-haired girl whose first gift to him, in the exchange of drug brands each regularly uses and now for each to try, is poison. Her treating physician informs us it was a "psychotic coup to defend herself against imaginary attack" (111).

Time travel comes up twice in the wake of Maren's death. Lars considers time travel as a way to encounter Maren again, even though he would have to wait fifty years to go back, because it is impossible to travel back in time right away into the recent past. Historically it is impossible. In fifty years the requisite warpage device will have been invented. But the requisite time will also have been allowed to pass. When Lilo attempts her first paradoxical intervention, counseling suicide rather than the long wait for reunion, Lars prepares to pop the poison pill (but it is his relationship to Lilo that is regressed on the upbeat, along which, through this reversal, he rolls the pill of decline). Maren's passing becomes the overdetermined occasion for Lars to grieve in excess, only then to double back and reformat the loss as access to Lilo, who wasn't the substitute but, from the start, the one. The point of his departure through dissociation and amnesia was his sense that Lilo had been obliterated in the showdown. That's not a death wish but common sense, as in goal. Lilo and Lars are on the same track. Maren's exit, like the loss of no love, trails an evil I as the displaced occasion for Lars to raise the essential questions of Dick's oeuvre:

"I just don't understand where the past goes when it goes. What happened to Maren Faine? . . . Where is she? Where's she gone?" (173)

Android Empathy

No engineer or chemist claims to be able to produce a material which is indistinguishable from the human skin. It is possible that at some time this might be done, but even supposing this invention available we should feel there was little point in trying to make a "thinking machine" more human by dressing it up in such artificial flesh.

—A. M. TURING, "Computing Machinery and Intelligence"

And Harrison Ford would say, "Lower that blast-pistol or you're a dead android!" And I would just leap across that special effects set like a veritable gazelle and seize him by the throat and start battering him against the wall. They'd have to run in and throw a blanket over me and call the security guards to bring in the Thorazine. And I'd be screaming, "You've destroyed my book!" ... They'd have to ship me back to Orange County in a crate full of air holes. And I'd still be screaming. . . . "Hollywood is gonna kill me by remote control!"

—PHILIP K. DICK in Boonstra,
"A Final Interview with Science Fiction's Boldest Visionary"

When Deckard busts an android network he senses that he, as the Form Destroyer, is impinging on a microcosm of life. Thus he rises to the occasion as overseer and death driver while the androids are miniaturized, in a sense, inside their representation of world or life. Truth be told, Deckard doesn't know the half of the ubiquity of androids crowding the passing lane on Earth. It would appear that most people in the android-making and the media entertainment industries are androids. This is where *Blade Runner* fits right in.

That the distinction between humans and androids, between empathy and psychopathy, traverses every human psyche is given in the opening scene of *Do Androids Dream of Electric Sheep?* which like an overture seems to contain all the novel's themes but set on a couple in need of counseling. Three gadgets dominate the couple's household or economy. In addition to the competing TV set and empathy box there is also the Penfield mood organ, which Rick Deckard likes to rely on as much as his wife Iran seeks to undermine it. In turn he tends to avoid the empathy box that she prizes above all. Like the television, the mood organ is a media device used both by humans and androids, often as weapons in their holy war. Iran's mistrust of the mood organ leads her to readjust it, via a series of trials, as extension of the depressive tendencies it was designed to cloak.

"At that moment ... when I had the TV sound off, I was in a 382 mood; I had just dialed it. So although I heard the emptiness intellectually, I didn't feel it. My first reaction consisted of being grateful that we could afford a Penfield mood organ. But then I realized how unhealthy it was, sensing the absence of life, not just in this building but everywhere, and not reacting—do you see? I guess you don't. But that used to be considered a sign of mental illness; they called it 'absence of appropriate affect.' So I left the TV sound off and I sat down at my mood organ and I experimented. And I finally found a setting for despair." (5)

Deckard warns her that it is " 'dangerous to undergo a depression, any kind' " (6). By the end of the novel, however, he will join her sensibility in which there was already that empathy for the hunted androids or andys, which he would add to the sensorium of testing. His wife Iran at the start of the novel accuses him of being a hired killer. When he protests that he has never killed a human being, she gets to the point way ahead of the novel's second thoughts: "Just those poor andys" (4).

When Deckard phones her later that day but cannot penetrate the depression she redialed after he left, he tips off his projected identification of her android nature, which, again by the end of the novel, he must reclaim and work through as his own. "For all intents he spoke into a vacuum. . . . I wish I had gotten rid of her two years ago when we were considering splitting up. I can still do it, he reminded himself" (94). She openly embraces the status of blow-up dolly to bring their morning altercation to a close (and to make him turn off the television). "I give up; I'll dial. Anything you want me to be; ecstatic sexual bliss—I feel so bad I'll even endure that. . . . What difference does it make?" (7).

Already in the same opening chapter, as he prepares to leave for work from the rooftop hovercar port, Deckard confesses to his neighbor that his sheep grazing nearby is in fact electric, the reproduction of the real sheep that died. When the neighbor promises to keep the secret of the sheep's artificial nature, Deckard finds himself under the influence of Iran's despair, her negative rhetorical questioning of difference. "Pausing, Rick started to say thanks. But then something of the despair that Iran had been talking about tapped him on the shoulder and he said, 'I don't know; maybe it doesn't make any difference'" (13). What makes the difference, again and again, is the turn to animals. Devastated by the execution he attended of the android Luba Luft, with whom he felt empathy, Deckard buys a living goat, which lifts his own and his wife's depression. After the android Rachael takes revenge by killing the goat, Deckard, after once again hitting bottom, makes it up out of the tomb world when, just like Mercer, he discovers animal life stirring in the dust. This time when the toad turns out to be another electric animal he can still draw from its being affirmation of life. It is over this acceptance of the electric toad and the care for it that will follow that the Deckard couple seems able or willing to contain the differences between husband and wife, the intermediary hub of coupling that Dick, too, set aside as one of the motors of mourning.

In the novel and more fully in the film version the android begins to enter the field of testing as object of empathy. The android seems constituted, however, as aberrant variant on or embodiment of mourning. Rachael stretches her so-called self-empathy to address the dynamic of interandroid relations. While she pulls up short before establishing compatibility with human empathy (which, by the way, she also doesn't really believe in), she fills in the blank with the human-all-too-inhuman predilections of murderous egoism.

"That goddamn Nexus-6 type," Rachael said, enunciating with effort, "is the same type as I am. . . . You know what I have? Toward this Pris android?"

"Empathy," he said.

"Something like that. Identification; there goes I. My god; maybe that's what'll happen. In the confusion you'll retire me, not her. And she can go back to Seattle and live my life. I never felt this way before. We are machines, stamped out like bottle caps."

Deckard extends the litter of the law of identical existence to androids. Maybe ants are similar to androids. But the ant—the AND—Rachael emphasizes typically, doesn't feel anything. What about identical twins? But, Rachael appears to admit, seemingly sadly, the android falls short of the profoundly empathic—even telepathic—relation obtaining in identical twinship.

As witnessed in the close quarters of Isidore's residence, the revolutionary nihilism of the androids in Dick's novel, publicly broadcast via Buster Friendly and His Friendly Friends, rejects empathic difference as merely ideological distinction that, right down to the overvaluation of animal life, which is but the roundabout formulation of the undervaluation of android life, serves to cover over and cover for android enslavement. However inadvertently, *Blade Runner* is by and large the propaganda film on behalf of this android worldview. In the novel the androids die because science has yet to solve the problem of cell replacement. In the film the androids are programmed to die young as yet another measure implemented to control them. In the novel the corporation implants false memories to influence or defer the outcome of the test. It is, we are assured, a desperate and pointless attempt. In the film, memories are used only to control the emotional life of the androids, which cannot be completely vacated or prevented.[1]

On the check-off list that counts down to discovery that the person I've been talking to is an android is, just one rung above the truth, the hypothesis that I'm dealing with a psychotic. "But he thought, It must be a delusion. She must be psychotic. With delusions of persecution" (148). Accordingly, the android Pris uses the hypothesis as last-ditch defense of her true identity: "Our trip was between a mental hospital on the East Coast and here. We're all schizophrenic, with defective emotional lives — flattening of affect, it's called. And we have group hallucinations" (161).

The Rosen organization already introduced this cover identity of the android as ruse whereby the testing apparatus would appear outmoded. The android Rachael was introduced as belonging to the small class of human beings who, because schizoid, must fail the Voigt-Kampff scale.[2] "This problem has always existed. Since we first encountered androids posing as humans. The consensus of police opinion is known to you in Lurie Kampff's article, written eight years ago, *Role-taking Blockage in the Undeteriorated Schizophrenic*" (38).

The androids in *Do Androids Dream of Electric Sheep?* — as clarified via their prehistory in *We Can Build You* and *The Simulacra* — were planned as next-door neighbors on Mars, as reassuring simulations of family values. As such, they were, however, misplaced. Life on Mars, even or especially artificial life, is profoundly lonely.

"You think I'm suffering because I'm lonely. Hell, all Mars is lonely. Much worse than this."

"Don't the androids keep you company? I heard a commercial on—. . . . I understood that the androids helped."

"The androids," she said, "are lonely, too." (150)

The screenwriters as well as the director and his team fixed the testing focus on Descartes's famous differentiation between humans and machines.[3] That Descartes treated machines and animals interchangeably however throws a wrench into the testable difference between man and machine that the undecidability established in the film cannot address. This undecidability set on the self-reflexivity of the film is not *gründlich*, in fact it is a limited edition not to be confused with the undecidability Derrida saw as sideswiped and displaced by every attempt to establish testable difference between man and animal. Dick was always open about his involvement with philosophy, theology, psychoanalysis. Descartes is almost never a key player in his studies. In fact *Do Androids Dream of Electric Sheep?* is in part a response to the Turing test. But as soon as the novel hits the screen, the surname Deckard sounds like Descartes, especially in earshot of the android Pris's recitation of Descartes's famous line as one of the things she can do. That outer-space colonies are referred to as off world (which resonates with "off screen") underscores the solipsism of the eye or ego that dominates the film's test site. Hence the all-importance of photography in the film for which there is no counterpart in the novel. The seeming perfect fit with Descartes would appear specific to the film medium. As epigraph to the science-fiction film *The Thirteenth Floor* (1999) we can read, therefore: "I think, therefore I am."[4]

Blade Runner interprets itself, as film, as the native habitat of androids via component stills that, however, can be perceived from all sides, even from the off. One innovation in *Blade Runner* without model in the novel is the Esper machine, through which the reproductive and illusory field of representation of or in a single snapshot can be virtualized and then explored from all sides.[5] The Esper scene gives a strong and literal interpretation of one of the opening lines from the start of the film in which a replicant is defined as "a being virtually identical to the human."

Virtual identity attends *Blade Runner*'s repeated introduction of the figure of the mother as measure of the untenability of human origin in its precincts.[6] The film begins with the shots that answer "Tell me about your mother." This breakdown in the animal objective of identification in Dick's test or text spawns the spider mother whose edible relationship to her own progeny foregrounds the same impossibility of identification that underlies the exchange of memory between Deckard and Rachael. It is just as likely that Deckard was programmed with the same implant as that he recognizes it as one of the implants from the storehouse of her model or maker. Rachael and Deckard share this spider memory (which is the film version of the android or psychopathic torture of the spider) from different levels of self-awareness that fall down as the bottom line (of film) that they are both androids. Like the photographic evidence illuminated and extended via the Esper machine, the scene of testing and shooting is contextless and at the same time retains the complete trace of wraparound context inside it.

Dick's story "Imposter" is thus a self-made film, *Impostor* (2002), in which the android medium declares itself in a punchline: I am an impostor. BANG! End of movie. While in the story the reader is aware that no one believes the protagonist (until a surprise spot of hesitation around the mechanical appearance of the corpse briefly tilts the standstill), in the film we are not alone in siding or identifying with the protagonist from the first accusation.

Screamers (1995) cuts into the flesh of undecidability between human and android on-screen only to vouchsafe the sadistic cutting as prolongable: the latest androids are tiny blood drops dolls. Dick's story "Second Variety" foregrounds the deregulated and autonomous self-production of androids as empathy-seeking missiles. In *Screamers* the machine beneath the love interest is revealed only via jealousy between android women who forget their android identities. Android films can't cut beyond the wraparound male gaze of Introduction to Film Studies.

A Scanner Darkly (2006) skirts the android = film issue by pulling the scramble suit over and through screened life. The scramble suit is the one component of the film that is (mostly) animation drawn from scratch. Otherwise the film is live action recast as animation through rotoscope. The director's name, Linklater, triggers association with the truly wonderful name of another media meister (and Disney throwback), Art Linkletter. While that name was *avant la lettre*, the filmmaker's is "-later." Rotoscope is a late arrival of that primal scene of animation Walt Disney delivered as *Snow White and the Seven Dwarfs* (1937).

The scramble suit, also the only sci-fi device in the novel, is a kernel of surveillance paranoia that has a history in the novel *A Scanner Darkly,* which is borrowed from the record of Dick's dreams and fears. Paradoxical intervention or paranoia: Dick was convinced that scary Republicans like Nixon were Communist plants (see *Radio Free Albemuth*). Like the inventor of the scramble suit, S. A. Powers, Dick once came out of a trance in which he had watched a slideshow on fast-forward of thousands of early modernist paintings. It's the Rosicrucians trying to warp my mind. But then Powers matches some paintings with those in the Leningrad museum collections. The Soviets were trying to contact or influence him telepathically. Beginning in the 1960s research in parapsychology was openly supported and so advanced in the Soviet Union because of the mistaken assumption that one of the U.S. nuclear submarines had been maintaining outside contact via telepathy. Through a slip or blip, then, the slack that was the impress of Stalinist prohibition of psychoanalysis could be picked up by the heirs of Spiritualism (Ostrander and Schroeder). The suit that scrambles the senses technologically the way drugs scramble them internally is pulled up from the Cold War and reformulated for the war on drugs. But like the communists being the anti-communists in Dick's view, those who enforce the war against drugs serve the interests of "drug terrorism" or, rather, drug capitalism.

Blade Runner departs from or exceeds the safe enclosure of its android self-reflexivity in the closing staging of finitude, for androids and humans alike. Like the males of so-called primitive societies whose first response to loss is to seek vengeance, as discussed by Freud in *Totem and Taboo,* Roy Batty smears Pris's blood over his torso as war paint and hunts or haunts the bounty hunter. As fitting retribution he commences his destruction of Deckard digitally—by breaking his fingers. But then he senses (digitally again) that he has begun to shut down. To extend the digital span he drives a nail through his hand. But then he accepts the inevitable, ceases his revenge, even rescues Deckard. The Christ imagery gathers momentum. But Deckard is saved to witness what cannot be witnessed, the loss that will be lost. Batty asserts that as our seeing-eye probe he has seen things that we cannot even imagine. His visual memories will be lost forever when he goes. "Time to die." The showdown between Deckard and Batty transpires in the attic spaces of Sebastian's building. Given his predilection for artificial life, perhaps he also constructed the pigeons roosting there. Otherwise, even in the film, which is less emphatic about the status of animals in its world, this upsurge of animal life would amount to a continuity error. But what is a continuity error in a self-reflexive film? We enter here an allegorical supplement to the film. The Christian signifiers refer as props to the storeroom of a world or screen in which redemptive systems of reference can only be found missing. When Batty dies what is given up is not the soul symbolized by the dove flying upward but the camera's movement toward the light, the very limit concept of this visual medium. She won't live, Deckard is advised by Gaff, a member of the police force who doubles as Deckard's guide out of retirement into the underworld of differentiation between human and android. Gaff is always making and leaving behind origami figures. His last piece represents a unicorn. In the course of his investigation of the photographs of the android Leon, Deckard nods off and, apparently, dreams of a unicorn. The unicorn is the mascot of the fantasy genre. It is pagan in origin but was subsequently reinscribed as a symbol of Christ. But here or now, at the close of *Blade Runner,* it attends finitude allegorically without redemption.[7] The woman no longer defined as not living or as never having lived but as one who won't live, who won't die, steps across the unicorn as she joins Deckard in their escape, not the escape of fantasy, but an escape into affirmed finite life.

Turing's test-case scenario advances from the question of decidability of gender (based on an unseen exchange with the questioner or tester) to another exercise posed, for the questioner, between human (or, literally, man) and the machine (which replaced the woman of the earlier setup). What exceeds Turing's conclusion regarding the equivalence of human and artificial intelligence in the context of interpersonal telecommunication is the exception he leaves open, the one that rules in Dick's future worlds. What could always queer Turing's test-proven total word domination by man the machine is telepathy. Telepathy casts its intrapsychic shadow across the interpersonal columns supporting the truisms of machine history. But telepathy doesn't only knock over the partitions in the lab space. Turing admits that if telepathy can be accepted (and he allows that scientific consensus on the reality of telepathy is already the up-and-coming trend), then we are also on the way to acceptance of the existence of ghosts. Thus on the sidelines of Turing's experiment we recognize the habitat of a whole caste of characters in Dick's works whose diverse occult abilities bound past boundary concepts as the joker in the package deal of control communications. While technologization of border states folds out as a kind of border patrol in Dick's world, communication with ghosts also becomes increasingly available. Even when time travel is the techno product that matches occult proclivities we also encounter that it finds itself in a blind spot via the influence of psychotelekinesis. Thus for every instrumentalization of occult abilities in the service of surveillance (for example) counterforces can be mobilized among those whose talent is the reversal and negation of what is positively given in the occult. In *Ubik,* for example, "inertials" vacuum up or pack the advance and advantage of telepaths or precogs. In lieu of the diversion of opposition or interchangeability, there is in Dick's fictional worlds diversification unto undecidability as to which "side" is given to score the advantage points.

The culture industry in Dick's future scenarios consists of recognizable variations on TV—including implantable programs that call up memory and forgetting as foreign embodiments—alongside assembly or receiving lines of artificial intelligent life. The juxtaposition suggests that android production and existence must represent in fact another variation on the metapsychological facts of life under conditions of visual mediation and liveness (as in surveillance). This latter development is located or confirmed in film versions based on narratives by P. K. Dick. What *Blade Runner* did for the androids who, coming complete with "artificial" memories, are us (or our suicide drive), *Total Recall* (1990) pulled up for TV's injection of memories in the receiving area of consumerism. While it remains patly undecidable whether the viewers will ever know Arnold Schwarzenegger's true memories as or as well as their own, in Dick's story "We Can Remember It for You Wholesale," a memory of a childhood fantasy or reality still holds the bottom line of reality's representation or repression in the word according to psychoanalysis. It is not the adult fantasy of being an Interplan undercover agent that the Interplan psychiatrist discovers in his patient, Mr. Quail, but a "most interesting wish-fulfillment dream fantasy" from childhood. Quail at age nine sees aliens resembling field mice land in a space vessel. The psychiatrist continues: " 'You halt the invasion, but not by destroying them. Instead, you show them kindness and mercy, even though by telepathy—their mode of communication—you know why they have come. They have never seen such humane traits exhibited by any sentient organism, and to show their appreciation they make a covenant with you.' Quail said, 'They won't invade Earth as long as I'm alive' " (49). But the "most grandiose fantasy" the policeman in attendance has ever encountered, since the lapse of his life into lifelessness brings down the world (50), turns out, they find out at the point of injecting him with the false memory of his being savior of the world, to be true.

Minority Report (2002) takes the least self-reflexive stance of Dick-inspired projections to date in relationship to its own medium nature as autistic or schizoid by-product of Dick's oeuvre. Only in a movie (in the movie inside the movie) can the future be edited out of the projective mythic imagery that the future has digitalized. The unpredictability of future crime opens up the prospect of the other's death as uncontrollable, unforeseeable, and yet inevitable. The film ends beside itself (it parts company with itself via the cheap shot of substitution) in the alternate present tension of mourning. If we bracket out the success with which mourning is rewarded, the film otherwise is a close tribute to the oeuvre by way of betraying "The Minority Report" (the story). The precogs turn the wheel of fortune in a world that makes good-enough use of the future. As brought to us by a word from our radio sponsor:

"... unanimity of all three precogs is a hoped-for but seldom-achieved phenomenon.... It is much more common to obtain a collaborative majority report of two precogs, plus a minority report of some slight variation, usually with reference to time and place, from the third mutant. This is explained by the theory of multiple-futures. If only one time-path existed, precognitive information would be of no importance, since no possibility would exist, in possessing this information, of altering the future." (85)

In Dick's story the snafu around majority versus minority reports reflects the consecutive time in which each report, each a minority report, was formulated. As head of operations, Anderton was in the unique position to interrupt the precogs and seize the first report of the gun he would use to kill Kaplan. Given time and the knowledge of Anderton's knowledge of the first report, the second view saw Anderton circumvent the showdown. But the second report also changed his mind back to the shooting range—especially once Anderton realized that the second report scenario was what Kaplan had planned, as a kind of taboo protection of his person.

Anxiously, Witwer trotted along beside the truck, his smooth, blond face creased with worry. "Will it happen again? Should we overhaul the set-up?"
    "It can happen in only one circumstance," Anderton said. "My case was unique, since I had access to the data. It could happen again—but only to the next Police Commissioner. So watch your step." (101)

Thus the Oedipal ban (which binds and excludes) attends transmission of the authoritative position with regard to the future.

"Paycheck" converts its tender into another currency of knickknacks that, like the small stones of Hansel and Gretel, lead the man with the recent past erased from his mind (the last two years) to safety. Because random events can impede the return path (like the birds eating the bread crumbs when the children ran out of stones), the relics are functionalized via the time scoop and mirror, which don't permit time travel, but do make previews of what's to come possible. What's repressed in the recent past—as Freud illuminates on the parallel track of his reading of Jensen's

Gradiva—is the protagnoist's bride-to-be. He even knew he had to keep his bargaining tip, the proof that her father is illegally pursuing technologies of time preview, safe from her filial loyalty to the firm, which he himself moves to keep intact by proposing marriage. "Seeing the future will destroy us" is the motto of *Paycheck* (2003). That it is destructive to act on the future as known is what *Minority Report* was getting across the year before. In *Paycheck,* world powers risk total destruction to obtain controlling interest in or via the techno-medium of prophecy. The protagonist sells timeshares in his gadget love, no more than two-to-three-month spans, to business interests eager to capitalize on already existing commodities (which they don't own) via their near-miss rip-offs that the engineer supplies with new and improved twists. As in Hollywood, so in the business world represented in a Hollywood film: the only good investment is in remakes of extant properties. After finishing his latest stint, followed as always by a chaser of zapped forgetfulness, the engineer gets the offer of a lifetime. Would he consider a project of two- or three-year duration? Soon the "or" is dipped into the sea of time and the offer is fixed at three years. The remuneration would be so immense that he could retire from his brain drain career. Three years are gone. But then you have the first day of the rest of your life. The day before he commences the time span that will be under erasure he hits on a scientist working for the corporation. When he is rebuffed, he flips from all to nothing in his approach to the other. But she programs the rebound: "You don't believe in second chances, do you?" On the other side of the three-year span, as he struggles to extricate himself from the fatal retirement plan the corporation had arranged for him—forgetting is not enough when the engineer building the time preview machine also takes it for trial spins—he learns that there is a second chance even for a ghost like him. His partner in the recent past remains mournfully attached to him even or especially in the absence of his memories of their time together. The dead or undead don't remember the loved ones left behind but must be brought back into a relationship to or through remembrance. The engineer saw not only his immediate peril, which prompted him to leave himself the trinkets of rescue and re-collection (he doesn't forfeit the money but hides it in advance of onset of the immediate contextlessness of his forgetting), but also the end of the world resulting from the marketing of time preview technology. The ultimate second chance dislodges a POV flash-forward from its flashback status as focused on the bullet coming at him: his former employer now encounters instead a bullet that was among the trinkets the engineer sent himself to lodge inside the apparatus powering the time preview machine. When its curiously industrial piston movement (already like the inner workings of a gun) presses down on the bullet, the explosion turns the whole machine into one big gun or pistol shot. It is also the shot of the camera that previewed a shooting that has been diverted from its immediate grammatical sentence or setting of subject and object but which, apparently, cannot itself be stopped in time.

In *Origin of the German Mourning Play* Benjamin cites Calderón as Baroque author of mourning plays that succeed where the works of the German dramatists failed precisely as mourning. The recurring theme of the blended boundary between dream (or delusion) and waking reality, to which the film reception of Dick would reduce his separate questioning of the difference between android and human, was summarized as successful mourning and as the secured succession of the sovereign's authority in the court of Calderón. *Life Is a Dream* fits our bill also because the dream theme must counter and contain the undue weight given prophecy. Simply put, dreaming projects the happy ending of Christianity while prophecy is linked to melancholia and related psy-fi states. Other differences between Calderón's stage and that of the German mourning play (as well as the stage of *Hamlet,* which, for all the difference or distinction of its Elizabethan setting, borders decisively on the origins in *Bildung* of the German mind-set) is that the lacing up of (melancholic) brooding with intrigue to preserve (paranoid) form is replaced by Calderón with the discourse of honor, to which interpersonal or social relation is surrendered. The torment of the German staging of mourning is circumvented in the trial offer so central to Calderón's world and the derangement of foretelling the future thus undermined.

As Arnie Kott surmised (in *Martian Time-Slip*), you don't die in your delusion or dream. Christianity is the community of believers sharing this delusion of a "no place" of death. Dick's understanding of metaphysics or rather of himself as metaphysical commits him to testify against his own Christian predilections. "I would define something as metaphysical as anything which, being observed by more than one person, those observers, plural, do not agree on what they have seen or experienced" (Anton and Fuchs).

Astrology, King Basilio's long-term interest or predilection, became dogma he could not curb when his wife's ominous dreaming of her own bursting belly death was fulfilled with their son's birth. All signs in the firmament and all the books in the fortune-telling section presaged the

Oedipal doom of paternal authority at the hands of the woundful heir. He decided to pronounce baby son dead for the record and deposit him in the tower for life.

But now that the sucker, I mean, successor is coming of age and more distant relations are lining up as next in line for the throne, he decides to put his following or understanding of the prophesied future to the test. "We know that evil is far more likely to occur than good / And good endings are never as plausible as bad" (21). Or again: "When a horoscope predicts / Misfortunes, it's generally correct: Any evil it predicts is certain: / Any good it predicts is dubious" (51). The king wishes to know whether the heavens never lie to the initiated or whether it could be instead that human beings have the power over their own destiny. Segismundo, the son in a tower, will awake from drugged sleep inside the castle as openly celebrated prince. How he flexes his sudden powers will determine the next step of the experiment. If he proves violent he will be knocked out again to awake back in the tower, but as though from a dream. The king provides the dream frame as buffer for the shock that might otherwise result from Segismundo's actual fall back inside the tower. All that happened before was no more than a dream. But the comforting fiction also reflects an understanding of life that runs smoothly: "Because in this world ... / Every one who lives is dreaming" (32).

King for a day, Segismundo loves acting out what they tell him can't be done. But he is warned not to be cruel: "It may turn out to be a dream" (49). Back in the tower, Segismundo is assured he must have been dreaming: "I think I'm still asleep ... / For if everything was a dream ... / Then anything could be a dream" (64). His memory of his violent acts cannot withstand the claim that it was all a dream. But his falling in love with a woman in the alleged dream strikes him as true, at least to the extent that while all the rest seems over, the love continues. Thus Segismundo decides to control his ferocity: just in case he is dreaming. He is learning that even or especially when you're dreaming, the good you do or experience is never lost. In the meantime the people are aroused to the point of monstrosity: they demand their natural born Prince instead of some distant relation and foreigner as successor to Basilio. When Segismundo hesitates, not wanting to fall for false power, a soldier assures him that great events are introduced by premonitions: thus if it seems a dream now, then that's because he dreamed it first. Prophecy doubles dreaming back onto waking life on one continuum of repetition or rehearsal, while dreaming contains prophecy, like that which Basilio had wrapped around his melancholia as symptomatic excess. Segismundo (set up as one of Hamlet's descendants in the history of tragedy or mourning play) should in turn excise remembering that proves in excess of these contours and parameters of dreaming.

If life is just a dream, and dreams are only dreams, then waking up introduces the sleep of death. The dream proved to be Segismundo's teacher: for dreams destroy illusions (101). An actor, too, plays the role of king, but when the play's over, he's at the mercy of strangers. These shadows have offended and the offensive must be mended, but in advance, as that good of happiness contained in dreams and brought into measured alignment with memories. The kind of happiness that lasts forever is, like every moment of happiness in the past, just a dream. Think back to some happy time: "It all feels like it was just a dream" (92). Thus one builds on the dream-memories of good times that which cannot be foretold but only remembered.

Homunculus and Robot

In differentiating between the two creations and their respective scientific traditions in "Homunculus and Robot" ("Homonkulus und Roboter"), Gotthard Günther follows the history of technological no-way know-how not in terms of the new and improved—of immediacy—but through all the mediations adding up not to machine history but to endopsychic allegory.

The creation of the homunculus inside a retort or test tube abbreviates the history of the world and mankind by withdrawing time and space from the whole process (though not completely, of course, since the test tube as last retort also takes up its share of space and time). To this extent, these are only the reduced conditions of the experiment. All the rest, the material stages of human development and so on, can be found in place and in process if the experiment is to succeed. But the homunculus is a utopian idea or fictional figure because it proves impossible to recapitulate on fast-forward the history of the world all the while leaving out the essential part. One cannot begin at the existential "beginning" because it is metaphysical not physical.

The mechanical brain by contrast rests on principles set against those of the metaphysical schema in which the idea of the homunculus is cooked up. The test-tube idea presupposes that life and consciousness are the historical results of being. Physical categories are primary, psychic categories are secondary—and the categories of signification follow only in last and (ontologically) least place. Cybernetically reformulated, we must consider that the classical scientific tradition views pure matter in its originary state as containing no "information." The originary state is materially allegedly chaos, which represents in itself no signifying links—no "information" in other words. But information is thus the existential form of mind. "If the classical technologist or engineer proceeds then from chaos, he means thereby that in every construction one can only begin ontologically with the physical system of the categories and that it is the scientific task of the constructor or chemist to derive after the fact the lesser categories of the psychic and the logical from the physical foundations of existence both theoretically and practically (chemically)" (196).

That the originary state of the world is to be imagined as chaotic is a dogmatic assumption based on a metaphysical concept ("chaos"), which plays its role only in classical traditions of the Western world because classical metaphysics or ontology is fundamentally monistic: only one logical-metaphysical foundation of the world is admitted, the being of being. In this case, then, the starter position as manifestation of the one cannot contain any "information," something secondary to the primordial in rank. The world as divine creation (out of chaos) is another way of saying that all information was in the beginning otherworldly and a divine consciousness exclusive not residing in the world itself. All relations of signification transcend reality as divine spirit. It is the task of history to integrate these relations within reality and to give them after the fact the same reality that matter had from the start.

The cybernetic view parts company with the classical tradition. What parts as company comes back as crowd: all physical existence contains from the start implicit "information" that can be explicated. The transclassical technologist operates within a triad: technically oriented thought possesses two material dimensions. There is the classical material and then there is the material of the second reality component named "information." As third party to the dimensions duo, transclassical technology introduces a second system of laws by modulating the mode of effectiveness of classical laws in the course of playing them off against transclassical lawfulness. The alchemical creator of the homunculus in seeking to imitate himself via magical laws that ran their course could only stand by passively watching and waiting for the results. For the cybernetical technologist the creation of a robot brain unfolds as the progressive modulation of classical non-reflexive lawfulness of being through the transclassical lawfulness of reflection of his own ego, which is set up on the former as overdetermination. The resulting mechanical consciousness is therefore an immediate result of human labor—which is not the case with the homunculus. In the test tube nature plays with itself. "In the creation of the electronic brain, however, man gives away his own reflection to the object and learns to understand his function in the world in this mirror of his self" (200).

Arthur Schopenhauer's explorations of empathy or *Mitleid* contemplate the lifting of the barrier between you and ego. As such they pay a close call to Günther's philosophical reflections on cybernetic futures. Empathy "presupposes that I suffer along with him his pain as such, feel his pain as otherwise I only feel my own. This requires that I identify myself with him in some manner, that is, that the complete difference between me and every other, on which my egoism is based, at least to some degree is overcome" (76–77). "This process is indeed remarkable, even mysterious. It is, in truth, the great mystery of ethics, its *Urphänomen* and the boundary stone beyond which only metaphysical speculation dares to step" (77). I cannot suffer the other's pain as my own. But I can suffer along with the other's pain as my pain but not in my person, but rather still in the other (103). Of the two opposing ways in which one can become conscious of one's own existence, empathy relies on the second order of the world. There is the external empirical view of one's vanishing point in a spatio-temporally limitless world. Then there is immersion in one's own interiority whereby one becomes aware of oneself as the only real being who for an encore sees himself in the other, a view given him from the outside, as in a mirror (144). The mirror that the other represents shows us that we are and remain what we are (Schopenhauer again quotes Mephistopheles). One's receptivity for empathy, selfishness, or mean-spiritedness is inborn. One's conscience speaks after the fact. This is the ethical fact of consciousness. Conscience is knowledge of one's own unchanging character by means of deeds. "Accordingly the course of life itself, with all its manifold activities, is nothing other than the external clockface of that inner originary mechanism, or of the mirror, in which is revealed to everyone's intellect alone the makeup of one's own will, which is one's kernel or essence" (141). In the Western tradition, Schopenhauer recommends his ethical system as the only one he can think of that is hospitable to animals.

As afterword to the 1952 German translation of Isaac Asimov's *I, Robot*, Günther addressed "The 'Second' Machine" ("Die 'zweite Maschine'"). Gotthard Günther draws a line between animal and man in order to pull in—hook, line, and thinker—the robot distinction. There are animals that pick up objects to use as mediating tools. But: "No animal projects itself as intelligence beyond the functional character of its own body and into an objective state of connection. For animal existence the boundary between inner world (microcosm) and outer world (macrocosm) remains unchanged. Nothing in the *Dasein* of the animal shows a tendency to cross this line."

Hegel already deemed the first stone tool primal man made and used objective spirit. A machine is (more or less) a tool that has attained autonomy in its functioning. In German you "handle" a tool, while you "serve" a machine. But a second order of machine is on the horizon. Already the servomechanism requires no more "service" but only, intermittently, "maintenance" *(Wartung)*. The electric transformer was probably the first type of second or transclassical machine (a machine, in other words, without moving parts).

The classical machine was modeled after the body with its moveable limbs. But for stage two we have taken the brain as model: this machine would function analogically to the human brain. Don't expect work from the second type of machine: it produces only information.

The math or logic whereby the mechanical brain can be described must be of a higher order than that which the robot brain itself uses to produce its concepts. Only a metalanguage can produce the language in which a robot thinks. A language that conceives of and articulates "I," "you," or "self" as logically relevant notions has no metalanguage.

The theological view of the unknown or X factor of consciousness as soul is correct as far as it goes. That it is a vague notion is witnessed by the theological debates regarding the relative immortality of the animal soul. Thus we return to Günther's starting point. The environment guides the animal. But the environment in regard to individual consciousness is transcendence. More specifically, the human soul is introscendent while the animal soul is extroscendent. In either case, the subject of consciousness does not reside at the level of consciousness determined by existence or action. Like animal consciousness, (possible) robot consciousness would have transcendence but no introscendence. There would be no I inside the consciousness. It would be extroscendent. The difference between animal and robot is location and relocation. While for the animal transcendence is located in the environment; for the robot it is the consciousness of its builder that is its transcendence locator. The robot's I is in the I of its creator. Even should it prove possible to couple logic-machine and math-machine, there would still be the requirement to fill of "transcendent" guidance. The mechanical brain would moreover require as guide a logic of a higher type than our normal classical Aristotelian logic. A logic superior to our own already exists in part. In theory it's coming around the bends of techno mutation.

At the same time the robot cannot know that it has mechanisms nor can it know the logic whereby they are integrated in its functioning. The human alone knows this about himself. That's why there is psychology or psychiatry by and for humans only. Ontologically speaking, all Is are identical from the vantage or vanishing point of that I one reaches at the end of an infinite regress. Empirically speaking, subjectivity is abyssal. Robot consciousness has a bottom—but it can never know this.

The mechanical consciousness needs access to certain metaphysical data. It needs to know that it was built by its creator, how it was built, that the creator set it in motion, and how he animated it. Without metabolization of this information, the mechanical brain would not be in a position to produce the mentational process of analogy—in analogy—to human consciousness.

Thus in the story or chapter "Reason" in *I, Robot,* the robot QT-1 (or "Cutie" as his humans call him) includes in its program the Oedipal triad of violence protection known as the Laws of Robotics, but no knowledge of its origins. Alone with its reason, it thinks, therefore it is at the service of the L-tube alone, which it is indeed supposed to service though not necessarily religiously as "master." The chance fit between Cutie's delusion and its work program renders the aberration functionally extraneous to the world order of man and machine.

According to Günther, Asimov's main theme is that a machine with consciousness requires, technically or functionally, a moral codex. Even borrowed thought implies spontaneity and therefore must follow ethical guidelines.

That Asimov and company view the final conflict as machinic is symptomatic, according to Günther, whose brain didn't drain, of the difference that marks the American people otherwise left out of the history of civilization, which is centered in the East. By banning history from Western psychic life inside thinking robots, history itself can be overcome.

Günther continues to develop this theme of the Western showdown without the East in another German-language syndication of his reflections on science fiction, this time as introduction to a collection of sci-fi stories. The intro's title: "The Discovery of America and the Case of Outer Space Literature" ("Die Entdeckung Amerikas und die Sache mit der Weltraum Literatur"). Günther would be making a common mistake if he were to restrict science fiction to the Cold War, but what he seems to be arguing instead is that science fiction has always been an American or anti-American exclusive. Science fiction is the first understanding of world culture (and beyond)—the repetition or rehearsal of primitive culture—which rejects the civilized past of the high cultures grounded in the East. While primitive culture has always been a planetary phenomenon, the high cultures were tied to specific geographically circumscribed areas they required, as Oswald Spengler put it, as their "mother earth." The horizon of high culture lies in the East. The West was only finally recognized as newly discovered (after the nth discovery had in fact already taken place) via the error of Columbus's stopover en route to a shortcut to the East. Westward Ho Ho Ho (no one wanted to go).

Science fiction via its ungrounded projection of artificial habitats based on reason alone and via its unabashed manipulation of time (as in time travel) is the first forum or form for Western cultural aspirations unbound by the Eastern past. The spaceship shatters the symbolism of classical metaphysics (by visiting upon the stars the hellish conditions of colonization) and thus abandons the classical form of life. The visions of outer space presuppose a universal planetary culture—and condition or determine a new nonclassical conception of reality. This conception goes beyond the home on the range of all metaphysical imaginings that belonged Back East. But the new idea in science fiction that Günther finds most fundamental is that of a soul, psyche, or self as something that stands in interchangeable relationship to its own content. In Eastern tradition such a notion was represented (and repressed) as the *Doppelgänger*. Günther deems the golem the ultimate incarnation of the double—as he understands or deconstructs it. Günther assigns to the golem, like the doorkeeper in relation to the man from the country in Kafka's parable "Before the Law," the doubling of each human crossing its path.

In *We Can Build You,* the demonstration simulacrum cost six thousand. Louis Rosen twice misremembers the sum, first as six hundred, then as six. If we reverse this diminishing return we hit the six-million point of no return. The simulacrum, though machinic, is also a sort of golem. Thus Louis is taken by surprise when his father is not so much fooled by as openly welcoming of the simulacrum.

It was impressive, the two old gentlemen standing there facing each other, the Stanton with its split white beard, its old-style garments, my father looking not much newer. The meeting of the patriarchs, I thought. Like in the synagogue. (17)

The name Rosen, which is German, that is, not necessarily German-Jewish, means, as a word, "roses." Rosen is the name of the head of the firm that builds the advanced androids Deckard hunts down. While his ethnicity or creed never comes up in Dick's novel, the film version avoids association with the Rosen name, preferring something as wasply neutral as a disc jockey's voice, something like the surname Tyrell. Rosen, then, as a name that's a given of assimilation, is itself a golem. Is it a word passing as a name, and therefore a name that sets apart? Names don't really "mean" anything. But when you're asked to make up a name, you may find yourself linking up existing nouns. Hence when Jews in the German-language world were encouraged in the late eighteenth century to take family names, the new surnames tended to resonate in earshot of the literal, which crosses the mind as image.

We Can Build You holds the place of a kind of prehistory to *Do Androids Dream of Electric Sheep?* Our attention is called to this relationship by the names to be recalled in the later work: the surname Rosen and the first name Pris. But Maury Rock's original old-world surname, Frauenzimmer, relates him to Maury Frauenzimmer, a character in the other novel, *The Simulacra,* in which artificial-life themes were rehearsed and repeated. Dick's first android novel, *We Can Build You,* supports the film *Blade Runner* (and the discipline of film studies that has accrued to it) inasmuch as artificial life is conceived, advertised, and constructed as indistinguishable from human being, indeed as more human than human. The assimilation drive is also routed through schizophrenia, which in this novel's setting is proclaimed the greatest health threat—good citizenship is earned in joining the cause of its healing or containment—while a common outcome of stabilization of the schizo outbreak, usually in the form of restoration to the earlier prebreak disposition, releases former inmates as the schizoids of everyday outpatient life, the other norm of our day in the future.

The alternate history choice that must have crossed Dick's mind when he contemplated *The Man in the High Castle*—it was his precedent in the new sci-fi subgenre—is checked off for *We Can Build You:* "What's on the mind of America, these days? . . . The Civil War of 1861. . . . This nation is obsessed with the War Between the States. I'll tell you why. It was the only and first national epic in which we Americans participated; that's why" (10–11). Imagining a different outcome of the Civil War was the primal alternate history to which American politics would seem, over and again, to have regressed. And yet the figure of civil war itself is associated throughout Dick's works with conflict that yields only losses.

Partner with the protagonist, Louis Rosen, in a firm building spinets and electronic organs, an enterprise marginalized by the advent (another prefiguration of *Do Androids Dream of Electric Sheep?*) of mood organs, Maury Rock urges production of a brand-new competitive product before there's no market left to corner.

> Maury had a point. What had undone us was the extensive brain-mapping of the mid 1960s and the depth-electrode techniques of Penfield and Jacobson and Olds, especially their discoveries about the mid-brain. The hypothalamus is where the emotions lie, and in developing and marketing our electronic organ we had not taken the hypothalamus into account. The Rosen factory never got in on the transmission of selective-frequency short range shock, which stimulates very specific cells of the mid-brain (6).

To enter the market of hypothalamus-stimulation organs, Maury had already hired an electronics engineer, Bob Bundy, who worked for the Federal Space Agency designing circuits for simulacra, synthetic humans or robots, until he was forced into retirement because he was a security risk after a touch of hebephrenia became apparent. He doesn't know from organs—which suits Maury just fine and his recovering psychotic daughter Pris, too, who joined her father in the master plan of launching and marketing reenactment of the Civil War with simulacra by building a demo, the simulation of Edwin M. Stanton, Lincoln's Secretary of War.

Once Louis Rosen falls in with a plan at least half-baked by the borderline psychotic Pris, it turns out he has committed himself to a complete unraveling around falling for Pris herself, who remains unmoved by his intentions. The name that would be given the cool or cruel android in *Do Androids Dream of Electric Sheep?* belonged first to a human in the schizoid holding pattern over the plummet into schizophrenia. Pris is also an eighteen-year-old graduate of the mental asylum; the onset of puberty was also in her case (we're assured it's the dominant pattern) the beginning of the psychosis that led, following routine testing, to hospitalization. The history of her illness seems to fold out of Binswanger's case study of Ellen West: "It was in high school that real trouble had begun. . . . She couldn't eat in public. Even if one single person was watching her, that was enough, and she had to drag her food off by herself, like a wild animal. . . . 'And remember,' Maury added, 'she was getting very fat. . . . Then she started dieting. She starved herself to lose weight. And she's still losing it. She's always avoiding one food after another; she does that even now'" (32).

Pris's identification with artificial life is reflected in her ideal, which is to be self-made, a success story that would belong to her image up in nightlights of the media. Thus she idolizes Sam Barrows, the most successful entrepreneur of the day, famous for his real-estate speculation on the moon. Pris's interest in the simulacra-building plan was always as a way to grab his interest. Barrows argues that the Civil War reenactment scheme would only work if one could bet on the outcome. Each enactment would then have the status, in theory, of alternate history. But the android is a plug for the live-effect of the mortuary palaces of collectability. Thus in *Now Wait for Last Year* robots people Wash-3 5, the souvenir setting simulated through the re-collection of authentic artifacts from this past of one man's hometown childhood. The best use of simulacra made according to the modifications that allowed simulation of Stanton and Lincoln would, Barrows concludes, be to give them away as the false security of friendly neighbors up in the lunar settlements.

Simulacra posing as human colonists, living on the Moon in order to create an illusion of prosperity? Man, woman and child simulacra in little living rooms, eating phony dinners, going to phony bathrooms . . . it was horrible. . . . And yet I could see Barrows's position. He had to persuade people in the mass that emigration to the Moon was desirable (111).

But when the men back away from the pressure of Barrows's negotiating style, Pris crosses over to his side of the table. It is at this vanishing point that Pris becomes supercharged for Louis as his one and only.

If schizoid Pris is less human than the simulacra she helped animate, then the blank of her departure must be filled not so much through identification or incorporation as via assumption of android identity. In going the distance with Pris, Louis can find an analogy for his psychic position only via a simulacrum's relationship to a time or place not his own.

I was like the Stanton simulacrum, like a machine: propelling itself forward into a universe it did not comprehend. . . . Trying somehow to re-establish a familiar environment, however unpleasant. I was used to Pris and her cruelty. . . . My instincts were propelling me from the unfamiliar back to the known. It was the only way I could operate. I was like a blind thing flopping along in order to spawn. (163)

The diagnosis that requires Louis's hospitalization was archetypically Jungian. The administrative part of the diagnosis is that his schizophrenia is situational. But what also makes this a milder form is that it is not stuck in the father-and-son relationship nor in relations with mother, but (as is made clear in the office of psychoanalysis in *The Simulacra*) on an image that the mass media Sensurround otherwise advertises to keep us low maintenance.

> The Magna Mater, the form you have, was the great female deity cult of the Mediterranean at the time of the Mycenaen Civilization. Ishtar, Cybele, Attis, then later Athene herself . . . finally the Virgin Mary. What has happened to you is that your anima, that is, the embodiment of your unconsciousness, its archetype, has been projected outward onto the cosmos, and there it is perceived and worshiped. . . . There, it is experienced as a dangerous, hostile, and incredibly powerful yet attractive being. The embodiment of all the pairs of opposites: it possesses the totality of life, yet is dead; all love, yet is cold; all intelligence, yet is given to a destructive analytical trend which is not creative; yet it is seen as the source of creativity itself. . . . When the opposites are experienced directly, as you are experiencing them, they cannot be fathomed or dealt with; they will eventually disrupt your ego and annihilate it, for as you know, in their original form they are archetypes and cannot be assimilated by the ego. . . . The archetypes of the unconscious must be experienced indirectly, through the anima, and in a benign form free of their bipolar qualities. (221–22)

Here we strike up the overture to the Magna Mater novels, too, though separated from the roll Dick would be on with this theme after the interval of one outer psychotic space novel and his idyll of survival by the word alone. However, only the other android novel, *The Simulacra,* will put it out there, also verbatim, as containable beside the crisis point of breaking psychosis that continues to press throughout the novel.

Louis's ultimate breakdown isn't bona fide psychosis. By the end of his stay at the mental health facility, his treating psychiatrist considers him a possible malingerer. But he has just pretended to see and think out loud what Pris, who is currently again hospitalized in the same facility, urges him to offer as evidence the psychiatrist will submit for his release. She asks him to trust her. While he does make it out of the facility, the part about Pris joining him isn't true. She's sorry, but she's much too sick to be released (246): end of novel. Up until he discovered Pris back in the hospital in the flesh, Louis was being treated via drug-induced hallucinations or fugue states in which a fantasy relationship to Pris was maintained and allowed to mature over the fictional passage of time chemically induced. The hallucination can be installed within the automatic momentum with which he flopped about, spawning himself, but as simulacrum, in her absence. To fall in love with someone is to overvalue that person. Thus the love we fall for is already a form of delusion—and a radical disappointment and downfall just waiting to happen. That's how Jerome interprets his son's condition. Louis sees himself making it with the hallucinated Pris while the shadowy presence of father and brother, who are actually in the room with him, is more an intrusion than a contradiction. Translating from the German, Jerome explains: "What I mean, he's asleep, my boy is, in the freedom of a night of love, if you follow me" (212).

Louis breaks through the middlebrow beat of borderline diagnosis and attains transferential recognition of his condition, which also runs counter to archetype, through his immersion in the case of Lincoln as manic-depressive (180):

Lincoln was exactly like me. I might have been reading my own biography, there in the library; psychologically we were as alike as two peas in a pod, and by understanding him I understood myself. Lincoln had taken everything hard. He might have been remote, but he was not dead emotionally; quite the contrary. So he was the opposite of Pris, of the cold schizoid type. Grief, emotional empathy, were written on his face. He fully felt the sorrows of the war, every single death. (182)

They've been working on the transference all mourning the long and the short of irreducible totemism. The android Lincoln debates (on behalf of the other manic-depressive) the psychopath (and idol of the part-time schizophrenic, full-time schizoid dark-haired girl). Lincoln the simulacrum challenges self-made man Barrows on the differences he assumes as manipulable among man, animal, and machine. Lincoln cranks up and through the age-old discourse on man-the-machine, which, at the tail end between its legacies, begins and ends with specism. He puts Barrows to the android test.

"Would you tell me, sir," the simulacrum said, "what a man is?" ...
    "A man can be defined as an animal that carries a pocket handkerchief." ...
    "But what is an animal?"
    "I can tell you you're not," Barrows said, his hands in his trouser pockets; he looked perfectly confident. "An animal has a biological heritage and makeup which you lack. You've got valves and wires and switches. You're a machine." ...
    "Then what, sir, is a machine?" the simulacrum asked Barrows.
    "You're one. These fellows made you. You belong to them."
    The long, lined, dark-bearded face twisted with weary amusement as the simulacrum gazed down at Barrows. "Then you, sir, are a machine. For you have a Creator, too. And, like 'these fellows,' He made you in His image. I believe Spinoza, the great Hebrew scholar, held that opinion regarding animals; that they were clever machines. The critical thing, I think, is the soul. A machine can do anything a man can—you'll agree to that. But it doesn't have a soul."
    "There is no soul," Barrows said. "That's pap."
    "Then," the simulacrum said, "a machine is the same as an animal.... And an animal is the same as a man." (107–8)

Louis asks his father Jerome, the novel's superego, who, like the Lincoln simulacrum, likes to cite Spinoza, whether it is true that Spinoza argued that animals were clever machines. " 'Did Spinoza really say that?' 'Regretfully I must confess it' " (113). Louis takes this confession on behalf of animals as the very measure of his father's so-called gentle humanism. Whatever humanism or even humanity may be, it begins and ends with the relationship to animals.

ALL OF YOU ARE DEAD. I AM ALIVE.

Around the square of vivid writing materializes the spray can a la Andy Warhol; the square of writing becomes its label, as in previous manifestations.... The two realities—the spray can versus the actual photographed events—merge into one ruin of particles, as if an entire planet had burst, and nothing remains of it but radioactive waste. It is as if the Warhol drawing of the spray can and the writing attempted somehow to stem the explosion and did so—but only for a moment; then it, too, was swept away. Even it was not enough.

—PHILIP K. DICK, *Ubik: The Screenplay*

In *The Three Stigmata of Palmer Eldritch*, adolescent or group psychology organizes the communion-like experience of fusion or translation that human colonists on Mars share when downing the drug Can-D and projecting themselves into the couple of dolls Perky Pat and her boyfriend Walt and into the doll layout, which represents life on Earth (or, more specifically, on the Coast).[1] Palmer Eldritch's competing experience of other worlds via his drug Chew-Z represents the psychotically heightened version of Can-D fantasy.

In Mercerism "fusion" was the highest attainment of empathic identification as group identification: clutching the empathy box one surrenders to the sending and receiving of one's mood, which whether upbeat or swinging low is group-formatted, reflected back as contained within the group experience. At the same time one sees Mercer on his hopeful/hopeless climb out of the tomb world and one feels the injuries he endures during this climb at the hands of adversaries who first assembled against him, according to the Mercer legend, to stop his interventions on behalf of animals. As Pris pointed out, however, conditions on Earth don't really hold a handle to understanding life on Mars. Thus the main difference between the fusion of Mercerism and the fusion or translation obtained via Can-D is that the importance of the tomb world is on Earth not as in the heavens or outer space. Viewed from the stricken world of Mars, Earth is the "other world" of fantasy.

Around the drug and the Barbie-doll-based small world after all of the Perky Pat layout colonists identify themselves as varieties of "believers." "It should be a purifying experience. We lose our fleshly bodies, our corporeality, as they say. And put on imperishable bodies instead, for a time anyhow. Or forever, if you believe as some do that it's outside of time and space, that it's eternal" (42). The sensualist position sees the drug as license to fantasize any and all illicit acts, which from the juridical standpoint are impotent wishes (42). Whereas this one wants to gain something, the other swears by the loss fundamental to fusion: "I admit . . . that I can't *prove* you get anything better back. . . . But I do know this. What you and other sensualists among us don't realize is that when we chew Can-D and leave our bodies *we die*" (42).

Whereas fusion in Mercerism was fundamentally the Christian Mass dismantled through the modifications that the all-importance of animals introduced, Can-D fusion is fundamentally adolescent, while analogies with the double Mass of Christianity and of mass-media consumerism are openly admitted. In the tight spot of small differences, official Christians nevertheless militate against the "religious" drug cults of fusion beholden to Can-D. Anne Hawthorne travels to Mars to try to convert drug users to the Neo-American Church: "You know how the eating of Can-D translates—as they call it—the partaker to another world. It's secular, however, in that it's temporary and only a physical world" (126). Her fellow passenger, Barney Mayerson, concedes that he would try Can-D before he joined her church: "I can't believe in that, the body and blood business. It's too mystical for me." But, Anne counters, tripping back to an Earth that you know isn't the real one also takes faith.

"It's experienced as real; that's all I know."
    "So are dreams."
    "But this is stronger," he pointed out. "Clearer. And it's done in—" He had started to say *communion*. "In company with others who really go along. So it can't be entirely an illusion. Dreams are private; that's the reason we identify them as illusion." (126)

In no time Anne gives up her mission and clamors to experiment with every manner of escape. But her first Can-D trip proves to be a disappointment:

> "How was it?" He asked her at last.
> "You mean being that little brassy blonde-haired doll with all her damn clothes and her boyfriend and her car and her—" Anne, beside him, shuddered. "Awful. Well, that's not it. Just—pointless. I found nothing there. It was like going back to my teens."
> "Yeah," he agreed. There was that about Perky Pat. (147)

In the layout, in California, world is reduced to two teenagers who go on dates. The dating teenager is at the threshold of the tension span between the group (which issued him his sexual license) and both the couple of parents (off-limits and out of it for the masturbating child or group of one) and the future couple the teen must form to secure the reproductive future for the group that has no reproducing plan of its own. The group medium awaits the science fiction of replication to externalize or futuralize its own and only medium of expansion or growth. This medium of group identification, on which midlifers flash to share fantasy escape or get religion, is what chooses the couple of teens (what dolls!) for temporary release or therapy. To this end several players can enter in one fantasy figure the layout of the land called California. In Chew-Z all that happens to you in a world in pieces is of one mind. Chew-Z advances to the psy-fi frontier of replication: "It seems nothing more or less than the desire of . . . an out-of-dust created organism to perpetuate itself." To make a comparison stop with Christianity: "instead of God dying for man, as we once had, we faced—for a moment—a superior—the superior power asking us to perish for *it*" (220). But every time Palmer Eldritch enters the delusional order he is, ironically, station break and word from the sponsor. He is thus at once internal to the frame and in excess of it.

Barney had been deferring his induction to Mars (via the psychiatric-psychoanalytic assessment of Dr. Smiley, who is on his case all the time via a communicating suitcase) when his firm P. P. Layouts gave him the covert assignment to take Chew-Z and then poison himself and lay the blame on the new drug. In exchange he will be able to return to Terra via a new identity (induction to Mars is otherwise one-way only). "Two, two and a half years from now," he'll be back at his job (154). The empty place thus set for mourning either lies beyond the end of the novel or is subsumed by the delusional worlds of Palmer Eldritch in which Barney is always on a role.

Whatever trip you take on Chew-Z you always can find Palmer Eldritch also in attendance. In Barney's case, he finds Eldritch frustrated with the scenario Barney has chosen. Since Barney opts to try to reunite with his estranged and divorced wife in the time trips, he remains inside an obsessive-compulsive order, and thus, by definitions current not only in Dick's understanding of psychosis, protected against the full-blown experience it also leads up to, through the disintegrative whammy of its order: the experience of Chew-Z as schizophrenia.[2] But then, in recognition of Barney's determination, Eldritch coaches him through the series of trips toward a season finale. Like hell, the worlds of Chew-Z are personalized. For Barney "it's an illusory world in which Eldritch holds the key positions as god; he gives you a chance to do what you can't really ever do—reconstruct the past as it ought to have been. But even for him it's hard. Takes time" (176). As Barney's fellow hovelists on Mars testify, Chew-Z fixes on the past, not as for most midlifers the Teen Age of Can-D, but one's own past backed up against the horizon of repetition compulsion and disintegration.

"Wow," Norm Schein said.
"Where'd you go?" Tod Morris demanded, thick-tongued; blearily he too stood, then assisted his wife Helen. "I was back in my teens, in high school, when I was on my first complete date—first, you get me, successful one, you follow?" He glanced nervously at Helen, then.
Mary Regan said, "It's much better than Can-D. Infinitely. Oh, if I could tell you what I was doing—" She giggled self-consciously. "I just can't, though." (177)

Chew-Z or Palmer Eldritch cuts off access to the communal world and puts the former translators into isolation, the isolation of his own head, which remains the outer limit of each fantasy world that Chew-Z induces. What's more, the Chew-Z trip is one-way. Chew-Z confines its consumers to its illusory worlds, compared now to "nets he casts," now to "Maya. The veil of illusion" (186). Not a taste of redemption but a reexperience of the Fall, the serial tripping relates to reality like a serial dream that, in time, begins to overlap with reality (204). But the question of reality is experienced again and again as showdown with one's nearest and dearest in which each accuses the other of being the phantasm.

"But this isn't real; this is a drug-induced fantasy. Translation."
"The hell it isn't real." Leo glared at him. "What does that make me, then? Listen." He pointed his finger angrily at Barney. "There's nothing unreal about me;

you're the one who's a goddam phantasm, like you said, out of the past. I mean, you've got the situation completely backward." (190)

A chorus of Palmer Eldritches welcomes Barney into the fold in time left open for loss that can't get lost:

"You're a phantasm, as Leo said; I can see through you, literally. I'll tell you in more accurate terminology what you are. . . . You're a ghost. . . . Try building your life on that premise. . . . Well, you got what St. Paul promises. . . . You're no longer clothed in a perishable, fleshly body—you've put on an ethereal body in its place. . . . You can't die." (193)

Palmer Eldritch gives himself all the identities and identifications in history down the corridors of his worlds within worlds. The one that sticks at the end is that of "creature," who sought to perpetuate itself through Chew-Z but who now longs for death. But if he is the creature, then death is a long way off. The staying power of the creature, however, is not about immortality. It is the immortal soul, only it's dead. The creature is out of context, out of time, the missing link that however endures, that should have perished and probably did, but like Kafka's "Hunter Gracchus" simply missed the boat, keeps on dying without end. As Hannah Arendt glosses the creaturely estate in *Love and Saint Augustine*:

The fact of being created has the structure . . . of having come to be, and thus has the structure of transience as such. Every creature comes from the "not yet" . . . and heads for "no more" . . . Heading for "no more," the creature refers forward to death . . . From the "not yet" to the "no more," life runs its course in the world. (70)

In the Christian setting there are positive developments to be inferred from all of the above:

The negation of life through the "not yet" has a positive meaning: it has to do with what followed upon the "not yet." The positive meaning of the "not yet" assures it of the eternity of its "whence." (71)

But what happens when, in the ruins of Christianity, the creature is "not yet" dead and yet burdened with the eternity of its "whence" and "whither"? The creature dates back to origins, original creations, and yet those same settings are withdrawn or lost. The creature is alone in the worlds and out of time. Thus the creature Eldritch "bore some relationship to God; if it was not God . . . then at least it was a portion of God's Creation" (225).

Without a receiving area in the deregulated zones of Christianization and (or as) secularization, our encounters with the creature are always horror feature.

"We have no mediating sacraments through which to protect ourselves; we can't compel it, by our careful time-honored, clever, painstaking rituals, to confine itself to specific elements such as bread and water or bread and wine. It is out in the open, ranging in every direction. It looks into our eyes; and it looks *out* of our eyes." (219)

The novel ends on the upbeat of Leo Bulero's madcap schemes to live on inside the inescapable illusory worlds while remembering all the while what's at the same time real. A guild of Protectors made up of "bubble-heads" like himself, individuals who have benefited from E-therapy, the acceleration of evolutionary adaptation, change, or mutation, will match and contain the advantages of Eldritch's advanced age via their own condensation of evolutionary time or the future for days.

But before reprisal on the upbeat, the novel ends with Barney Mayerson's realization that there is no way for him to be restored to his "original condition—dimly remembered, such as it was—before the late and more acute contamination set in":

Because he held a terrifying insight, simple, easy to think and utter, which perhaps applied to himself and those around him, to this situation.
There was such a thing as salvation. But—
Not for everyone. (225)

Benjamin was interested in schizophrenia, but not as an insider. Instead he engaged in a series of hashish "experiments" or "sessions," alone and with participants, which he recorded in "protocols." He sets up shop at an intersection that Max Dessoir described in 1889 as intrinsic to the new field of research that Spiritualism had opened up.

One can identify dreams as the normal form of hallucination, or waking hallucinations as the pathological form of the dream and consider as intermediary the fantasies of the hashish high. (2)

Benjamin experienced on a couple of occasions how the hashish trance broke through to the allegorical pageants or bardo states of psychosis from which theoretical reflection is gained in doing the aftermath. In his protocol written January 1928, Benjamin addresses the "aftereffect":

Despite my recurring depression, my writing has recently displayed a rising tendency, something I have never before observed. Can this be connected with hashish? A further aftereffect: on returning home, I tried to fasten the chain, and when this proved difficult my first suspicion (quickly corrected) was that an experiment was being set up. (88)

This session was dominated by what Benjamin refers to as its satanic phase, not in the mode or sense of destructiveness, he adds, but as knowledge, satisfaction, and calm. It is the relationship of devil's advocacy that Freud adopts in *Beyond the Pleasure Principle* when contemplating frankly infernal scenarios for the understanding of the death drive: even instincts for self-preservation, for example, serve to keep the organism on course toward the death that indwells it. Freud dismisses this devilish arrangement as contradicted by the sexual instincts. By not signing up with the devil but only advocating for his view, Freud never settles on any one of the exemplifications he gives for the death drive. At the point "that the roots of addiction, the collusive knowledge about nonbeing, can be boundlessly intensified by increasing the dose," Benjamin refuses to recognize in the creaturely pageantry of his surroundings "the ambiguous wink from Nirvana" that nevertheless comprises and gives him "satanic satisfaction" (86). *Winke, winke* (the German imperative to wave good-bye to departing loved ones, even after they pass out of sight by train or by car): rather than pass to the death drive behind it, he observes in the gap between "'outside' and a person's visual space, however extended it may be ... the same significance ... as the relationship between the stage and the cold street outside has for the theatergoer" (87).

The pageant in the satanic phase, which relentlessly allegorizes history with and as stage props, also has a "dime-novel aspect" (88). Now the room winks at him: "What do you think may have happened here? The connection between this phenomenon and cheap literature." Next he summarizes this aspect with the caption, "Cheap literature and subtitles," and then goes on with its show:

To be understood as follows: think of a kitschy oleograph on the wall, with a long strip cut out from the bottom of the picture frame. There is a tape running through the batten, and in the gap there is a succession of subtitles: "The Murder of Egmont," "The Coronation of Charlemagne," and so on. (88)

This brings Benjamin to the conclusion of his reflections on the ways in which the "profoundest truths" conspire in being reflected "in the irresponsible dreamer"—end up, in other words, contributing to the fantasy genre to which they owe the suppression of their depth charge, their dead charges.

The connection between cheap fiction and the profoundest theological intentions. They reflect it through a glass darkly, transpose into the space of contemplation what is of value only in the case of active life. Namely, that the world always remains the same (that all events could have taken place in the same space). Despite everything, that is rather a tired, faded truth in the realm of theory (for all the sharpness of perception it contains); but it is spectacularly confirmed in the lives of the pious, for whom all things turn out for the *best*, much as the space of the imagination subserves the *past*. So profoundly is the realm of theology submerged in that of cheap fiction. (89)

The Three Stigmata of Palmer Eldritch elaborates as satanic phase a certain relationship to addiction as knowledge about nonbeing in the midst of ambiguous winks from Nirvana and up against the dime store of theology.

In his hashish protocol from March 1930, Benjamin reflects on aura in the terms he used to describe the unique stabilization of Schreber's delusional system. He commences by turning up the contrast with occult and mystical views he knows well enough to recognize their links and limitations:

First, genuine aura appears in all things, not just in certain kinds of things, as people imagine. Second, the aura undergoes changes, which can be quite fundamental, with every movement the aura-wreathed object makes. Third, genuine aura can in no sense be thought of as a spruced-up version of the magic rays beloved of spiritualists and described and illustrated in vulgar works of mysticism. On the contrary, the characteristic feature of genuine aura is ornament, an ornamental halo, in which the object or being is enclosed as in a case. (328)

Aura, which, Benjamin's protests notwithstanding, belongs to the category of ghostly doubling, excess, or emanation, assumes the form of ornamental encasement. The life-and-a-half span of aura as encapsulation undergoing change is another formula for half-life in Dick's *Ubik*.

Written within the same year as *Do Androids Dream of Electric Sheep? Ubik* pursues testing, which skips its assigned place and function, and withdraws into worlds within worlds of mass marketing, commodification, religious belief in other worlds, and psychic steady states of projection in the context or contest of life versus death drives. The protagonist of *Ubik*, Joe Chip, is the electrical tester for a Prudence Organization, an allegorically titled and entitled line of work that seeks or markets neutralization of occult mediations of surveillance.

After the catastrophe or turning point (of undecidability) he is left testing the difference between half-life and full life.

Joe's skill at testing for the range and intensity of psionic activity is what, allegedly owing to lack of time, the fateful commission of an emergency group mission on Luna succeeds in bracketing out as unnecessary prep work. The commission was a trap. Once Joe covertly tests the field and finds it empty the trap is already sprung: the employer they were meeting face-to-face turns out to be a humanoid bomb that explodes.

The trap was also set that morning with the rapid-fire hire of Pat, a new type of anti-psy, whose time warping powers can contain the effects wrought by precogs without alerting them to their containment. Unlike your typical anti-precog who robs the precog of the luminosity whereby one can read which of the alternate futures is chosen, and thus alerts the precog to the anti-influence (27), Pat, whose own parents were precogs who never even suspected her talent (29),[3] changes the past itself thereby allowing the precog to keep the future choice and lose it, without knowing it, too. The scout, who was inevitably in on the plot ultimately hatched by Ray Hollis, head of the leading rental office for covert mediums of surveillance, to set back the neutralizing countermoves of the Runciter anti-psionic undertaking, brings Pat to Joe as his greatest find to be tested and passed on to the boss for employment as one of his inertials. But Pat uses her talent to prove to Joe that she's got it and doesn't need to be tested for it. More specifically, the first time around he tested her and found her empty; this time around she wants him to fill out the scorecard in affirmation of her talent. She appears psionically empty in the present tense of testing, she explains, because her talent is activated and evident only in or as the past (33). But even as he complies, Joe signs the positive evaluation sheet with positive-looking icons that, decoded however, signify that she is a danger to the firm. In her second demo, while being introduced to Runciter, Pat creates an alternate world that intervened two years ago, in which she married Joe. When she withdraws her influence she holds onto the wedding ring as keepsake from the simulated past (that everyone else, along for the time ride, must in no time forget).

"I had a group of eleven inertials in here and then I suggested to her—"

Joe said, "That she show the group what she could do. So she did. She did exactly that. And my evaluation was right." With his fingertip he traced the symbols of danger at the bottom of the sheet. "My own wife," he said.

"I'm not your wife," Pat said. "I changed that, too. Do you want it back the way it was? With no changes, not even in details? That won't show your inertials much. On the other hand, they're unaware anyhow... unless some of them have retained a vestigial memory as Joe has. By now, though, it should have phased out." (56)

Just the same, though Pat is nominated again and again as master villain-ess,[4] even after her role in the in-between bardo states of half-life can be written off as projection (including her own), this process of elimination doesn't clarify her only remaining role, the one she plays in the original plot—unless, of course, her purpose was to circumvent the role of testing, which Pat would then have helped bring about twice over.

By the end of the novel, the struggle to crack the code of its chaos seems to rest with the lodgment of all the volatility in our typeface on one side of the glass in half-life, leaving the other side, by implication and exclusion, to Runciter, who lives on. But in the closing chapter Runciter finds that his own coins have turned into the kind of funny money that attended his "manifestations" inside the half-life world whereby he sought to influence its random course from the outside, from his external advantage point.

I wonder what this means, he asked himself. Strangest thing I've ever seen. Most things in life eventually can be explained. But—Joe Chip on a fifty-cent piece?

It was the first Joe Chip money he had ever seen.

He had an intuition, chillingly, that if he searched his pockets, and his billfold, he would find more.

This was just the beginning. (216)

Like the Chew-Z worlds of the creature Palmer Eldritch, half-life proves an uncontainable perspective in which we struggle to defer our inevitable grounding—our being ground up—inside the tomb world. But in this ultimate application for the awarding of significance to alternate worlds or times, half-life is not under psychotic pressure. In the world of *Ubik* half-life designates the receiving area in which we keep in touch with our dead. Between the first death and the final one, there is half-life, a period of mourning that is organized around continued communication with the "deceased" stored in cold pac but wired to media outlets and receivers. Via half-life, then, the relationship to our dead is Spiritualism attained.

In the earphone words, slow and uncertain, formed: circular thoughts of no impor-tance, fragments of the mysterious dream which she now dwelt in....

"Hi, Ella," he said clumsily into the microphone.

"Oh," her answer came, in his ear; she seemed startled.... "Hello Glen," she said, with a sort of childish wonder, surprised, taken aback, to find him here. "What—" She hesitated. "How much time has passed?"

"Couple years," he said....

"I was dreaming," Ella said. "I saw a smoky red light, a horrible light. And yet I kept moving toward it. I couldn't stop."

"Yeah," Runciter said, nodding. "The *Bardo Thödol,* the *Tibetan Book of the Dead,* tells about that. You remember reading that; the doctors made you read it when you were—" He hesitated. "Dying," he said then.

"The smoky red light is bad, isn't it?" Ella said.

"Yeah, you want to avoid it." ...

"It's so weird. I think I've been dreaming all this time, since you last talked to me. ... I think that other people who are around me—we seem to be progressively growing together. A lot of my dreams aren't about me at all." ...

"Well, like they say, you're heading for a new womb to be born out of. ... You're probably anticipating your next life, or whatever it is." He felt foolish, talking like this; normally he had no theological convictions. But the half-life experience was real and it had made theologians out of all of them. (12–14)

Both Dick's favorite borrowed systems—the Tibetan guided journey of the dead in transit as well as the tomb versus aetherial worlds (Ella describes her state as floating away from the gravity or grave of the earth into the firmament and beyond)—appear to be up and running. But then there is a glitch. A certain Jory gets on the line. Together with Runciter, we learn of the inevitability of more vital residual psyches permeating the more accessible, weakening psyches. When Runciter demands that Ella be separated from Jory's influence, Herr von Vogelsang, the head of the Swiss moratorium, explains that they place the storage batteries of half-life close to each other for a reason: half-lifers enjoy wandering through each other's minds.

This disruption on the inside of the perfectly functioning establishment of Spiritualism is the flaw in the appointment the survivor tries to keep according to a schedule of one and a half lives. It is this in-between space of disruption that the survivors of the blast must inhabit. That their environment of survival is out-of-joint is first indicated by replacement of brand-new consumer items by their aged and decayed versions. But then they find their currency is turning into funny money with Glen Runciter's portrait on the bills and coins. From deep inside their disjointed relationship to the world of commodities, the anti-psi operators or inertials begin to discern that they are being subjected to two processes.

"One is a going-away, so to speak. A going-out-of-existence. That's process one. The second process is a coming-into-existence. But of something that's never existed before." (106)

Going-away has the stronger pull. But its process, too, follows two trends. Symptoms of decay alternate with (and stabilize as) products that are obsolete. But then individual members of the group dry up in a few hours into mummy crisps.

The form *TV set* had been a template imposed as a successor to other templates, like the procession of frames in a movie sequence. Prior forms, he reflected, must carry on an invisible, residual life in every object. The past is latent, is submerged, but still there, capable of rising to the surface once the later imprinting unfortunately—and against ordinary experience—vanished. The man contains—not the boy—but earlier men, he thought. History began a long time ago

The dehydrated remnants of Wendy. The procession of forms that normally takes place—that procession ceased. And the last form wore off, with nothing subsequent: no newer form, no next stage of what we see as growth, to take its place. (132)

What jumps the slippage is the expiration date that cannot stop the decay and which doesn't add up to but only subtracts itself from the procession of forms unto rebirth.

That a dynamic of mourning links Glen Runciter to Joe Chip comes across between the lines of the TV's restarting itself. Runciter almost comes across through the white noise, static, or snow typically attending the media manifestations of ghosts. First news broadcast announces Runciter's funeral.

With his foot Joe Chip tripped the pedal which controlled the TV set; the screen faded and the sound ebbed into silence.

This doesn't fit in with the graffiti on the bathroom walls, Joe reflected. Maybe Runciter is dead, after all. The TV people think so.... They all consider him dead, and all we have that says otherwise is the two rhymed couplets, which could have been scrawled by anyone...

The TV screen relit. Much to his surprise; he had not repressed the pedal switch. And in addition, it changed channels: Images flitted past, of one thing and then another, until at last the mysterious agency was satisfied. The final image remained.

The face of Glen Runciter. (126–27)

And then Runciter advertises Ubik, even addressing Joe at one point by name. When Joe asks if they are two-way, Runciter announces that he is on tape recorded two weeks ago. "He felt all at once like an ineffectual moth, fluttering at the windowpane of reality, dimly seeing from outside" (129). Runciter makes contact—with only the glassy partition between them. Either Runciter feels to Joe like the ineffectual moth or Joe feels like moth drawn to the pane/pain. Communication that does and does not take place bypasses Joe's repression of the on/off pedal of electric life.

What is Ubik? In a German translation of *Ubik,* the advertising spot in which "Ubik" declares itself to be Logos was rendered in keeping with the series of "Ubik" ads traversing the novel and culminating in the Logos declaration, which is already sustained throughout in the service of a double Mass medium. In German its station identification as Logos was translated as "brand name," a name that in German bears *Marke*, both a commodity brand and, on the side, a marking. Had he translated the Gospel according to St. John, I suppose it would have come out as:

When all things began, the brand name already was. The brand name dwelt with God, and what God was, the brand name was" ("How to Build a Universe That Doesn't Fall Apart Two Days Later," 278).[5]

Up to this point of entry into the plotline as Logos or brand name, ad copy–like epigraphs pitching various Ubik commodities began each chapter, but precisely did not interact with or tie into the chapter itself, keeping its place just like an ad or station break.[6] When Ubik steps down from the epigraph horizon into the narrative (its underworld), it is a cure-all product, perhaps the essence of the Ubik commodities encountered above, which Runciter now pitches as the force that can contain or defer entropy.

"One invisible puff-puff whisk of economically priced Ubik banishes compulsive obsessive fears that the entire world is turning into clotted milk, worn-out tape recorders and obsolete iron-cage elevators. . . . You see, world deterioration of this regressive type is a normal experience of many half-lifers, especially in the early stages when ties to the real reality are still very strong. A sort of lingering universe is retained as a residual charge, experienced as a pseudo environment but highly unstable and unsupported by any ergic substructure. . . . But with today's new, more-powerful-than-ever Ubik, all this is changed!" (127)

What Runciter is talking about here is memory. But whose memory of whom?

Runciter appears both as the external source of manifestations, advice, and directions addressed to his employees and as his own corpse laid out for burial in his place of birth, Des Moines, in the 1939 world unto which the dynamic of reversion has brought the surviving inertials. After a series of close calls, the outsider finally gets across and saves Joe with the cure-all Ubik. But now it becomes clear that Runciter does not really know what's going on in the 1939 world. Yes, Runciter is probably alive sitting next to the Snow White coffins in which the inertials are suspended in half-life, trying to communicate, but he does not control, not even in the mode of knowledge, the disruptions that have made it so difficult to put through the connection all this time.

The struggle all along has been between the fifteen-year-old Jory and Ella exclusively on the turf of half-life. Jory pulls himself out of inertial Denny to introduce himself to Joe. He already turned Denny into Dennys.

He specializes in "eating" fellow half-lifers to obtain yet more energy for the task of pushing back degenerescence. Ella represents eros: Ubik is her invention and legacy. Her sojourn in half-life is coming to an end. She wants Joe restored so he can take her place as Runciter's advisor from the other side. Ella can give Ubik—in other words, time, a lifetime supply— but she cannot take Jory away.

"Maybe in time you can learn ways to nullify him. I think that's really the best you can hope to do; I doubt if you can truly destroy him—in other words consume him— as he does to half-lifers placed near him at the moratorium. . . . And—there are Jorys in every moratorium. This battle goes on wherever you have half-lifers; it's a verity, a rule, of our kind of existence. . . . It has to be fought on our side of the glass," Ella said. "By those of us in half-life, those that Jory preys on. You'll have to take charge, Mr. Chip, after I'm reborn. Do you think you can do that? It'll be hard. Jory will be sapping your strength always, putting a burden on you that you'll feel as—" She hesitated. "The approach of death. Which it will be. Because in half-life we diminish constantly anyhow. Jory only speeds it up. The weariness and cooling-off come anyhow. But not so soon." (206–7)

Go with the Flow

Flow My Tears, the Policeman Said is the scattershot estimation of the prospects for mourning when every interpersonal connection has been lost and your social context no longer recognizes you back. The protagonist Jason Taverner endures a loss of reciprocity that would resemble the psychotic break or the half-life of a ghost if reality did not continue to compute but only one way. It turns out that social reality was displaced by a relationship that crossed fantasy with realization of the wish through alterations in time and space. Alys Buckman, it turns out, reduced the world she swallowed whole with her drugs to her relationship to Taverner, famous TV personality and singer, otherwise unknown to her but the object of her fantasy communion.

"It was Alys. Taverner, like the rest of us, became a datum in your sister's percept system and got dragged across when she passed into an alternate construct of coordinates. She was very involved with Taverner as a wish-fulfillment performer... But although she did manage to accomplish this . . . , he and we at the same time remained in our own universe. We occupied two space corridors at the same time, one real, one irreal." (211–12)

Flow My Tears, the Policeman Said picks up *Ubik*'s society-wide coordinates of relations with the after- or higher life, but displaced to the periphery of Alys's boundary-blending wish fulfillment. The empathy boxes of *Do Androids Dream of Electric Sheep?* are again pressed into service, but this time to raise consumerism to the power of the "phone grid" of Passion, with sadomasochism legibly inscribing the legend to this remapping of Christianity onto exhaustible surfaces of embodied life.

"Your—everybody's—sexual aspects are linked electronically, and amplified, to as much as you can endure. It's addictive, because it's electronically enhanced. People, some of them, get so deep into it they can't pull out; their whole lives revolve around the weekly—or, hell, even daily!—setting up of the network of phone lines. . . . Most of them have been doing it two, three years. And they've deteriorated physically— and mentally—from it. . . . But don't put down the people. . . . For them it's a sacred, holy communion." (153)

The new medium spans the recent past of two, maybe three, years (during which time teenagers at heart are sentenced to midlife). Taverner's spell of nonexistence in the Is of his beholders in an environment he alone recognizes as his own lasts two days. The countdown of mourning is orthogonally twisted around and away from the duo dynamic of one twin's wish fulfillment. Alys, the acting-out, world-warping twin sister of Felix Buckman, one of the generals of this police state, can be seen as Jane Dick's representative in her own brother's work. What if Jane's world doesn't admit mourning, identification, or recognition but entertains only fantasies by association with the mediatic environment? What if she is the author with the Dick surname? Jane, see Dick run. Her portrait, however, is highly ambivalent not because Alys herself or the incestuous relationship to her brother is so illicit, but because she dies within the vehicle of her comeback.

What Alys and Jason Taverner do have in common however is, if only by dint of what the industry calls continuity error, they could both be already dead. That Alys dies an instant ancient skeleton suggests, not only in the lexicon of Dick's collected work, that she may already have been dead. And then Jason wakes up in the two-day world to which he does and doesn't belong from what was going to be emergency surgery for removal of an extraterrestrial parasite's tentacles. Never again is the operation, the emergency, the near-death mentioned, let alone accounted for.

Alys's consumerism turns identification as recognition value into identification with that which she recognizes as other. The object is creaturely or thingly in the range of selection. Alys craves contact with celebrities. Plus Jason Taverner is, as a so-called six, genetically enhanced stock, which means, however, since the plan of experimentation to which he owes his status was long ago abandoned, that he is collectible. At the hub of twinship we find a collection unconscious that sifts through and preserves that which is functionally or futurally extinguished. The novel ends with a sighting of the blue vase that, having passed through several exchanges in Taverner's narrative, ends up both as decontextualized marker of the past that can no longer be summoned or cited with specificity and yet as the hub of identification renewal:

The blue vase . . . wound up in a private collection of modern pottery. It remains there to this day, and is much treasured. And, in fact, by a number of people who know ceramics, openly and genuinely cherished. And loved.

Taverner's double condition requires the work of analogy. He is like one dead to his world, which does not, however, remember him, dead or alive. Like the psychotic he loses his world—except in his case, his world loses him, since he still knows where he lives, even if no one else knows even that he lives or once lived. He is like a ghost summoned at séance who must convince the participants not that he is who he says he is but that he ever existed at all. Taverner is pulled through this psychotic voiding of existence into the position of double mourning, which only others can fill in, as the blanks in their own grieving lives.

The first sentence of *Flow My Tears, the Policeman Said* announces what would seem to be the slightest possible loss or lag, but in programming that presumably exceeds that of the TV show the gap demanding filler knocks whole worlds out of sync. "On Tuesday, October 11, 1988, the Jason Taverner Show ran thirty seconds short." To help pick up the slack Jason announces the next show, *The Adventures of Scotty, Dog Extraordinary,* for which the audience should stay tuned.

At the opener the novel finds filler for an error in the continuity of time. In no time continuity will err, wander, drift into split-off parts that no longer communicate with one another. In the alternate present that seems to pass on through nothing but continuity errors, there will be one exchange of experiences of time, reading time, which remains a near miss, but one that the protagonist Jason Taverner will inexplicably pine for pointlessly. Jason asks the forger and police informant Kathy how far she got into Proust's *Remembrance of Things Past* when he sees a copy lying about.

"To *Within a Budding Grove.*" . . .
　　"That's not very far," Jason said.
　　Taking off her plastic coat, Kathy asked, "How far did you get into it?" . . .
　　"I never read it," Jason said. "But on my program we did a dramatic rendering of a scene" (35).

Proust's work of remembrance is for the man out of time at once unread and acted out. According to Benjamin in "The Image of Proust," Proust's materials were, just like this exchange between Jason and Kathy, the stuff of an insignificant dream that someone bothers to recount in conversation. Is there anything more painfully forgettable than someone's halting attempts to relate to you a disconnected and pointless dream? But he raised the forget-together of everyday life to the power of elegy: "the eternal repetition, the eternal restoration of the original, the first happiness. It is this elegiac idea of happiness . . . which for Proust transforms existence into a preserve of memory" (204). Proust discovered that it is smell, that which no one remembers, that will trigger an interminable relay of memories. Through cultivation of the forgotten as memory prop or trigger, Proust dedicated self or corpus to the *actus purus* of recollection itself. "An experienced event is finite—at any rate, confined to one sphere of experience; a remembered event is infinite, because it is only a key to everything that happened before it and after it" (202).

But the work of remembrance cannot be readily maintained as such. Proust kept it going only at crisis point: "the threatening, suffocating crisis was death, which he was constantly aware of, most of all while he was writing. This is how death confronted Proust, and long before his malady assumed critical dimensions—not as a hypochondriacal whim, but as a 'réalité nouvelle,' that new reality whose reflection on things and people are the marks of aging" (214).

Like smells, the marks of aging comprise the layering of forgetting and remembrance. "The eternity which Proust opens to view is convoluted time, not boundless time. His true interest is in the passage of time in its most real—that is, space-bound—form, and this passage nowhere holds sway more openly than in remembrance within and aging without" (211). "Involuntary memory" releases "the rejuvenating force which is a match for the inexorable process of aging." When the past comes to be reflected in the fresh instant "a painful shock of rejuvenation pulls it together once more." Proust carried out "the tremendous feat of letting the whole world age by a lifetime in an instant. But this very concentration in which things that normally just fade and slumber consume themselves in a flash is called rejuvenation" (211).

Before he swaps with Kathy souvenirs of the unread, at the end of the day that he held together by inserting the adventures or investigations of a dog into the gap in the continuity of live TV, Jason is at a loss—of identity and of the world held in common with others. Instead he finds himself surrounded by police officers and psychotics who have no idea who he is but are just the same attracted to his nonexistence.

Reality always already begins to return, even if only on the terms of the world that never knew him as TV star. It is the hurt that gets him hurdling over the "bottom of life" (where the time slack dropped him) into the space of new beginnings. But it's not, not yet, his grief. The first niche of his lost world that he can reenter belongs to former actress Ruth Rae, whose general amnesia mixes him into some alcohol anonymous recollection, even though in the former world she knew him well. The only thing he thinks he remembers about her from their past together on his time was that she couldn't abide animals. When he carelessly or symptomatically insults her as too old for him, he finds that he couldn't love her or leave her but now must live her hurt. Ruth sets before Jason a mourning pageant of loss totemically dedicated to dead animals. Ruth has given up on love, which for her began and kept on ending with animals. But giving up amounts to consuming herself in the flashback of a lifetime, in which she has been following the dead into the internal/eternal moment of their first contact with loss (or rejuvenation).

"Their lives are so short. Just so fucking goddamn short. Okay, some people lose a creature they love and then go on and transfer that love to another one. But it hurts; it hurts."

"Then why is love so good. . . . You love someone and they leave. . . . After that until you're dead you're carrying around this huge hunk of love with no one to give it to. And if you do find someone to give it to, the same thing happens all over." . . .

Ruth said, "Love isn't just wanting another person the way you want to own an object you see in a store. That's just desire. . . . When you love you cease to live for yourself; you live for another person." . . .

Jason said, "But why is it good to go against the instinct for self-survival?" . . .

"Because the instinct for survival loses in the end. . . . You can never accomplish what your survival instinct sets out to do, so ultimately your striving ends in failure and you succumb to death, and that ends it. But if you love you can fade out and watch . . . with happiness, and with cool, mellow, alpha contentment, the highest form of contentment, the living on of one of those you love."

"But they die, too." . . .

"But you can grieve. . . . Grief is the most powerful emotion a man or child or animal can feel. . . . Grief causes you to leave yourself. You step outside your narrow little pelt. And you can't feel grief unless you've had love before it—grief is the final outcome of love, because it's love lost. . . . But to grieve; it's to die and be alive at the same time." (109–12)

Readers of *Do Androids Dream of Electric Sheep?* have marked down the high value of pets in that novel's world following upon the near extinction of animal life as market value only. And yet, if we heed Benjamin, the commodification of nearly extinct animals only underscores their allegorical significance. In *Flow My Tears, the Policeman Said,* the continuum of mourning that is opened around interspecial relations traverses this world without Watergate in which Nixon resides on the right side of the father God. African Americans are objects of veneration under special protection following their near extinction during the Second Civil War. Even now, under cover of planned parenting or parenthood, their extinction, though interrupted, is being administered just the same, just over time, via the requirement that for African Americans there be no more than one child per couple. Even in housing that permits pets, more than one per family is either discouraged or disallowed. The family with one only child is *the* Christian family. Still warnings are issued regularly, especially in white culture, against the self-imposed plan by couples to reproduce only one child. The desire for or dread of planned obsolescence meets the backfire of projected violence halfway. The medium of the exchange is Christianity.

But the cynical alignments of valuation and extinction begin to break down by coming to grief. Felix Buckman found that the planned parenthood of his own incestuous coupling with Alys pulled him out of the original merger. Loving his only child opened up that innermost part of him where he had something to lose. Like Alys, he is alone with the love of the child experienced as one-way flow that never reverts and if interrupted by loss could never be recovered (136). Thus when his twin dies, he doesn't die with her. Instead Buckman takes his grieving to an unknown black man. The two protagonists, Taverner and Buckman, connected only through subjection to Alys's world, both come to grief via the other's ability to acknowledge mourning. Ruth and her lost ones, with her dead pets at the front of the line, guide Taverner, while the black man at the gas station in the middle of the night, as member of an endangered race, enables Buckman's grief to recognize itself. It is in the relationship to one's pets that human beings are given second chances to renew vows with life. For a white man to form a friendship with a black man in a racist society is hard working through. Is that why white American expatriates in Europe will express their pining for the former environment's inclusion of substantial numbers of blacks?

The specism of our societies becomes immediately evident with the death of an adopted animal. There is no context, community, continuity for the remembrance of dead animals. It's not just that you are alone with the loss—whereas before the poor critter's death everyone stopped to pet the best friend or make a fuss over the little one. It is rather that the living bond becomes derealized after the fact. Even the photographs, like the records of Taverner's existence before he was dragged inside Alys's world, become blurred, unidentifiable, and unrecognizable.

Embracing the black man, Buckman is able to break through the murder in idealization—which is, after all, an acceptable description or goal of mourning work. All along as police general he exhibited a kind of hobbyist resistance to the full pogrom of law enforcement. He found loopholes through which the losers of the civil war could escape incarceration or execution. At this point of breakthrough, however, the exception no longer fits one man's intention or personality but opens wide as structure. The police state will become too monolithic to prove effective. The student underworld or counterculture will come to an end not because it was wiped out but because the lines of opposition left over from the civil war will not be needed. No breeding regulations can be enforced. It is through the diversification of investments and holdings in mourning beyond planned relationality that Dick recognizes as inevitable that even the constitutive boundaries of political and psychotic control will come to grief as defective, permeable, already let go.

The novel occupies or cathects the two worlds given in the title and an indefinite number more. Written up to the crisis point of the 1974 mystical revelations or psychotic breakthrough, *Flow My Tears, the Policeman Said* offers the only immediate introduction available for assessing Dick's state just prior to coming under the receivership of healing flows of information. In his *Exegesis* Dick finds his work revalorized in light of these illuminations: "My writing deals with hallucinated worlds, intoxicating & deluding drugs, & psychosis. But my writing acts as an antidote, a detoxifying—not intoxicating—antidote. This is a fascinating realization. My writing deals with that which it lessens or dispels by—raising those topics to our conscious attention" (*In Pursuit of Valis*, 184). *Flow My Tears, the Policeman Said* and *A Scanner Darkly* have in common the raising to consciousness of something that is real, not only psychotically but also politically. As Dick underscores in the *Exegesis*, "because the fictional or phantastic element is virtually lacking," both novels "are obviously semimimetic" (181). That element, indeed lacking (or, rather, withdrawn inside the media record) in *A Scanner Darkly*, is pressing in *Flow My Tears, the Policeman Said*, but pressing to the point that it must be countered and contained.

Dick's 1978 essay "How to Build a Universe That Doesn't Fall Apart Two Days Later" grants *Flow My Tears, the Policeman Said* a span of reality that exceeds the two days of Taverner's sojourn in Alys's world. The essay inhabits a splitting of the ambivalence otherwise engaged in his fictions. In the first half, Dick points to television's synchronization of words and perceptions as already the realization of many sci-fi forecasts of mind control.

> TV viewing is a kind of sleeplearning. An EEG of a person watching TV shows that after about half an hour the brain decides that nothing is happening, and it goes into a hypnoidal twilight state, emitting alpha waves. This is because there is such little eye motion. . . . Recent experiments indicate that much of what we see on the TV screen is received on a subliminal basis. We only imagine that we consciously see what is there. The bulk of the messages elude our attention; literally, after a few hours of TV watching, we do not know what we have seen. Our memories are spurious, like our memories of dreams; the blank spaces are filled in retrospectively. And falsified. We have participated unknowingly in the creation of a spurious reality, and then we have obligingly fed it to ourselves. (265–66)

But at the end of the essay he turns the TV around to address the children, let them come unto him, they are fraudulence proof. Sure they want to eat the fast food and play with the toys advertised on TV "but the deep heart beats firmly, unreached and unreasoned with" (279). Children are quicker than adults, time is speeding up, time is going to end.

We have here Arthur Clarke's vision of an ending in *Childhood's End*. In his essay "Man, Android, and Machine" from 1976 Dick explicitly summons the "Overmind" from Clarke's science fiction when it's time to collapse before the reality revealed when our ontological categories fail and we wake up out of veil reality into the reality of oneness (219). In a summation of the ongoing *Exegesis* that he separated out for advance preview in 1980 under the title "The Ultra Hidden (Cryptic) Doctrine: The Secret Meaning of the Great System of Theosophy of the World, Openly Revealed for the First Time," Valis is itself, once disclosed, presented as another Overmind: "the situation is over; you are bound for heaven or hell, but the midrealm of *purgatorio* is shut to you forever" (339). Dick introduces this "situation" along the lines or lives of his fiction: "we are dead but don't know it, reliving our former lives but on tape (programmed), in a simulated world . . . where we relive in a virtually closed cycle again and again until we manage to add enough new good karma to trigger off divine intervention, which wakes us up . . . so that we can begin our renascent back up to our real home" (337–38).

For the time being, all that there is to describe is the intermediary realm that is the bane of ghost scholars who must accommodate the Christian hierarchy (if only for reading orientation). But it is the point of legibility or transference without which there can be no study of where the dead go. For Dick as for Freud, the fake world of our repetition compulsion is the rack of retraumatization but also the scratch from which one can begin again. In an earlier summary of the *Exegesis* process, "Cosmogony and Cosmology" (1978), one again cannot pull his plug for isomorphic realization of the Urgrund (another Overmind, as formulated by Jacob Boehme) from the outlet that sustains the intermediate position, which is occupied by the artifact, now a projector, now a computer-like teaching machine responsible for our world, which functions "as a sort of mirror or image of its maker, so that the maker can obtain thereby an objective standpoint to comprehend its own self" (281). We are thus controlled or guided "as we act without awareness of it within our projected world" (281). The prospect of overcoming life as replay is lodged (like another projection) inside this ghostly, transitional realm of media technologization.

Thomas, Dick's alter ego from the early days of Christianity, is bound to Dick by having done precisely what he or Dick did not do the first time around. This is the break we get—between alternate worlds. "Only this not-you act or acts could save you, actions without a history.... For it was with 'Thomas' that the new and unprogrammed veered off from what happened the first time, and there indeed was a first time." Thomas's act without ideation, the act Dick would not have done, prompted Dick's realization: "THERE IS ANOTHER PERSON IN ME" (340). Dick also still lives in the era of the Book of Acts. All the alternate realities inhabit the wait for Christ's return in which (at least in their alternation) early Christians like Dick hide out from the Roman Empire (associated in Dick's day with Nixon's government). But as alternative plan, Christianity would also be kept from making the transition to being the first "world religion" coextensive with the infrastructure of the Empire (including the postal system and the network of roads). But there's no early to late delay external to Christianity, which is constitutively media savvy. Why else is the New Testament comprised of epistles or letters?

If all this is indeed in his mind, which is double, the guiding part "speaking out of a ghostly realm where what is is also what is not" (347), then thought proceeds double time, exchanging what was original for what is automatic or new and improved. Dick is trying to articulate the motive force of what we do not know in our lives in repetition. The mind inevitably errs. When the mind abandons the A solution, because it didn't work, it moves to the next solution, B. "The mind when it comes to employ the

B solution does not have to think. The thinking took place in a realm or track that has been abolished; when that realm was erased the thinking was erased with it, leaving only the motor and speech centers active. The mind, when it employs the B solution, is its own machine, . . . acting out a solution that was not the primary one" (347). Because we change our minds, we admit the intermediary machine that erases the recent past of original thought, which, however, erred in the first place.

If it isn't all in your mind, however, then time disruption as possibility changes everything: "This theory about time disruption replaces the theory . . . that we are dead but don't know it." Disruption of time can break down "the twin-tape synch system that makes of us little more than DNA robots" (348). Major erasure and reinscription can take place. But time disruption, in Dick's case, was not done by Dick but by another Dick who lived through to the end of his life, died, and returned to an earlier stage of his life, but now under taped conditions. "It would not be correct to say that the second time around, things are different from the first time around; both times are the same time, through an orthogonal intervention of needed information" (349). Yet this is what makes "taped conditions . . . a combination of servitude and opportunity" (348). To be of two minds means a second chance: "the B solution is a feedback system that monitors the failure of A with the absolute wisdom of hindsight" (349). Where there was repression, let there be or let it become retrospective intelligence.

In his 1977 essay "If You Find This World Bad, You Should See Some of the Others," Dick, while contemplating a cosmos that does nothing but think, shares a thought that crossed his mind one day, which "undermined" his own "marvellous pantheistic monism" (234):

What if there exists a plurality of universes arranged along a sort of lateral axis, which is to say at right angles to the flow of linear time? (234)

The "Undermind" chooses then not to pass into the light or night of oneness but opens up concessions to finitude in lateral realities. In contrast to the reading light of remembrance, the light according to Christianity loses the recognition value of the dead in the short attention spam of advertising, the news or the gospel. Dick's fiction finds the undermining of linear time an improvement on the old saw of eternity seen last as the (suicidal) merger with the Overmind in Clarke's *Childhood's End*. But we're in nonfictional Dick now. Just the same, after dismissing this sci-fi conceit as an absurd notion at large, Dick again asks his audience or readership to assume for the moment that alternate universes do exist, though such an assumption lies outside our right minds.

Then, if they do, how are they linked to each other, if in fact they are (or would be) linked? If you drew a map of them, showing their locations, what would the map look like? For instance (and I think this is a very important question), are they absolutely separate one from another, or do they overlap? . . . I am saying, simply, if they do indeed exist, and if they do indeed overlap, then we may in some literal, very real sense, inhabit several of them to various degrees at any given time. . . . It may not merely be that our subjective impressions of the world differ, but there may be an overlapping, a superimposition, of a number of worlds so that objectively, not subjectively, our worlds may differ. . . . It may be that some of these superimposed worlds are passing out of existence, along the lateral time line I spoke of, and some are in the process of moving toward greater, rather than lesser, actualization. These processes would occur simultaneously and not at all in linear time. (237–38)

PART V

Room for Thought

Aby Warburg filed for release on his own consciousness to the surprise of Ludwig Binswanger, who, when he considered the patient's disorder, was cureless. Like Heidegger, like Jung, Binswanger was a technophobe who saw delusions of reference to technologization as the chronic endpoint of psychotic regression. Contrariwise, Freud, in his Schreber reading, saw the point of any delusion, which invariably and endopsychically ranged from underworlds to the cosmic or galactic projections of techno-futures, as being the point of return to world, no longer the world lost in the breakdown but a Sensurround of cathected relations all the same.

Jung was still on the future track of transference when he inspired Freud's inside view of delusions as attempts at recovery: Freud credited Jung's early work on schizophrenia, in which flights of ideas and motor stereotypies were analyzed as relics of former object-cathexes. But when the transference was negated, object relations were ditched for the big picture of the Unconscious bigger and older than the two of us, self and other. The technical contours of a certain genre of psychotic delusion were too tightly strapped to the transference onto Freud he had abandoned. The technical connection is too interpersonal for Jung (for reasons of his own). Heidegger viewed outright technologization in thought or delusion as the original provenance of application to which psychoanalysis belonged as techno theory. Binswanger stayed on the same side as Freud of the Jung divide but staggered their neighborhood via strict zoning distinctions between schizophrenia and melancholia, for example. In the mapping around this example one recognizes Benjamin's Freudian affiliation.

Like Schreber, Warburg only had to prove through performance of his professional duties and thus also in writing that his right to reside in the (former) world was back, back up and functioning. In his presentation on "The Serpent Ritual," Warburg moreover reclaimed his techno disorder as order of the world in decline against which he delivered the prehistory of and antibody to our relationship to the shock of heirs in the face of primordial relations with nature. In drawing on encounters with honest Indian cultures, which he sought out during his visit to the United States twenty-seven years earlier, going native in reaction to the horrors of the middlebrowbeat Back East, Warburg attended to a span of commemoration of his career that he intended to delegate as rededicated to a new discipline of study not to be confused with art history, which he considered abandoned with this talk.

By the end of his presentation Warburg comes full circle within the span of tension that he is documenting and reclaiming when he touches down in San Francisco via his snapshot of a businessman—Warburg refers to him as an "Uncle Sam"—who, together with the electrical wires overhead, bisects the foreground in front of brand-new neoclassical buildings that could have been erected in Germany at that same time. In this photo Warburg was able to capture "the figure of overcoming of the snake cult and the fear of lightning, the heir to the aboriginal peoples and the gold-seeking suppressor of the Indian" (58). The electrical wire or "copper snake" signifies Edison's wresting of lightning from nature. But Warburg revalorizes the wire Americans suspend outside and the Central European sensibility tucks away underground as openly repressed line to pagan beliefs. "The American of today fears not the rattlesnake. It is killed, certainly it is not worshipped as divine. What is offered as countermeasure is extinction. The lightning bolt ensnared in the wire, the impersonal electricity, has engendered a culture that has put the pagan past away." The German phrase, *mit dem Heidentum aufgeräumt,* also means, literally, to clean up "with" or "by means of" paganism.

What does our new techno order of the world set in the place of paganism overcome? The forces of nature are no longer viewed in anthropomorphic or biomorphic contexts but rather as endless wavelengths that obey the touch of the human hand. In this way, the culture of the machine age destroys that to which the sciences, growing out of myth, had painstakingly laid claim, the space or room of contemplation *(Andachtsraum),* which laid the foundation for thinking space *(Denkraum).* "The Mnemnosyne Atlas" alone would indicate that Warburg was gadget lover enough to have a more differentiated relationship to this prose and cant of technophobicity. Warburg brackets out (and implicates as one of the likely frames of his former delusional world) Spiritualist recourse to the media of live transmission for communication with the departed. This is most likely where he had to leave behind those techno relations syntonic with his p-unitive delusions and, by translating them back into animism proper, secure his return to the former world. The password is dismissal of technologization as applied science (science still being a good thing) and original American sin.

If the futility of Germany's position in the Great War triggered, by all accounts, Warburg's breakdown,[1] then the entry of the United States into the world conflict must have been the last raw material that broke Germany's back to back with Warburg's breakdown. The new order of the world is thus essentially American: the modern Prometheus is Franklin and the modern Icarus, the Wright brothers. These neo occupants of old positions, however, destroy the sense of distance and lead the world again into chaos. "Telegram and telephone destroy the cosmos. Mythic and symbolic thought together create in the struggle for the spiritualized connection between man and environment the space for contemplation or thought which the electrical instantaneous connection murders" (59). Warburg's struggle for sanity or release required that his techno-delusional system pull apart along the projected lines of a conflict as worldwide as what Warburg at the same time raises as questionable, the genealogy of media or values.

In pockets deep inside the United States of techno culture, Warburg found enclaves of primitive paganism, which maintained themselves in hardship but just the same as resistant via and for the magical practices that were pressed into the service of agriculture and the hunt. The juxtaposition of fantastic magic and sober purposeful activity could strike one at first as "schizoid." (Warburg uses this term throughout along the lines of dissociation rather than of detachment.) But not so for the Indians: it is the liberating experience of possible relationality between man and environment. The three types of mask dance follow the sliding scale of valuation: animal dance, tree dance, and the dance with living snakes, viewed as developmental stages, correspond to the procession from primitive paganism via the paganism of Antiquity to modern humanism.

The masked dancers are represented in every household as kachina dolls. A dancer wearing the matching artificial head is so much more terrible for being recognizable as the well-known unmoveable doll head. "Who knows whether our dolls were not originally such demons" (33). In vertical contrast to the dolls we find in one of the photographs Warburg took back then a straw broom of utility up against the wall of assimilationist American mass culture (or of resistance to it). Still inside the Indian home, we find that the pottery decorations reflect a level of abstraction that demands to be read rather than looked at. We attend here to the intermediary stage between iconic imagination of reality and the written sign. We can discern in the cosmological ornamentation on pottery, walls, and textiles not only steps and ladders symbolizing the struggle to move up or down in space but also the snake, which symbolizes the rhythm of time.

The steps of ladder or stairway ennoble man's vulnerability as upright walker on two legs over against the animal's groundedness on four legs. "Gazing at the heavens is blessing and curse of mankind" (24). "The Indian relates to the animal internally completely differently than the European. He views the animal as a higher being, since the unicity of its animalness makes it a much more powerfully gifted being in contrast to the weaker human" (27).

The world house the Indian pitches above his vulnerability rises up by steps and ladders. But the mistress of his house remains the uncanniest of animals: the snake (24). The design abstraction in the figuration of certain animals underscores their totemic significance. The snake, however, is specifically and directly tied to lightning via magical causality.

In the process of linking up with the utmost in extrapersonals, the mask dances represent the farthest-reaching subjection to an alien being. Here imitation serves the cultic enactment of devoted loss of self to this being. The bearer of the mask believes he metamorphoses into the object or objective of the ceremony—but as still under his control. At the same time as hunter or farmer he seeks the same objectives (which again seems, all together now, "schizoid"). The cohabitation of logistics and fanatical magical causation underscores the situation of the Indians as hybrid or transitional. They are not primitive grabbers, without any relation to the future of their actions, nor are they technologically pacified Europeans whose future is under control. They stand between magic and logos, and their medium is the symbolic connection. Between the grasping man and the thinking man stands the man who conjoins symbolically. The metamorphic way of thinking is the preamble to our natural-scientific interpretation of the world. The totemic view of animals as ancestors of clan members is not so different from Darwinism. The Indians don't hand it all over to autonomous nature but seek explanations instead through deliberate conjoining with the animal world. "It is . . . Darwinism through mythic elective affinity" (27).

With their mask dances, the Indians offer "the primary pagan form of response to the big painful question of the why of things: the Indian thus offers up in contrast to the unfathomability of processes in nature his will to grasp or understand so that he becomes himself such a cause of things. Instinctually he posits for the inexplicable consequence the cause as easy to grasp and see. The mask dance is danced causality" (54).

The snake ceremony stands between imitative mimetic empathy and bloody sacrifice. The animals themselves, and not their representations, are in fact introduced into the ceremony not to be sacrificed but as petitioners for rain. The snake not sacrificed is rendered in the dance a delegate to the souls of the dead to seek the release of stormy weather in the form of lightning. (Right after the dance movement is over, the dancer runs off with the snake to release it in the plains text of transmission.)

The snake is the mascot of a "process of sublimation in religion" whereby bloody sacrifice is left behind in the developmental progress of religion from East to West (44). Via the contribution of the snake one can distinguish the fetishistic from the purely salvific nature of belief systems.

In the *Laocoön* sculpture the terrible strangulation of father and sons by the serpent of the gods symbolizes Antiquity's passion: "Vengeful death through demons without justice and without hope of redemption" (45). But in time the demonic snake of the pessimistic worldview faces a snake divinity, Asclepis, who shows a beautiful aspect of humane healing, which bears or shares the traits of world savior. (Warburg sees the crucifixion emerge from snakes and ladders.) But Asclepis commenced his ascent in the underworld as god of the dead. The snake ringing around the stave is the soul of the departed living on as snake. (The stacking of identifications invites association with Christianity: the deceased is represented by the snake, is the snake, while the snake is at the same time the god. The relationship to the deceased is close but even more so far far away.) By acts of approximation turned into hieroglyphs Asclepis climbs yet higher than the humane and reaches the stars as astrological sign under which doctors and prophets are born. Thus the snake god becomes a sublimated totem: *verklärten Totem*. Already in the astrology of Antiquity mathematics and magic are on the same page of skywriting. The snake god in the heavens becomes a mathematical measure of mass. Asclepis ends up at once fetish holder or niche and mathematical limit concept. The snake is an international icon that points out where in the world elemental destruction, death, and suffering come from. But how can mankind overcome this compulsive conjoining with a poisonous reptile? The natural-scientific enlightenment clears away mythological causation (literally, in the German, this enlightenment clears away "with" mythological causation) and in its application, as technologization, takes away the fright factor. But can one *not* respond to the questioning of existence?

This open question is Warburg's free act, which can be seen as emerging from, while reformatting the violent acts that first required his hospitalization. Between acts Warburg immersed himself in a delusional system or project that we can begin to discern between the lines of the Serpent Ritual lecture. Binswanger privileged the aberrant act as assertion of living relationality, even if only in its *Verfallsform,* whereby this breaking point is where the psychotic can still break through. In his case study of Ellen West, Binswanger valorized even his patient's suicide as ill but freeing act. The aberrant act, the last try by *Dasein* to come to itself, become itself, takes the form, in the case of Ilse, of letting one's own hand burn slowly in the oven in order to draw the attention of a loved one. Ilse thus marked the onset of her breakdown by handing the sacrifice to her father and leading Binswanger by this hand to her stabilization. After thirteen months at the institution, she can return home completely cured of her acute psychosis. The hand she gave her father and extended through the father transference to her treating clinicians was not as decontextualized as the sacrifice Binswanger interprets but already belongs to the relay of tests through which she passed during what Freud would consider her recovery. Regarding Ilse's endopsychic perception of this relay of testing and torture that also characterized her stay at the asylum, Binswanger rushes to reassure us in a footnote that this so-called treatment was the patient's delusion. No "psychoanalytic" experiments were in fact conducted using Ilse as human subject. Suzanne Urban may not get out of the rut of her martyrology, but Ilse helps herself to the restoration of reality testing, the egoic function that determines animation or motility, but as an on/off switch internal to memory. Reality testing and transference define psychotic states by process of their elimination. If they can be *found* missing, they draw the borderline of legibility between neurosis and psychosis inside psychosis. It is via the intermediary position of the Indians—and of symbolic linking itself—that Warburg picks up the slack of reality testing within his own delusional system of global torment.

Caduceus

Dr. Futurity entitles the medical profession to raise the healing snake emblem above all other totems in an alternate future of mankind. The protagonist, Parsons, is a physician who time slips into the future where healing and surviving are outmoded personal effects readily sacrificed to the future life of the race, species, or kind. Parsons was summoned or met halfway by a renegade Indian clan seeking to restore the family values of reproduction in a Teen Age that cooks up its future generation out of the frozen stock taken from boys fixed in preadolescence. Sexuality is thus charged with child abuse. Not only did the Indian chief Clothis escape castration and introduce family resemblance into future generation, living on into midlife, but even his mother, the *Urmutter*, continued to live (on arrested grief). In the world around these renegades the average age is fifteen. Parsons, who is the other unfixed male in the cooped-up clan headquarters, becomes a reproductive part of this family society. He sires twins, a boy and a girl, who replace the wolf totem of the clan with the caduceus in honor of their ancestry, which escaped via time travel the fixings of progress: "crossed snakes twining up a staff topped by open wings. The caduceus. The ancient sign of the medical profession" (159).

Parsons arrives by California freeway in another time zone—the neck of the woulds and shoulds in which the only answer is death. As he struggles to survive the hit-and-run attempt, Parsons recognizes the young drive-by's shocked confusion: "the boy thought I wanted to be run down!" (8). He merges on the freeway heading for the future on suicide drive. The future is a hub of time-traveling connections between past and future times, which is porous to the flow of past times and again. All it takes is "displacement" for frogs, an extinct species, to fall in the streets

(20). The future has a history that Parsons can identify: it's more of the same, only with the slant eyes of mixed color. Are there no black people in California, compared to East Coast population centers, or is it more to the point that whole Back East country clubs of white people are missing? In the future, everyone's of color. The teens speak a kind of polyglot that's less language and more jargon. They have the attention spans to match. "There are no spirits"—just the high spirits of the forever young who, no matter what shade of off-white the color, still view themselves, via their ego ideal, as beached blank bimbos. The kids go by tribal names, totems painted on their car doors. (I brake for Mickey Mouse.) A series of contests reorganized the world along these lines following the H-war. Al Stenog, who has a last name, turns out to be the wild card in deregulated time travel. He aims to make the legacy of the last name last and to put white into the future mix, too.

Clothis thought he alone was using time travel to make adjustments to the history of white colonization of the new world. Ahead of Pisarro and Cortez in the lineup of terrible adventurers is a certain Drake who landed on the West Coast. As the *Urmutter* explains: "So my son went back. To the first New England. Not the famous one, but the other one. The real one. In California" (101). Clothis goes back to assassinate Drake. But he is mortally wounded instead. When rewind and playback functions don't succeed in averting the mishap, time travel is used to bring a physician from the past to the rescue. In the future it is a crime to avert death. When Parsons saves the life of a seriously wounded young woman he is charged with a crime that, as a term, is the mongrelization of Nazi German: *Rassmort* (35). Stenog explains that the only life that counts is the life stored in all its potential perfectibility—their version of immortality—as billions of zygotes frozen inside "the cube." "'Our total seed. Our horde. The race is in there. Those of us now walking around—' He made a motion of dismissal. 'A minute fraction of what's contained in there, the future generations to come'" (45). Parsons recognizes that the minds of future teens inhabit their posthumous future (so bright they are shades) and not the present. One man's mysticism is future man's science: "Those to come, in a sense, are more real than those who are walking around now" (45). But can death be posited as the cause of life?

Parsons said slowly, "We may ignore death, we may immaturely *deny* the existence of death, but at least we don't court death."

"You did indirectly," Stenog said. "By denying such a powerful reality, you undermined the rational basis of your world. . . . So war *happened* to you; it was like a natural calamity, not man-made at all. It became a force." (48)

Secreted away in the headquarters of the Indians, a miniature cube contains not the seed but the man, suspended in otherwise doomed animation: "Instead of a hundred billion zygotes and developed embryos, this small cube contained the preserved body of a single man, a fully developed male perhaps thirty years old" (78). Midlife criticism thus balances its acts with those of the Teen Age. The body, dead or alive, as the occasion for mourning or reproduction, is kept at the heart of the resistance in or to the future. But when the good doctor Parsons removes the feathered arrow and restores Clothis to life, a heartbeat later another arrow is piercing his heart. At that point, at the latest, the Indians realize that they are not alone in deployment of time travel.

The Before Stenog, in contrast to the After Stenog who stitches up history through time travel to save the time or momentum of the death drive, dismisses time travel as an "always already" or as contradiction in its terms:

"That is, if you wanted to invent a time machine, all you'd have to do was swear or prophesy that when you got it working, the first use you'd put it to would be to go back into time, to the point at which you got interested in the idea. . . . And give your earlier self the functioning, finished piece of equipment. This has never happened; evidently there can be no time travel. By definition, time travel is a discovery that, if it could be made, *would already have been made.*" (36)

There is a limit to travel into the future. The first time Parsons takes a ride he accelerates all the way to this end point, where he encounters a plaque on monumental stone bearing instructions addressed to him for a more differentiated and calibrated use of the time device. As the novel closes, he sets out to set up this monument of instruction so that he can stay in the loop between different times across centuries, which function, however, as alternate presents. The limit in the future is also a warning label, after the fact, associated with efforts to change the past. If the past could be altered, wouldn't the aftershocks wipe out the present or future? "There is a general tendency for the vast, inertial flow to rectify itself. To seek a sort of level. It's almost impossible to affect the far future" (113). At the same time, the multiple returns from the future to the spot one is in with the past in the future turns each agent of history's redemption into "a ghost," "Haunting this spot, seeking a way to change the flow of past events" (128).

After he slips on the freeway onto death drive and then joins the eros club of resistance to what drives the future world as "pre-dead" (77), the coordinates of Parsons's lifetime consist of life with wife and children in twentieth-century California and another family pack of lifetime in the postapocalyptic future in California. In between, he inhabits the time loop back to sixteenth-century California, which is, however, so manipulated by the players in the future as to be the history of this future: at once entirely contrived after the fact and compatible with known history, which can be repeated, rehearsed, but not altered. Time travel only thickens the plot. Drake, for example, is Al Stenog, who goes back in time to ensure the transmission of what they call death but he calls life. "All the tampering had already been done," Parson reflects. "And, by going back, he would simply observe, not alter" (114). Each of the explorers who trailblazed colonization turns out to be "a man transplanted from the future, an imposter. Using equipment from the future" (128). "'It was a fatal blow to us to discover that the man whom we had selected as the epitome of the conquering whites was actually a man from our own time. Born in our culture, adhering to its values. Stenog went back into time to protect our culture. That is, the aspect of our culture that he had taken the job of supporting. Our tribe, as you know, does not follow their system of birth or death" (162).

Before Parsons enters the plot as substitute engenderer of a line rededicated to healing, the line Clothis was giving was postcolonial criticism as redemption of the terrible past. Mastery itself would have been overturned through his application of time travel: "And it would not have been mastery over slaves. The supremacy of one race over another. It would have been a natural relationship: *the future guiding the past*"(110). Won over to this cause, Parsons elects to go back to the moments of miscarriage of Clothis's time trip to protect the chief and ensure his plan of assassination of Drake. Rather than the specialized medical talent and training for which he was summoned, Parsons feels that he thus becomes a whole person. But it turns out that he was the one (in fulfillment of the Oedipal logic of whodunit) who, always already, killed Clothis as a result of the latter's misunderstanding and in his own defense. This killing is revalorized by his brood-to-come: to protect the new lineage of healing, the twins stab Clothis post-op with another synthetic arrow from their time in the future. Parsons went back again, into his recent past in the future, to do it himself—but he cannot deliberately commit murder. Thus his status as ancestral healer is secured as good as only the dead or Dad can be. That past is as much in the future as the future is in the past.

Jump

Time travel serves as outer limit of long distance. In other words or worlds, it offers a model for the mode of transportation—beyond distance—that interstellar travel necessarily requires. Gotthard Günther contemplates in another science fiction spread of three installments the meaning of motion that gets seconded or skipped in the space-warp notions of outer-space fiction and is already concept-limited to the paradox of Achilles's futile race against the tortoise. Logically, in terms of denumerable material units of distance, the tortoise must remain, since in constant motion, one point ahead of its pursuer. Achilles could catch up with and overtake the tortoise only if, like the mode of transport interstellar travel would entail, he could move with infinite speed and thus cover the distances between identifiable points in zero time. The race would be overcome or won—or one—from start to finish: "if there is a race—with finite speeds for the racers—no overtaking could ever take place" (I, 3). "The day of interstellar space travel will be here when Achilles overtakes the Tortoise in our thoughts as well as in nature. In other words, when we have unravelled the secret of motion" (I, 13).

We have always only been getting around infinity, which is left off limits as "unthinkable for human thought" (I, 4), while harnessing motion and seconding it as function of common sense. The space warp of science fiction designated a new frontier of motion in terms of something other than distance or time units. Günther turns to Cantor's golemesque introduction of "transfinite" numbers, set off and set apart by the first letter of the Hebrew alphabet, Aleph. To initiate interstellar travel the notion or law of relativity—that nothing can move in space faster than light—must be overcome as limitation. Cantor's "transfinite system of real numbers" "provides us with a picture of space which is allowed to shrink with-out limits" (II, 7). Distance must be shrinkwrapped. "Interstellar travel is, theoretically speaking, an undeniable certainty because the secret of motion is that it does not happen on the basis of quantized physical con-ditions where distances gradually pile up to almost immeasurable orders of magnitude" (II, 8). Günther quotes John W. Campbell's summary of Cantor's intervention: "a line of any length is equal to a line of any other length" (II, 9). Only in this way can we shoot for the stars—once matter proves to be as relative as space and time.

"In our present universe time has two directions. It stretches toward the past as well as toward the future. But in an empty universe time would have only one direction—toward the future. A past would not exist. The possibility of 'passing' time demands the presence of matter" (III, 7). But if you keep on adding matter, "then gravitation becomes stronger than expan-sion, and the universe will start to shrink" (III, 8). "Distance is a property of quantized matter but not of a continuum like space or time" (III, 10). Günther quotes from an Asimov novel *(The Stars Like Dust):* "It is only the Jump which makes interstellar travel possible" (III, 11).

Of the three components of the universe, two are continua (space and time) and one is regularly quantized. In the continuum, however, length of distance or interval is meaningless. A technique is required for the elimina-tion of the quantized component "by substituting non-quantized features" (III, 13). We are operating here according to the logic of inoculation or elimination by proxy. It is an artificial state of existence that the three components support. However, as artificial, this state of existence is based, bottom line, on an operation that needs to be raised to consciousness as the fourth basic component. We thus enter a redundancy that allows omis-sion of one of the four interchangeable components. (Oh my God! The universe is transference!) If we eliminate the operation or process (P), then "we have the universe just as it is without man's action" (III, 13). "Of course, P is still there as far as the objective world is concerned but it is distributed over MST." At the same time as the introduction of P as inde-pendent parameter, "as a fourth degree of freedom for action, we add human creative procedure to the natural events as a means of producing something which has not existed before." Thus the special case of space flight can be *conceived*—as swift as thought, the Faustian momentum of the creative act. "The addition of P permits us to eliminate the proper-ties of one of the other components by substitution." "This is possible because all human technique and action is two-valued" (III, 14). "If we add a fourth parameter we gain a technical dimension in which the laws of a three-parameter-world are not abolished but capable of modulation." Zeno could not define motion because it was neither a thing nor a nothing. "Motion is an event or process." The transfinite numbers do not apply to a three-parameter universe but call for a fourth parameter. Thus we ultimately return to and rearticulate the famous fourth dimension: through P the first three parameters can be rotated at will. For the properties of one parameter one can substitute those of the other three. The stars are as near as we think them.

Günther opens this third and final part—a parting of the ways with matter through one universal transference neurosis—with media technical prehistory, complete with totemic mascot:

In the pioneer days of wireless telegraphy the wife of one of the scientists engaged in developing the new invention was asked by her friends whether she could explain to them what her husband was doing. "Of course," she said, "my husband explained it to me just yesterday. Imagine a very long dog. His forelegs are in Washington when his hindlegs are still in New York. If you pinch this dog in New York, he will bark in Washington. Wireless telegraphy is exactly the same—but without dog."

Still

Dr. Johann Heinrich Jung, who in later years added to his name Stilling, which he borrowed from an uncle, as indication that he was happy or, in any event, tranquil in the prospect of the next life, published *Theory of the Doctrine of Ghosts (Theorie der Geisterkunde)* in 1808. Goethe had already published the first part of Jung-Stilling's memoirs, an act of ghost publishing that would appear to be the reverse of the occult act of plagiarism. We have the body of work that is reckoned as the onset of the *Entwicklungsroman,* the other novel of development, on Goethe's author-ship. But on this role Jung-Stilling kept on publishing, and late in his public career released his ghost treatise.

"Through magnetism, nervous illness, long-term states of concentra-tion, and through other hidden means a yet living person, if he otherwise has a natural inclination in this regard, can untie his soul to a certain higher or lesser degree from its bodily organization" (367). The untying is what Jung-Stilling designates in German as *Entwicklung,* the word for "devel-opment" that literally also means "to untie" or "to unwrap": the shroud from a mummy or a baby's diaper. But as the opening up of the liminal realm of earthbound spirits it identifies what is stowaway or repressed in the genre of *Entwicklungsroman* that Jung-Stilling unknowingly origi-nated under Goethe's direction.

Jung-Stilling essentially gives counsel on how to help ghosts find the path into the light of dissolution or redemption. He still has his work cut out for him. Good spirits will try to guide him in what to do to claim the Heavenly good. He must cleanse his imagination (and remembrance) of all images of his former life, indeed of the very love of earthly things (297).

It's hard on Mr. Between who's not yet been given a taste of Heaven and yet must give up the shadowy aftertaste of the world (298).

The spooky apparitions that divine justice must, in time, condemn hover on the border between this and the next world as cautionary examples for the living (332). The ghosts pull together their apparitions as shape to come from the same seed of resurrection hidden away inside the living (300–301). Yet the eternal love that sent us away from paradise also cut the open line to the spirit realm. If that had not happened, we would have gone to the Devil or become demons (377).

Jung-Stilling also counsels the living to prepare for a Christian death and thus go directly to the afterlife and not pass through ghostliness, the between state that hangs over life lost as though still depending on it. The powers of imagination increase after death but their realization at the same time proves empty, mere dusty projection (373). Transmigration of souls is a misguided belief. The spiritual realm has enough cleansing action without return trips to or through the life of the senses (374). You don't have to do time in Hades, dear reader. As long as you don't leave behind unreconciled blood debts and guilts or ruling earthly passions and sensual dependencies—you'll swing straight on up into the light (296). The suffering in Hades is homesickness for the world of senses irretrievably lost. It is hard after death to shake passions that have taken root in this world. You have to give these problems over to death here in this world (327).

Jung-Stilling addresses haunting as a therapeutic issue but not within a preexisting interpersonal or intrapsychic relationship. Thus none of his examples includes the return of an identified loved one, with whom one identifies. The reason ghosts hover about waiting to make contact with relative strangers, or stranger relatives who are generations removed from the ghost's former lifetime, is because they must find someone who is sensitive, attuned, and otherwise gifted in the matter of contact with the spiritual realm. But the spiritual realm itself must not be reduced to the range of haunting. It is the ghosts who compromise the spiritual realm by importing leftover imaginings or memories of materiality, corporeality, and worldliness for the purpose of getting their communications across (185). Thus ghosts are our doubles in a loss we, all together now, can't acknowledge or let go.

Jung-Stilling teaches by example or anecdote. According to the lengthy account written by the father, his son was regularly approached by a spook for help with unfinished business. Son like father responded with Christian

wariness. They enjoined the specter to turn to Christ, who alone can alleviate undead fixations on this world. In the course of negotiations, since
father and son can't exchange words with him, they communicate with
him in writing. Can he be an evil spirit from Hell if he enjoins them to help
him in the name of Christ? The spirit claims he will go straight to Heaven
upon completion of the task he has been hovering over now for centuries.
Father and son counter that nothing here can stop him: he right now can
go straight to Heaven. The son is the next in the spirit's own bloodline
to possess the intuitive capacity for contact. The ghost asks for delivery
from thoughts about hidden funds, which their excavation and proper
delegation to the heir will bring about. When the boy passes the spot of
the assignation he will not or cannot keep, he glimpses allegorical figures,
blackamoor and dog, on top of the buried treasure mound (238). The
spirit also rages when his contact person denies him aid: his fingers spark
fire and leave behind burn marks that are skeletal, like X-rays, not fleshed
out (like fingerprints) (244). It was the spirit's own leftover portion of
earthly superstition that supplied the special manifestations seen attending
or guarding the spot of treasure as well as the mission to retrieve it (259).

The pastor they bring in as consultant concludes, among other points,
that to demand of a Christian that which can be carried out only with
dubious conscience goes against love. Hence the ghost is to be rejected as
temptation to evil. Jung-Stilling begins his commentary. Since the spirit
can't speak, the son acted as medium, like a somnambulist. Rapport with
the spirit could come about only when the son was in a certain sense somnambulistic: the spirit then transferred to him his thoughts right into the
auditory organ, just as when one hears speech in dreams (257). Jung-Stilling
implicates himself toward the end of the treatise when he notes his own
inability to talk to the reader, even as he turns to the form or forum of direct
address. He, too (also like the father who provides the record of haunting),
can give only written instruction (312).

How did the ghost read the written communications? As a somnambulist reads what is placed over his heart. The spirit is tied to the aetherial
shell that influences us as light, electricity, galvanism, or magnetism. The
Hellish sparks were not Oriental metaphor but reality and truth (261).

The apparition is our brother and we are not indifferent to his fate. But
we must understand what our duties are—which is the purpose of Jung-
Stilling's instructions manual (288). Every news flash from the departed is
of no help to the living: except as the thoughtful reflection and self-collection

that follows the shock of ghost contact (290). Whosoever has the intuitive ability to receive spirit communications must not value this gift or inclination that is contrary to nature. If you do come to value the contact, the range of reception grows. Your health will then suffer the consequences and you yourself will enter the spirit realm way ahead of schedule (299). Ignore even their standard requests for proper burial or reburial! These are a person's errors set in the psychic rigor mortis of his last hours of life, which become like the Furies for his spirit after death. Those who died in their fleshly sentient condition remain dependent on their bodies, especially if they take with them superstitions about proper and improper burial (349). Then there is the ghost, like the famous apparition of the white lady, who appears before another kinsman dies to give him pause and cause to collect and prepare himself. But Jung-Stilling declares her mission aberrant, indeed against the order of God. Rarely if ever is anyone instructed by an apparition. Usually a frightful panic is the result (359–60).

Once the soul slips out of the body what we call space, body, extension, distance, et cetera no longer count. And yet the soul or spirit still remembers the world of the senses but no new data can be received, except secondhand from the newly departed. The basic forms of imagination, space and time, are eternal but emptied of what was sensed in this world. Instead the soul senses the objects of the spirit realm, also in terms of space and time, but with the big difference that everything is up close and nothing distant. Hence the soul can know what happens in the future (274).

Ghosts can disclose only the imminent future. But effective ghost seers must be pious and have the good Christian sense to consult only good spirits in securing the forecast (174–75). The atmosphere is populated mainly by evil spirits and spirits who are good only in a mediocre way, but in their illuminated shape, even though they are aberrant, they can seduce the living. The soul still positioned inside the "fleshly prison cell" is not yet able "to test the spirits" (370).

Since the turning point of Christ's victory over Satan there can be no evil spirit as such. But whether or not evil spirits still have great powers, evil individuals can without question summon these spirits by their natural disposition or by a developed intuitive capacity (190). Sometimes to foresee and guarantee the immediate future one must give them the worst (and fulfill a death wish, the primal groove Christianity's happy ending is stuck in). Therefore corpse seers, who never go beyond the range of death and burial, should be forbidden by law to disclose their visions (182).

The spirit between father and son could hardly have been keeping watch all those years waiting for the descendant with the talent to serve as medium. No, some recently deceased person who knew the young man must have informed the spirit. (The mother is doubly missing from the son and father household.)

And yet the spirit was wrong. He was able to find peace without the raising and transfer of the loot. The rest came with his turn, at last, to the redeemer while at the same time letting go of his dependency on earthly mothers, I mean matters. But the son was right, which is more to the point. The fear that rendered the ghost's descendant speechless must have come as aid from on high: thus son and father were scared away from contemplating the fulfilment of the specter's request (259).

The homesick ghost seeks to comfort himself by imagining all former treasures or pleasures. But these bygones be bygones and can be realized only as dream images without substance. This is the seed of Hell the ghostly dead carries inside. The specter still knows all the old songs. In 120 years he hasn't learned anything new. He was accordingly fixated on the transmission of the treasure to an heir, whose most proper qualification is that his intuitive capacity tunes in ghosts. The spirit was thus fortunate to run into such pious people in whom he could confide. Otherwise he would have grown unhappier still (266).

And yet souls that have to be led to the light don't attain the same bliss as do the souls that were prepped in life for direct ascension to Heaven. The balking point concerns the redeemer's declaration that the sin against the Holy Ghost will not be forgiven in this world or the next, while all other sins can be forgiven in the afterlife. Proximity to the one sin that doesn't ever go away is the gravest consequence of putting off ethical cleansing until the living end. The presumption involved in ghostly pursuit of earthbound missions comes very close to the sin against the Holy Ghost (266–67).

A craftsman and his apprentice enjoyed talking together about the state of souls after death and in particular about the restoration of all things lapsed into lifelessness. When the apprentice became consumptive, the craftsman tended him. He only asked that the young man return to him, if permitted, to assure him of the process of restoration in the beyond. After two such visits, the craftsman became convinced that it was presumptuous to seek contact with the dead (267–68).

A female ghost, who introduces herself as good, so not to fear, cannot yet enjoy the complete face-to-face with God because her husband wasn't willing to be reconciled with her before she died. He felt remorse over this refusal and passed on in true albeit weakened belief in Jesus Christ (318). Only someone from her future family can reconcile them. Her husband was jealous because she secretly met with a pious cavalier to discuss spiritual matters. The mediator she was looking for performed the reconciliation. But when he passed on it turns out he had stipulated that his body be buried in lime (323). Jung-Stilling points out it was all the woman's fault: at the latest when she noticed it riled her husband she should have cancelled the meetings with the cavalier. The result was that conflict kept both wife and husband in Hades, their imagination stuck on this earthly matter. Jung-Stilling once again enters the liminal border zone of direct address to the reader, which in the absence of speech renders this writing like communication with the other side, to counsel the reader, however, to beware of the writing on the wall of the crypt: reconcile yourself with everyone around you before you check out. Bad vibes don't fly heavenward but, like gravity in the grave, keep you earthbound (325). Thus the mediator in the couple's therapy made sure he would be buried in such a way that his body would decay on the spot he was in with his successfully reconciled spirit couple (331). What's worse than death is to be dead and yet not to be able to die.

In another instance of haunting, a ghost mimed a magic lantern show by holding up a sign resembling an image with a hole in the middle and putting his hand repeatedly through this opening. In this case the deceased had borrowed slides from a merchant to try them out but then his own mortality kept him from returning them to the owner (309). But these ghostly figurations out of twilight and mist by imagination alone give us a foretaste of the powers of imagination awaiting the soul in Heaven (315–16). Homesickness gets the spirit stuck in the door to other worlds. But don't fear the spirits or defend against them. Empathize with the predicament of their erring passage and give them directions not for finding and returning the magic lantern slides but to the address of the redeemer (316).

Hamlet had to ignore the possibility that his father's ghost was a demon from Hell to take down the injunction to remember the departed other as undead. Protestantism, which is what Jung-Stilling in this regard must also overlook, deemed the evidence of ghosts pulled up short before their purposive goals (Heaven or Hell) untrue or restricted in its provenance exclusively to that of evil spirits (221). But Jung-Stilling can cite scripture against this inflexible view of all haunting as evil in origin. He thus argues against his own religion at the border it shares with the Enlightenment or secularism. The secular view that denies the reality of specters thus admits its own decline. Is it possible to identify the ghost phenomenon as superstition? He aims to show instead how one can comport oneself both reasonably and as Christian in the course of keeping up with apparitions.

From the start Jung-Stilling rejects scientific enlightenment in spiritual matters. In our dealings with ghosts we must be guided by Providence via the Bible. The spectral realm, as proven as the existence of electrical matter and galvanism and their participation in and influence on embodied nature, transmits continued revelations of the truth of the Christian religion (185). He enlists the ghosts themselves in support of his rejection of the Enlightenment. There is too much evidence to dismiss the existence of ghosts as unfounded. Jung-Stilling is particularly amazed that irreligious types accede to the ghost evidence but can't follow Gospel. Surely ghosts prove that the soul is immortal. But, and thus the ambivalence begins, surely not!

The doctrine of *Seelenschlaf,* of the unconscious sleep of souls lasting until resurrection day, is not supported by scripture but only by prejudice that believes the soul needs the body to be effective at all. Magnetic experience and ghostly apparitions prove the contrary (376). Modern therapeutic reformattings of ghost seeing in terms of animal magnetism offer the secular mindset opportunities for expanding its finite horizon. The anti-Christian sensibility fears apparitions (and yet seeks them out) (311). What confusion awaits us when the living learn how to manipulate the in-between realms! Christianity sought to offer a stay to this application. But leave it to the Enlightenment to plunder these holy secrets (366). There are free spirits and mechanical philosophers who have undeniably been in contact with ghosts of dead persons they knew and yet they continued to doubt the continuity of life and self-consciousness, specifically the transfer in the Christian sense (360). In the German original there is a literal ambiguity: what's questionable to the philosophers could be either their own continued existence or that of the spirits.

A Wake

I think or rather I dream of Walter Benjamin.
— JACQUES DERRIDA, *Archive Fever*

Surprised — it always surprised him to find himself awake without
prior notice — he rose from the bed.
— PHILIP K. DICK, *Do Androids Dream of Electric Sheep?*

Exiting Kreuzlingen (a slight toss of the word salad gives you *Kreuzigung*
or "crucifixion") Warburg had determined to abandon art history and set
out on a new path marked by totemism, allegory, and the technological
relation. The technophobicity of the Serpent Ritual presentation belonged
to the fever pitch for release. Judging by Warburg's emphasis and by the
reluctance on Binswanger's part to let him go — since both moves reflect
the scale of valuation Binswanger applied to delusional systems, according to which technological delusions occupied the incurable living end of
psychosis — we get a good idea of how proximate Warburg's break chance
was to Schreber's own endopsychic allegory. But during his asylum stay
Warburg's students had established an institute in his name, which was
dedicated as research facility to serve the art-historical institution. During
his student embodiment (which he could not not acknowledge as transferential gift) Warburg pursued his Mnemosyne Project (with which only
Benjamin's *Passagen-Werk* suggests compatibility).

Consider the work of Panofsky as legacy of the student betrayal of
Warburg's commitment to a new field of study beyond the "border police"
of art-historical scholarship in his day and to this day. While Warburg's
post-Kreuzlingen work addressed the edges of context as destabilized and

unassumable, Panofsky incorporated a context, which was at the same time a reception, whereby his scholarship proved exemplarily accessible without appearing compromised (the definition of "academic"). Panofsky taught art history at Harvard. His essay "Et in Arcadia Ego" is admirable also or in particular as a teaching tool. As context and frame of reception he incorporated your average Harvard undergraduate and with this inward turn the standard of what Jacob Taubes referred to as American "half *Bildung*." The Harvard BA is the stopgap at the end of about two years of intensive culture training to which, on average, next to nothing is added in the time of his life. He also has little background (other than prep work) and none of that background that reaches back into childhood. He has no mother tongue. Made coterminous with American half *Bildung* already in Warburg's lifetime, art history was far removed from the melancholic brooding that watched over its prehistory and even further removed—mediocrity always cements the irreconcilability between opposites that it itself is—from the new frontier Benjamin and Warburg reached via their Schreber pardons and which they (plus a few others) alone cathect or occupy.

Can you see it? A way of theorizing here's looking at you, kids, that must operate in the tight spot we are in with economies of sacrifice or inoculation. That the problem with the control-release of violence through shocks or shots of inoculation must lead, on the sidelines of its efficacy, its tracks record, to new autoimmunity crises, was addressed by a select relay of thinkers who raised (in place of the interdisciplinary exchange of the password "Death") questions of or to the dead and undead. Consider, as Benjamin did, the surfeit of immunization that Karl Kraus foresaw as rendering impossible any encounter whatsoever with the reality shock of the new. As Benjamin underscored in his essay "Karl Kraus," the artistic intervention that Kraus championed drew itself up and onward within a frame of archaic, overcome, illicit references: cannibalism, plagiarism, incorporation. It is in the accidental overlap between the sound shapes of the German words for "dream" and "trauma"—*Traum* and *Trauma*—that the span of intervention that Benjamin sought to administer can begin to be discerned.

In "On the Program of the Coming Philosophy" ("Über das Programm der kommenden Philosophie"), Benjamin let roll four instances of identification in a row. The examples of preanimistic primal man who identifies himself with and as animals and of the soothsayer who receives the perceptions of others as his own are on the level with his own coming philosophy of media. While the madman who is said to identify with objects of his perception limps along inside philosophical anthropology—and is overtaken on the scale of madness by Benjamin's next example of the patient who identifies his bodily pains not as his own but as originating in other creatures—the force of exemplification shows that Benjamin in 1912 is a reader of anthropology (both as the modern science Freud analyzed in *Totem and Taboo* and as philosophy's miscellaneous drawer) and the occult. In the receiving area of modern anthropology, Benjamin, Freud, and Warburg renewed vows with the mimetic relation.

According to Benjamin, mimeticism, though child's play, reflects the impulse not only to imitate and identify but also to conceive the whole world as governed by a system of correspondences or nonsensuous similarities (which are based on the name as the primal form and forum of language). Like Warburg, like Benjamin: astrology is the correspondences school. According to Warburg, our cognitive oscillation moves time and again between imagistic and semiotic positing of origins or causes. Inflationary imagery leads to ascendancy of mathematics. The significance of astrology derives from this span of to and fro. In the meantime disconnected abstractions supply our frame of reference. The doctrine of astrological sympathies fortified the hangover of a primitive metaphysics of occult affinity.

Ambiguity is the medium of modernity's incessant citation or summoning of primeval history. Ambiguity supplies the image of dialectics standing still, which is also a dream image out of primal time. The commodity is this dream image ready-made. The skewer passing through dream, dialectics, commodification, prehistory, and ambivalence is modern allegory still standing.

Charles Baudelaire's ultimate understanding of allegory inhabits the tension span between the distant memory of mimetic experience or *Erfahrung* and the degraded *Erlebnis* of modernity. (In German, *modern*, meaning "modern," is also the verb meaning "to decay.") The "correspondances" *chez* Baudelaire are the key to late allegory, in which *Andenken* replaces the corpse or *Leiche*. In the *Origin* book the measure of the symbol's withdrawal is given finally as the extinction of the eidos, the dissipation or passing away of the *Gleichnis*. The *Leiche* at the allegorical art of postsymbolic figuration is raised to the power of remembrance, but in the border zone of commodification: *Andenken*, for example, also means "souvenir." The basis of the allegorization Benjamin considers in Baudelaire is the destructiveness of mass consumerism.

Benjamin repeatedly underscores that the "correspondences" were lifted from the occult corpus of Immanuel Swedenborg.

In the course of analyzing the possibility of relations with spirits, as exemplified in particular within Emanuel Swedenborg's occult writings, Immanuel Kant arrives, like Columbus, in another place, that of metaphysical knowledge of the limits of human reason, which neither bend nor give way before the questions of ghosts as of life after death. Although Kant suggests that the soul is a completely different conception than the spirit, since the latter is of this world and the former, like God, is out of it, he also admits that we tend to believe in ghost seers because we hope that there will be another life of the soul after death. Ghost seers cannot keep imagination and reality apart. And yet to go just one step further and grant imagination the status of reality is simply error or surely mental illness.

With Kant, Swedenborg falls through the cracks of knowledge that only knows what it knows, while with Karl Jaspers the case of Swedenborg the schizophrenic must be read through the cracks that are already also "inside" him. Jaspers identifies the various accounts of the onset of Swedenborg's occult beliefs (following a distinguished career as natural scientist) as on the hallucinatory setting. In one account he started seeing on the screen of his suddenly darkened eyesight reptilian animals writhing around all over the floor. This pattern recognition soon gave way to large-scale variations parading animals past him worthy of *Fantasia*. The intensified darkness parted to let a man address him directly. Back home the man was back: he was the Lord Almighty with big plans for Swedenborg, who followed suit, severing his ties to worldly scholarship and science and devoting himself instead exclusively to spiritual matters, in the course of which he received instruction that he was to pass on (111–12). When he also kept on making out "the Word" behind or above all inscription, Jaspers is reminded of the mentally ill who typically find hidden meanings in newspaper ads, which they then round up as coherent system (116). Swedenborg fits the low-maintenance type of schizophrenic often found at the center of sect-like activities but with no other psychotics around. According to Jaspers, such a schizophrenic could convince one hundred healthy people to follow him before he succeeded in convincing even one other crazy person (109).

By the end of his exercise, Kant puts the whole ghostly matter as far-flung piece of metaphysics to the side as finished: he will have nothing more to do with it. But he declares the reader of ghost chronicles free to judge for himself.

Someone had to rewrite Kant's "Dreams of a Ghost-Seer" ("Träume der Geisterkunde"). Schopenhauer's "Essay on Seeing Ghosts" ("Versuch über das Geistersehn und was damit zusammenhängt") identifies itself as the one. This lineage of philosophical investigations into occult claims passes through Freud's *Interpretation of Dreams* with the dream side turned outward (and the ghost side turned inward).[1] Schopenhauer begins with the dead in our dreams (280). Whereas Freud will cite the example of the deceased father making a comeback in your dreams because he doesn't know that he's dead, Schopenhauer's examples place the forgetting that the dead are dead in the court of the dreamer. Because such a breakdown of memory can happen in dreams, the dream is tantamount to a brief bout of psychosis *(Wahnsinn)* (281).

Schopenhauer opens up possibilities that Kant foreclosed. Thus he turns to Goethe's Urphänomen to draw a line between experience or *Erfahrung*, as a justifiable mode of inquiry, and the inexplicable nature of the phenomenon experienced. It's related to what Freud would designate as a metapsychological fact (of life), which emerges out of the (experience of the) transference. Such a fact or phenomenon, then, is that we can see and hear without perceiving anything external. What the Scots call second sight finds its justification in dreaming. Thus Schopenhauer designates as the "dream sense organ" *(Traumorgan)* the alternative to our external sense organization. Through the dream sense organ a connection or communication directly to the brain without the mediation of the senses is possible (289).

Somnambulists are most clairvoyant when deeply asleep (290). What we see in our dreams is really there as dream perception. Thus the German word for perceiving, *Wahrnehmen*, which separates out as "true" and "taking," models Schopenhauer's neologism *Wahrträumen*, "true dreaming," perceiving through the *Traumorgan* (291). And yet to see with the body, as somnambulists claim to be able to do as gut or chest feeling, specifically through the *Herzgrube* (the "hollow" in the chest over the "heart"), is as impossible as making a daguerreotype in an open camera obscura (297).

The only way to explain something like magnetic influence, therefore, is via Schopenhauer's own equation of body and will (according to which the body is the image of the will arising in the brain) (299). Somnambulists who can see the future at a steady rate or state appear to Schopenhauer to have reached that hidden mechanism or source where that which is seen externally, that is, "through the optical glass 'time,'" as coming in the future is already now and present (318–19).

Animal magnetism, sympathetic cures, magic, second sight, prophetic dreams, seeing ghosts, and all kinds of vision are related manifestations, "branches of one trunk," and give clear indication of there being a "nexus of beings that rests on another order of things than does nature, which has as its basis the laws of space, time, and causality" (319). The agent in all such phenomena is the will, which thus identifies itself as the *Ding an sich*. Schopenhauer cites Szapary, a known *magnitiseur* who, in his study of animal magnetism, was inspired by this truth, though independently of Schopenhauer's or any other philosophy. Via his empirical or medial method, Szapary turns to the will as the bottom line of all corporeal and spiritual life (321). Philosophically, animal magnetism is the greatest discovery ever: "it is truly practical metaphysics" (323).

While it seems congruent to postulate an open mind among the living, once the dead are included we face a contradiction in the underlying division between material and immaterial realms. Schopenhauer turns to the indexical and the mediatic registers to motivate reproduction of images of the dead. It is fairly certain, Schopenhauer admits with care, that visions that bring the past, namely the shapes of formerly living persons, before the dream sense organ, but in the waking state, can be occasioned by the proximity of *Überreste der Leichen* ("leftovers of the corpses") of the same (339). That's why spooks are zoning-restricted to certain places, like haunted houses. Retrospective second sight, as inexplicable experience or *Erfahrung*, serves, then, as *Urphänomen*. To have more than one *Urphänomen* means you can start stacking them until there is only one, as also happened, for example, when mineral magnetism was derived from electricity (341). As with the doctrine of electricity, then, Schopenhauer proposes organizing manifold phenomena around one completely inexplicable experience or *Urphänomen,* namely retrospective second sight or *rückwärtsgekehrte Deuteroskopie* (346).

The ability to perceive events in the "night of the future" is reversed in the case of seeing ghosts, though the reversal of projection becomes less inexplicable when accompanied by material influence, by *Überreste* or leftovers, like the clothes of the deceased (342). But similarly, when a clairvoyant somnambulist (as documented in Justinus Kerner's book) seeks to ascertain the health of an absent but living person, a corporeal connection, a piece of cloth worn by the patient on her body or a lock of her hair, is required to establish long-distance rapport. Already the ancients hid and sought the dead (or undead) in the realm of shadows. One doesn't see the departed himself but rather his shadow or image, which arises in the dream sense organ on account of some leftover, a trace that's left behind. It has the reality of the image of someone who sees himself or is seen by others in the place where he is not (343). Thus the "dumb shew" of ghosts Schopenhauer cites or summons joins the doubling procession folding out of the mirror or psyche. But the dumb show is a tomb show and the mirror opens onto the inverted world of the dead (or undead). And yet the vestigial connection doesn't transfer. Thus the mirror image is indexical, like every image that through reversal can never again be superimposed onto the original. Thus the seemingly objective indexical occasions for haunting play the same role in recognizing the departed through the medium of the dream sense organ that in normal thought the *nexus idearum* plays in relation to objects of thought (347). As long as the person is still living there is, for Schopenhauer, no difficulty in accepting transfer of thoughts, as when the dying appear to their nearest and dearest, often several at once, before departing (348). The will is effective in the live transmission of apparitions of the still living (351). Schopenhauer thus reformulates the indexical proof of haunting, again with care. With regard to the *Doppelgänger* sent, often unwittingly, by absent but living persons as proxy to stand before another person as apparition or vision Schopenhauer states that this transmission does not necessarily require or presuppose an immediate real presence. The indexical *requirement,* which rests on the point of view of Spiritualism instead of on that of Idealism (which is where Schopenhauer was all along heading), is the basic flaw in every theory of haunting to date. It is the same flaw inherent in the assumption that man consists of two radically different substances, a material one, the body, and an immaterial one, the so-called soul (351). After separation in death, the material side supposedly continues to appear in spirit just the same. If we recognize an inner being of man as untouched by death and existing outside time and space, then any influence on the living could be arranged only via many, many mediations, all on the live side, with the result that it would be hard to determine how much of the influence was really the input/output of the deceased (367).

This flexibility allowed in the theory or construction of the ghost, as gap of exception to the indexical or technical series of its being, is also the hole in the argument through which all evidence of the extra senses empties out. While Schopenhauer is willing to entertain as hypothesis that the reversal of the vibration of brain fibers has ultimate bearing on *Urphänomen* second sight (356), the indexical proof of ghostliness, by contrast, runs counter(intuitive) to the gesture and frame of the debate on seeing or influencing at a distance, according to which the evidence or experience is never charged with being not true but rather not possible (362). Whatever the experience of ghostliness may signify, this meaning must go with the flow of the relativity of the difference between objectivity and subjectivity (359).

Where there's will there's a way to communicate immediately and at a distance with the will of another. The organism itself is but the image of the will in the brain (364–65). The underlying identity of the *Ding an sich* in a world of appearances accommodates the often observed contagiousness of visions, second sight, and ghost sightings (366). You can think in my brain while yours sleeps deeply, Schopenhauer offers, because the *Ding an sich* is the same in all beings. To the extent that will is *Ding an sich*, the will cannot be destroyed through death (367). The will alone is metaphysical (369).

But in German as in English one speaks of the last will as testament, which signs off in the groove or grave of the indexical relation. Where Freud reinscribed the dream sense organ or *Traumorgan* as trauma organ, Nietzsche reintroduced the Eternal Return of the Same as the indexical burial grounding of the will (as will to power). In his reflections on ghost seeing, Schopenhauer includes, almost as drop scene, the opinion of some young priest as doubly laughable, one, for coming from England, the land where one earns a "living," and, two, for his phobic view of magnetism, which Schopenhauer, just the same, repeats: whosoever believes in animal magnetism cannot believe in God (324). This brief encapsulation of the question of God's existence, taken down at the priest's word to ward off insular resistance to occult research (and continental philosophy), admits secularization, which, like Schreber's delusional system, must take foreground or background to other belief systems that can thus be acknowledged, even if one doesn't subscribe to them, as equally real or extant. The scar tissue of this healing of the rift between the returning ego and the host of miraculated bystanders leaves behind the psychic dotted line along which Dick's signature alternate present realities fold out as conceivable.

A month before Lou Salomé left Nietzsche, never to return, they attended a séance together in Leipzig presided over by a medium, whom the astrophysicist Zöllner had found satisfactory (in Hagen, *Radio Schreber,* 43, n. 117). In preparation for the experience Nietzsche wrote down reflections "On the Explanation of the So-called 'Spiritist Manifestations'" ("Zur Erklärung der sogenannten 'spiritistischen Erscheinungen'"). Nietzsche projected a theoretical grid, indexical or analogical, wired through both the "unconscious" and electricity, whereby the occult transmissions could be conceived. Nietzsche finds the transference of thought between persons no weirder than the transmission, in the course of stumbling, from brain to foot in one body. Even a deceptive medium is mediated by the unconscious: "What happens to or through us is essentially unconscious, and the rogue is unconsciously a hundred times more and more often rogue than he is consciously." That he was in the end disappointed by the séance doesn't cancel his attempt to grasp communication with ghosts from within the interdisciplinary mix that was his lab space at the time for exploring and shoring up the Eternal Return of the Same as scientific doctrine. "The belief in reunion with the dead is the precondition of Spiritism. It is a kind of free thinking. Truly pious persons don't require this belief." That Lou Salomé, Nietzsche's intended heiress to his doctrine of Eternal Return, was dispatched shortly after the occult interlude supports her unwitting/structural role as link, more specifically as the *fort/da* bouncing ball, between Nietzsche and Freud, between Eternal Return and repetition compulsion (and so on).[2] A relationship to or through Schopenhauer can now be added to this transmission. On its sidelines, which his own trajectory of reception of Freud occupies or cathects, Benjamin allegorizes and remediatizes the unprovable experience of return of the dead.

The "correspondences" Benjamin holds with Baudelaire hold fast to a concept of *Erfahrung,* which contains cultic elements. Their memorial function operates in a preserve of early cultic experience. The "correspondences," as data of remembrance, are not historically but rather prehistorically given. Thus the term, translated into German, fully enters Benjamin's lexicon at the high point of articulation of endopsychic allegory where the *Korrespondenzen* obtaining between the world of modern technology and the archaic symbolic world of mythology meet and cross over (*Passagen-Werk,* 576).

Once upon a time, human experience—*Erfahrung*—had not yet been transformed into *Erlebnis* (the mediation or building blockage of mimetic assimilation). Their independence in theory was secured by entering prehistory and the state of dreaming into the equation. Just like a natural phenomenon, technologization put Europe to sleep, to dream, as its "time" or era within which mythic powers reemerged.

Even though perception is always mediated, the shocks of the new, in particular at the forefront of urban massification, heighten the process of screening. A good defense straddles the fence between *Erfahrung* and *Erlebnis*—however only ultimately to block the former and fulfill the concept of the latter. Benjamin's model of our lateral way of seeing histo-ricizes Freud's defense contract with perception.

According to its syndication in Freud's thoughts—which Kafka on his own sets into play most prominently via the traveling explorer in his story "In the Penal Colony," who is, not only etymologically, the agent of *Erfahrung*—the mere receptivity of *Erfahrung* glances along the world of obser-vation like a traveling shot. Both Kafka and Freud, though in very different doses and from contrary provenances, had already supplied testing as the "activity" or immersion of this open-headed passivity.

Benjamin finds the ultimate test site, which he otherwise transports to the film studio as its original setting up, within a more primal-time cor-respondence between the distraction or dissemination before the screen and the moment of awakening. "There is one completely unique experi-ence of dialectics. The determining, drastic experience that contradicts all makeshift universality of becoming and proves all apparent development to be its eminently composed dialectical reversal is the moment of awak-ening from the dream state" (*Passagen-Werk*, 1006). Only thus, through the breaking up of the connection between dreaming and waking states, can one "break through into the heart of discarded things in order to interpret the contours of the banal as picture puzzles *[Vexierbilder]*. . . . Psychoanalysis has already uncovered picture puzzles as schemata of the dream work. We however are with such certainty on the track less of the soul than of the things. We seek the totem tree of objects in the thicket of primal history" (281).

Baudelaire sought to give the lived or throwaway experience of moder-nity the weight and wait of *Erfahrung*. Going on extinction, the flâneur occupies the threshold of his endangered status. Urban existence—the crowd—is the veil, the lure, drawing the modern allegorist onward. It is his Eternal Feminine at the front of the chorus line that proclaims tran-sience (as well as, according to Nietzsche, immutability) but as *Gleichnis*. In allegory, *Gleichnis geht ein:* it perishes and enters the allegorical process of brooding immersion. "The last journey of the *flâneur*" or late allegorist is through death to the new. While allegory can be seen to offer a stay to novelty's PR campaigns, allegory also shares a continuum with novelty, which is the former's update. "The illusion of novelty is reflected . . . in the illusion of perpetual sameness" ("Central Park," 171).

The Eternal Recurrence of the Same as sign of the times joins the com-modity on the assembly line along which allegory too can return. Thus only in eternity could a continuity shot of recurrence get past or outlast the catastrophe. The doctrine, Benjamin also points out, projects as imminent/immanent prospects in the technologization of biological reproduction ("Central Park," 182). What is returning when the same returns? That which returns, those who return, are the dead. That's where our dead are, in the eternal return of the same. The concluding lines dance of the Eternal Feminine rings in the eternal return of the same. Faust is the designated death denier. He never mourns; he doesn't really even die. In the course of the tragedy the women in his life first do the dying for him, and then they do the mourning for him.

Benjamin says: Baudelaire, like the surgeon, unlike the Baroque allegorist, does not come to a full stop before the corpse as primal allegory but knows the corpse inside out. The interior of the "same," of *Gleiche,* its skeleton, *Gestell,* or X-ray, is *Leiche.*[3] Allegorically speaking, it is the *Leiche* or corpse that returns in or as the *Gleiche,* "the same." I suppose it is God's corpse. But there are so many corpses that would be closer to home. If the recent past is that immediate context that we all inhabit and tend to repress, then who but the recently departed could be returning as the returning same or corpse. The immediate or imminent future (in which they return) is, as one of Dick's precogs can testify, a "static" display of known possible futures. While the immediate future cannot be known for sure, much that comes our way in the mode of imminence is recognizable or will be recognizable as déjà vu.

Spätwerk

Among the dreams Adorno recorded for his unfinished dream book, there is one that turns up the contrast with the daytime recording of seemingly resolved and remembered transference proceedings. It's a school dream about a school day. But the high school is now fifty years old and former student Adorno has been invited to contribute to the *Festschrift* thus occasioned. In his dreams the musical direction of the high school is ceremoniously transferred to him. That the transference is where the heat still is becomes evident via the physical return of his "repulsive" music teacher, who honors him. "Afterwards a grand gala ball was held. I danced there with a huge yellow-brown hound—in my childhood such a hound dog played an important role. He walked upright and wore a frock coat. I followed the hound's lead completely and, though I am otherwise without any talent whatsoever for dancing, I had the feeling that for the first time in my life I could dance, sure-footed and uninhibited. Occasionally we kissed, the dog and I. Woke up highly satisfied." (mid-September 1958, *Traumprotokolle*, 70).

In his "Fichus" lecture (held in Frankfurt on the occasion of his receipt of the Adorno Prize in 2001) Derrida contemplated his "dream" of a book he wished to compose in seven interminable chapters in which he would explore and establish his relationship to Adorno, Benjamin, and the Frankfurt School. "The seven chapters of this history, of which I dream, are already writing themselves, of this I am confident. What we today share with one another, testifies to it without doubt." Derrida attends carefully to the many factors one most likely might at first anticipate as separating deconstruction from the Frankfurt School. By the third chapter, however, we arrive at a plan for establishing common ground, namely the interest in psychoanalysis that Derrida shared with Adorno and Benjamin. But it is not until chapter 7 that there appears a direct hit of proximity or continuity between Derrida and Adorno.

This chapter proposal doubles as the plan for Derrida's *Spätwerk*.

Now I come to the chapter that I would take the greatest pleasure in writing, because it would open a path that is the least traveled, if it has even been opened yet, but which, it seems to me, counts among the most significant for a future reading of Adorno. It concerns that which one designates with a general singular noun, something that always shocks me anew, as the animal. As though there were only one. Beginning with scattered sketches or references . . . I would attempt to show . . . that we are dealing here with premises that must be unfolded with great care, indeed with the appearance at least of a thinking and acting revolution of which we are in great need in living together with those other living beings called animals. Adorno recognized that this new critical ecology (I would prefer to speak of it as "deconstructive") would need to confront two fearsome powers that at times are opposed to each other, at other times stand allied.

On one side the most powerful idealist and humanist tradition of philosophy. "Human domination of nature," Adorno clarifies, "is directed against animals. . . . Animals play virtually the same role for the idealist system that the Jews play for the fascist system." The animals would be the Jews of the idealists, who thus would be nothing other than virtual fascists. Fascism begins when one verbally abuses an animal, indeed the animal in man. To scold the animal in man or "abusively call man an animal—that is genuine idealism." Twice Adorno speaks of "schimpfen" [to scold, abuse verbally, name call, insult].

On the other side, however, . . . one would need to confront the ideology that conceals itself behind the dubious interest that in turn, on occasion all the way to vegetarianism, the fascists, the Nazis and their Führer seemed to take in animals.[1]

The last time I saw Derrida was my first opportunity to introduce my dog Elli to him. I like to think that Elli was the first animal to sit in his public audience. During the closing panel discussion, Derrida asked several times and with emphasis where Elli was in the audience; he wanted to know that she was there; he wondered whether she was listening or whether she would perhaps respond. In the course of the discussion Derrida underscored that he had all along sought to reinscribe the response, the call, responsibility, in short all the figures in philosophical discourse exclusive to human speech, as effects of the trace whereby all of the above would be open to animals, too.

In 1997 at Cerisy Derrida lectured for days on "the autobiographical animal" (the title of the conference, which was devoted to his work). Derrida read the philosophical oppositions separating animal and man—those between reaction and response, or between first-grade deception and the deception that is deceptively deceptive—as defensive attempts to disown in each case a fundamental undecidability. Derrida could moreover pull out from between the lines, whether in Descartes or in Lacan, the regular sideline effect of philosophical animal testing, according to which the attempt to establish a fundamental distinction between animal and man pulls up short before a supplementary distinction that places the animal suddenly nearer to God than thee (or humanity). Thus reading with Lacan but against Lacan's philosophical specism, Derrida identified a certain "*divinanimalité*" as that which meets all the conditions of an otherness that for Lacan, too, must remain irreducible to contact with or via the interpersonal columns. If we are indeed able to break with the imaginary duel of mirror resemblance, then the other cannot be our fellow man, partner, or sibling. Therefore the symbolic father and the law occupy interchangeable places with the animal.

In one of the tail-end sections of *Dialectic of Enlightenment* Max Horkheimer and Theodor Adorno pursue the reversal of the philosophical topos of man versus animal by considering behavioral psychology as symptom of the antithesis topping off the topos at each station of the crossing out of animal existence. "The antithesis is still accepted today. The behaviorists only appear to have forgotten it. The fact that they apply to humans the same formulas and findings that, without restraint, they force from defenseless animals in their nauseating physiological laboratories stresses the contrast quite adroitly. The conclusion they draw from mutilated bodies applies not to animals in the free state but to man as he is today. It shows that because he does injury to animals, he and he alone in all creation voluntarily functions as mechanically, as blindly and automatically as the twitching limbs of the victim which the specialist knows how to turn to account" (245). But the highly visible process whereby unreasoning creatures have thus encountered reason, beginning with the primeval hunt, "conceals the invisible from the executioners—existence denied the light of reason, animal existence itself." Horkheimer and Adorno reclaim this existence as life governed by mental impulses, the proper topic of psychology, which can explain man only in his disordered state. What has been identified as "animal psychology," however, loses itself and its purpose in its mazes and traps: "it is to the animal alone that psychology can turn to discuss and conceive the soul or psyche."[2]

In the corner of every encampment on the frontier of his thought's estrangement from the behaviorism of American consensus or from the jargon of authenticity we find in Adorno the relationship to the animal, often the child's relationship to or through the "death" of the animal. It is this "death" that Auschwitz could not cancel. Roadkill throws up "first" contact with finitude denied or otherwise revalorized in the sensibility of fairy tales. In *Minima Moralia: Reflections from Damaged Life (Minima Moralia: Reflexionen aus dem beschädigten Leben)*, Adorno recalls, from childhood, a folk song in which the topsy-turvy world stops short of reversal and falls down between death and life. A kind of happiness, too, is possible in this second example under the title "Regressions":

As long as I have been able to think, I have derived happiness from the song "Between the Mountain and the Deep, Deep Vale": about the two rabbits who, regaling themselves on the grass, were shot down by the hunter, and, on realizing that they were still alive, made off in haste. But only later did I understand the moral of the story: reason can only endure in despair and extremity; it needs absurdity, in order not to fall victim to objective madness. One ought to follow the example of the two rabbits; when the shot comes, fall down foolishly, half-dead with fright, collect your wits and then, if you still have the breath, show a clean pair of heels. The capacity for fear and for happiness are the same, the unrestricted openness to experience amounting to self-abandonment in which the vanquished rediscovers himself. What would happiness be that was not measured by the immeasurable grief at what is? For the world is deeply ailing. He who cautiously adapts to it by this very act shared in its madness, while the eccentric alone would stand his ground and bid it rave no more. He alone could pause to think on the illusoriness of disaster, the "unreality of despair," and realize not merely that he is still alive but that there is still life. The ruse of the dazed rabbits redeems, with them even the hunter, whose guilt they steal. (266)

In *The Open: Man and Animal*,[3] Giorgio Agamben summons Benjamin to the rescue. In stretches of Heidegger that Derrida already dog-eared (in *Of Spirit*) as overdetermining the animal, via a series of untenable contrasts with man, to take up the unique position of undermining (in theory) the implementation of the deconstruction of ontology begun in *Sein und Zeit,* Agamben comes up with two or three conclusions, two by Heidegger (though by two I mean, of course, the most interminable number you will ever know) and one by Benjamin, which, according to Agamben, lies resolutely, incongruously outside the tradition Heidegger is thinking through. Agamben's close reading of Heidegger on man and animal (in a nihilistic setting of surprise scientific influence, that of Jakob von Uexküll) issues in the flat line that bare life is the last stand or understanding of man and animal—of man as animal—in the only context left for our consideration of the social relation, that of Foucault's biopolitics. But the nonmachinic android Dick introduced at this juncture as figment of our Teen Age, revalorizes bare life as electro cute and thus issues with the group psychology, as Nietzsche did in his detours through Christianity, the extended warranty of legibility and possibility. Without animal access or in circumvention of the totemic work of mourning, the rebel androids nevertheless forge their in-group bond experimentally out of live or life transmissions: drugs, disease, and media.

In the close quarters given "rescue" between "saving" and "redemption," Agamben sends Benjamin to head the Heidegger reading off at its impasse by conjuring up a "rescued night" *(gerettete Nacht)* or (via the German etymon of *Nacht, Nichts*) "rescued nothingness." Of course this night or nothingness can't be saved or redeemed, but it does qualify for allegorical rescue. Agamben thus gives Benjamin the last word as outside chance of pulling up short before "the nothing," even though or especially because Benjamin is dead set up as outgunned by the momentum and weight of the Heidegger reading or, rather, by the dynamic of its Before and After, its history. But in giving Heidegger the floor Agamben can't floor it anymore, but must spell out the in-appropriation of the animal that Heidegger saw himself up against. Thus there is an extra or supplemental alternative, the not-offered one, the one avoided or denied (or *vermieden,* which Derrida in *Of Spirit* reads as Heidegger's unconscious gesture). In *The Open* it is up to Heidegger to admit the Freudian tradition of contemplation of man and animal (which incorporates Darwin and was inherited by the Frankfurt School, the station stop missing from Agamben's itinerary of Benjamin's thought). "At work in both Nietzsche and Rilke is that oblivion of being 'which lies at the foundation of the biologism of the nineteenth century and of psychoanalysis' and whose ultimate consequence is 'a monstrous anthropomorphization of . . . the animal and a corresponding animalization of man'" (58). Rilke's poetic word thus "falls short of a 'decision capable of founding history,' and is constantly exposed to the risk of 'an unlimited and groundless anthropomorphization of the animal,' which even places the animal above man and in a certain way makes a 'superman' of it" (59).

When trying to hold onto Agamben for bare life it's easy to skip to the modern section of his reading, the horizon of his interpretation of vital signs. The early arcane section is, in vertical contrast, selected from the stockpile of the venerable unread. And yet the piled up preamble contains the germ of what should be Agamben's "own" notion of bare life as life unsuitable for sacrifice. The horizon or continuity of reading in the longer run of the modern part (which is, any way, one big jump cut) is the effect of rapid intercuts. In fact "bare life" is buoyed up amidst cosignatories to a close reading that never took place. Quality reading time with one corpus belongs, presumably, to development. In production, according to the cuts we are served, it is Agamben's own contribution of sometimes a great notion that is the continuity shot. The back-and-forth among Carl Schmitt, Heidegger, Foucault, and Benjamin wraps around this notion the mantle of the reworked tradition of contemporary theory. But it's a wrap. Like Paul de Man, like Agamben: resistance to psychoanalysis (and thus to the transferential setting) is strapped to parallel tracks of disavowal of the technical settings of arguments summoned to underwrite the introduction of "homo sacer" as Everyman (for himself). The technical frame just the same returns as internalized double feature of Agamben's style of screening entire traditions, which pass before our eyes exclusively as editing effect.

The double tracking of transference and media technologization is on location with the totem animal. Animal sacrifice is not considered in *Homo Sacer*. And yet, as Warburg underscores in "The Serpent Ritual" as main motivation for the revaluation of sacrifice that commences with the Old Testament, originally (in ancient Egypt for example) human sacrifice was made to animal deities (whose living delegates, whole ibis colonies, were granted protected existence). *The Open* thus gives animals a hearing or clearing supplemental to their absence in *Homo Sacer*.

Agamben's notion of bare life literally applies to Kafka's "The Metamorphosis." The *Ungeziefer* into which Gregor Samsa finds himself transformed upon awakening spells out, etymologically, the condition or status of "the unclean animal not suited for sacrifice" (Corngold, *The Commentators' Despair*, 10). Stanley Corngold reads the continued metamorphosis of Gregor as allegorical stations of crossing over and out: He dies in time for the resurrection of Christ. But it is not so much that his sacrifice has not been accepted; rather the symbol is metamorphically and metaphorically untenable in writing that aims for (or falls short of) autonomy. Thus Gregor's ultimate transformation into a decorporealized translucent page of parchment is trashed and repressed.

The story closes—and Kafka would in time find the concluding paragraphs loathsome—with the vital signs of the surviving family members on a second wind rising up from evacuation of the wound of Gregor's kinship. One of the properties of Gregor's near-miss assignation with the Christ symbol is the apple, thrown at him by his father, which catches him in the back and, festering there, allows the family to treat him as horror-proofed and invalid-ated. The *Ungeziefer* slithers through the condemned site of formerly functional belief systems.

Kafka's animals inhabit the allegory of writing (of being writing). Kafka's libidinal investment in being writing or being literature carries over into Deleuze and Guattari's "becoming-animal." Indeed D and G's monograph on Kafka is by far their best effort, which does not lend its excellence to application. The main reason for the enigmatic force of the D and G reading as success story lies in the excluded proximity to Benjamin, whose interlinear reading of Kafka's animals remains powerfully implicit.

Let the Dead Be

"Goodbye, sweet Tulip," I would say and, returning to her, raise
the pretty disconsolate head that drooped so heavily in my hands,
and kiss her on the forehead. Then I would slip out into the darkness of Witchball Lane. But the moment the door had closed
behind me she would glide back into our bedroom, which was on
the front of the bungalow, and rearing up on her hind legs at the
window, push aside the curtains with her nose and watch me pass.
This was the last I would see of her for five days, her gray face, like
a ghost's face, at the window, watching me pass.

—J. R. ACKERLEY, *My Dog Tulip*

As Binswanger comes close to working through a phenomenology of the
psychotherapeutic setting toward a social ontology based on Heidegger's
ontology—in 1945—he turns to von Uexküll's animals. Mankind inhabits countless worlds while holding a world in common. But the psychotic,
in forgoing the common world, fits the worlds within worlds von Uexküll
claims for the animals. Psychiatry wasted time assessing the divergence
between delusional systems and the common world. Instead we must follow
Freud and focus on the private world of the psychotic on its own terms.

Just as we would say that it is not possible to describe the psychosis of a person if
one has not first thoroughly traversed his worlds, just so von Uexküll says: "It is not
possible to describe the biology of an animal if one has not completely circumscribed
the circles of its function." And as we would say furthermore: therefore one is justified to assume as many worlds as there are psychotics, von Uexküll says: "Therefore
one is fully justified to assume as many surrounding worlds as there are animals."
(Binswanger, "Über die daseinsanalytische Forschungsrichtung," 237)

To communicate with these radically singular worlds, those of psychotics as of animals, is already to be in a relationship of commemoration. In Rollo May's edited collection, which included the case study of Ellen West, we also find this position paper on *Dasein*-analytical research. "The Attempted Murder of a Prostitute," which is essentially a case study of aberrant mourning, also appears in this volume. Its author, Roland Kuhn, was referred to in *The Simulacra* by the novel's identified psychotic Kongrosian as one of the existential analysts who would understand him (but not help him).

First Kuhn sets up Freud as all about successful mourning and substitution without complications or consequences.

We must, hereby, differentiate between the mourning affect which consists in the emotional experience in the bereaved touched off by that loss, and mourning in the sense of a profound and lasting transformation of existence which replaces the mournful affect, if the deceased has been loved in the full meaning of the word. Thereby, "mourning work" in the Freudian sense—namely a withdrawal of libidinal energy from the lost object and a turning to other objects—does not occur; but rather (as particularly shown by Binswanger) the mourner himself, by bidding farewell to the departed, gets into bidding farewell to his own earlier way of existence, and the bereaved takes over somehow the being of the deceased. (405–6)

To demonstrate what actually occurs in mourning, Kuhn cites the passage from *Being and Time* that consigns the dead, ultimately, to forget-together (though Kuhn like Binswanger draws "existential mourning" out from under Heidegger's sentencing). To be together means to be together in the same world. The dead however are out of it. For a living being to be with the dead requires that he too depart from this world. Though he thus excludes relations with the dead (and with their interrelations) Heidegger still comes not to raise but to bury them.

To care for the deceased in the time span of burial rites is to treat the deceased as more than "stuff at hand." And yet the deceased is no longer there. There is a time limit to mourning precisely because joining the dead in being out of it has its limits. Mourners tend to play dead. Kuhn advises that a survivor assume forms of movement that he knew in the deceased. Once memory becomes movement the mourning affect can be overcome "and mourning in the existential sense commences" (407). The bottom line of relations with the dead would then be the borderline along which psychotic worlds are set apart, like the singular animal worlds according to von Uexküll. The skewering of these denizens of singular worlds tells us more about the outer limits of our perception in repression. Thus the psychotic no doubt multiplies and separates worlds for the same reason the schizophrenic, according to Arieti, multiplies, fragments, and reassembles words: the risk of fragmentation is undertaken to break down and thus multitask piecemeal what would otherwise be the world of high anxiety. The singular worlds of psychotics drift apart from our common world through unmourning, theirs or our own, while it is in our relationship to animals that we are totemically called back to our dead. It is in this sense that the animal empathy test in *Do Androids Dream of Electric Sheep?* is a reality test.

Following the alignment between animals and psychotics Binswanger nevertheless pulls up short before von Uexküll's twofold mix-up. On the one hand von Uexküll posits animal as subject and environment as object; on the other hand he emphasizes the complete interconnectedness or union of these two factors within the so-called blueprint of a given animal. If you reverse the ordering of von Uexküll's argument—subjecting it thus to the "Kantian-Copernican revolution"—and begin with transcendental subjectivity, proceeding from there to *Dasein* as transcendence, then you go directly to *Dasein*-analysis without walking in von Uexküll's blueprints.

Von Uexküll, Binswanger underscores, is no philosopher. "So it should not be held against him that he, like most natural scientists, makes light of the essential difference between animal and man" (239). Human *Dasein* is not limited to its blueprint but contains countless possibilities of being or being able. For example, he can be a hunter, an enthusiast, or a tradesman. Different world and self-designs (or projections) can moreover transcend being or make it accessible to itself.

Binswanger's save for philosophy after almost losing one replays as passage through the closing scene of Theodor Fontane's *Effi Briest*. Effi has managed to die without openly committing suicide. The surviving parents are seated near their daughter's grave, which has been integrated within the family home's garden (where the novel also begins and now, we're on the last page, ends). The dead woman's dog, Rollo, guards the site of burial:

Mrs. von Briest had in the meantime poured the coffee and looked out at the circular flower patch. "Look, Briest, Rollo is lying again in front of the stone. It affected him more profoundly than it did us. He also isn't eating any more."

"Yes, Luise, animal life [literally, "the creature," "*die Kreatur*"]. That is what I'm always saying. We're not as great as we believe ourselves to be. We're always talking about instinct. In the end it is after all what proves better than all the rest."

"Don't go on like that. When you philosophize . . . don't take it personally, Briest, but you don't have the talent."

Philosophy, "too wide a field," marks father Briest as brought up short before his own limits at the moment he concedes funeral rights to the creature. For Mrs. von Briest, however, "philosophizing" properly can only be a question of talent or style, which her daughter's ex, Baron Innstetten, masters with his largely Spiritualist discourse. The spirit discourse whereby Innstetten sought to keep his I on his younger wife conveys only sexual ghosts. Mrs. von Briest is the same age as her ex-son-in-law, whom she knew (and wished to marry) when they were both younger then. He, however, liked them younger. Fontane's late contribution to the adultery series featuring Tolstoy's *Anna Karenina* and Flaubert's *Emma Bovary* is the only one out of three that hides its haunted state by directly thematizing Spiritualism as timely fad that an older husband uses to intimidate his child bride. But the control freakishness of Baron Innstetten doesn't explain away the effects of haunting (just as it can't alone motivate Effi Briest's openly concealed suicidality). Into the breach of exposure, which always accompanies and facilitates Spiritualism's monopolization of ghostliness as its ultimate medium, the creature steps forward to mourn.

Play Bally

For the complex of readings that have become the environment of von Uexküll's corpus it is the notion of the moment in a world of marking or noting that commands these pages as the very translation scene of their words or worlds of difference. Here we restore what Agamben in *The Open* leaves out of his close paraphrase of the tick passage from the 1933 pamphlet *Excursions through the Environments of Animals and Humans (Streifzüge durch die Umwelten von Tieren und Menschen)*, through which von Uexküll popularized the work that had established his reputation twenty-five years earlier. At the close of his presentation of the tick's environment or perceptual field as impoverished but secure world, von Uexküll notes that from this one inside view one can derive the basic traits for the construction of environments that would apply to all animals. But there is an additional capacity characterizing the tick, which, von Uexküll promises, "opens up for us a yet wider insight into the environments" (29). The tick is able to wait for indeterminate spans of time for the survival of its species. Then von Uexküll notes that for which Agamben was lying in wait: in the Zoological Institute in Rostock a tick has been kept ticking eighteen years and counting simply by depriving it of nourishment. Agamben lets this reference, which concludes a section of *The Open*, resonate indefinitely, deprived of its environment in the text, von Uexküll's introduction of the moment as the smallest possible and most basic span of time during which the world stands still. Stylistically at least, as transition, the tick here is almost Freudian. The eighteen years of the Rostock tick calls up the same number in another setting, namely one-eighteenth of a second, which is how long the moment of man lasts. At this moment a footnote delivers the proof: "The proof of this is provided by cinema. During the screening of a strip of film the pictures must leap forward jerkily one after another and then stand still. To show them as sharply as possible the jerky leaping forward must be made invisible with the aid of a filter. The darkening which thus occurs is not perceived by our eyes if the standing still of the picture and its darkening transpire within one one-eighteenth of a second. If more time is taken intolerable flickering ensues."[1] The duration of the moment differs from animal to animal. But however we compute the moment of the tick, it is beyond possible to endure an unchanging environment for eighteen years. At this point Agamben misreads or mistranslates von Uexküll's assumption that a sleeplike state suspends the tick's long time, a state to which we humans have recourse, according to von Uexküll whenever we must wait for extended periods of time, but according to Agamben every night when we sleep. That we should sleep, like Ellen West, only to cut the loss of waiting in half indeed loses von Uexküll's attentiveness to the knowledge in the waiting of animals.

What Benjamin referred to as the optical unconscious was opened up through opportunities available in filmmaking and projection, for example, for speeding up and slowing down our perceptual field. Benjamin's examples might be found summarized in the 1953 Disney film *The Living Desert*. Just add rainwater and the hatching, crawling, blossoming, and pollinating across the desert surface can be viewed on-screen in no time. But von Uexküll underscores that the opening up of the range of our seeing ego probe, which no longer need stop short before invisibility, extends to the animal environments that whiz by us or just drag along, but which now can be made perceptible to us through their technically possible calibration.

That a perceptual environment can be, at least as far as timing goes, another world is what we learned first from animals and psychotics and which, according to von Uexküll, cinema proved. In *Martian Time-Slip* the autistic boy Manfred, who is growing up schizophrenic, is considered a case for testing new theories from Switzerland about the relative slowness of the psychotic perceptual environment, which registers the normal environment or common world only as unbearable fast-forwarding. Manfred leaps so far ahead that it's the future—and you only know it's the future, unmediated by wish fulfillment or fantasy, if it's the tomb world. Jack Bohlen, a recovered schizophrenic, is hired to build a machine that translates the input of the common world as audio and video recordings slowed down to fit Manfred's perceptual environment. The boy's communications would then in turn be up to speed by the time they reached our ears.

This time machine modifies the environment or perceptual field to unblock communication the way training lays claim to trainability. In the closing chapter of her study *Adam's Task*, Vicki Hearne introduces autism research into the interdisciplinary exploration of how training of dogs and horses meets their trainability more than halfway as ennobling test. Autism may indicate that something like training or, better yet, trainability is the more fundamental criterion of relationality and possibility than speaking or not speaking. Yet this human illness, like boredom, the Heideggerian supplement that Agamben also tries to take against the animalization and technologization of mankind as supplies, doesn't commit us to sharing one continuum with the trainable animal. Whereas animals are so generous in answering us, the constitutively human ability to speak can also always mean not to answer, not to be answered by, the other.

Hearne wagers that the first time we find that the request we were taught to pronounce is insufficient to guarantee the response of the other, the paradoxes and muddles that thus begin to arise drive us to philosophy and poetry. The resulting focus on certain aspects of our intellect and imagination, to come full circle within what is human, ends up manifesting, though in less extreme form, autistic self-stimulation behavior. The autistic child would thus appear to be the by-product of our unique evolutionary development, according to Ivar Lovaas according to Hearne. The trainable animal matters, Hearne adds, to "a tribe as lonesome and threatened most of the time as ours is" (265). Because the animal answers, training is what we offer in exchange to enact and exact our gratitude.

In his study of animals and humans, first published in 1945, psychoanalyst Gustav Bally entered a field overcrowded with precursors, mainly von Uexküll and his students, which as too much information or overstimulation in the animal's perceptual field would guarantee for the animal, by veiling the single-minded goal, a freer play of mental faculties. Expanding on this anxiety in influence, Bally summarizes findings that prove that in animal testing the best results are obtained through a noncatastrophic but unexpected stimulus. A measured electrical shock is most effective. Animals learn better under more difficult rather than easier circumstances. The alarm effect of unknown factors opens up the animal's immediate environment and differentiates it. In the field, then, in which the animal is born free, the startle response as alarm signal is beneficial up to a point, but goes into reverse when a reaction to catastrophe replaces it (40). Animal testing and the study of animal behavior and learning are sometimes on the same field. Stimuli that are punitive make the animal more careful, expand the view of the surrounding environment, and lead to new solutions.

Uexküll, the figure Agamben followed into corners in which Heidegger backed up animals, is at the top of a long list of researchers Bally consults on the animal side of his study. On the human side, play is still largely in Schiller's court.

According to Bally, the centrality of the all-important *Annäherung* or approach between animal and man rests on the section titled "Das Stutzen" (a term that signifies an animal's "startled hesitation," which interrupts the action up to that point). The animal's startled hesitation opens up the field of goal-directed focus to its innately possible variations. Inhibitions of movement toward the goal enrich the field with markers. In addition to the inner inhibitions Bally has already summarized and discussed—those provided, for example, by satiation and relative security from foes—external, more-or-less random blockers cause the animal to halt and contain itself in the mode of startled hesitation. Keep in mind Dick's notion of "balking" as the empathic or ethical measure of resistance that distinguishes humans from androids according to his animal reality test.

Right before the moment of startled hesitation, as the dog took after the quarry, there was no image of the consequent detour. It must therefore have emerged in the moment of startled standing still. Startled hesitation places the animal in a singular relationship to things in the field. The flow of movement is stopped with a jerk. What is more, the movement transforms itself up against the blocking force into tension. And moreover into a tension in which the possibility of the detour first emerges. This tension, so we can assume, derives on the one hand from the motoric beginnings of the goal-directed movement. On the other hand it derives from the motoric impulses, which newly emerged in front of the hindrance and have the character of going back. It signifies therefore the result of two opposing strivings. This antagonism leads, motorically speaking, to standing still of the movement with retention of the corresponding inner-vations. The startled animal stops in its tracks. Psychologically, however, startled hesi-tation signifies a changed position in the field. A sudden being-distant from the goal with which the animal already represented in the aimed-for movement a (dynamic) unity *[Einheit]*. In this being distant the detour is conceived. Only in it can the overview of the field be attained. . . . There are in the flow of the appetence-behavior, that is, in the approximation area of an instinctual goal, longer or shorter moments, in which the movements suddenly make room for a tensed stance. The animal stops short. When it proceeds, the manner of the momentum has changed. . . . The animal has not become, as one might assume at first sight, entirely the function of its sensory apparatus, like someone submerged in meditation. It is entirely—possible movement. Through the eye in this moment *[Augenblick]* the tensed apparatus of movement tests its possibili-ties or chances in a field confused by impediments. . . . Often whole sequences of move-ment are executed as in an experiment *[wie zur Probe]*. . . . Animals think through movement. Thinking, says Freud, is a testing activity *[Probehandeln]*. (36–37)

The animal as test subject breaks away from behavior modification and suffers thought. Every displacement of the direct path to the goal demands attentiveness to its overcoming and, to be sure, the relationship to the things in one's immediate environment is thus enriched. The question posed to the animal is not, what sort of thing is this blocker? but rather, "how do I materialize the vectors even in the most difficult field?"

We must conclude from the excited behavior that becomes visible in startled hesitation and securing *[Sichern]* that here a new total *[Gesamt]* situation has suddenly emerged.... Whereas before the field was narrowed in focus on the attainment of the instinctual goal, it widens itself now.... Suddenly the rapid answering of many and manifold questions intervenes as vitally important.... This passing illumination of the field is only possible thanks to the sudden pausing in the flow of movement toward the goal, thanks to the excited securing and the tensed startled hesitation. (38)

In the field of animal behavior and learning, which, as noted, seems interchangeable or coterminous with the field of animal testing, stimuli that are punitive make the animal more careful, expand the view of the surrounding environment, and lead to new solutions. However, they do not open up the field of play in which the animal approaches the thing in the field in relative freedom with regard to instinctual goals. The distinction drawn earlier between the consequences of external inhibitions and those of the inner follow from this:

The external inhibition of the goal-striving flow of movement leads certainly to an excitement that "illuminates" the surrounding field and promotes learning.... This greater wealth of what has been learned always however remains tightly bound to an instinctual goal. The inner inhibition in contrast subdues, as we saw, the actual instinctual act in securing protection from enemies and in securing nourishment, without however bringing about expression of the appetence-activities, which belong to the spatio-temporal Gestalt of the instinct.... The living being is not alarmed in any way, it is rather freely entrusted to its inner impulses through the relaxation of the push toward the instinct goal. (41)

The appetence-activities run through or past on empty or rev up in neutral gear. "It is precisely this behavior that can be characterized as being in neutral gear *[Leerlauf]* in the loosened-up field that finds new goals, which we in fact can no longer address as instinct goals" (41–42). In sum: "If von Uexküll says that the immediate environment *[Umwelt]* poses questions to the animal which it answers with the instinct action, whereby it extinguishes the question, then we must say here that the *Umwelt* asks questions of the one playing which through the movement of play not only are not extinguished, but are indeed deepened and enriched" (42).

In the second half of the study reserved for humans at play Bally singles out the dog as singularly ready for the good impressions that even chimps can't make (65). Even a puppy can observe and follow human sleight of hand and remember which hand holds the food. The canine ready positioning for receiving the impressions of training or testing exceeds a one-way field of behavior study and modification to include a mode or model of communication, one (or more) modeled in fact on interspecial exchange.

Das Hund

If it were not for Structuralism, we might have noticed already that Freud's famous pronouncement that we do not find our love objects but only re-find them is at least as melancholic as it would be Oedipal (or symbolic). But ambivalence accepts this as law of desire. While the diagnostic handbooks decree that zoophilia always substitutes for a missing human connection (which is presumably a blocked outlet that can be open to treatment), we can also say, in reverse, that every beloved animal—every pet—is, without the synthesis of ambivalence but as melancholic chain operation or compulsion, a RePet. This cloning industry in the foreground of the film *The 6th Day* (2000), which is downgraded with plot points to strategic diversion but then proves to be the true bottom line, raises commodification to the powers of allegory also in keeping with P. K. Dick's undercover brilliance in ad copy and marketing over skills.

It all begins with our not wanting to let the other go. But then there are those who don't want to go themselves: these are the dangerous ones, while the former are forever going through a change of heart.

Dr. Weir invented the successful procedure for cloning humans in order to give his marriage for the sake of all others a new lease on life and wife. His business partner, Drucker, applies cloning to his own risk-free life or death. What the doctor only discovers over his wife's clone's expired body is that Drucker has also programmed via congenital defects that fatal disease will cut short everyone celebrating a comeback. Thus those who prove unreliable, disloyal, et cetera die anyway, while the chosen can be brought back again for a fuller brush with fate. When the wife's clone starts dying after four more years, she implores her husband to let her go this time: she's not afraid. Dr. Weir follows her lead and declares that he will never again bring someone back as clone. But it's too late: Drucker applies the cure-all. He kills Dr. Weir so he can bring him and his wife back without the new fears and resolutions. According to the logic of the film, this is possible because Dr. Weir and his wife were longstanding test subjects with archives of symcordings (pictures taken of the mind), which were made at various moments. Because you are cloned with or through your symcording, your renewed memory (or sentient life) picks up where the symcording left off. Thus Drucker can choose a mind picture from a period prior to the wife's determination to die. The shades of mourning need no longer fall upon the couple's once and future memories. The recent past would have been, to this end, completely elided. But it's too late for the cure-all, too late for Drucker, too. Arnie and his clone tricked Drucker with the symcording evidence: one didn't look at the other as they advanced on cloning headquarters. With the imprint of the other out of sight, it's out of the mind picture being read as narrative of only one Arnie to deal with. But with two Arnies as insiders, the whole apparatus of replacement and reanimation begins to break down. Arnie, home a clone, can flex the momentum of alternate presents and disrupt Drucker's equation between elimination and cloning. In the shoot-out Drucker is mortally wounded. But as he proceeds to provide his own cloning replacement, he finds he can go only so far: he clones himself only incompletely, either as not yet fully born or as zombie. In either case, the next in the Drucker line begins taking off the former Drucker's clothes to complete the transfer. Can't he wait until the first guy's dead? But the former Drucker gets to die embracing himself, the clone who slimed him.

The evil masterminding in the movie's replication plot is restricted to Drucker's attempt to keep cloned life on a short lease. But when everything is over and fixable, Arnie's clone doesn't want to know about his deadline: "we all have to die some day." This was Mrs. Weir's message in the bottled up affect of her husband. But up to the point of Drucker's subcontracting out the renewal of living to Death, we, too, learn to accept the message of cloning on the upbeat. Christianity is defined as that which says "No" (in spite of its fateful bid for resurrection) to the cloning of humans. We start getting around the Christian "No" via pets. The cloning industry in exile started running RePet at or as the loss that would form dependency of the populace on replication as way of life around death. Two further inroads that circumvented the prohibition restocked wildlife (and thus added the full range of totemic significance, from haunt to hunt) and created spare organs. Cloning pets relieves the pain of survival in the smaller world of childhood totemism. Drucker readdresses the cloning of organs as on the way to saving the unmournable child from death or deposit. What if your son has a tumor? The brain can't be cloned: you can save the boy only by cloning the whole body. (I guess the brain is the body without organs.) Ergo: to clone a person is no more than to clone his or her brain.

Behind the scenes, already, valuable or influential individuals are cloned by accident. Thus a valuable football player breaks his back but then is back with the news that the injury had been slight. (It's his clone.) Before he gets cloned by mistake (on his birthday he agrees to let his copilot fly his mission for him, but then the copilot is killed, but in Arnie's name) Arnie resists cloning his daughter's dog who had to be put to sleep that morning. It's his birthday and not only can't he die if he wants to, but he also can't let the dog go. Arnie says the dog will live on in their memories. Wife says their daughter is too young to understand that. Later we discover that Drucker decided that all those working for him need to be their own spare parts: routine eye exams are in fact the means for taking pictures of their brains. Arnie's brain was shot while he was still against RePet. That the Arnie we've been following since he took the day off for his birthday might be the clone was suggested by the jump cut of his waking up in the cab momentarily decontextualized. When we are shown his perceptions and memories they are moreover interchangeably rendered in the techno vibe generally given irreality or the occult in film. But then the copilot (who in the meantime is the copilot's clone) notes that Arnie still has the saving, shaving nicks in real time. A clone lacks all physical markings applied from without. But they updated his appearance down to the wire of the memories current at the time of symcording. However the eyes are dotted each time you've been a clone. Our seeing I Arnie, our delegate in the narrative about one's own clone, is the clone. "Kind of takes the fun out of being alive, doesn't it?"

Arnie's clone comes home to his birthday celebration bearing the gift of an android doll, a sympal his daughter wanted. But he doesn't bring the clone of the dog his wife requested on the daughter's behalf. Instead he's rehearsing breaking the news to his daughter of her dog's death. But when he arrives the dog greets him. Inside his clone is being celebrated. His daughter is clutching her sympal. (We learn via the copilot's home life that it is possible to live with and love even a hologram, in his case his live-in girlfriend.) By the end it's the clone who had to come around to accepting RePets. While finitude is still credited with being necessary for human reckoning and relating, the RePet is allowed to rest in one piece continuity-shot through with replication. The mourning and substitution a loved pet brings home throw the high beam on lives kept too brief by some design on our freedom. In *Valis* it is averred that the dead pet in the street is the strongest imaginable argument against God's existence. But with Faustian extensions added to our totemic delegates, human life, even when doubled, becomes worthy of affirmation. Only thus can the death-wish overview of the other's lifespan be made to pull its punchlines, which are all on you.

It is characteristic of Schwarzenegger's image control that he should play the part of a man and his clone (and himself) without succumbing to the crisis of uncanniness. He secured the first in his long series of Oedipal roles by producing *Total Recall*. In *The 6th Day* the programming of moviegoers with a sense of Schwarzenegger's all-Americanism begins, however oddly, via cloning. After they have rescued wife and daughter from Drucker, original Arnie assures his clone that he risked his life to protect wife and kid: "If that isn't proof of humanity, I don't know what is." Original Arnie is a pilot flying a futural type of helicopter suggestive of war or law enforcement. The clone has signed up with a destroyer that sets out for sea while Arnie flies overhead. One if by land, two if by air and sea. Arnie is a military of two.

In Stephen King's *Pet Sematary* the prehistorical turf of reanimation of animals precludes extension of the same rites to humans (who must first be withdrawn from the Christian comfort zone before being made into RePets). Protagonist Louis Creed finds that the tour of the pet cemetery was the second major initiation for his young daughter Ellie: first there was where babies come from, now there's where the dead go. But Ellie's second question is reformulated before it can ever (never) be answered: why don't pets live as long as people? (49).

The pet cemetery is the preamble or cover for the second cemetery, which is secret. This ancient Indian burial ground harbors the magic of reanimation. When the family cat dies, Louis carries the corpse there to change it with a spare for Ellie. Reanimated animals bear a shadow. And they're always farther away than they stink. They're off somehow, but we can still live with the shades of their undeath. When the RePet in turn dies, it's time to go (on the Faustian schedule). That no pet is brought back a second time is not a contradiction, nor is it an admission of failure, but really it's the whole point.

But when it's a human child you can't let go, the revenant coming back through the RePet metabolism is simply murderous. "Sometimes dead is better." But which time? The boy's mother lost her sister in childhood while wishing her gone. When she sees her undead son she is sure it is Zelda back from the dead inexplicably wearing the suit in which her boy was buried (387). In other words, the whole machinery of projection, through which the reanimated corpse is thrown for a loopy return, enters the field of survival as life-or-death struggle between the newly dead and those who can't let go. Louis Creed struggles to bring back his son against the momentum of mourning and substitution. Even as he digs him up out of his grave he realizes he no longer remembers what the boy looks like (334). Earlier he imagined a scenario two years from now with daughter Ellie successfully picking up where they lost the boy. "But would that not be the same as murdering his son? Killing him a second time?" (299). But when he does finally put his reanimated son to sleep by injection (just like a pet) "for a moment Louis saw his son—his real son—his face unhappy and filled with pain" (402). When the father resolves to bring back his wife (murdered by their zombie son) we are left hoping that her comeback will be the continuity shot we have been denied. The ultimate hope is the contradiction by mourning rites on which the novel closes or breaks. Since it's the end of the novel, how she turns out when she turns up again, back from the dead, is largely a blank unfilled.

While Vicki Hearne tacked onto her philosophical study a brief afterword calling for extension of the rights of seeing-eye dogs to all trained companion dogs, Donna Harraway has been seeking to rewire relations with our "companion species" along the functional lines to which we owe our working relationship. I'm in support of putting the shepherding dogs back to work in a clearing provided ultimately by Web site politics. But while I want to bark back in support, I cannot get around the primal time that inevitably mediates our first interspecial relations and renders them profoundly allegorical on or in a stage of mourning play. Let this be my intervention.

In Benjamin's *Origin of the German Mourning Play,* the dog or *Hund* casts its breath and shadow on the *Und*—the And. The dog emblematizes the dark side of melancholia via the rabid or manic issue of the fragile spleen's degeneration in melancholic humans and in afflicted dogs.[1] But on the lighter side, as Benjamin concludes this emblem label, it is also the dog's perseverance and sagacity *(Spürsinn)* that inspired the image of the inexhaustible brooder, the other melancholic. This double significance of the dog as melancholia mascot finds another outlet at the same time in Kafka's "Investigations of a Dog." The canine protagonist is bipolar, if you take his history, but remains throughout the story the melancholic brooder whose endlessly erring path of investigation is accordingly ascribed at one fragmented juncture to an aberration that the "primal fathers" set in motion. Josef K.'s death "like a dog" (as I've argued more intricately elsewhere)[2] is interchangeable with the other "as if," that the shame would survive him, because etymological crosstalk links *Scham* ("shame") and *Leichnam* (a ceremonial word for "corpse," reserved, like corpus, for that of Christ, for example). The mourner's survivor guilt is the melancholic's mourning shame. The *Und* that *Hund* breathes on belongs to the undead siblings Kafka carried for his mother. Like an And—it was as if the covered corpses would outlive him. Thus we remain within the loop of Josef K.'s initial mourning arrest.

In a letter dated December 17, 1934, Adorno responded to Benjamin's "Kafka" by twice intervening from within the lexicon of Benjamin's own *Origin* book. In Kafka, according to Adorno, the creature, from which the things took all words, is unbound in gesture, which, in turn, gestures toward music. This double creaturely gesture is the last link, says Adorno, perhaps the missing link, to silent film, which, he emphasizes, disappeared at the time of Kafka's death. Odradek is not an archaic figure emerging out of the primeval world and guilt. The assertion alone is archaic. Because Odradek dwells in the house of the father as his "care" *(Sorge)* and "danger," we are given here, according to Adorno, the prefiguration of the overcoming of the creaturely relationship to guilt. Thus *Sorge*—"truly a Heidegger placed on his feet"—is the promissory cipher of hope. "Of course Odradek is, as the backside of the world of things, the sign of deformity—but as such a motif of transcending, namely, the removal of the boundary and reconciliation between the organic and the inorganic or the overcoming of death: Odradek 'survives'" (translation modified). Benjamin replies on January 7, 1935, with gratitude: now for the first time he finds he can address Kafka's "Investigations of a Dog" (which he misremembers in its title as "Notes *[Aufzeichnungen]* of a Dog" and thus places in the position of communication). Prior to Adorno's intervention, he found that this particular story, like a foreign body, withheld from him its "genuine word" ("eigentliches Wort").

In the recent past investigation into the origin of the *Hund/Und* was in the news.[3] Given in evolutionary or sci-fi terms, the hypothesis (even if only as phantasm) challenged received notions of evolution as ascending line that put a chimp on our shoulders. Something like an alternate reality shot up the sidelines when, as the new theory presented it, sudden mutation (and not domestication) turned a small number of wolves into a new species driven or programmed to read and follow our nonverbal communications.[4] Presumably the relationship had to undergo a few trials or tests. The dogs approached our encampment to engage us only to be severely tried by our incomprehension and hunger. Freud's primal father myth thus goes to the dogs.[5] In East Asia, according to DNA test results, is located the single place of origin of all the dogs in the world today. It is also the place where the ambivalent relationship to dogs still gets acted out. Just like (or precisely as) the primal father once devoured by his sons, the canine readers and teachers introduced, following their mistaken consumption as voluntary quarry, mourning as problem, condition, and legacy (for which their dog heirs then, as emblems of melancholia, served as mascots).

In Wagner's *Tristan und Isolde,* Isolde curses the *Und* that binds her to Tristan and separates them—but also lets them live. She seeks to eradicate the *Und* in their *Liebestod.* "Yet this little word *and*— / were it destroyed, / how else than / with Isolde's own life / would Tristan be given death?" (act 2, scene 2) Nothing circumvents mourning (or unmourning) quite so immediately as mass self-destruction. Only with the survival, the passing, of adolescence does the unique evolution of man transmit.

In Bergson's *Creative Evolution* the "cinematographic method" that organizes ordinary thought and ancient and modern science stumbles over an excess piling up on the cutting-room floor: "there is *more* in the transition than the series of states, that is to say, the possible cuts—*more* in the movement than the series of positions, that is to say, the possible stops" (314). It is the philosophy of Ideas that the cinematographic method applies and maintains. But the "nothing" in "nothing but Ideas" doesn't go away.

> In right, there ought to be nothing but immutable Ideas, immutably fitted to each other. In fact, matter comes to add to them its void, and thereby lets loose the universal becoming. It is an elusive nothing that creeps between the Ideas and creates endless agitation, eternal disquiet, like a suspicion insinuated between two loving hearts. (317)

On the stage preliminary to every cinematographic method, Isolde seeks to deliver the "nothing" from the "and," the additive "between."

The superman, Freud corrects Nietzsche, belongs in the past, not to the future. What stands above us remains the primal father of prehistory. But there is also another prehistory, Adorno advised Benjamin in a letter dated August 2–4, 1935 (again in deference to the *Origin* book): the recent past is the most repressed period of time, which therefore always appears as prehistory and comes toward us only as catastrophe and return. This repressed recent past is excavated in the time of mourning. Darwin's theory of evolution tends to be received as progressive development of species, which climbs up over corpses that are not counted individually but count only as part of a milieu for the selection of survivor traits. In the span between the recent past and mourning over those closest to us, however, the theory of evolution can be seen at the same time as leaving open the possibility of rapid fundamental changes, as can follow, for example, from the invention and introduction of new technical prostheses. According to Freud, the first takeoff of artificial flight already programmed the First World War as consequence of this technical extension of the fields of vision and battle. Applied to technological changes, the theory of evolution inspired countless fantasies and fictions of close encounters with animal, plant, and machine species that advanced beyond us via the rewind and playback functions of evolutionary time.

The fantasy of time travel also reckons with the new units of time brought to us by technical evolution. For the most part, however, time travel fictions show us the past in the future from which we are given the chance to swerve thanks to the warning. Changes are introduced into one's own past in order to alter the future.

P. K. Dick further differentiated and internalized time travel in his fictions. Here one travels mainly through the recent past in order to pull the dead into media-technological real time or extended lifetime where they can still be visited. As with his administration of time travel, Dick hitched his use of alternate history or alternate reality to the present going on the recent past. Dick dismissed fascination with past lives as generic fantasy. He promoted instead his conception of alternate present realities (which, through time travel, interconnect in the recent past, which can be staggered through alternation but never altered). Within an expanding archive of finitude, then, Dick dismantles the present as vanishing point of the recent past, the big repressed where the dead are.

If the andy is our close-to-home tendency to repress mourning in the course of building up the in-group bonds of rebellion and denial, then the *Und* of mourning, we must admit, doesn't come easy: it comes toward us—for example via mutation across species—as the other, the answering other.

In *Ubik* "half-life" is a variation on the itinerary through alternate times whereby the dead and the survivors keep in touch. In the condition of half-life, the deceased is suspended as ghostly interlocutor between first and second deaths. As technological fulfillment of modern Spiritualism half-life control releases the tomb world around the leak it keeps springing on the survivors and the undead alike. The teenager at the heart of undeath drives apart the best laid plans for reunion and remembrance. Jory, who died a teenager, acts out among the half-lifers by devouring the ones he's with and thus denying finitude even in the secular afterlife of half-life or haunting. Thus for all others he reverses the deferral of the second death and turns the liminal realm of half-life back into the tomb world, which reaches inside the world of full-life.

One character proclaims that he is not dead, that he resides within "full-life," that the other hangs out in half-life. He is trying to contact him, that is, to manifest himself in the half-life world of the other. But the other character saw the first one as corpse inside his ostensibly delusional world, which belongs to an earlier era. In half-life one still dies, but not so fast, or rather the finality is displaced through contextlessness, as in the creaturely state of the Hunter Gracchus. Whenever the full-life world is proclaimed as alternative, Dick halves it through inclusion of a detail possible only in the delusions comprising half-life. And for those who believe themselves to be immersed in half-life, their relation to those in the full-life world seeking to make contact appears only as ghostly connection.

We are served by organic ghosts, he thought, who, speaking and writing, pass through this our new environment. Watching, wise, physical ghosts from the full-life world, elements of which have become for us invading but agreeable splinters of a substance that pulsates like a former heart. (213–14)

Dick's alternate reality of mourning or unmourning as half-life views the deceased and the survivor as always having in common that they both lost each other. Therefore it proves possible to travel through a time in which one cannot decide who died on whom. For the near future, the living and the and-dead, *die Und-Toten* (the "and-dead"), just like the present and the recent past, remain in interchangeable but incalculable contact.

Notes

All translations into American English, unless stated otherwise, are by the author.

Introjection

1. Originally written for a conference at Cerisy titled "Reorganization of the Senses," this meditation appeared as "Endopsychic Allegories" in *Postmodern Culture*. The publication in some ways previews the first two chapters. Two more preview publications are "Veil of Tears" (in *What Does the Veil Know?* edited by Eva Meyer and Vivian Liska), which covers the readings of the tomb world more fully developed in Part II, and "Take Me to Your Reader," my contribution to *Reading Ronell,* which includes the essence of my reading of *A Scanner Darkly* in Part I.

2. My recasting of sci fi as an impulse or drive is what the respelling here refers to. It is where, in addition to bona fide science fictions, psychoanalysis, psychosis, and psychological warfare meet and cross over.

3. See Rickels, ed., *Acting Out in Groups,* 199.

4. It is conceivable that Dick would have tracked the first serious writing on his work—Fredric Jameson's article on *Dr. Bloodmoney* (collected in *Archaeologies of the Future*)—to the author's frame of references. In this depot *The Prisonhouse of Language* was already available, in which the importance of being a reader of Benjamin's own melancholic brooding was on center stage.

5. Ronell's multiple choice of Nietzsche as her designated thinker is the condition of the original attention she gives the widest possible span of "the test."

6. Guided by artist Eran Schaerf's declared interest in test situations (and readymades) I composed a brief essay, "All of the Above," which skewered together Freud's observations on fear of testing in school and his asides on reality testing, suggesting that the trauma theory of *Moses and Monotheism* can be seen as the graduate of these test theories. It marked the third installment of art catalogue essays on testing. In 1999 I responded in "Just Testing" to Mike Kelley's "Test Room Containing Multiple Stimuli Known to Elicit Curiosity and Manipulatory Responses" and, two years earlier in "Die Prüfung Unica

Zürns," to the Wartegg test sheets artist Zürn filled out in the course of her treatment as schizophrenic. My reading of the cite-specific explications of (reality) testing in Freud and in Benjamin lies in the background of this reading of Dick's test situations in the contexts of his immediate research (from Binswanger to Jung). It is enough for this course of study that we know what we think we know about Freud's notion or "device" of reality testing. And who hasn't read Benjamin on the testing of moviegoers who are at the same time experts in their own gadget love?

7. In my *Aberrations of Mourning* Rank's essay is one of the many references in Freud's work through which I tracked the underworld of psychoanalysis. For my first book I immersed myself in the collected works on mourning and melancholia in the Freudian psychoanalytic tradition. I track these references only if I have again worked with and on them. If they accompany this study as corpus memory I don't cite them. In an important sense I have forwarded my former immersion in the context of Freud's melancholia to *I Think I Am,* which enters or encloses the new work like the ectoplasm of my first writing assignment. Albert Kümmel received postdoctoral support as Feodor Lynen Fellow from the Alexander von Humboldt Foundation to examine under my advisorship the literature of modern German Spiritualism. Our contact had in a sense already sent me back inside one of the underworlds of *Aberrations* shortly before I read the Valis trilogy.

8. I am revisiting yet another cluster of interreferences embedded inside my *Aberrations of Mourning,* which are also openly identified in the index. Freud included Sadger's reading in his analysis of the case of Leonardo da Vinci.

9. See in this regard volume 2 of my *Nazi Psychoanalysis: Crypto-Fetishism.*

Endopsychic Allegories

1. Rickels, "Suicitation: Benjamin and Freud." This article has since been called to reassembly within my study of placements of psychoanalysis within literary theory appearing soon as *Resistance in Theory.*

2. This would then be the reversal of the trauma timeline: "The real danger, the ultimate horror, happens when the creating and protecting, the sheltering, comes first—and then the destruction. Because if this is the sequence, everything built up ends in death. Death hides within every religion" (177).

3. Rickels, "Sui-citation," 148.

4. I explore these missing links—these links with the missing—at far, far greater length in *Aberrations of Mourning: Writing on German Crypts.*

5. A recurring figure in science fiction, "four-dimensional space-time" (Dick, *Valis,* 40–41) is invoked in *Valis* via Wagner's *Parsifal* not in order to imagine time travel, for example, but rather to accommodate the religious insights or delusions of Horselover Fat.

6. "What is the point of all our laboriously attained inventions if Spiritism can be proven right? If, as Askakov tells it, the odic spirit can leave the body of a girl lying in somnambulic sleep and greet someone far away, or if, according to Du Prel's informant Dr. Stuffli, the spirit of a sleeping girl can turn off the light in another house, what's the point, then, to telephone and telegraph? . . . Just the same it is for other reasons to be regarded as beneficial that our exact natural sciences may be inclined to concern themselves more thoroughly with the occult sciences than before. It is highly likely that we will gain

valuable insights into the psychic life via the careful study of such psychopathic states" (Kreusner, "Der moderne Gespensterglaube,"653).

7. Specifically, he "loses" Benjamin's reference to Schreber's press in a footnote in passing, writing it off as minimizing and passing reference on Benjamin's part, one that Hagen moreover blames in good measure for the lack of interest taken in this Spiritualist context by Schreber scholars (110 n.307).

8. Allegory came into being because the Christian Church could not excise the gods from the memory even of the faithful. Allegory was originally hell-bent on "exorcising" the surviving remnants of pagan antiquity, and its original figure was the Devil. But with the Devil's overt reclamation of authorship of allegory, allegory comes to its end, at once cessation and Christian purpose, and the pagan remnants return to the Christian Church as infernal elements that diversify its holdings (and which can be successively exorcised, even or especially if only over and over again). The Devil's other role as major player in allegory is covert: he guarantees that there will be an intermission within the fallenness of the world for affirmation of finitude. See my *Devil Notebooks*.

9. In 1908 Freud noted in passing that paranoia emerges from the sadomasochistic component of libido.

Schreber Guardian

1. In these remarks (in interview with Philip Purser) lie gap and overlap between *Time out of Joint* and Peter Weir's film *The Truman Show* (1998).

Belief System Surveillance

1. What also fits this frame is a reading of Ronell's *Crack Wars*, which I pursue between *A Scanner Darkly* and the Frankfurt School in an essay titled "Take Me to Your Reader."

2. In 1939 Hennell offered his services as artist to the British war effort. He died at the hands of terrorists in Java in 1945.

3. Deleuze and Guattari's discussion of faciality can be found in their *Thousand Plateaus*.

Deeper Problems

1. Freud at one point in their correspondence characterizes Binswanger's atrocious handwriting as the psychotic patch in his personality, while Binswanger simply keeps on hoping (before he turns to transcription) that a positive transference (he actually suggests this to Freud) was the only decoder ring required.

Veil of Tears

1. Sutin, *Divine Invasions*, 300.

2. The strategic emplacement of unbirth within Christianity is the main reason we find so many psychotics applying for the savior position.

Go West

1. "When her physician chanced upon her reading 'Faust I' during a medium-strong manic phase, the patient explained that she was very happy that Goethe had lived before her, otherwise she would have had to write it all!" (Binswanger, "Melancholie und Manie," *Der Mensch in der Psychiatrie*, 406).

2. "In 1916 I felt an urge to give shape to something. I was compelled from within, as it were, to formulate and express what might have been said by Philemon. This was how the *Septem Sermones ad Mortuos* with its peculiar language came into being. It began with a restlessness, but I did not know what it meant or what 'they' wanted of me. There was an ominous atmosphere all around me. I had the strange feeling that the air was filled with ghostly entities. Then it was as if my house began to be haunted.... The experience has to be taken for what it was, or as it seems to have been. No doubt it was connected with the state of emotion I was in at the time, and which was favourable to parapsychological phenomena. It was an unconscious constellation whose peculiar atmosphere I recognized as the nume on an archetype. 'It walks abroad, it's in the air!'" In a footnote we are reminded that the citation is from *Faust II*.

3. The other two are "able-to-be" or existence and "allowed-to-be" or love.

Glimmung

1. In his *Exegesis* Dick joins the lineup: "Christ was born in me, literally him, and now firebright slumbers, the product of our union (with me as female host). (as impregnated bride, wedded to Christ as Bridegroom.)" (*In Pursuit of Valis*, 183).

Spiritualism Analogy

1. At the start of the study, Jung stressed that with schizophrenia we leave daydreaming behind and enter the dream state: "the course of association in dementia praecox ... is very superficial and proceeds by way of numerous clang associations. The disintegration is so marked, however, that we can no longer compare it to normal daydreaming, but must compare it directly to a dream. Indeed, the conversations we have in dreams sound very like this" (15–16).

2. This chapter in the psychoanalysis of media in their encrypted settings is titled "Necrofiliation" and can be found in my *Aberrations of Mourning*. The reading of Tausk's study is fully developed there and will hence not be revisited here.

3. We will return to Binswanger's animal analogue (which he receives from von Uexküll and rewires for his understanding of psychosis) toward the end of this study.

Hammers and Things

1. Barbara's problem with Hook Operating began in the other Southern region gone with the wind of carpetbagger-attended changes. Hinton, as adolescent rebel, marks the spot Barbara was in down south when she found that she was more Scarlett than Melanie. By the time she recognizes "jungle qualities" in her place of work or life her adaptation doesn't serve survival because it was made to fit by "burying" elements of herself that would

have marked her as "different." But the beast of this jungle is, no surprises here, double-backed. Why the hook? The hook knows. During the delusional phase of her recovery she had to go to court to learn to face her crummy opponents properly and legally. She learns to sue and to be sued. This activity whereby Operators settle contests among themselves is termed, in the learning phase or phrase of Barbara's observation of the Operators, as listed among the definitions included in the Appendix, to "judicate."

Umwelt, *Mitwelt*, and *Eigenwelt*

1. *Perceval's Narrative* heralds the overuse of "perversion" to this day—as common as the misspelling of murder as "homocide." Lunacy itself is "the perversion of the understanding" (216). In his "Introduction" Bateson also characterizes the deliberately outlandish behavior of schizophrenia (into which Perceval obtains insight) as "perverse" (xvii). There is a strong undercurrent of homosocial excess that Perceval must (literally) wrestle with. For example: "Later in the year, a young handsome lad used to invite me to box with him every evening in my bedroom, striking me in sport a few blows: at length, I expressed a kind of awkward resentment at it. I have perhaps written enough on this subject" (139). In Perceval's case "perversion" means that his mind is open and shut to nonreproductive desires. Perceval's presenting problem, by all accounts, involved overstudy of religious books. But he gives a more arcane diagnosis: "Begotten in love to woman, and not to man, I have great difficulty in arranging my ideas" (222). As I argued in *The Case of California*, perversion is the negative of psychosis, a reformulation of Freud's claim that neurosis is the (photographic) negative of perversion. In the missing place of transference, perversion supplies a kind of legibility to psychosis: the splitting between media-technologization and its analogue relations (ultimately with transference and mourning) introduces into delusion endopsychic insight into (Freud's theory of) the functioning of the psychic apparatus.

The German Introject

1. The first version, under the title *The Unteleported Man*, written 1964–65, was published in differing book forms in 1966, 1983, and 1984. Yet more revision pages were discovered in 1985, which contributed to the reconstruction of Dick's 1979 intended remake in 2004.

A Couple of Years

1. Ursula K. Heise holds onto this distinction with readerly loyalty. Dick of course put us to the test by raising the stakes of the Android distinction to life or death. Somehow capital punishment of androids, though they be antisocial psychos, doesn't solve the problem (of adolescence).

2. Reflecting on the case profile of Roy Baty, the group leader of android rebellion, Rick gives us the only indication in the novel that the difference between androids and humans has been deliberately contrived in order to keep them separate: "The account had a pathetic quality. A rough, cold android, hoping to undergo an experience from which, due to a deliberately built-in defect, it remained excluded" (185).

Android Empathy

1. The film's streamlining of the difference between human and android finds explicit syndication in *Blade Runner*'s film studies reception. Kaja Silverman sees the androids as confronting "the arbitrariness and the violence of what passes for 'difference' within any given culture" (113). Oddly in her reading any self-assertion of difference must be tested to determine if it is not in fact inhabited by something artificial or ideological that only passes for difference. Equally odd but in tandem is her assertion that the film represents a "deconstruction of difference" (121). In regard to the empathy standard as measure of difference in the future world of *Blade Runner,* Silverman asserts: "The two primary forms of difference in our own culture that depend upon a similar visual and biological rationalization are of course the sexual and the racial" (114). Rather than copying or reflecting a privileged model, the replicants, like their marginalized counterparts in our own culture, live "out more fully and more consciously than their makers the basic conditions of subjectivity" (114).

2. Rachael's strongest response is to a scenario involving abortion (50). Her other strong response, in the novel as in the film version, is to the scenario of the husband's attachment to the poster of a nude woman (49). Clearly in the film and more ambiguously in the novel, Rachael's strong rejection is of the other woman. In the film she misses the detail to which she should respond: the nude is sprawled out on a bearskin rug. But when Rachael keeps on referring to the owl as "it," Deckard is convinced that the test results were accurate after all. Pro forma he asks her one last test question. It's a conversational rhetorical question that he slips in as trick question before the testing has officially begun. The question could well be improvised. It concerns the manufacture of his briefcase out of human babyhide. She reacts, but a slight delay gives her away.

3. According to Catherine Liu's literary-theoretical reading of the film, *Blade Runner* offers an ironic revision of certain conclusions Descartes reaches during the Second Meditation (in *A Discourse on Method*). Descartes turns to the example of clockwork robots to illustrate how easily we deceive ourselves. We assume we know what we've seen in the scene on the street below. But what if the people were in fact robots and their activities programmed? (This is *the* psychotic question.) Liu comments: "It is the power of judgment that resides in his mind/esprit and not in his senses that allows Descartes to affirm that under their hats and coats, the creatures he sees from his window are not fake men but real ones. In order to arrive at the certainty of his judgment, he must pass through the moment of 'hyperbolic doubt'. . . . Deckard's dilemma has to do with no longer being able to judge the difference between human beings and their replicas either by his sense or by his intellect. The difference is evaluated by 'scientific' means, by the Voigt Kampff test . . . , but even with the empirical results provided by such a test, Deckard remains uncertain as to the difference between the replicant and the human being; he continues to doubt" (41–42). Of course, as Liu also notes, Derrida's quarrel with Foucault relied on the unstoppability of the momentum of doubt—all the way to dream and psychotic hallucination—as already uncontained within Descartes's own text.

4. The insight or revelation via *Blade Runner* that everyone is an android is, according to Jameson, symptomatic of what he terms the "'android cogito': I think, Therefore I am

an android" (374). Thus we find reversed "the external issue of testing into a permanent rift within self-consciousness itself." As advertised on TV.

5. A scholar with the wonderful name Deutelbaum reads the Esper machine as high point in the process of layering and retrofitting that underlies the construction of the future world as accretion of visual memories. Deutelbaum can show that the virtualized photo is constructed via interreference with early Flemish paintings that highlight optical manipulation within the new frames of perspective. As representation of progress that builds up upon the layers of its history, the Esper scene is comparable thus to Sebastian's apartment, which, crowded with automata from all stages of the history of manufacture of artificial beings, serves as the setting for our closest encounter with replicants.

6. Elissa Marder tracks the untenability of the mother as origin or definition of humanity as the truth the film reveals not only about its own medium. However she shows her stripes (between stills or frames) when she opens with a pet shot at *E.T.*'s "cozy humanism, . . . which treated the alterity of the extraterrestrial with the familiarity of a domesticated pet." No accident that Marder in the film buff sounds like she sees the movie *E.T.* treating the alien the way a pet might treat it.

7. Ridley Scott's classic fantasy film *Legend* (1985), in which we find unicorns up in highlights, turns up the contrast to his sci-fi film and thus confirms some of the reservations made by Dick regarding the irreconcilability of the two genres. Just the same, it is possible to track the relationship to finitude in *Blade Runner* as the systematic overtaking of novelty by allegory.

ALL OF YOU ARE DEAD. I AM ALIVE.

1. "Under a Christmas tree, Phil and Anne exchanged little volumes of pious teachings. Hattie got a Barbie doll equipped with several outfits, hair ornaments, makeup, and a boyfriend—Ken. Once he suppressed his initial impulse to make fun of these risible caricatures of the American dream in good ex-Berkeleyite fashion, Phil found Barbie and Ken an endless source of fascination. He tried to imagine what future archaeologists—or Martians—would make of them and how they would reconstruct our civilization based on these artifacts alone. Like a connoisseur hunched over a miniature, he marveled at the details, delighting in their precision and amused by what the dolls' designers chose to leave out. Barbie's hair dryer seemed more sophisticated and, all things considered, more realistic than Anne's did. Her bra hooked in the back just like a real one—and was no easier to unhook—but the breasts it held lacked nipples. And if (he waited until Anne had turned her back) one dared to pull down her panties and give her a quick look, nada, there was nothing there, no pubic hair, nothing at all. The archeologists of the future would scratch their heads trying to figure out how twentieth-century humans managed to reproduce. On the other hand, maybe they would find nothing odd at all about Barbie and Ken, for the simple reason that they would look exactly like them. Ken and Barbie prefigured the humanity of tomorrow, those who would replace us. Or else maybe—why not?—they were the vanguard of an extraterrestrial invasion" (Carrère, *I Am Alive and You Are Dead*, 105). However, as Norman O. Brown established around this same time, it is the resurrected, reanimated, or otherwise undead body that constitutively lacks its former visual-genital center (just take a look at Osiris making his comeback).

2. Chew-Z as insanity is always a comparison stop away from the shared delusion (as Freud put it) of religious belief. The world that Chew-Z exceeds is immersed in psychoanalysis and its mass media analogues or cultures. Stress can be measured in terms of Freuds (6), temperature is marked in Wagners, humidity is measured in Selkirks, and glaciers recede by degrees of Grables (8). This is established early on at or as the origin and essence of this future world.

3. "Quite a few new and potential inertials were children, having developed their ability in order to protect themselves against their psionic parents" (22).

4. Consider her description in *Ubik: The Screenplay:* "She is too pretty—black hair, large intense eyes . . . —but her expression is thin and rigid, a mean look, a bitch look, a look of power rather than warmth. It is a clouded face, obscured by an aura of disturbance; there is intelligence here, and the capacity to be kind, but the motor which drives her is one which seeks domination rather than relationship with those around her. . . . It's as if we are seeing a teenager who has grown in strength and judgment but not in wisdom" (34). By obscuring the guilt of this dark-haired girl he lets her go on—and then lets her go.

5. And yet one wonders why Dick felt that this novel could be remade for the screen. Did he know, just like the German translation, that God's immersion in the finitude of Mass culture was as irreversible by now as our creaturely estate on Chew-Z?

6. As Mark Poster points out, the final epigraph, in which Ubik declares itself to be the divinity, the word, doesn't break ranks with the logic of advertising—which Dick was not alone in marking (or marketing), for example in *The Ganymede Takeover,* as "a world where dreams were for sale, where youth and health came in a box, and all pain and suffering were smoothed over with long, beautiful, slow-motion hair" (132). The spiritual force of the commercial, which is not the commodity itself but only the hot air that tries to get the consumer where he reads, hears, breeds, leads Poster to gloss Katherine Hayles's interpretation of *Ubik* as Dick's privileging of "the word" of his own being-writing. Poster quotes the following words from Hayles: "*Ubik*'s distinctive achievement is to represent simultaneously the performative power of language and the mediated, uncertain relation of language to the material world while also mapping this difference onto an 'inside'-'outside' boundary that hints at the complexity of communication between self and other, conscious and unconscious. The hope *Ubik* holds out is that although boundary disputes will never disappear, inside and outside can be made to touch each other through the medium of writing that is no less valuable for infecting our world with all manner of epistemological and ontological instabilities" (Hayles, *How We Became Posthuman,* 188). Poster gives the media-therapeutic treatment of advertising as spiritual force and passes the allegorical baton to Hayles, who reads it as Dick's own ad or ID.

Room for Thought

1. Marazia and Stimili's edition of the case record doesn't reveal much more than what was already known about the battle of the diagnoses. While Binswanger identified his patient as schizophrenic with a poor prognosis to match, Kraepelin, who was brought in as second opinion by the Warburg family, recognized a manic-depressive disorder with an improved prognosis. It was into this breach that Warburg aimed his request to pass the test of the

presentation. And yet the case record does show in the details it gives of Warburg's persecution—he and his loved ones were being rounded up pogrom-style—how the projection in the delusion was also a precog forecast. In a letter to Warburg's brother about a projected biographical study of the then-deceased former patient, Binswanger notes that he picked up back then on similarities between features of the delusions and the themes in the published work. Is this the influence of Warburg's lecture on Binswanger's sense of the case as a whole?

A Wake

1. Herbert Silberer, the completely mediumistic figure in the background of the inner circle around Freud, is summoned by Freud in *The Interpretation of Dreams* to conjure or perform the ghost reading that is silent as the grave of references that includes Schopenhauer at once on ghosts and on the dream sense organ. Silberer supplemented Freud's dream theory by catching the process of transformation of thoughts into images in the act of awakening. He tended to experiment on himself: he tried forcing intellectual work on himself while in a state of fatigue. The resulting image represents not the thought but the fatigue itself. (So often the media record of one's recollection of a dream, for instance, plays back only the forgetting as injunction or resistance.) Silberer gives the example of forcing himself to contemplate a philosophical problem. "I wanted to compare the views of Kant and Schopenhauer upon Time. As a result of my drowsiness I was unable to keep the arguments of both of them before my mind at once, which was necessary in order to make the comparison" (in Freud, *Standard Edition,* 5:503). He keeps on trying. Then he emphatically impresses Kant's deductions upon his mind with all the strength of his will (as he puts it). But after he switches to Schopenhauer, there's no going back to Kant. "This vain effort of recovering the Kant dossier which was stored away somewhere in my head was suddenly represented before my closed eyes as a concrete and plastic symbol, as though it were a dream picture" (503–4). He's standing before a disobliging secretary asking for information. Instead of complying, the secretary gives Silberer a disagreeable look. (This primal scene of the death wish was lodged at or as the origin of the uncontainability of madness and haunting in *The Cabinet of Dr. Caligari.*)

2. I examine this two-way influence through Lou in "Friedrich Nichte" and at greater length in the first chapter of my *Aberrations of Mourning.*

3. I pursued this col-lapsus in Nietzsche once upon a time by philosophizing with a stammer.

Spätwerk

1. Even for Blondie the living wasn't easy. According to Horkheimer and Adorno, in the section "Man and Animal": "The Fascist's passionate interest in animals, nature, and children is rooted in the lust to persecute. The significance of the hand negligently stroking a child's head, or an animal's back, is that it could just as easily destroy them" (*Dialectic of Enlightenment,* 253). One of the decrees issued against the German Jews on the way to their exclusion and eradication concerned pets, which Jews were no longer allowed to keep. The confiscated animals were immediately exterminated.

2. 246. In *Dialectic of Enlightenment* bare life is the social relation as symptom. That the bottom line is psychic life (for better or worse) is thus guaranteed by animals (and the "and" in the coupling antithesis "man and animal"). Superego says: so, you want to dominate nature. Then be, your self, debased nature, mere life.

3. Agamben cites Heidegger's reading of Rilke's eighth "Duino Elegy" against the background of the more extensive argument Heidegger developed ten years earlier in lectures on "The Fundamental Concepts of Metaphysics: World, Finitude, Solitude."

Play Bally

1. Von Uexküll organizes the entirety of the section on "Movement" ("*Bewegung*") in *Theoretische Biologie* around the cinematograph as analogue. However it is in this popularizing and illustrated version that the technical device advances to the status of proof.

Das Hund

1. A dog that becomes dangerously violent in our midst is not viewed as having returned to its animal nature but instead as afflicted by serious illness, including psychosis. Like man, like dog: both tend to be identified (historically) as the result of an eclectic mix of heredity and upbringing.

2. See my chapter on Kafka, "Warm Brothers," in *Aberrations of Mourning*.

3. We have begun to traverse a text I originally wrote in German for a film by Eva Meyer and Eran Schaerf *(Flashforward)*. Meyer and Schaerf invited a group of artists and writers to contribute a performance and/or text and enact or read it for the film. Elli and I performed this first version of "Das Hund" following Elfriede Jelinek's reading procession. It was in this contribution that I conceived of the revision of the primal father myth.

4. I couldn't find the brief article in the *Los Angeles Times* that I have eidetic memories of reading along these lines. What I was able to find in the archive of the *Times* (an article dated November 22, 2002) is more tentative. Thus it is suggested that the genetic change that is evidently innate (closer readers of us even than chimps, for example, puppies already will watch us and immediately understand where we have placed or hidden the food) might have resulted, as a form of adaptation, over the many years of our relationship. (Even the name or call is something the dog responds to from day one.) But there are researchers also cited who identify the transformation of a few wolves into dogs as first-generation "Eves." For better or worse, we learned from dogs that interspecial relations were possible. This marks the onset of our ready-positioning for technologization. Better prostheses than our tools or weapons, dogs came in for the hunting skills they improved. The dog's pack psychology is stronger than our own. The sense of territory or property that is innate with dogs (control, by contrast, seems to be the innate human sense) could very well have inspired us to set up the first boundaries around domesticated herbivores. Lippit follows the logic of the evil eye when he identifies animal spectrality as the fallback position for the encounter animal communication calls out in us. The animal in exchange may not be understood (until slain by us) but will not be ignored, especially in the prolonged span of parting. Also see "Pet Grief," my contribution to the catalog accompanying an exhibition of Diana Thater's work.

5. Konrad Lorenz's *So kam der Mensch auf den Hund* ("Thus Man Went to the Dogs") postulates the birth of dogs out of jackals but then sets apart certain more wolf-like dogs, including some of his best friends: these over-dogs survive in the stricken world of the closing days of the Reich on the Eastern front, flexing a dignity that the last phase of German propaganda recommended for losers, but which the people couldn't deliver, strapped as they were to the laugh tracks of Celine's inside view of "Gone with the Blitz."

Bibliography

Ackerley, J. R. *My Dog Tulip*. New York: New York Review Books, 1999 [1965].

Adorno, Theodor W. *Kierkegaard: Construction of the Aesthetic*. Trans. Robert Hullot-Kentor. Minneapolis: University of Minnesota Press, 1989.

———. *Minima Moralia: Reflexionen aus dem beschädigten Leben*. Frankfurt am Main: Suhrkamp Verlag, 1969 [1951].

———. *Traumprotokolle*. Ed. Christoph Gödde and Henri Lonitz. Frankfurt am Main: Suhrkamp Verlag, 2005.

Adorno, Theodor, and Walter Benjamin. *The Complete Correspondence, 1928–1940*. Ed. Henri Lonitz. Trans. Nicholas Walker. Cambridge, Mass.: Harvard University Press, 1999.

Agamben, Giorgio. *The Open: Man and Animal*. Trans. Kevin Attell. Stanford, Calif.: Stanford University Press, 2004.

Anton, Uwe, and Werner Fuchs. "So I Don't Write about Heroes: An Interview With Philip K. Dick." *SF EYE,* Spring 1996: 37–46.

Apel, D. Scott, and Kevin C. Briggs. "Philip K. Dick Interview" (June 20 and July 23, 1977, in Sonoma, Calif.). In *Philip K. Dick: The Dream Connection*, ed. D. Scott Apel, 31–110. San Jose: Permanent Press, 1987.

Arendt, Hannah. *Love and Saint Augustine*. Ed. Joanna V. Scott and Judith C. Scott. Chicago: University of Chicago Press, 1996 [1929].

Arieti, Silvano. *Interpretation of Schizophrenia*. New York: Robert Brunner, 1955.

Arnold, Hans. *Wie errichtet und leitet man Spiritistische Zirkel in der Familie?* Leipzig: Verlag von Max Spohr, 1892.

Asimov, Isaac. *I, Robot*. New York: Gnome Press, 1950.

Bair, Deirdre. *Jung: A Biography*. Boston: Little, Brown, 2003.

Bally, Gustav. *Vom Spielraum der Freiheit: Die Bedeutung des Spiels bei Tier und Mensch*. Basel/Stuttgart: Schwabe & Co, 1966.

Bateson, Gregory, ed. *Perceval's Narrative: A Patient's Account of His Psychosis: 1830–1832*. Stanford, Calif.: Stanford University Press, 1961.

———. "Toward a Theory of Schizophrenia." In *Steps to an Ecology of Mind*, 201–27. Chicago: University of Chicago Press, 2000 [1972].

Beers, Clifford Whittingham. *A Mind That Found Itself*. Pittsburgh: University of Pittsburgh Press, 1981 [1906].

Benjamin, Walter. "Bücher von Geisteskranken: Aus meiner Sammlung." In *Gesammelte Schriften*, ed. Rolf Tiedemann and Hermann Schweppenhäuser, 4:615–16. Frankfurt am Main: Suhrkamp Verlag, 1972–1989 [1928].

———. "Central Park." Trans. Edmund Jephcott. In *Walter Benjamin: Selected Writings, Volume 4, 1938–1940*, ed. Howard Eiland and Michael Jennings. Cambridge, Mass.: The Belknap Press of Harvard University Press, 2006.

———. "Goethe's Wahlverwandtschaften" [1925]. In *Gesammelte Schriften*, 1, pt. 1: 123–201.

———. "Hashish, Beginning of March 1930." Trans. Rodney Livingstone. In *Selected Writings*, vol. 2, pt. 1, *1927–1930*, ed. Michael W. Jennings, Howard Eiland, and Gary Smith, 327–30. Cambridge, Mass.: The Belknap Press of Harvard University Press, 1999.

———. "The Image of Proust." Trans. Harry Zohn. In *Illuminations*, ed. Hannah Arendt, 201–15. New York: Schocken Books, 1968 [1929].

———. "Karl Kraus." In *Gesammelte Schriften*, vol. 11, pt. 1:334–67.

———. "Das Kunstwerk im Zeitalter seiner technischen Reproduzierbarkeit" [1936]. In *Gesammelte Schriften*, vol. 1, pt. 2: 471–508.

———. "Main Features of My Second Impression of Hashish." Trans. Rodney Livingstone. In *Selected Writings*, vol. 2, pt. 1, *1927–1930*, ed. Michael W. Jennings, Howard Eiland, and Gary Smith, 85–90. Cambridge, Mass.: The Belknap Press of Harvard University Press, 1999.

———. *Das Passagen-Werk*, Vol. 1. Ed. Rolf Tiedemann. Frankfurt am Main: Suhrkamp, 1982.

———. "Über das Programm der kommenden Philosophie" [1912]. In *Gesammelte Schriften*, vol. 2, pt. 1: 157–71.

———. "Über einige Motive bei Baudelaire." [1939]. In *Gesammelte Schriften*, vol. 1, pt. 2: 607–53.

———. *Ursprung des deutschen Trauerspiels* [1928]. In *Gesammelte Schriften*, vol. 1, pt. 1: 203–430.

Bergson, Henri. *Creative Evolution*. Trans. Arthur Mitchell. Mineola, N.Y.: Dover Publications, 1998 [1911].

Binswanger, Ludwig. "Der Fall Ellen West." In *Der Mensch in der Psychiatrie*, in *Ausgewählte Werke*, vol. 4. Heidelberg: Roland Asanger Verlag, 1994.

———. "Der Fall Lola Voß." *Schweizer Archiv für Neurologie and Psychiatrie* 63 (1949): 29–97.

———. "Der Fall Suzanne Urban." In *Ausgewählte Werke*, 4:210–322.

———. *Dream and Existence*. Trans. Jacob Needleman. Ed. Keith Hoeller, special issue of *Review of Existential Psychology and Psychiatry* 19, no. 1 (1984–85).

———. "Insanity as Life-Historical Phenomenon and as Mental Disease: The Case of Ilse." In *Existence: A New Dimension in Psychiatry and Psychology*, ed. May, Angel, and Ellenberger, 214–36.

———. "Mein Weg zu Freud." *Ausgewählte Werke*, 3:17–33.

———. "Melancholie und Manie." In *Der Mensch in der Psychiatrie*, in *Ausgewählte Werke*, 4:351–428.

————. "Über die daseinsanalytische Forschungsrichtung in der Psychiatrie." In *Ausgewählte Werke*, 3:231–58.

Boonstra, John. "A Final Interview with Science Fiction's Boldest Visionary Who Talks Candidly About *Blade Runner*, Inner Voices, and the Temptations of Hollywood." Rod Serling's *The Twilight Zone Magazine*, 2/3 (June 1982).

Braun, Wernher von, and Willy Ley. *The Exploration of Mars*. New York: Viking Press, 1956.

Brown, Norman O. *Love's Body*. Los Angeles: University of California Press, 1990 [1966].

Byron, Lord. *Manfred*. In *Poetical Works*. Oxford: Oxford University Press, 1970 [1817].

Calderón de la Barca, Pedro. *Life Is a Dream*. Trans. John Clifford. London: Nick Hern Books, 1998.

Carrère, Emmanuel. *I Am Alive and You Are Dead: A Journey into the Mind of Philip K. Dick*. Trans. Timothy Bent. New York: Henry Holt and Company, 2004 [1993].

Clarke, Arthur C. *Childhood's End*. New York: Random House, 1990 [1953].

Corngold, Stanley. *The Commentators' Despair: The Interpretation of Kafka's "Metamorphosis."* Port Washington, N.Y.: Kennikat Press, 1973.

Cover, Arthur Bryan. "*Vertex* Interviews Philip K. Dick," *Vertex* 1, no. 6 (February 1974): 34–37.

Deleuze, Gilles, and Felix Guattari. *A Thousand Plateaus: Capitalism and Schizophrenia*. Trans. Brian Massumi. Minneapolis: University of Minnesota Press, 1987.

Derrida, Jacques. *The Animal That Therefore I Am*. Ed. Marie-Louise Mallet. Trans. David Wills. New York: Fordham University Press, 2008.

————. *Archive Fever: A Freudian Impression*. Trans. Eric Prenowitz. Chicago: University of Chicago Press, 1996.

————. *Fichus: Discours de Francfort*. Paris: Éditions Galilée, 2002.

————. *Of Spirit: Heidegger and the Question*. Trans. Geoffrey Bennington and Rachel Bowlby. Chicago: University of Chicago Press, 1989.

————. "Two Words for Joyce." Trans. Geoff Bennington. In *Post-structuralist Joyce: Essays from the French*, ed. Derek Attridge and Daniel Ferrer, 145–59. Cambridge: Cambridge University Press, 1984.

Dessoir, Max. "Gespenster Lebender." *Über Land und Meer* 10 (1889), two pages.

————. *Vom Jenseits der Seele: Die Geheimwissenschaften in kritischer Betrachtung*. Stuttgart: Enke, 1916.

Deutelbaum, Marshall. "Memory/Visual Design: The Remembered Sights of *Blade Runner*." *Film Literature Quarterly* 16, no. 1 (1988): 66–72.

Dick, Philip K. "The Android and the Human." In *The Shifting Realities of Philip K. Dick*, 183–210.

————. *Clans of the Alphane Moon*. New York: Vintage Books, 2002 [1964].

————. *Confessions of a Crap Artist*. New York: Vintage Books, 1992 [1975].

————. *The Cosmic Puppets*. London: HarperCollins, 1998 [1956/57].

————. "Cosmogony and Cosmology." In *The Shifting Realities of Philip K. Dick*, 281–313.

————. *Counter-Clock World*. New York: Vintage Books, 2002 [1967].

————. *The Crack in Space*. New York: Vintage Books, 2005 [1966].

————. *The Divine Invasion*. New York: Vintage Books, 1991 [1981].

———. *Do Androids Dream of Electric Sheep?* New York: Ballantine, 1996 [1968].

———. *Dr. Bloodmoney.* New York: Vintage Books, 2002 [1965].

———. *Dr. Futurity.* New York: Vintage Books, 2005 [1960].

———. *Eye in the Sky.* New York: Vintage Books, 2003 [1957].

———. *Flow My Tears, the Policeman Said.* New York: Vintage Books, 1993 [1974].

———. *Galactic Pot-Healer.* New York: Vintage Books, 1994 [1969].

———. *The Game-Players of Titan.* New York: Vintage Books, 1992 [1963].

———. "How to Build a Universe That Doesn't Fall Apart Two Days Later." In *The Shifting Realities of Philip K. Dick,* 259–80.

———. "If You Find This World Bad, You Should See Some of the Others." In *The Shifting Realities of Philip K. Dick,* 233–58.

———. "Imposter." In *The Collected Stories of Philip K. Dick,* vol. 2, 299–310. New York: Carol Publishing Group, 1995 [1953].

———. *In Pursuit of Valis: Selections from the Exegesis.* Ed. Lawrence Sutin. Lancaster, Penn.: Underwood-Miller, 1991.

———. "Introduction to *Dr. Bloodmoney.*" In *The Shifting Realities of Philip K. Dick,* 80–83.

———. *Lies, Inc.* New York: Vintage Books, 2004.

———. "Man, Android, and Machine," In *The Shifting Realities of Philip K. Dick,* 211–32.

———. *The Man in the High Castle.* New York: Vintage Books, 1992 [1962].

———. *The Man Who Japed.* New York: Vintage Books, 2002 [1956].

———. *Martian Time-Slip.* New York: Vintage Books, 1995 [1964].

———. *Mary and the Giant.* London: Gollancz, 2005 [1987].

———. "Minority Report." In *The Collected Stories of Philip K. Dick,* vol. 4, 71–102. New York: Carol Publishing Group, 1991 [1956].

———. *Nick and the Glimmung.* London: Piper Books, 1988.

———. *Now Wait for Last Year.* New York: Vintage Books, 1993 [1966].

———. "Now Wait for This Year." In *Philip K. Dick,* ed. Joseph D. Olander and Martin Harry Greenberg, 215–27. Writers of the 21st Century Series. New York: Taplinger Publishing Company, 1983.

———. *Our Friends from Frolix 8.* New York: Vintage Books, 2003 [1970].

———. "Paycheck." In *Paycheck and Other Classic Stories by Philip K. Dick,* 279–308. New York: Citadel Press, 1987 [1953].

———. *The Penultimate Truth.* New York: Vintage Books, 2004 [1964].

———. *Radio Free Albemuth.* New York: Vintage Books, 1998 [1985].

———. "Schizophrenia and *The Book of Changes.*" In *The Shifting Realities of Philip K. Dick,* 178–82.

———. "Second Variety." In *Second Variety and Other Classic Stories,* 373–410. New York: Citadel Press, 1987 [1953].

———. *The Shifting Realities of Philip K. Dick. Selected Literary and Philosophical Writings.* Ed. Lawrence Sutin. New York: Vintage Books, 1995.

———. *The Simulacra.* New York: Vintage Books, 2002 [1964].

———. *Solar Lottery.* New York: Vintage Books, 2003 [1955].

———. *The Three Stigmata of Palmer Eldritch.* New York: Vintage Books, 1991 [1965].

———. *Time out of Joint.* New York: Vintage Books, 2002 [1959].

———. *The Transmigration of Timothy Archer.* New York: Vintage Books, 1991 [1982].

———. *Ubik.* New York: Vintage Books, 1991 [1969].

———. *Ubik: The Screenplay.* Burton, Mich.: Subterranean, 2008.

———. "The Ultra Hidden (Cryptic) Doctrine: The Secret Meaning of the Great System of Theosophy of the World, Openly Revealed for the First Time." In *The Shifting Realities of Philip K. Dick,* 337–50.

———. *The Unteleported Man.* New York: Berkley Books, 1983 [1966].

———. "Upon the Dull Earth." In *Second Variety and Other Classic Stories,* 203–20. New York: Citadel Press, 2002 [1954].

———. *Valis.* New York: Vintage Books, 1991 [1981].

———. *Voices from the Street.* New York: Tor, 2007.

———. *Vulcan's Hammer.* New York: Vintage Books, 2004 [1960].

———. "We Can Remember It for You Wholesale." In *The Collected Stories of Philip K. Dick,* vol. 2, 35–52. New York: Carol Publishing Group, 1995 [1966].

———. *What If Our World Is Their Heaven? The Final Conversations of Philip K. Dick.* Ed. Gwen Lee and Doris Elaine Sauter. Woodstock and New York: The Overlook Press, 2000.

———. *The World Jones Made.* New York: Vintage Books, 1993 [1956].

———. *The Zap Gun.* London: HarperCollins, 1998 [1967].

Dick, Philip K., and Ray Nelson. *The Ganymede Takeover.* London: Severn House Publishers, 1988 [1967].

Dick, Philip K., and Roger Zelazny. *Deus Irae.* New York: Vintage Books, 2003 [1976].

Du Prel, Karl. "Ein Wort über den Spiritismus." *Vom Fels zum Meer: Spemann's Illustrierte Zeitschrift für das deutsche Haus* 2 (1887): 264–74.

Fichtner, Gerhard, ed. *The Sigmund Freud–Ludwig Binswanger Correspondence, 1908–1938.* Trans. Arnold J. Pomerans. New York: Other Press, 2003.

Fontane, Theodor. *Effi Briest. Sämtliche Werke,* vol. 4. Ed. Walter Keitel. Munich: Carl Hanser, 1962 [1896].

Freud, Sigmund. *The Standard Edition of the Complete Psychological Works.* Trans. and ed. James Strachey. 24 volumes. London: The Hogarth Press, 1958.

Gebsattel, V. E. von. "The World of the Compulsive." In *Existence: A New Dimension in Psychiatry and Psychology,* ed. May, Angel, and Ellenberger, 170–87.

Goethe, Johann Wolfgang von. *Wilhelm Meister's Apprenticeship.* Trans. Eric A. Blackall. Princeton, N.J.: Princeton University Press, 1995 [1796].

Gombrich, Ernst H. *Aby Warburg: An Intellectual Biography.* London: The Warburg Institute, University of London, 1970.

Günther, Gotthard. "Achilles and the Tortoise." 3 parts. Günther Electronic Archive, www.thinkartlab.com/pkl/archive.htm. Originally published in *Astounding Science Fiction* 32, no. 3 (1954).

———. "Aristotelian and NON-Aristotelian LOGIC." 4 parts. Günther Electronic Archive. Originally published in *Startling Stories* 32, no. 1 (1954).

———. "Can Mechanical Brains Have Consciousness?" www.vordenker.de. Originally published in: *Startling Stories* 29, no. 1 (1953).

———. "Die Entdeckung Amerikas und die Sache mit der Weltraum Literatur." www.vordenker.de. First published as preface to *Weltraum-Bücher,* a collection of science fiction edited by Günther. Düsseldorf: Verlag von Karl Rauch, 1952.

———. "Homunkulus und Roboter." In *Das Bewusstsein der Maschinen: Eine Metaphysik der Kybernetik,* 195–200. Baden-Baden: Agis Verlag, 2002.

———. "Idealismus, Materialismus, und Kybernetik." In *Das Bewusstsein der Maschinen: Eine Metaphysik der Kybernetik,* 123–94. Baden-Baden: Agis, 2002.

———. "The SEETEE Mind." 4 parts. Günther Electronic Archive. Originally published in *Startling Stories* 31, no. 3 (1954).

———. "The Soul of a Robot." 4 parts. Günther Electronic Archive. Originally published in *Startling Stories* 32, no. 3 (1955).

———. "The Thought Translator." 4 parts. Günther Electronic Archive. Originally published in *Startling Stories* 33, no. 1 (1955).

———. "Die 'zweite' Maschine." www.vordenker.de. Originally published as "Nachwort" to Isaac Asimov's *Ich, der Robot,* 1952.

Häberlin, Paul. "Sexualgespenster." *Sexual-Probleme: Zeitschrift für Sexualwissenschaft und Sexualpolitik* 8 (1912): 96–102.

Hagen, Wolfgang. *Radio Schreber: Der "moderne Spiritismus" und die Sprache der Medien.* Weimar: Verlag und Datenbank für Geisteswissenschaften, 2001.

Harraway, Donna. *The Companion Species Manifesto: Dogs, People, and Significant Otherness.* Chicago: Prickly Paradigm Press, 2003.

Hayles, Katherine. *How We Became Posthuman: Virtual Bodies in Cybernetics, Literature, and Informatics.* Chicago: University of Chicago Press, 1999.

Hearne, Vicki. *Adam's Task: Calling Animals by Name.* London: Heinemann, 1987.

Heidegger, Martin. "Die Frage nach der Technik." In *Vorträge und Aufsätze.* Pfullingen: Verlag Günther Neske, 1954.

———. "Die Kehre." In *Die Technik und die Kehre.* Pfullingen: Verlag Günther Neske, 1954.

———. *Parmenides.* In *Gesamtausgabe,* vol. 54, ed. Manfred S. Frings. Frankfurt am Main: Vittorio Klostermann, 1982.

———. "Wozu Dichter?" In *Holzwege.* Frankfurt am Main: Vittorio Klostermann, 2003 [1946].

Heise, Ursula K. "From Extinction to Electronics: Dead Frogs, Live Dinosaurs, and Electric Sheep." In *Zoontologies: The Question of the Animal,* ed. Cary Wolfe, 59–81. Minneapolis: University of Minnesota Press, 2003.

Hennell, Thomas. *The Witnesses.* Hyde Park, N.Y.: University Books, 1967 [1938].

Horkheimer, Max, and Theodor W. Adorno. *Dialectic of Enlightenment.* Trans. John Cumming. New York: Continuum, 1997 [1944].

Jameson, Fredric. *Archaeologies of the Future: The Desire Called Utopia and Other Science Fictions.* London: Verso, 2005.

Jaspers, Karl. *Strindberg und van Gogh: Versuch einer vergleichenden pathographischen Analyse.* Munich: R. Piper and Company Verlag, 1949.

Jefferson, Lara. *These Are My Sisters: A Journal from the Inside of Insanity.* Garden City, N.Y.: Anchor Press / Doubleday, 1975.

Jung, C. G. "Foreword to the *I Ching.*" In *Psychology and the East,* trans. R. F. C. Hull, 189–208. Princeton, N.J.: Princeton University Press, 1978 [1950].

———. *On the Psychology and Pathology of So-Called Occult Phenomena.* In *Psychiatric Studies,* trans. R. F. C. Hull, 3–88. Princeton, N.J.: Princeton University Press, 1983.

———. "Psychological Commentary on *The Tibetan Book of the Dead.*" In *Psychology and the East,* trans. R. F. C. Hull, 59–76. Princeton, N.J.: Princeton University Press, 1978 [1935].

———. *The Psychology of Dementia Praecox.* In *The Psychology of Dementia Praecox,* trans. R. F. C. Hull, 3–151. Princeton, N.J.: Princeton University Press, 1974.

———. "Schizophrenia." In *The Psychology of Dementia Praecox,* trans. R. F. C. Hull, 178–93. Princeton, N.J.: Princeton University Press, 1974.

———. "The Seven Sermons to the Dead." In *Memories, Dreams, Reflections,* trans. Richard and Clara Winston, 189–91. New York: Vintage Press, 1989.

———. *Symbole der Wandlung: Analyse des Vorspiels zu einer Schizophrenie.* Vol. 5 of *Gesammelte Werke.* Ed. Lilly Jung-Merker and Elisabeth Rüf. Zürich: Walter-Verlag, 1996.

Jung-Stilling, Johann Heinrich. *Theorie der Geisterkunde; in einer Natur-, Vernunft- und Bibelmäßigen Beantwortung der Frage: Was von Ahnungen, Gesichten, und Geistererscheinungen geglaubt und nicht geglaubt werden müsse.* Nürnberg: Verlag der Raw'schen Buchhandlung, 1808.

Kant, Immanuel. "Träume eines Geistersehers, erläutert durch Träume der Metaphysik." In *Vorkritische Schriften bis 1768,* vol. 2., ed. Wilhelm Weischedel, 923–1000. Frankfurt am Main: Surhkamp Taschenbuch, 1977 [1766].

Keller, Gottfried. *Gesammelte Werke.* 5 volumes. Munich: Nymphenburger Verlag, 1981.

Kerner, Justinus. *Die Seherin von Prevorst.* Stuttgart: J. F. Steinkopf Verlag, 2007 [1829].

Kierkegaard, Søren. *The Sickness unto Death: A Christian Psychological Exposition for Upbuilding and Awakening.* Trans. Howard V. Hong and Edna H. Hong. Princeton, N.J.: Princeton University Press, 1980.

King, Stephen. *Pet Sematary.* New York: Signet, 1984.

Klein, Melanie. "The Importance of Symbol Formation in the Development of the Ego." In *The Selected Melanie Klein,* ed. Juliet Mitchell, 95–111. New York: The Free Press, 1986 [1930].

Kohut, Heinz. "On Empathy." In *The Search for the Self: Selected Writings of Heinz Kohut: 1978–1981,* vol. 4., ed. Paul H. Ornstein, 525–36. Madison, Conn.: International Universities Press, 1991.

Kreusner, Kurt. "Der moderne Gespensterglaube: Eine Studie über den Spiritismus." *Westermanns illustrierte deutsche Monats-Hefte für das gesamte geistige Leben der Gegenwart* 84 (1898): 645–53.

Kristeva, Julia. *Black Sun.* Trans. Leon Roudiez. New York: Columbia University Press, 1989 [1987].

———. "Stabat Mater." In *The Kristeva Reader,* ed. Toril Moi, 160–86. New York: Columbia University Press, 1986.

Kuhn, Roland. "The Attempted Murder of a Prostitute." Trans. Ernest Angel. In *Existence: A New Dimension in Psychiatry and Psychology,* ed. May, Angel, and Ellenberger, 365–425.

Lacan, Jacques. "Desire and the Interpretation of Desire in *Hamlet*." Trans. James Hulbert. In *Literature and Psychoanalysis: The Question of Reading: Otherwise,* ed. Shoshana Felman, 11–52. Baltimore: The Johns Hopkins University Press, 1982.

Lippit, Akira. *Electric Animal: Toward a Rhetoric of Wildlife.* Minneapolis: University of Minnesota Press, 2000.

Liu, Catherine. "What's the Difference?" In *Copying Machines: Taking Notes for the Automaton,* 21–48. Minneapolis: University of Minnesota Press, 2000.

Lorenz, Konrad. *So kam der Mensch auf den Hund.* Munich: Deutscher Taschenbuch Verlag, 1965.

Lupoff, Richard A. "A Conversation with Philip K. Dick." *Science Fiction Eye* 1, no. 2 (August 1987): 45–54.

Marazia, Chantal, and Davide Stimili, eds. *Die unendliche Heilung: Aby Warburgs Krankengeschichte.* Berlin and Zurich: Diaphanes, 2007.

Marder, Elissa. "*Blade Runner*'s Moving Still." *Camera Obscura* 27 (1991): 91–106.

May, Rollo, Ernest Angel, and Henri F. Ellenberger, eds. *Existence: A New Dimension in Psychiatry and Psychology.* New York: Basic Books, 1958.

Minkowski, Eugene. "Findings in a Case of Schizophrenic Depression." Trans. Barbara Bliss. In *Existence: A New Dimension in Psychiatry and Psychology,* ed. May, Angel, and Ellenberger, 127–38.

Nietzsche, Friedrich. "Zur Erklärung der sogenannten 'spiritistischen Erscheinungen.'" In *Sämtliche Werke,* vol. 10, ed. Giorgio Colli and Mazzino Montinari, 16–17. Munich: Deutscher Taschenbuch Verlag, 1980.

O'Brien, Barbara. *Operators and Things.* New York: Ace Books, 1958.

Ostrander, Sheila, and Lynn Schroeder. *Psychic Discoveries behind the Iron Curtain.* New York: Bantam Books, 1971.

Pike, James, with Diane Kennedy. *The Other Side: An Account of My Experiences with Psychic Phenomena.* Garden City, N.Y.: Doubleday, 1968.

Poster, Mark. "Future Advertising: Dick's *Ubik* and the Digital Ad." In *Information Please: Culture and Politics in the Age of Digital Machines,* 250–66. Durham, N.C.: Duke University Press, 2006.

Purser, Philip. "Even Sheep Can Upset Scientific Detachment." *London Daily Telegraph* 506 (July 19, 1974): 27–30.

Rickels, Laurence A. *Aberrations of Mourning: Writing on German Crypts.* Detroit: Wayne State University Press, 1988.

———, ed. *Acting Out in Groups.* Minneapolis: University of Minnesota Press, 1999.

———. "All of the Above." In *The Promise, The Land: Jewish-Israeli Artists in Relation to Politics and Society,* ed. Thomas Edlinger, Stella Rollig, and Roland Schöny, 146–49. Catalogue for exhibition held at OK Zentrum. Vienna: Folio Verlag, 2003.

———. *The Case of California.* Minneapolis: University of Minnesota Press, 2001 [1991].

———. *The Devil Notebooks.* Minneapolis: University of Minnesota Press, 2008.

———. "Friedrich Nichte." In *Looking After Nietzsche,* ed. Laurence A. Rickels, 137–58. Albany: State University of New York Press, 1990.

———. "Just a Test." In *Mike Kelley,* 29–36. *MAGASIN,* Exhibition catalogue for Centre National d'Art Contemporain, in Grenoble, 1999.

———. *Nazi Psychoanalysis*. 3 volumes. Minneapolis: University of Minnesota Press, 2002.

———. "Pet Grief." In *Diana Thater: gorillagorillagorilla*, 64–73. Cologne: Walther König, 2009.

———. "Die Prüfung Unica Zürns." In *Unica Zürn: Bilder, 1953–1970*, 193–98. Berlin: Verlag Brinkmann und Bose, 1998.

———. "Suicitation: Benjamin and Freud." In *Benjamin's Ghosts: Interventions in Contemporary Literary and Cultural Theory*, ed. Gerhard Richter, 142–53. Stanford, Calif.: Stanford University Press, 2002.

Rickman, Gregg. *To The High Castle: Philip K. Dick, A Life 1928–1962*. Long Beach, Calif.: Fragments West/The Valentine Press, 1989.

Róheim, Géza. "After the Death of the Primal Father" [1923]. *The Psychoanalytic Study of Society* 11 (1985): 33–60.

———. *Magic and Schizophrenia*. Ed. Werner Muensterberger. Bloomington: Indiana University Press, 1962.

Ronell, Avital. *Crack Wars: Literature, Addiction, Mania*. Urbana: University of Illinois Press, 2004.

———. *The Telephone Book: Technology, Schizophrenia, Electric Speech*. Lincoln: University of Nebraska Press, 1989.

———. *The Test Drive*. Urbana: University of Illinois Press, 2005.

Sachs, Hanns. "The Delay of the Machine Age." *Psychoanalytic Quarterly* 11, no. 3/4 (1933): 404–24.

Schopenhauer, Arthur. *Über das Mitleid*. Ed. Franco Volpi. Munich: Deutscher Taschenbuch Verlag, 2006.

———. "Versuch über das Geistersehn und was damit zusammenhängt." In *Parerga und Paralipomena: Kleine philosophische Schriften*, vol. 1, 273–372. Frankfurt am Main: Suhrkamp, 1986 [1850].

Schreber, Daniel Paul. *Denkwürdigkeiten eines Nervenkranken*. Leipzig: Mutze, 1913.

———. *Memoirs of My Nervous Illness*. Trans. Ida Macalpine and Richard A. Hunter. Cambridge, Mass.: Harvard University Press, 1988.

Silberer, Herbert. "Über die Behandlung einer Psychose bei Justinus Kerner." *Jahrbuch für psychoanalytische und psychopathologische Forschungen* 3:724–29.

Silverman, Kaja. "Back to the Future." *Camera Obscura* 27 (1991): 109–32.

Sutin, Lawrence. *Divine Invasions: A Life of Philip K. Dick*. New York: Citadel Press, 1991.

Taubes, Jacob. *Die Politische Theologie des Paulus*. Munich: Fink Verlag, 2003.

Tausk, Victor. "Über die Entsehung des 'Beeinflussungsapparates' in der Schizophrenie." In *Gesammelte psychoanalytische und literarische Schriften*, ed. Hans-Joachim Metzger, 245–86. Vienna: Medusa, 1983 [1919].

The Tibetan Book of the Dead. Trans. Francesca Fremantle and Chögyam Trungpa. Boston: Shambhala, 1987.

Tolkien, J. R. R. "Foreword to the Second Edition." In *The Lord of the Rings*. London: Ballantine, 1966.

———. "Introduction." In *Sir Gawain and the Green Knight, Pearl, and Sir Orfeo*, trans. J. R. R. Tolkien, 13–24. Boston: Houghton Mifflin Company, 1975.

———. "On Fairy-Stories." In *The Monsters and the Critics and Other Essays,* ed. Christopher Tolkien, 109–61. London 1983 [1947].

Uexküll, Jakob von. *Streifzüge durch die Umwelten von Tieren und Menschen: Ein Bilderbuch unsichtbarer Welten.* Hamburg: Rowohlt, 1956 [1933].

———. *Theoretische Biologie.* Frankfurt am Main: Suhrkamp Verlag, 1973 [1928].

Warburg, Aby M. *Schlangenritual: Ein Reisebericht.* Berlin: Verlag Klaus Wagenbach, 1988.

Laurence A. Rickels moved to the Coast in 1981 upon completing his graduate training in German philology at Princeton University. While in California he earned a psychotherapy license. He has published numerous studies of the phenomenon he calls "unmourning," a term that became the title of his trilogy: *Aberrations of Mourning, The Case of California,* and *Nazi Psychoanalysis* (Minnesota, 2002). He has also written two "course books": *The Vampire Lectures* (Minnesota, 1999) and *The Devil Notebooks,* (Minnesota, 2008).